SUSTAINING THE MILITARY ENTERPRISE

Series on Resource Management

Rightsizing Inventory
by Joseph L. Aiello
ISBN: 0-8493-8515-6

Integral Logistics Management: Operations and Supply Chain Management in Comprehensive Value-Added Networks, Third Edition
by Paul Schönsleben
ISBN: 1-4200-5194-6

Supply Chain Cost Control Using Activity-Based Management
Sameer Kumar and Matthew Zander
ISBN: 0-8493-8215-7

Financial Models and Tools for Managing Lean Manufacturing
Sameer Kumar and David Meade
ISBN: 0-8493-9185-7

RFID in the Supply Chain
Judith M. Myerson
ISBN: 0-8493-3018-1

Handbook of Supply Chain Management, Second Edition
by James B. Ayers
ISBN: 0-8493-3160-9

The Portal to Lean Production: Principles & Practices for Doing More With Less
by John Nicholas and Avi Soni
ISBN: 0-8493-5031-X

Supply Market Intelligence: A Managerial Handbook for Building Sourcing Strategies
by Robert B. Handfield
ISBN: 0-8493-2789-X

The Small Manufacturer's Toolkit: A Guide to Selecting the Techniques and Systems to Help You Win
by Steve Novak
ISBN: 0-8493-2883-7

Velocity Management in Logistics and Distribution: Lessons from the Military to Secure the Speed of Business
by Joseph L. Walden
ISBN: 0-8493-2859-4

Supply Chain for Liquids: Out of the Box Approaches to Liquid Logistics
by Wally Klatch
ISBN: 0-8493-2853-5

Supply Chain Architecture: A Blueprint for Networking the Flow of Material, Information, and Cash
by William T. Walker
ISBN: 1-57444-357-7

ERP: Tools, Techniques, and Applications for Integrating the Supply Chain
by Carol A. Ptak with Eli Schragenheim
ISBN: 1-57444-358-5

Introduction to e-Supply Chain Management: Engaging Technology to Build Market-Winning Business Partnerships
by David C. Ross
ISBN: 1-57444-324-0

Supply Chain Networks and Business Process Orientation
by Kevin P. McCormack and William C. Johnson with William T. Walker
ISBN: 1-57444-327-5

Collaborative Manufacturing: Using Real-Time Information to Support the Supply Chain
by Michael McClellan
ISBN: 1-57444-341-0

The Supply Chain Manager's Problem-Solver: Maximizing the Value of Collaboration and Technology
by Charles C. Poirier
ISBN: 1-57444-335-6

Lean Performance ERP Project Management: Implementing the Virtual Lean Enterprise, Second Edition
by Brian J. Carroll
ISBN: 0-8493-0532-2

Integrated Learning for ERP Success: A Learning Requirements Planning Approach
by Karl M. Kapp, with William F. Latham and Hester N. Ford-Latham
ISBN: 1-57444-296-1

Basics of Supply Chain Management
by Lawrence D. Fredendall and Ed Hill
ISBN: 1-57444-120-5

Lean Manufacturing: Tools, Techniques, and How to Use Them
by William M. Feld
ISBN: 1-57444-297-X

Back to Basics: Your Guide to Manufacturing Excellence
by Steven A. Melnyk and R.T. Chris Christensen
ISBN: 1-57444-279-1

Enterprise Resource Planning and Beyond: Integrating Your Entire Organization
by Gary A. Langenwalter
ISBN: 1-57444-260-0

SUSTAINING THE MILITARY ENTERPRISE

An Architecture for a Lean Transformation

DENNIS F.X. MATHAISEL

Professor, Babson College, Massachusetts, USA
Research Engineer (Former), Massachusetts Institute of Technology, Massachusetts, USA

CRC Press is an imprint of the
Taylor & Francis Group, an **informa** business

Auerbach Publications
Taylor & Francis Group
6000 Broken Sound Parkway NW, Suite 300
Boca Raton, FL 33487-2742

Printed in the United States of America on acid-free paper
10 9 8 7 6 5 4 3 2 1

International Standard Book Number-13: 978-1-4200-6224-3 (Hardcover)

Library of Congress Cataloging-in-Publication Data

Mathaisel, Dennis F. X.
Sustaining the military enterprise : an architecture for a lean transformation / Dennis F.X. Mathaisel.
p. cm.
Includes bibliographical references and index.
ISBN 978-1-4200-6224-3 (alk. paper)
1. United States--Armed Forces--Equipment--Maintenance and repair. 2. United States--Armed Forces--Weapons systems--Maintenance and repair. 3. United States. Dept. of Defense--Management. I. Title.

UC263.M345 2007
355.80973--dc22 2007043430

Visit the Taylor & Francis Web site at
http://www.taylorandfrancis.com

and the Auerbach Web site at
http://www.auerbach-publications.com

Contents

Preface .... **xi**

Acknowledgments .... **xiii**

About the Author .... **xv**

Chapter 1 The Current Military Sustainment System **1**

1.1 Introduction 3

1.2 Characterization of the Current Military Sustainment System 7

1.3 Analysis of the Current Military Sustainment System 13

1.3.1 System-Level Factors Affecting Sustainment Efficiency and Responsiveness 18

1.3.2 Depot-Level Factors Affecting Sustainment Efficiency and Responsiveness 25

1.4 Ramifications and Conclusions 29

Chapter 2 A Lean Model for the Military Sustainment Enterprise **33**

2.1 Introduction 33

2.2 The Lean Sustainment Enterprise Model 36

2.3 Benefits of and Challenges to the Lean Sustainment Enterprise Model 40

2.4 A Case Study: The Joint CAD/PAD Program 42

2.5 Conclusion 44

Chapter 3 A Lean Enterprise Architecture for Military Sustainability **45**

3.1 Introduction 46

3.2 The Life Cycle of an Enterprise 46

3.3 Why Is an Enterprisewide Transformation So Important? 47

3.4 The Process of Architecting an Enterprise 50

3.5 Enterprise Architectures 54

3.6 A Lean Enterprise Architecture for Military Sustainability 60

3.6.1 Definitions 60

3.6.2 The Lean Enterprise Architecture....61
3.6.3 Phase 1: Transformation Strategic Planning....63
3.6.4 Phase 2: Transformation Acquisition and Integration....63
3.6.4.1 The Requirements Package....63
3.6.4.2 The Acquisition Plan....66
3.6.4.3 The Integration Plan....66
3.6.4.4 The Change Management and Communications Plan....67
3.6.5 Phase 3: Transformation Implementation....68
3.7 The Role of Systems Engineering in the Lean Enterprise Architecture....69
3.7.1 The Conceptual Design Task....70
3.7.2 The Preliminary and Detailed Design Tasks....70
3.7.3 The Implementation Task....72
3.7.4 The Operation Task....72
3.8 Enterprise Transformation Engineering and the Lean Enterprise Architecture....72
3.9 Preference for a Performance-Based Transformation....75
3.10 Applications of the Lean Enterprise Architecture....76
3.11 Case Study: The Lean Enterprise Architecture Implementation Process in the U.S. Air Force....80
3.11.1 Organization of the Implementation Process....80
3.11.2 Responsibilities and Activities at the Air Logistics Center Levels....84
3.11.2.1 The Air Logistics Center Level....84
3.11.2.2 The Wing/Organization Level....87
3.11.3 The Depot Maintenance Transformation Board....88
3.11.4 Transformation Area Team Meetings....90
3.11.5 Transformation Evaluation Steps and Criteria....91
3.11.5.1 Determining Transformation Feasibility....91
3.11.5.2 Methodology/Evaluation Tools....92
3.11.5.3 Transformation Planning Questions....92
3.11.5.4 Criteria....93
3.11.5.5 The Business Case Analysis/Return on Investment Process....93
3.11.6 Project Identification and Coordination....93
3.11.7 Impact Analysis....94
3.11.8 The Integrated Master Plan/Integrated Master Schedule....94
3.11.9 Enterprisewide Business Case Analysis/Return on Investment....94
3.11.10 Prioritization and Selection of Projects....96
3.11.11 Documentation, Communication, and Change Management....96

3.11.12 The Transformation Project Life Cycle 96
3.11.12.1 The Project Template 97
3.11.12.2 Metrics 97
3.11.12.3 Communication 99
3.11.12.4 Implementation 99
3.11.12.5 Measuring Results 99
3.12 Conclusions and Future Directions 99

Chapter 4 Continuous Process Improvement Initiatives for Military Sustainability 101
4.1 Transformation 103
4.1.1 What Is Transformation? 103
4.1.2 The Transformation Process 109
4.1.3 Measuring Transformation 112
4.2 Continuous Process Improvement Initiatives for Transformation ... 113
4.2.1 Total Quality Management 114
4.2.1.1 Awards for Quality Achievement 117
4.2.2 Six Sigma 118
4.2.3 Business Process Reengineering/Redesign 119
4.2.4 Quick-Response Manufacturing 122
4.2.5 Agility 125
4.2.5.1 The Agility Forum 125
4.2.5.2 Agile Manufacturing 126
4.2.6 Variance Reduction 128
4.2.7 Lean Production 130
4.2.8 Value-Stream Mapping 131
4.2.8.1 The Value Stream 132
4.2.8.2 The Value-Stream Mapping Process 132
4.2.8.3 Value-Stream Mapping as it Relates to Lean Sustainment 135
4.2.8.4 The Benefits of Value-Stream Mapping 135
4.2.9 Cellular Manufacturing 136
4.2.10 Total Productive Maintenance 138
4.2.11 The Theory of Constraints 140
4.2.12 Flexible Sustainment 142
4.2.13 Conclusions on the Continuous Process Improvement Initiatives 143
4.3 Case Studies 146
4.3.1 A Case Study on Process Improvement Initiatives in the U.S. Air Force 146
4.3.2 Value-Stream Mapping Case Studies 146
4.3.2.1 Commercial Avionics High-Level Value-Stream Map 147

4.3.2.2 F-15 Heads-Up Display High-Level Value-Stream Map 181
4.3.2.3 A Comparison of Air Force and Commercial Avionics Repair 186
Appendix: Performance Metrics for the Transformation of a Depot Maintenance Base....... 187

Chapter 5 Best Sustainment Practices 191
5.1 Benchmarking 192
5.1.1 Best Sustainment Practices: A Definition 193
5.1.2 Reasons for Searching for Best Practices....... 193
5.2 Objectives of This Chapter....... 194
5.3 A Methodology for Benchmarking 195
5.3.1 Identifying the Best Practices 195
5.3.1.1 Conducting a Survey....... 195
5.3.1.2 Websearches 197
5.3.1.3 Reports and Papers....... 197
5.3.2 A Framework for Identifying and Classifying the Best Practices 197
5.3.2.1 Step 1: Defining the Issue or Problem 197
5.3.2.2 Step 2: Identifying Solutions to the Problem: Higher-Level Practices....... 199
5.3.2.3 Step 3: Identifying the Enabling Practices and Their Sources....... 201
5.3.2.4 Step 4: Listing the Best Practice and Its Related Tasks 202
5.3.3 Generic Benchmarking Categories 203
5.3.4 Key Operations, Functions, Processes in Sustainment to Be Benchmarked 203
5.3.5 Performance Characteristics/Metrics to Be Benchmarked...205
5.4 Conducting Site Visits to Witness the Best Practices 205
5.5 Mapping the Best Practice to the Appropriate Task in a Transformation Project 206
5.6 Summarizing and Reporting the Results 210
5.7 Implementing the Best Sustainment Practices 211
5.8 Schedule Plan for Executing the Seven-Step Benchmarking Process....... 213
5.9 Best Sustainment Practice Case Studies....... 215
5.9.1 Pratt & Whitney....... 216
5.9.1.1 A Case Study in Implementing Enterprise Resource Planning Systems at Pratt & Whitney Space Propulsion 216

5.9.1.2 A Case Study on Cellular Repair and Overhaul at Pratt & Whitney's San Antonio Engine Center 218
5.9.1.3 A Case Study on Depot Production Operations at Pratt & Whitney 222
5.9.2 The U.S. Army 223
5.9.2.1 The Corpus Christi Army Depot 223
5.9.2.2 The U.S. Army Maintenance Center–Albany 227
5.9.2.3 The U.S. Army Materiel Command 228
Appendix: Benchmarking Questionnaire 232
Section A: Performance Metrics 233
Section B: Customer Interaction and Performance Levels 235
Section C: Service Processes 237
Section D: Information Infrastructure 239
Section E: Business Practices 244
Section F: General Background Information 247

Chapter 6 Lean Enterprise Transformation Activities: A Guide 249
6.1 Activity 1: Establish an Integrated Product Team (IPT) 252
6.1.1 Senior Management Involvement and Support 252
6.1.2 Empowerment 253
6.1.3 Composition of the IPT 253
6.1.4 Stakeholders 254
6.1.5 Communication 255
6.1.6 Change Management Plan 255
6.1.7 Integration Plan 256
6.2 Activity 2: Define the Need and Describe the Problem 257
6.2.1 The Need 257
6.2.2 The Requirements 258
6.2.3 Is the Transformation a Product or a Service? 259
6.2.3.1 Product Type of Contract 260
6.2.3.2 Service Type of Contract 260
6.2.4 Synopsis of a Transformation Initiative 260
6.3 Activity 3: Transformation Preliminary Design—Possible Solutions 261
6.4 Activity 4: Transformation Detailed Design—Performance Work Statement or Statement of Objectives? 262
6.5 Activity 5: Transformation Detailed Design—Measuring and Managing Performance 263
6.6 Activity 6: Transformation Implementation—Source Selection 264
6.6.1 Source Selection Documents 265
6.6.2 Evaluating the Proposal Responses 266

6.7 Activity 7: Transformation Implementation—Managing Performance and Risks 268
6.7.1 Risk Management 268
6.7.2 Create a Training Course 269
6.8 Activity 8: Transformation Operation 270
6.9 Conclusion 270
Appendix A: Useful Websites 271
Government Websites 271
Market Research Websites 272

Notes 273
Chapter 1 273
Chapter 2 274
Chapter 3 274
Chapter 4 274
Chapter 5 275
Chapter 6 275

References 277
Chapter 1 277
Chapter 2 279
Chapter 3 280
Chapter 4 284
Chapter 5 288
Chapter 6 289

Index 291

Preface

An increased military operational tempo, aging weapon systems, an aging workforce, limited financial resources, and new technologies are some of the reasons why the military needs an aggressive sustainment transformation plan. *Sustainment* is defined as the maintenance, repair, and overhaul (MRO) practices that keep the systems (the products of the military enterprise) operating and up to date (via new technology upgrades) throughout their entire life cycle. The goal is to achieve a quantum leap in sustainment throughput and efficiency by transforming military depot workload and processes into those of a best-in-class commercial-type facility. In order to produce a successful transformation, military depots require an integrated set of activities and support methods that execute their strategic vision, program concepts, acquisition strategy, schedule, communications plan, and implementation strategy. To accomplish this objective, this book describes a lean enterprise architecture (LEA) strategy to transform the MRO industrial enterprise. LEA is a structure to organize the activities for the transformation of the enterprise. It is the application of systems architecting methods to design, construct, integrate, and implement a lean enterprise using maintenance engineering methods and practices. The design process incorporates lean attributes and values as design requirements in creating the enterprise. The application of the LEA is designed to be less resource intensive and disruptive to the organization over the traditional lean enterprise transformation methods and practices.

The Office of the Secretary of Defense of the U.S. government has recognized the need for process improvement and directed all Department of Defense (DoD) logisticwide initiatives to undergo a transformation by adopting commercially proven practices and strategies. This directive is a radical departure from the traditional military paradigm, and it is aimed at all enterprises that perform DoD work. These enterprises include contractors such as Boeing, Honeywell, IBM, Lockheed Martin, and Raytheon. These logistic transformation objectives include the implementation of many commercial best practices, such as lean and cellular manufacturing, systems engineering, and supply-chain management. Transformation offices have been established in the military to implement these new strategies. The problem is that these offices have no condensed, user-oriented context to refer to in the search for the necessary tools with which to implement the strategies. The rush to field new products and systems without using sustainability requirements continues to plague projects in the government, as well as the commercial sectors of our economy.

The intent of this book is to help develop the management and technical skills necessary to design and implement cost-effective, integrated, sustainment networks and agile organizational structures. At the same time, new tools are needed to help address the unique problems facing the military sustainment community. These problems include aging systems and commercial off-the-shelf life-cycle support challenges. For example, the Lockheed C-5 military transport was designed in the 1960s with a life expectancy to the year 2000. Because of cutbacks in new DoD systems procurement, its life was extended well into the 21st century. How does such old technology sustain itself well beyond its expected life? Another example is the V-22 Osprey tilt-rotor aircraft program, which initially had significant operational test and evaluation problems. Most of these problems have been overcome, but what performance-based logistics maintenance support program design is best for this new system?

Commercially proven supply-chain management and lean enterprise practices have significantly benefited the manufacturing and retail industries, but they have been difficult to apply in the defense industry because of the high degree of variability in both source material and low-volume production requirements. Under ideal conditions, a sustainment supply chain network would be responsive and flexible enough to meet varying demand conditions. The right types of material and parts would be available in the right quantities, at the right place, at the right time, and at an affordable cost. Parts and material shortages, coupled with increased maintenance requirements, are just some of the issues facing the sustainment community today. The logistic transformation from a (Cold War) mass-production model into a "lean and agile" model requires significant management and technological change. In much the same way, commercial enterprises supporting the military need to ascertain how to sustain themselves during transformations in the DoD enterprise.

The author has investigated many of these problems and the application of new technologies, tools, and strategies that could be leveraged in providing leaner and agile sustainment networks. This book focuses on the various process-improvement initiatives that are available to help sustain the military enterprise, and it presents a lean enterprise architecture to accomplish that objective. It is the first volume in the *Sustaining the Military Enterprise* series. Future volumes by the author will provide the sustainment community with the required maintainability, reliability, supportability, and logistics practices and technologies, and it will also present the necessary principles of maintenance and systems engineering that are required for military sustainability.

Acknowledgments

First and foremost, special gratitude must be extended to my wife, Clare Comm, for her love, patience, and encouragement throughout the long and arduous production of this manuscript.

My sincere appreciation must also be extended to two individuals without whom this book would not be possible: Mario F. Agripino, president of EC Systems Engineering (http://www.ec-systemsengineering.com); and Timothy P. Cathcart at the Naval Undersea Warfare Center in Newport, Rhode Island. Each of these individuals possesses over 20 years of hands-on experience in the sustainment field. This collective experience proved invaluable to the production of this book. They contributed generously to the ideas contained within, and they provided support and feedback during its production. Furthermore, it was Tim Cathcart who first encouraged me to write this book. My thanks to you both!

Finally, I would like to thank the Massachusetts Institute of Technology, the U.S. Air Force, and Babson College. It was my involvement in the Lean Sustainment Initiative at MIT in collaboration with the U.S. Air Force that provided the incentive and knowledge that led to the production of this manuscript, and the Babson College Board of Research provided the funding that enabled me to benchmark the institutions used as case studies in this manuscript.

About the Author

Dennis F. X. Mathaisel is professor of management science in the Department of Mathematics and Science at Babson College, and holds a doctor of philosophy degree from the Massachusetts Institute of Technology. For 20 years he was a research engineer at MIT. He was also cofounder and president of Scheduling Systems Incorporated, a computer software firm, and in the early 1970s he was a branch manager at the McDonnell Douglas Corporation.

Dr. Mathaisel's interests focus on the sustainability of complex and aging systems. He is an expert in lean sustainment, and was an MIT colead for the Lean Sustainment Initiative for the U.S. Air Force. Dr. Mathaisel has written several papers on lean sustainment and enterprise transformation. Through his experience working with several government and commercial organizations he has learned how an effectively designed and executed enterprise transformation plan can promote the vision, commitment, sense of urgency, senior leadership buy-in, and shared goals and objectives that are necessary for a successful adaptation of enterprisewide lean sustainment.

Dr. Mathaisel has consulted for the Federal Aviation Administration, the National Aeronautics and Space Administration, the U.S. Air Force, and the U.S. Department of Transportation (Office of the Secretary); Pratt & Whitney; FedEx, the Flying Tiger Lines, Continental Airlines, Garuda Indonesia Airline, Hughes Airwest, Iberia Airlines, Northwest Airlines, Olympic Airlines, Pan American World Airways, Trans World Airlines, and USAirways, among many other institutions. These assignments have focused on enterprise sustainment, the application of lean manufacturing to sustainability, decision support systems, maintenance and logistics, scheduling, fleet and route planning, and transport systems analysis and engineering.

Dr. Mathaisel is a private pilot and an owner of a Cessna 182 aircraft based at Hanscom Air Force Base, near Concord, Massachusetts.

Chapter 1

The Current Military Sustainment System

Some believe that with the United States in the midst of a dangerous war on terrorism, now is not the time to transform our armed forces. I believe that the opposite is true. Now is precisely the time to make changes. The war on terrorism is a transformational event that cries out for us to rethink our activities, and to put that new thinking into action....

As we prepare for the future, we must think differently and develop the kinds of forces and capabilities that can adapt quickly to new challenges and to unexpected circumstances. We must transform not only the capabilities at our disposal, but also the way we think, the way we train, the way we exercise and the way we fight. We must transform not only our armed forces, but also the Department that serves them by encouraging a culture of creativity and prudent risk-taking. We must promote an entrepreneurial approach to developing military capabilities, one that encourages people to be proactive, not reactive, and anticipates threats before they emerge.

—Donald H. Rumsfeld, "Secretary's Foreword," in U.S. Department of Defense, *Transformation Planning Guidance*

Transformation has become the new buzzword within the U.S. Department of Defense (DoD). In fact, the National Defense Authorization Act for fiscal year

2005, Title VIII, Subtitle F, requires the secretary of defense to provide the department's plans to increase the emphasis placed on lean manufacturing technologies and processes in acquisition programs, and the potential for broader application of such technologies and processes throughout the department—in particular, sustainment. *Sustainment*, or *depot maintenance activity*, is defined here as the means by which the military enterprise is enduring. It also is defined as the maintenance, repair, and overhaul (MRO) practices that keep systems (the products of the enterprise) operating and up to date (new technology upgrades) throughout their entire life cycle. Depot maintenance activity involves repairing, overhauling, and modifying and upgrading defense systems and equipment. It also includes the limited manufacture of parts, technical support, modifications, testing, and reclamation as well as software maintenance.

In addition to the "war on terrorism," an increased military operational tempo, aging weapons systems, an aging workforce, limited financial resources, inadequate resource management, and the availability of new sustainment technologies are only some of the reasons why nearly every MRO depot has conducted a study of its sustainment enterprise to become more efficient. Most of these studies focus on individual elements of this system, such as transforming a turbine engine blade shop using lean principles and cellular nanufacturing concepts, or instituting a purchasing and supply-chain management (PSCM) initiative. However, to more effectively solve the sustainment problem, research should be conducted on the whole enterprise, from raw-material suppliers to delivery of the repaired/overhauled system.

This volume focuses on the tools and processes that management, product development, systems engineering, and operational support teams should consider in the design, development, operation, and improvement of their depot maintenance systems that are cost effective in all phases of the product's life cycle, "from cradle to grave." The goal is to minimize non-value-added activities throughout the entire sustainment enterprise.

To counter the challenges currently facing the sustainment system, military maintenance, repair, and overhaul depots must implement an aggressive transformation plan for the future. The DoD 2001 Quadrennial Defense Review has described the need to reduce the logistics footprint, improve DoD global mobility, and increase the reliability of DoD weapons systems. In addition, the new DoD Defense Acquisition Management series directive 5000.1 (Defense Acquisition System) and instruction 5000.2 (Operation of the Defense Acquisition System) are oriented toward achieving these objectives while also reducing the time required for development and deployment of needed war-fighter capability through implementation of evolutionary acquisition strategies and spiral development processes. The goal of all these directives is to achieve a quantum leap in sustainability throughput and efficiency by transforming depot workload and processes into those of a "best in class" facility using best practices, process improvement initiatives, and advanced manufacturing/sustainment processes and layouts.

A question arises as to whether to transform the entire enterprise (either the entire depot or each strategic business unit) all at once or to incrementally repair one cell at a time. This volume contributes to the question by defining and describing a lean enterprise architecture for the transformation of the entire MRO enterprise. Three disciplines guide the design: the application of current process improvement initiatives in the transformation, enterprise architecture, and systems engineering concepts.

Professionals involved in sustainment need a parallel set of skills and tools. One set should focus on the management aspects of the integration of the support elements and the sustainment issues with other program management functions. The other set should focus on the engineering aspects of sustainment. To date, no condensed, practical, and user-oriented text has been available to meet these two needs. To address this void, the author has researched new approaches specifically designed for the problems currently facing the sustainment community. These papers provide the essential technical skills, methods, and tools needed to implement many new strategies and principles that are required in order to effectively sustain the military enterprise and the products created by that enterprise. The present volume is the result of these efforts.

1.1 Introduction

Since 1990, the DoD has reduced its budget by 29 percent. This reduction has greatly impacted weapons system acquisition and in-service support (Cordesman 2000). Reduced budgets have forced the branches of the military to extend the life of current legacy systems with significant reductions in acquisition of replacement systems. In addition, current weapons systems are faced with escalating operations and maintenance costs. These sustainment costs are due to

- Increased operational tempo
- Increased mean time between maintenance cycles due to increased operational requirements
- Increased life extension of existing weapons systems due to delays in new-system acquisition
- Unforeseen support problems associated with aging weapons systems
- Material shortages because of diminishing manufacturing resources and technological obsolescence
- An aging MRO workforce, one-third of which is eligible for retirement in the next five years
- The development and introduction of new sustainment technologies, such as advanced systems electronics and failure detection
- Reduction of the organic infrastructure due to base realignment and closure
- Insufficient investment in the current plant and equipment

As sustainment costs increase, there is less funding available to procure replacement systems. An analysis conducted by the DoD (Gansler 1999) has concluded that unless mission requirements and the operational tempo are reduced or there are significant increases in the budget, the operational maintenance cost portions of the budget will equal the total current (net present value) budgets by the year 2024 (see fig. 1.1). This chain of events has been illustrated and characterized in figure 1.2 as the "DoD death spiral." To waive off this death spiral, the DoD must find innovative solutions to support legacy systems that are cost effective and flexible. The DoD must economically manage these system life cycles in order to address obsolescence and modernization issues without degrading readiness, cost, and performance objectives.

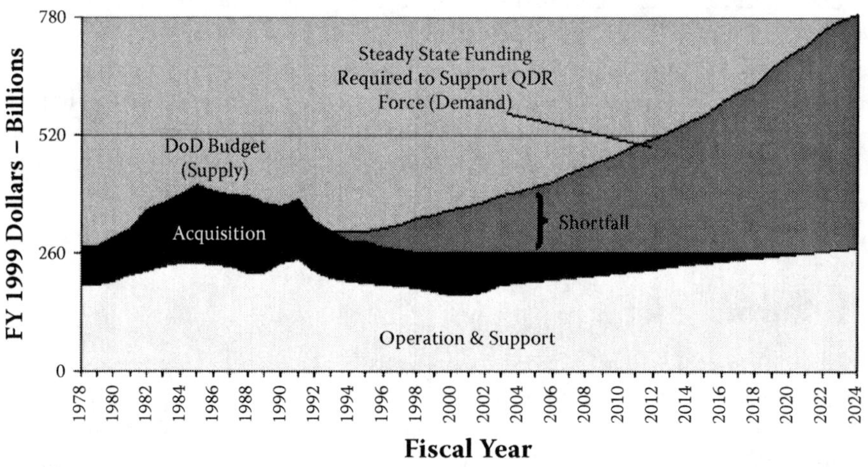

Figure 1.1. The DoD Budget Profile (from Gansler 1999).

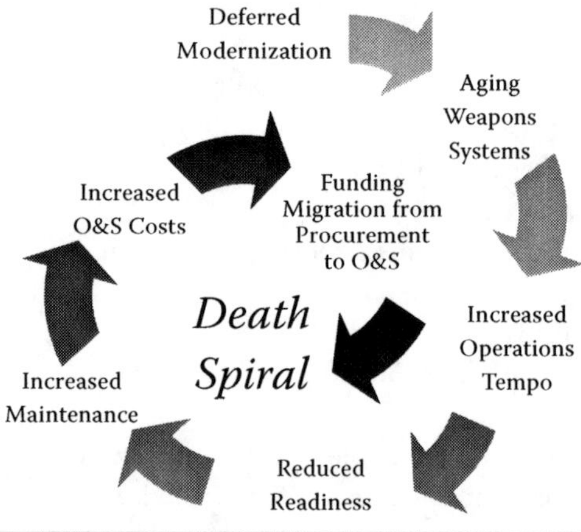

Figure 1.2 The DoD "Death Spiral" (from Gansler 1999).

Along with DoD budgets, the defense industry sector has shrunk dramatically. In order to effectively compete in a significantly smaller market, the industry has seen a large number of corporate mergers. With the restructuring of the new industry base, many of the supply chain networks no longer exist. Second- and third-tier supply-chain businesses have gone out of production. The defense industry sector is changing, and their associated supply-chain network is eroding rapidly.

With over 60 percent of the total aircraft system life cycle cost associated with operations and aircraft maintenance, and as aircraft systems age, there is great opportunity to optimize sustainment costs (Blanchard and Fabrycky 1998). With some degree of success, industry and government partnerships have been formed to attempt to address these issues. Examples include agile combat support (Eady and Williams 1997), flexible sustainment (Performance-Based Business Environment 1997), the U.S. Army's Modernization through Spares program (Kros 1999), the Lean Aerospace Initiative,[1] and the Lean Sustainment Initiative.[2] These initiatives focus on three primary areas:

1. Modernization through commercial off-the-shelf technology solutions ("technology refreshment" and "technology insertion")
2. Manufacturing, production, and logistics methods (the "just in time," lean, and agile initiatives).
3. Modernization of the industrial base (the flexible manufacturing system, material resource planning systems, and advanced manufacturing technologies).

However, these initiatives focus on individual elements of the sustainment system, not the whole enterprise; thus, the question arises, are these efforts coordinated? Organizations have the mind-set that if it was not invented here it has no value. Therefore, the results of independent efforts often are not used by organizations other than those that are the target of the investigation. These projects overlap, and in many cases multiple initiatives are conducted on the same research areas (Warren 1998).

The forces depend upon a highly responsive sustainment system to ensure that well-maintained equipment is ready and available to the warfighter. The variance in the demand for these resources places an increased responsibility on the depots. Existing depot maintenance production methodologies need to be made more flexible to meet these varying demand requirements. However, the supporting facility infrastructure, equipment, processes, and personnel are operating with less-than-optimal flow processes, facility constraints, and outdated equipment. Current batch-and-queue methods of production are task oriented and functionally isolated (Sharma and Moody 2001). Current systems are designed and arranged as separate elements, which results in excessive travel time and distance for parts. Past performance-improvement efforts were concerned with the process, not the product. There is a big distinction between process flow and product flow. Process flow was instituted to ensure that each process was operated efficiently without regard to end item support to the customer. The process flow approach was deemed a mistake and, ultimately, expensive. In addition, some portion of the industrial processing equipment is aging and is at the point of needing refurbishment or replacement. The equipment is prone to excessive downtime due to long lead-supply items, out-of-business contractors, and obsolete parts.

To effectively respond to this increased, yet unpredictable, demand for mission-ready resources, the depots must confront the challenges with an aggressive transformation plan for the complete industrial complex and processes. The focus should be on increasing throughput and customer support, with the additional benefits of reducing flow time, and increasing available capacity and labor productivity, so that the depot can achieve more productive work. The transformation entails changes in repair processes, material support, financial accounting systems, and management mind-set. The industrial space needs to be transformed to function with commercial efficiencies through the use of process improvement initiatives like lean manufacturing (Lamming 1993; Liker 1997; Womack and Jones 1996; Maskell 2003). Recent U.S. Air Force initiatives, such as the Air Force Materiel Command's depot maintenance transformation and PSCM, have already adopted commercially proven lean MRO transformation methodologies and practices. These methods and practices facilitate increased capacity, higher quality, and higher productivity while simultaneously reducing inventory and costs (Liker 1997). Also applicable to the transformation effort are the principles of cellular manufacturing (Levasseur, Helms, and Zink 1995; Mungwattana 2000; Sekine 1992; Singh and Rajamaani 1996). The integration of people, machines, and the control and manufacturing processes that bind them together within "cells" reduces cost, material scrap, workforce requirements, lead times, reworking, and flow times, and it optimizes the use of floor space. Such changes must be foundational and fundamental to the way depots conduct business. Limited resources and significant cultural changes compound the transformation process. Further, the necessity to provide continuing support to operations throughout the transition process increases the challenge.

Lean enterprise engineering and cellular manufacturing, particularly in a large depot organization, is a complex task that requires a critical balance be maintained within four major areas during all stages of transformation:

1. The lean and cellular MRO strategy
2. An infrastructure that supports a lean/cellular operation
3. Change management: a symbiotic relationship between the decision-making personnel and the operating personnel to establish ownership of lean goals and the responsibility of the government to provide additional education and training required to effect change.
4. Continued support of the MRO requirements during the transformation

These interrelated functional areas are key to a transformation, from conceptualization through acquisition planning and integration, and on into the support phase of the implementation.

The transformation also requires an architecture that portrays the overall "flow" of the action phases necessary to initiate, sustain, and continuously refine the enterprise transformation that would result in the implementation of the lean/cellular principles and practices (Brown 2000). Should this architecture be enterprisewide? Or, should the architecture support an incremental, cell-by-cell, transformation?

1.2 Characterization of the Current Military Sustainment System

The DoD depot maintenance program was at its peak in 1987 in terms of workload, people, and facilities. It has changed significantly since then. The primary event that framed these changes and put certain key actions into motion was the end of the Cold War and the associated force-structure downsizing. A number of other diverse but interrelated factors—such as threat changes, new war fighting plans, and changes in maintenance concepts—influenced defense downsizing. With these change agents in the works, the DoD began restructuring its depot maintenance program. This restructuring primarily has been achieved through three series of actions: (1) the base realignment and closure (BRAC) process, which was designed to reduce the DoD's infrastructure; (2) increased reliance on the private sector for depot maintenance support; and (3) a major downsizing of depot maintenance personnel. Today, the DoD has a smaller depot structure (see fig. 1.3) with three Air Force air logistics centers, five Army depots, two Marine Corps multicommodity maintenance centers, three Navy aviation depots, four naval shipyards, one naval surface warfare center in Indiana,[3] and the aerospace maintenance and regeneration center in Arizona.[4]

Thus, as a result of the BRAC process, in 2001, 19 of the 38 public-sector maintenance depots that existed in 1987 remain in operation as government-owned and -operated activities, primarily supporting DoD maintenance but with several diversifying to also support commercial customers. Additionally, most of the remaining military depots are smaller in size since 1987 as equipment has been consolidated and facility footprints downsized. Some of the prior military facilities were privatized, such as the San Antonio, Texas, air logistics center, and continue to function with important maintenance activities. During the period 1987–2001, depot maintenance personnel have been reduced by 59 percent, the third highest percent of any category of DoD civilian personnel (U.S. General Accounting Office 2001a). Also, while the number of systems being maintained has declined since 1987, system complexity and age have increased, thus increasing the amount of depot maintenance work required for many systems. For example, in 2001 the average amount of time for a C-141 overhaul was about 9,200 hours, or one-third more than the average amount of time in 1987.

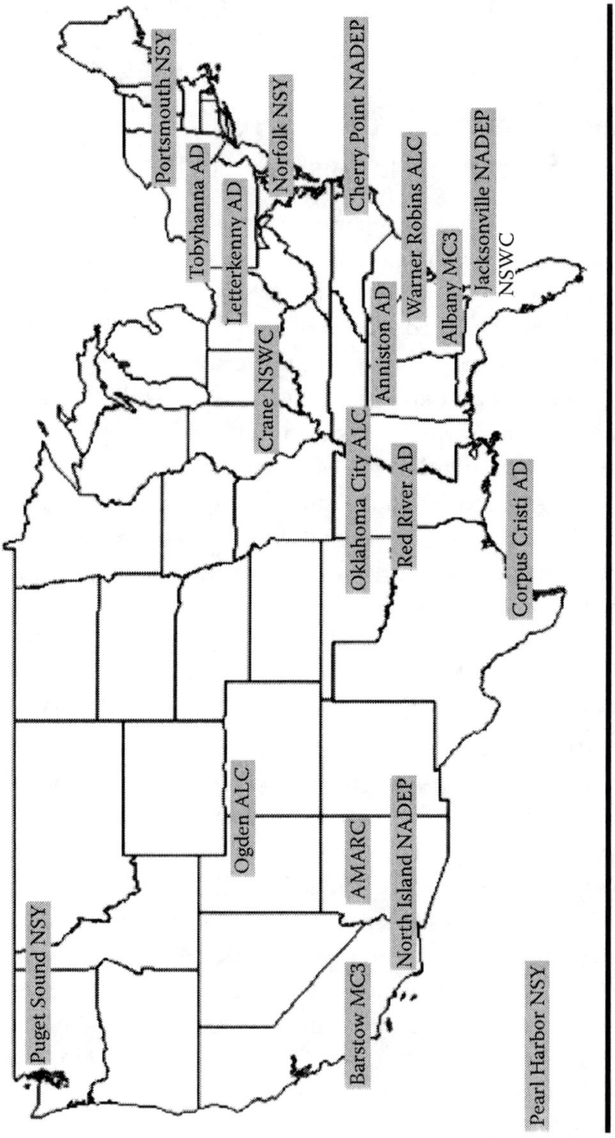

Figure 1.3 The DoD Depot Maintenance System.

In terms of defense contractors, information is not available regarding the number of contractor facilities in which the tens of thousands of depot-level maintenance contracts are being performed or the value of the equipment that is involved. Increasingly, the DoD is contracting for a variety of logistics activities that may include supply and weapons system support, engineering, configuration management, maintenance, and a variety of other functions. As recommended in various studies, the DoD has implemented a policy change placing increased reliance on defense contractors for depot maintenance and related logistics activities. While no central database provides reliable information about depot maintenance contracting, contractors' share of depot maintenance funding has increased by 90 percent while the military depots' share of funding has declined by 6 percent in the period 1987–2001 (U.S. General Accounting Office 2001a). Although workload production data is not available for contract work, the military depots' production hours were down 64 percent during this period. This policy shift to the private sector has most directly affected workloads for new and upgraded systems, because work on these is largely going to the private sector.

In terms of the amount of money being spent on sustainment, depot maintenance activities are funded through the Defense Working Capital Fund (DWCF) budget. The fiscal year 2006 DWCF budget was $112.1 billion, of which $58.8 billion was for supply management and $14.6 billion for depot maintenance activities (shipyards; Navy aviation; and Air Force, Army, and Marine depots; Donnelley and Proctor 2005). The depot maintenance program funds the overhaul, repair, and maintenance of aircraft, missiles, ships, submarines, combat vehicles, and other equipment.

The current military sustainment system is complex, but it can be characterized in a simple way as comprising four major elements: supply support, intermediate/depot maintenance and operational support, integrated logistic support, and the in-service engineering process. This characterization, illustrated in figure 1.4, demonstrates the necessary coordination among the various sustainment organizations.

Starting on the right side of figure 1.4, the supply support function consists of the supply chain, the supply system, and the Government Industry Data Exchange Program. The supply chain is comprised of the vendors (V) and suppliers (S) that provide consumable materials and refurbishment services to the supply system and depot. The item manager has overall responsibility for inventory management, handled through inventory control points. Inventory locations are referenced as designated stock points, which maintain spares and consumable inventories.

The intermediate and depot maintenance functions consist of those maintenance organizations responsible for keeping weapons systems in a serviceable condition. The designated overhaul point, also known as the organic military depot, performs maintenance that includes servicing, inspection, test, adjustment and alignment, removal, replacement, reinstallation, troubleshooting, calibration, repair, modification, and overhaul of weapons systems and components (Blanchard, Verma, and Peterson 1995; Jones 1995). Maintenance data and failure analysis are provided

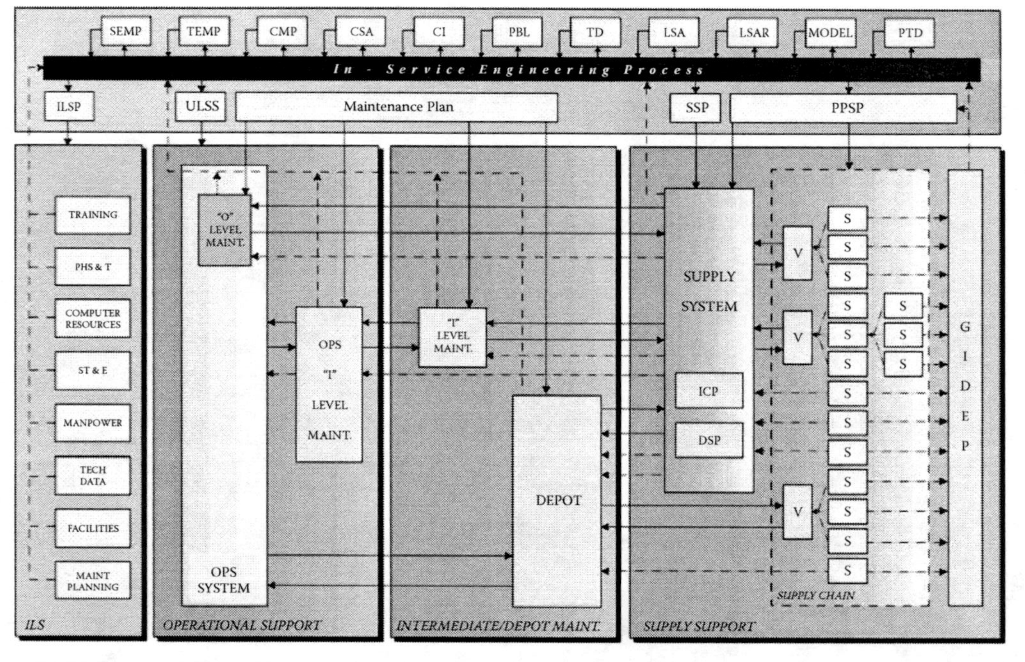

Figure 1.4 The Current Military Sustainment System.

Key: CI = configuration item; CMP = configuration management plan; CSA = configuration status accounting; DSP = designated stock point; GIDEP = Government Industry Data Exchange program; ICP = inventory control point; I-Level = intermediate level maintenance; ILS = integrated logistic support; ILSP = integrated logistic support plan; LSA = logistics support analysis; LSAR = logistics support analysis record; O-Level = operational level maintenance; PBL = product baseline; PPSP = postproduction support plan; PTD = provisioning technical documentation; S = supplier; SEMP = system engineering master plan; SSP = supply support plan; ST&E = special tools and equipment; TD = technical data; TEMP = test and evaluation master plan; ULSS = users' logistics support summary; V = vendor.

to the in-service engineering process. Intermediate maintenance organizations provide operational support services at the customer's base of operations. Depot maintenance organizations perform MRO services to the weapons system and its associated components. The depot procures consumable materials from the supply system and commercial sources.

The integrated logistics support function on the far right of figure 1.4 is a composite of all support considerations, including system design for sustainability and the logistics infrastructure that is necessary to assure effective and economical support of a system throughout its existing life (Blanchard 1998). The primary objective is to achieve and maintain readiness objectives. Logistics include all of the support elements necessary to sustain the weapons system, including such elements as training and support; packaging, handling, storage, and transportation; and computer resources and support.

The in-service engineering process, at the top of figure 1.4, is responsible for maintaining the system configuration of the product and identifying postproduction support problems and product improvements associated with the operation, maintenance, and integrated logistic support of all weapons system support elements. Other responsibilities include the evaluation, definition, and testing of solutions to possible postproduction support problems using systems engineering processes in an effective and expeditious manner to support required readiness objectives for the remainder of a weapons system's life cycle (INCOSE 1998).

To illustrate the inefficiency and complexity of the current military sustainment system, figure 1.5 shows the system from the perspective of the distribution channel and the supply chain. In that figure, the distribution channel on the left includes the processes necessary to provide a ready-for-issue (RFI) spare part to the war fighter, including the technical maintenance services provided by the maintenance sustainment organizations. The supply channel on the right includes the processes necessary to replenish the RFI stock inventory required to support the distribution channel. This process includes replenishing the consumables, the MRO of RFI spares, and the associated lower-level supply-chain activities. Note that there are seven levels for the distribution and supply chain. Another perspective of this complexity is also illustrated in figure 1.6, which places the item manager in the center of the complicated supply-channel and distribution-channel activity. Such a model is good for the support of large, slowly changing platforms and systems, but it possesses negative characteristics, such as:

- It is a seven-tier sustainment system: there are too many links in the supply chain
- It contains uncoupled processes
- It has fragmented organizational structures
- It possesses uncoordinated supplier and distribution channels
- It is a push-oriented, not pull-oriented system, which violates one of the fundamental principles of lean sustainment
- It is not responsive in today's MRO environment

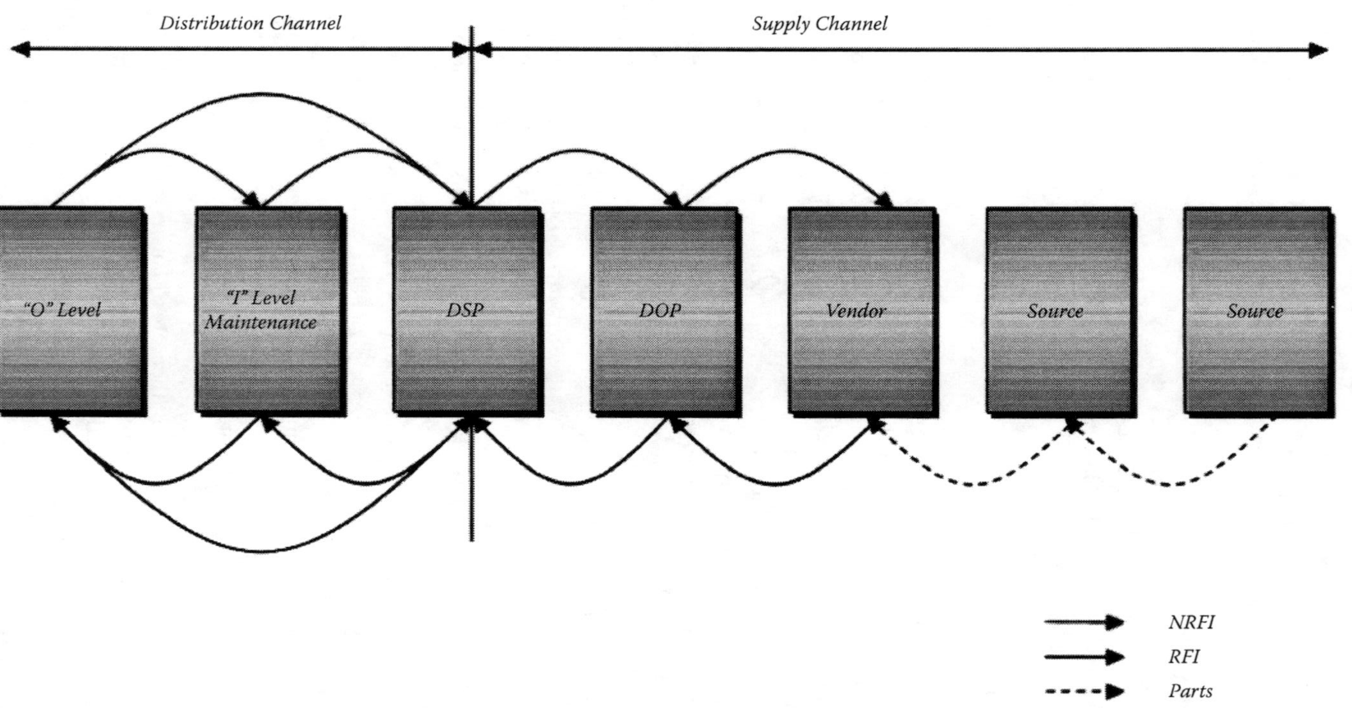

Figure 1.5 The Current Military Sustainment Supply Chain.

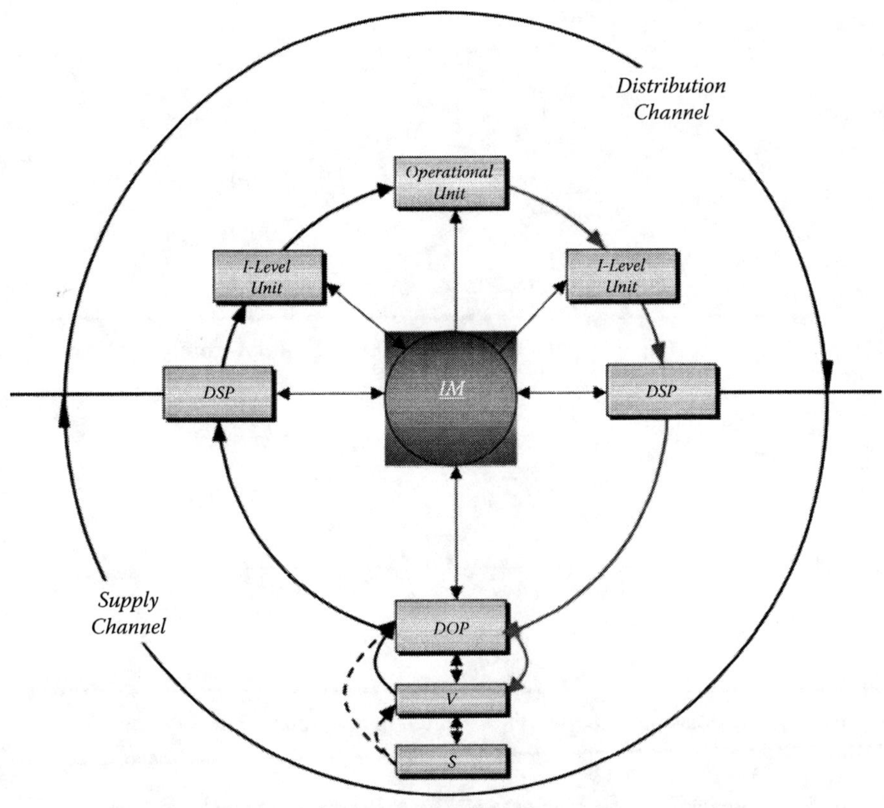

Figure 1.6 Current Military Sustainment Distribution and Supply Channels.

The complexity of the channels in figures 1.5 and 1.6 indicate that there is an opportunity to integrate many of the system functional elements to effectively meet supply system and fleet requirements concurrently.

1.3 Analysis of the Current Military Sustainment System

One key measure of military sustainment performance is the availability of weapons systems to carry out their missions. The high-level metric that is most often tracked is the mission capable (MC) rate and its associated full mission capable (FMC) rate. These rates are the percentage of time a weapons system can perform at least one (MC) or all (FMC) of its assigned missions. The U.S. General Accounting Office (GAO) has examined key DoD aircraft MC and FMC rates, and whether the respective services have been able to meet their MC and FMC goals. What the GAO found was that the average annual MC and FMC rates for fiscal years 1998–2002 was about 77–83 percent for the Army and the Air Force,

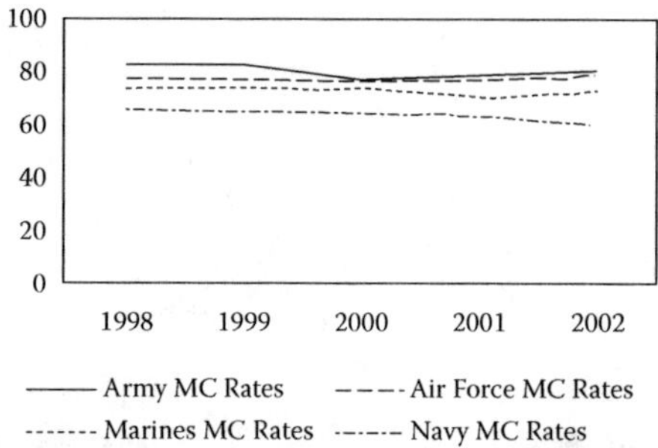

Figure 1.7 Mission Capable (MC) Rates (from U.S. General Accounting Office 2003).

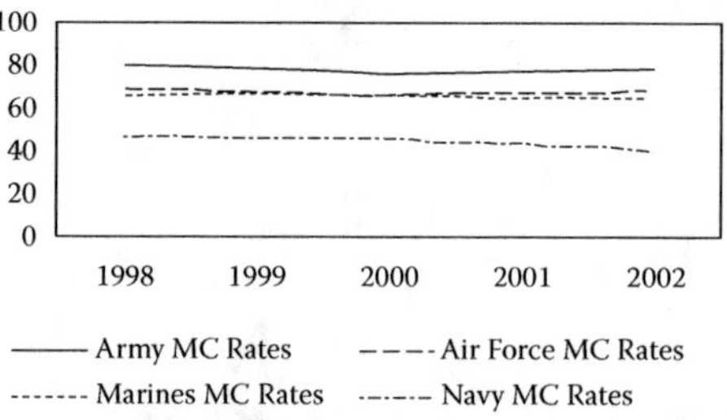

Figure 1.8 Full Mission Capable (FMC) Rates (from U.S. General Accounting Office 2003).

about 71–75 percent for the Marines; and 61–67 percent for the Navy (see fig. 1.7). A similar pattern follows for the average FMC rates for the services (see fig. 1.8). Average MC and FMC rates varied by service and type of aircraft. Among aircraft types, the average MC rates varied from 60 to 80 percent. Average MC rates were the highest for helicopters, followed by cargo aircraft and tankers, fighter/attack aircraft, bombers, and electronic command/control aircraft (U.S. General Accounting Office 2003).

The GAO also found that less than one-half of 49 key active-duty aircraft models that it had reviewed met their MC or FMC goals during fiscal years 1998–2002. In most cases the actual rates reported above were at least 5 percentage points below the goals. The difficulties in meeting the goals are caused by a complex combination of logistical and operational factors. One big factor is the age of the weapons systems. For example, the average military aircraft age is 21 years, which, of course, varies considerably by platform (see table 1.1; Michaels 2004).

As these systems age, spare-parts shortages adversely affect the performance of assigned missions (MC and FMC rates) and the economy and efficiency of maintenance activities. For instance, table 1.2 shows the reported rates for U.S. Air Force aircraft that were mission capable and those that were not mission capable due to the shortage of spare parts to repair them.

Table 1.1 Aircraft Age

Aircraft	*Age (in Years)*
B-52 Bomber	41
KC-135 Refueling Tanker	40
C-5 Transport	35
UH-1 Helicopter	31
C-130 Transport	25
F-16 Fighter	13
NH-90 Helicopter	5

Table 1.2 Reported Rates for Aircraft that Were Mission Capable and Not Mission Capable

Fiscal Year	*Aircraft Reported as Mission Capable (Percent)*	*Aircraft Reported as Not Mission Capable Due to Supply Problems (Percent)*
1996	78.5	11.0
1997	76.6	12.6
1998	74.3	13.9
1999	73.5	14.0
2000	72.9	14.3
2001 (1st Quarter)	72.9	14.0

Source: U.S. General Accounting Office 2001a.

Spare-parts shortages are pervasive throughout the military sustainment system. The majority of reasons cited by item managers at the maintenance facilities for spare-parts shortages were most often related to more spares being required than were anticipated by the inventory management system and delays in the Air Force's repair process as a result of the consolidation of repair facilities. Other reasons included (1) difficulties with producing or repairing parts, (2) reliability of spare parts, and (3) contracting issues. For example, the anticipated quarterly demand for a machine bolt for the F-100-220 engine was 828, but actual demand turned out to be over 12,000. As a result, some F-100-220 engines were not mission capable because they were waiting for more bolts to be obtained. In another case, a contractor produced sufficient quantities of a visor seal assembly for the C-5, but the parts failed to meet design tolerances. As a result of this production problem, demands for this part could not be met for the Air Force (U.S. General Accounting Office June 2001b). Similar results are reported for the Navy (GAO July 2001c). The Army reports that the fact that actual demands for parts were often greater than anticipated, delays in obtaining parts from a contractor, and problems concerning overhaul and maintenance were the main reasons for the unavailability of parts. For example, because a cracked gear in a Chinook transmission was discovered during an overhaul, the entire fleet was grounded in August 1999. As a result, the demand for the part has been much greater than anticipated. Also, Defense Logistics Agency records show that as a result of a contractor's late deliveries of Apache shear bolts, the agency did not have the parts available for Apache users. Additionally, due to a shortage of parts the Army experienced problems that prevented it from repairing and overhauling Blackhawk T-700 engines in a timely manner. Furthermore, according to Army and Defense Logistics Agency officials, a contributing factor to the shortages was the Army's inability to obtain parts for these aging aircraft from the original part manufacturers, who may no longer be in business (U.S. General Accounting Office 2001d).

One tangential result of the parts shortage problem is cannibalization. When parts are not available to repair a malfunctioning aircraft, and the aircraft is needed to fly a mission, the cannibalization of another aircraft for parts is often seen as the answer. In the broadest sense, cannibalizations are done because of pressures to meet readiness and operational needs and because of shortcomings in the supply system. A Navy study also found that cannibalizations are sometimes done because mechanics are not trained well enough to diagnose problems or because testing equipment is either not available or not working. In these cases, parts are swapped from one aircraft to another until the larger problem is solved. All the military services use cannibalization extensively as a routine aircraft maintenance practice. In fiscal years 1996–2000, the Navy and the Air Force reported about 850,000 cannibalizations (see fig. 1.9), requiring about 5.3 million additional maintenance hours. For the Army, while the Apache, Blackhawk, and Chinook helicopters generally met their mission-capable goals, indicating that parts shortages have not affected their mission capability, supply availability rates and the cannibalization of parts from one aircraft to another indicate that spare-parts shortages have indeed been a problem. The numbers, however, are incomplete because the Navy's data are reportedly understated by as much as 50 percent, the Air Force underreports cannibalizations, and the Army

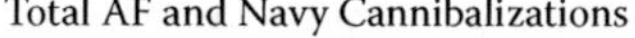

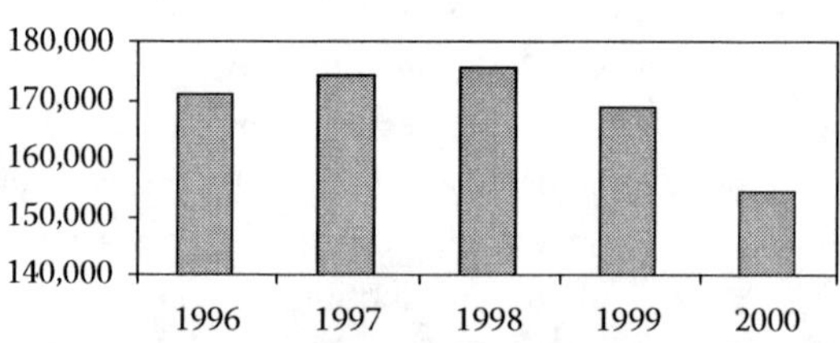

Figure 1.9 Total Air Force and Navy Cannibalizations for Fiscal Years 1996–2000 (from U.S. General Accounting Office 2001e).

does not collect servicewide figures.[5] As a result, neither the DoD nor the individual branches of the armed forces know the overall magnitude of the practice.

Cannibalizations have several adverse impacts. They increase maintenance costs by increasing mechanics' workloads, affect morale and personnel retention, and sometimes take expensive aircraft out of service for long periods of time. Cannibalizations can also create additional mechanical problems. The effects on workloads seem the most serious: over half of all aircraft maintenance personnel report working more than 50 hours a week, and some report working 70 hours or more. A Navy study has noted that the additional work generated by cannibalizations adversely affects morale and lowers reenlistment rates. However, because the services do not track how much time they spend on cannibalizations, they cannot assess all of the consequences (U.S. General Accounting Office 2001e).

Another factor contributing to the MC and FMC rates is inadequate resource management. For instance, the GAO reports that the U.S. Army is not effectively maintaining its equipment to ensure maximum mission capability at the least cost. A long-standing problem is poorly performed maintenance and repairs at the user level. In addition, inadequate record keeping and reporting provide Army management a more optimistic picture of equipment condition and status than actually exists. Ultimately, these conditions stem from inadequate supervision, training, and resource management at the local level, and insufficient monitoring of organizational maintenance operations by Army management (U.S. General Accounting Office 1987). Other principal findings in the GAO report note that

- Equipment deficiencies were often not detected and reported
- Inadequate maintenance is creating many equipment failures, greater maintenance costs, and unnecessary downtime
- Optimal effectiveness of organizational maintenance is hindered by inadequate supervision, training, and resources
- Maintenance records are being improperly maintained
- Although the Army purchased several million dollars worth of diagnostic equipment (and is buying more) to isolate and identify failures, organizational mechanics are not using it to troubleshoot vehicle failures
- Army managers lack sufficient visibility over monitoring the performance of organizational maintenance

While such MC, cannibalization, and resource-management observations seem to paint a negative picture of the current military sustainment system, it is important—and only fair—to take a balanced perspective when examining depot efficiency and responsiveness. A good starting point is to recognize that the MRO depots, taken together as a public enterprise, are embedded within a large and complex institutional, organizational, and management structure spanning the various materiel commands (e.g., the Army Materiel Command, the Air Force Materiel Command), the Defense Logistics Agency (DLA), and reaching well into various other parts of the DoD. They are also constrained by numerous government policies, regulations, rules, and practices. Even though these larger government-induced policy factors are not explicitly addressed in this volume, they represent a major constraining factor and require a more detailed analysis. It is also important to carefully sort out the various factors and influences impacting depot repair efficiency and responsiveness, at different levels, to identify major barriers and key strategic options to overcome these barriers, and to implement a comprehensive road map resulting in fundamental change by building upon steps already being taken. The guiding long-term purpose is to design a world-class, efficient, and responsive agile combat support system that meets both the peacetime and wartime needs of the nation's war fighters (Lean Sustainment Initiative 1998).

The summary of efficiency and responsiveness of the military sustainment system that follows consolidates the results from the Lean Sustainment Initiative at the Massachusetts Institute of Technology and integrates specific observations as they pertain to depot repair efficiency and responsiveness.[6] Key factors impacting depot repair efficiency and responsiveness, at the system level as well as at the depot level, are summarized, the latter incorporating shop-floor issues. The observations at different levels are highly interrelated and serve the purpose of presenting salient results in a structured manner. Meanwhile, it is important to recognize that the MRO depots, at the front lines of improving their efficiency and responsiveness, have little if any control over a number of key system-level factors, while other issues at the depot and shop levels can be addressed by the depots with support at the DoD level.

1.3.1 System-Level Factors Affecting Sustainment Efficiency and Responsiveness

> The excessively complex, multilayered, stove-piped, institutional, organizational, and management structure within which the depots are embedded is constraining efficiency and responsiveness.
>
> **—Lean Sustainment Initiative, "Depot Repair Efficiency and Responsiveness"**

Effective interorganizational interfaces and coordination mechanisms are lacking in the face of numerous stovepipe organizational units driven by quite different and often conflicting objectives and performance metrics against which they are evaluated. The functional interrelationships linking these organizational entities are complex, many-layered, and virtually impenetrable. The lack of visibility or transparency contributes to a lack of trust, impedes the development of a shared vision, and poses an obstacle to building mutually advantageous cooperative relationships. Further, roles and responsibilities are poorly defined, often making it difficult to discern who is working for whom or for whose benefit.

These interorganizational coordination problems are particularly acute in the case of financial interrelationships at various levels, starting with the development and management of the Defense Working Capital Fund (DWCF). The DWCF is further decomposed into funds for the respective services. For example, the Air Force business area is now called the Air Force Working Capital Fund, consisting of both Air Force managed activity groups and Air Force Materiel Command managed activity groups. The latter includes the Supply Management Activity Group (SMAG) and the Depot Maintenance Activity Group (DMAG). The DMAG is responsible for providing repair services to the SMAG and other customers. The DMAG bills the SMAG for these services, which can be performed organically at one of the depots, by a commercial source or by other service providers. Without a funded project order or customer order acceptance list from the SMAG, the DMAG would not induct assets into the repair process to get them fixed. For all practical purposes, the SMAG acts as the customer to the DMAG. However, the SMAG also serves as a support function, providing the DMAG with materials and supplies. This dual role played by the SMAG may be a source of conflict in its responsibility and accountability. Also, the daily interactions between the SMAG and the DMAG, concentrating on the organic workload execution process through funds application and project order processing, are largely governed by an excessively transaction-intensive bureaucratic process, where managing the process as currently structured may be running the risk of detracting from more directly focusing on customer needs and priorities.

Other interface problems permeate the relationships between the sustainment community and the DLA, for example. The DLA serves as the primary centralized supplier of DoD's consumable items, parts, and supplies needed for logistics and sustainment by all services. Employing over 30,000 people, the DLA operates a logistics system containing about four million items with a total inventory value of $89.2 billion (in 2005). In recent years, the DLA has been under increasing pressure to achieve significant savings through efficiency measures to make it possible for the DoD to find the much needed additional resources for weapons system modernization. Consequently, the DLA has embarked on a set of initiatives, such as outsourcing and privatization, acquisition reforms, organizational restructuring, and process reengineering to achieve savings in its support functions. In this connection, DLA has employed a number of commercial practices—such as its prime vendor, local distribution/supplier parks, and integrated supplier initiatives—to reduce logistics costs and meet sustainment needs more efficiently. However, the logistics and sustainment system can benefit from more extensive and far-reaching DLA efforts to modernize its operations, particularly by more aggressively pursuing the integrated supplier concept and by demonstrating greater flexibility in its support functions.

In an earlier study, this author has found that "[s]ome of the existing military policies and regulations concerning the procurement of materials and parts are either not properly implemented or are no longer effective in today's environment" (Mathaisel 2001, page 5).

Under ideal conditions, the right types of materials and parts would be available in the right quantities, at the right place, at the right time, and at affordable cost in order for the military sustainment system to provide the required services efficiently, flexibly, and responsively under varying demand conditions. However, materials and parts shortages have led to a number of critical systems having an unusually long "awaiting parts" (AWP) status during normal MRO operations. The situation has caused high rates of cannibalization of working weapons systems for parts and has caused long cycle times for MRO operations for some critical systems. In a few cases, the AP problem has been documented to be a reason for poor mission capability rates on associated weapons systems and was having a tremendous impact on MRO production operations.

Field studies conducted by the Lean Sustainment Initiative have revealed, for instance, that although military MRO operations are just as efficient as commercial operations, the AWP situation for the military was not as favorable as for the commercial counterparts. One of the team's observations was that cycle times for military MRO functions (such as testing, the actual repair process, and retesting) were favorably comparable to those in the commercial sector. In fact, lessons can be learned by the commercial sector from successes on the military side. In terms of these functions, at a high level, military MRO operations are just as efficient as commercial operations. The one exception, however, was when there was an AWP situation. For example, average time in AP status for avionics systems was 160 hours for commercial operations versus 848 hours for military operations.[7]

In its investigation into the underlying reasons for these parts-availability problems in the military sector, the team studied C-141 skin panels and F-15 heads-up displays (HUDs) and revealed the following:

- Parts were not cataloged in the DLA system. The program office systems engineers had revised the construction material for the panels, but it had not notified the DLA in Battle Creek, Michigan, for cataloging.
- The depot manufactured 14 of the parts in the last two years and had not completed the transaction process to record the demand.
- No forecasts were generated for the number of panels that needed to be repaired in the future. Thus, the DLA did not have warning on future requirements.
- Demand for HUDs increased by a factor of between three and four in the years of the team's investigation. This caused overreaction in the DLA ordering process.
- The depot repair-induction computer system continued to induct additional HUDs, which were not necessarily needed to satisfy Mission capable aircraft. In the end, the DLA had ordered 446 power supplies to satisfy this perceived demand, which was greater than actual need.

- The reason for the recent high demand in the HUD cables was unknown to the DLA. When contract negotiations were initiated with the sole source supplier of the parts, the supplier initially was "unresponsive" to the increased demands. When the supplier ultimately did respond, there was an "unsubstantiated" price increase of 38 percent, according to the DLA. The supplier stated that it had a problem getting deliveries of a component from one of its subsuppliers.
- The depot does not own any of the data packages for the HUD cable, so it cannot manufacture the cable on its own. Thus, it must rely on the sole source supplier.

After the assessment of the findings above, the following have been deemed to contribute to the root causes of the parts availability problem:

- Existing policies/procedures (demand transactions, configuration management) are not being followed.
- Forecasting procedures are not effective. With the thousands of national stock numbers (NSNs) that must be managed, no one in the system (depots, the DLA) can efficiently look at the demand data for low-volume items to ask why the demand is changing.
- There are no effective criteria for triage (early problem identification) on aging systems.
- Existing policy allows some sole source contractors to be nonresponsive; and, when the military does not own data packages on these systems, it relies on these sole source contractors to perform.
- The DLA's safety stock algorithm penalizes low-volume, mission-critical, high-cost items.

These root causes can be summarized into the following conclusion: existing military policies and regulations are either not properly implemented or are no longer effective in today's environment. Some policies violate the fundamental principles of being lean, and these adverse policies have an impact on materials and parts availability. Current contracting practices allow a sole source supplier of key parts to be nonresponsive to a call for increasing demands, so cycle time goes up and costs increase. Further, configuration management policies don't provide for new technology insertion practices to be communicated to the DLA, so the DLA does not have a warning on new demands. As the Lean Sustainment Initiative has noted, "Basic goals, objectives and performance metrics are not clearly and uniformly defined and communicated, thus impeding the ability of the depots to maximize both efficiency and responsiveness" (1998, page 6).

A coherent MRO strategy linking goals, objectives, and metrics to the MRO process is essentially missing. Performance measures currently being used (e.g., mission capability, or MICAP, hours and incidents; customer wait time; base-issue effectiveness' depot shop flow time; the awaiting of parts) are helpful as directional performance indicators, but they lack clear and direct connectivity to explicit weapons systems availability targets. These traditional measures must be subordinated to availability metrics. They are also not a substitute for a well-thought-out sustainment strategy that translates the overall goals, objectives, and metrics into an efficient as well as effective operational system for depot activities.

Available statistical data provide measures on planned versus actual performance (e.g., "on time" percentages), as well as planned versus actual flow-time performance (i.e., flow day variance, which is different from the technical measure of "variance" used in statistics). It is not obvious, however, whether "planned" numerical values (e.g., flow days) represent business targets or stretch goals (see note 2). As a result, it is not possible to evaluate the measurable effects of specific actions at different levels on the achievement of overall aircraft availability targets or for evaluating progress. For example, over the period October 1996 through December 1997, both aggregate Depot Repair Enhancement Program–related MICAP incidents and MICAP hours increased. During the same period, aggregate customer wait time (average number of days) increased while total AP times—as well as total AP times greater than 90 days—declined. How these measures are linked to the achievement of specific weapons system availability targets during this period is difficult to ascertain, particularly in light of the conflicting results that are presented. What, in reality, are the effective performance targets for fully mission-capable weapons systems? What are the priorities? Are all assets in the inventory of equal importance? To what extent does repair priorities reflect the relative scarcity of the warfighter assets? Clear answers to these questions have not been observed.

Moreover, associated business or process improvement targets—such as reducing maintenance costs per flying hour, reducing mean unit cost of maintenance and repair, reducing the mean program depot maintenance (PDM) shop flow time, and reducing the statistical variance in both unit cost and flow time—do not appear clearly defined. System-level efforts in such areas as reengineering, continuous improvement, and environmental control are made considerably weaker as they are presented without realistic agreed-upon targets or milestones. Operational plans seem to have concentrated more on those shops that need to be brought into these improvement initiatives and less on hard reference ("as is") and future ("to be") performance targets.

In such a complex organizational environment, part of the problem may well be that the yardsticks used for evaluating the performance of different organizational units are not synchronized with a consistent set of enterprisewide objectives and metrics. The objectives and metrics may not be sufficiently visible throughout the value stream. Some objectives and metrics, although counterproductive, may be allowed to persist. This could well lead to decisions driven by forces and objectives dissociated from customer needs, resulting in local optimization. For example, it has been observed that some managers seem to focus on internal efficiency and quarterly production rather than on effectiveness; the item manager seems to concentrate on MICAPs and distribution; the DLA seems focused on inventory; and the comptroller seems mostly concerned with obligations and budget allocation. Separate DMAG and SMAG organizational structures, creating a complex transactional environment, stress budget allocation and sales performance rather than fostering a cost-minimization discipline. The pricing regime for repair and maintenance services, together with handing over a checkbook to the different field units, may be encouraging excessive cannibalization of systems for spare parts and higher aggregate systemwide costs that might be avoided through alternative cost accounting, pricing, and financial management strategies. Further, Defense Business Operations Fund (DBOF) fences promote a functional mentality, and the many different "colors of money" impede integrated performance metrics as well as a clearer measure of progress toward achieving greater efficiency.[8]

Also, in such a complex organizational and management environment, it is common that a lack of effective communication appears to be an important factor impeding the creation of a common set of clearly defined goals, objectives, and metrics throughout the sustainment enterprise. A consistent difference between top management and middle management on the existence, clarity, and meaning of goals, objectives, and metrics has been made strongly evident. Field studies conducted by the Lean Sustainment Initiative have revealed, for instance, that top management responsible for a PDM shop at one of the depots showed no cognizance of other initiative objectives long after an improvement initiative had been launched. At another depot, the top leadership responsible for reengineering to accomplish its objectives had no metrics with which to evaluate performance outcomes. Consequently, in a particular case where both shop flow time and unit cost had been reduced, these outcomes could not be linked to any particular initiative-related practices.

The clear and uniform definition and communication of goals, objectives, and metrics presents a particularly difficult challenge in light of the complex and multilayered organizational environment that characterizes the military system. The different materiel commands (e.g., the Army Materiel Command) have evolved cascading strategic plans that link command-level goals, objectives, and quality-performance indicators to center-level objectives and action plans. Also, numerous measures of merit (e.g., MICAP hours and incidents, customer wait time, base-issue effectiveness, depot shop flow time, AWP times) do not appear clearly synchronized or linked to the achievement of the overall weapons system availability targets. The flow down of specific metrics are not unambiguously defined and quantified. Further, measures relating to customer satisfaction do not seem directly linked to operational, cost-performance, and financial targets at the system, depot, and shop levels in the form of realistic, agreed-upon metrics and milestones.

World-class lean enterprises in a wide array of industries have developed and effectively communicated a clear and consistent set of enterprisewide goals, objectives, and performance metrics driving their performance at all levels and embracing all activities ranging from product development to customer support. Lean companies take a "value stream" view of their operations by mapping out the value of all of their support activities and suppliers. Goals concisely articulate the central long-term purpose and direction of the enterprise. Objectives define the strategic actionable thrusts for achieving the goals. Metrics represent a cascading set of consistent, repeatable, and valid measures of performance that enable assessment of progress toward the achievement of goals and objectives, foster understanding and motivate action for continuous improvement, and facilitate comparative evaluation of performance relative to other enterprises.

Goals, objectives, and metrics can be both qualitative and quantitative; they are expected to be more quantitative at finer levels of organizational or functional granularity. They must also be accompanied by a clear and complete set of planning assumptions, including the most likely anticipated future environment as well as (physical, human, budgetary, and technological) constraints. In the most effective companies the goals, objectives, and metrics are few in number and are clearly traceable from the top down; all stakeholders, ranging from suppliers to shop-floor workers, know them and understand how their individual efforts contribute to the overall enterprise goals. They must also be sufficiently stable over time in order to induce the desired behavioral response and adaptation throughout the value stream. Conflicts must be eliminated, any variations must be explained, and subsequent changes must be effectively communicated to remove any appearance of inconsistency.

The Lean Sustainment Initiative has noted that "[t]he apparent absence of a comprehensive and well-coordinated transition plan to bring about fundamental enterprise-wide change has impeded accelerated progress by the depots to achieve significant measurable improvements in sustainment efficiency and responsiveness" (1998, page 6).

The various MRO continuous process improvement (CPI) initiatives that have been instituted by the depots have triggered an important change process to improve depot efficiency and responsiveness. These initiatives appear to have achieved some localized improvements, but they have not been able to bring about systemic change in the depot MRO process as a whole. Enterprisewide effects of the changes initiated by these initiatives remain to be seen and are difficult to quantify, particularly in terms of any hard evidence showing discernible improvements in the availability of fully mission capable weapons systems. However, even such a statement must be carefully qualified. Because of the rather fragmented organizational and management structure of the military sustainment system, it is a difficult matter to show unambiguously why the currently established weapons systems availability targets seem so difficult to achieve on a routine basis. It is important to recognize, nevertheless, that even the localized successes resulting from the CPI initiatives were achieved against formidable, entrenched, obstacles.

1.3.2 Depot-Level Factors Affecting Sustainment Efficiency and Responsiveness

A central issue affecting sustainment efficiency and responsiveness concerns the perceived lack of a coherent and clearly articulated strategy driving the depot MRO process.

—Lean Sustainment Initiative, "Depot Repair Efficiency and Responsiveness"

The depot MRO process that involves prioritizing repair tasks represents neither a "pull" nor a "push" system. For example, one depot that was investigated has been using a "deepest hole" method in prioritizing repairs, which approximates a "pull" (repair-on-demand) system. while another depot employed the "availability based" method, which approximates a "push" (forecast-based) method. Most depots appear to firmly believe that the repair of assets should be based on forecasts of weapons systems availability and not on requisitions (repair on demand). Batch repair appears to be preferred where setup time to repair and test items is significant. The availability-based method is not conducive to supporting batch repair. These examples and practices highlight a broader question: In the face of considerable demand variability, what is the best way to design and manage a robust depot-repair process that can flexibly respond to fluctuations in demand on a routine basis without causing service disruptions or workplace dislocations? Some believe in a "just in time" (repair-on-demand) system; others believe in a "just in case" (forecast-based) philosophy.

At the command level, the existence and operational use of "supportability" modules within computer-generated repair prioritization processes reveals an inherent conflict between meeting war fighter requirements and maximizing sales for the depot. Prioritized repair tasks, on the basis of the sort values that are generated, are subjected to the supportability test, including budget availability. On any given day, repairable assets with sort values falling below the cutoff point may not be inducted into the shops for repair. In effect, repair tasks are "rationed" in light of constrained resources. The most important constrained resource or limiting factor is the availability of funding for repair and maintenance; that is, the demand for repair services exceeds available funds. Therefore, the most likely cause of the inherent conflict between maximizing weapons systems availability and maximizing sales is the shortfall in available budget resources.

This creates an environment in which "maximizing" aircraft availability leads to an ambiguous situation. It prevents a clear-cut definition of accountability on the part of the Air Force Materiel Command (AFMC) while it also results in customer dissatisfaction. A solution satisfactory to both the AFMC and its customers would require the establishment of expectations and hard performance objectives grounded in a clear definition and understanding of cost-performance trade-offs at various levels of systemwide efficiency. Meanwhile, the AFMC must cover the costs of sustainment through sales revenues derived from its customers. There are a number of options through which this may be possible, and these options are defined below. It is worth noting here that the AFMC is well on its way toward realizing not marginal but significant operational efficiency gains, as well as increasing effectiveness, in the face of overwhelming obstacles. It is not obvious, however, that the current aircraft availability targets can in fact be met with the currently available budgets.

As the Lean Sustainment Initiative has noted, "The lack of an overarching cost minimization and continuous productivity improvement (CPI) mindset, discipline, or forcing mechanism is slowing down progress toward achieving significant efficiency gains in the depot repair process" (1998, page 10).

For instance, since the implementation of the Aircraft Repair Enhancement Program (AREP) in the Air Force at the F-15 PDM operations at the Warner Robins Air Logistics Center, the flow time required to complete the PDM work on the aircraft has been reduced from an average of 108 days to 88 days or less. However, cost reductions are more difficult to track or to demonstrate. One problem involves the timely availability of accurate cost data, as a result of which plans have been initiated to adopt activity-based costing (ABC) practices. On the other hand, having timely and accurate cost information is only the first step toward minimizing costs. It is here that more fundamental questions arise: What is the logic driving the pricing regime within the sustainment system, encompassing all depot functions? How are prices related to actual costs? In a comparatively sheltered market environment in which many depot operations remain largely unaffected by the competitive commercial market pressures outside, what principles and incentive mechanisms should be adopted to drive down costs on a continuous basis while also reducing factory (shop) flow time and maximizing weapons systems availability?

Currently, prices charged to customers for depot-level reparables are structured to recover the costs associated with performing the required services, or for replacing nonserviceable assets, plus overhead costs that include allocation of cost items not directly related to repair operations. The available information suggests that prices far exceed the marginal costs of providing such services, thus signaling customers to minimize their own local costs in a variety of ways. These may include, for example, performing test and repair operations at the base rather than sending recoverable items for repair to the depots. Alternatively, they may be induced to continue using systems or components until they reach a "hard broke" condition before sending them to the depots for repair. More generally, the current pricing regime may have induced the customers to minimize their own local costs, but this may have resulted in higher aggregate systemwide costs. Also, the current pricing regime may have created disincentives for customers, discouraging them from using the repair services provided by the depots.

The general issue of adopting an efficiency-inducing pricing regime concerns not only how to price services to "outside" customers but also to "inside" customers (i.e., among the depots or shops) through the adoption of appropriate transfer prices. The issue of transfer prices is particularly acute in light of the relatively sheltered market environment for many shops.

The separation of the SMAG and DMAG functions may also have created a bureaucratic, transactional environment not conducive to the creation of an overall efficiency-maximization discipline or mechanism. This is evidenced by how the setting of "burn rates,"[9] and the decisions made as to whether a specific repair task should be inducted into repair, reflect budget allocation decisions where SMAG authorizes DMAG to perform specific repair assignments. The project order processing, certification, acceptance, and related tasks essentially represent an "on-off" funds application process and fail to foster a systemic discipline for maximizing internal efficiency. Perhaps only tangentially it might be argued that only by becoming more efficient can shops expect to be assigned more work, since greater efficiency would presumably reduce the "burn rate" and leave more funds available for later use. However, simply being able to do more work does not provide a compelling reason for inducing greater efficiency.

At a more fundamental level, it is simply insufficient to remove existing sources of inefficiency and waste. The longer-run challenge is to optimize resource allocation to bring about significant productivity improvements. This means closer examination of optimal combinations of both labor and capital, to identify opportunities where substitution of capital for labor, in a tight labor market environment, would result in higher productivity. This leads to the issue of technology insertion and modernization of the existing capital stock at the depots, which will be addressed more fully in the case studies later in this book.

As the Lean Sustainment Initiative has noted, "The lack of an integrated supplier network proactively designed to implement a clear and coherent sustainment strategy has a significant negative effect on current depot efficiency and responsiveness" (1998, page 11).

Field research has revealed that a lack of parts, as well as tools, is a serious problem across the various depots and in many of the shops. Lack of visibility by the repair prioritization processes into DLA operations has been noted as a major impediment to timely availability of materials and consumables needed by the depots to perform their required repair tasks. Recent DLA initiatives (e.g., the prime vendor approach, local distribution centers and supplier parks, and integrated supplier programs), which have been implemented to reduce logistics costs and also to deliver parts and supplies on a "just in time" basis, are found to have resulted in improved delivery of high-volume, standardized, consumable items. However, difficulties have been noted in being able to apply such a model to the procurement of unique (one-of-a-kind) but critical parts and components, particularly in cases involving parts obsolescence and diminishing manufacturing sources.

On many occasions, contracting officers and material managers have noted how much more smoothly the supply-chain management process works when those responsible have a workable knowledge of the parts and the systems that are involved. A general problem concerns the relatively simple task of issuing a procurement subcontract, which often takes months from requirements definition to contract award. Other issues involve the inability of workers at the shops to order parts and supplies before repairable assets have been inducted into the repair process, causing an obstacle to reducing costs and factory flow time. In addition, due to regulations or policies, the depots or the shops are often unable to discontinue the services of suppliers performing poorly.

Often, because of poor supplier performance, the lack of availability of relatively simple parts causes inordinate delays in completing the required repair tasks. A telling anecdotal example involves the five-month-long wait for obtaining a bushing for a C-130 nose landing gear at the Ogden (Utah) Air Logistics Center landing gear repair shop. Also at Ogden, at one point in mid-March 1998, 844 parts (representing 92 different types of parts) caused work stoppage due to NSN parts shortages, affecting landing gear repair for A-10s, B-1s, B-52s, C-5s, C-141s, F-4s, F-15s, F-16s, and KC-135s. The magnitude of the AP shortages problem can be put into the proper context by noting that the Ogden landing gear shop manages approximately 15,000 different NSN parts and services, supporting repair and overhaul services for 30 aircraft platforms. Other examples, elsewhere, include end items that have remained in AWP status for longer than 90 days (e.g., NSN 1270-01-364-3118 detector/cooler, 212 days; NSN 1270-01-365-9471 laser transmitter/receiver, 205 days). In other cases, delays in obtaining specific shop-replaceable units and various piece parts (e.g., NSN 1270-01-286-9512 Pockels cell driver assembly, 173 days; NSN 1240-01-416-6726 wavelength switch, 205 days) have driven delays in repairing a specific laser transmitter/receiver (i.e., AAQ-14, PDN 38124A).

The issue of integrated supplier networks involves internal, as well as external, suppliers. For example, many back shops effectively serve as suppliers to PDM operations. In fact, as a major enabler of the AREP, the PDM Scheduling System was designed to support PDM with an automated, task-by-task, scheduling system by helping to synchronize PDM operations with all aircraft logistics support and PDM-related component repair services in the back shops. However, the linkages among the AREP, the Depot Repair Enhancement Program, and the Contractor Repair Enhancement Program (CREP) thrusts do not appear to be tightly synchronized. While it would appear that aggressively pursuing the CREP thrust would have helped to accelerate the infusion of best commercial practices through the adoption of modern supply chain management practices, this was observed as the least advanced among the CPI initiatives.

"Inadequate workforce education and training, along with inflexible personnel practices and a general lack of incentives for career advancement, are impeding the development of a highly-motivated and productive workforce," notes the Lean Sustainment Initiative (1998, page 12).

The depots have experienced and capable workforces, but they generally lack the comparatively higher levels of commitment that can be found in the commercial sector toward continuous formal worker education and training aimed at fostering the development of high-performance work teams. Structured educational programs in the commercial sector stress improvements in a number of essential areas, such as basic skills (reading, writing, mathematics), critical thinking and problem solving, interpersonal and leadership skills, technical skills (e.g., statistical process control and computer literacy), general business skills (e.g., accounting and finance), and related areas (e.g., quality control, business ethics, environmental policies and regulations, and health and safety issues). Workers in enterprises with structured human resource development programs are multiskilled, embrace teamwork, have joint responsibility for the workflow, influence decisions on workplace organization and management, and are able to rotate jobs within the work group, across work groups, and across departments.

For example, cross-training and multiskilling could provide substantial performance improvements at one of the sites examined in detail. However, at this site, ideas of multiskilling and multitasking have met strong resistance. Unions have made this a bargaining issue. Primarily, workers do not wish to be transferred to performing "more menial" tasks when there is a reduction or slowdown in their workload. There is also a general lack of incentive for workers to seek further education and training or to strive to improve productivity. At this site, the average age of the workforce is close to 50. The typical employee has reached his or her maximum pay grade and has no further visible potential for advancement, because promotion from the shop floor to a management position is not available. Production incentives are not allowed, and the awards program has effectively been eliminated due to lack of funds. Workers are also well set in their ways and are resistant to change. In this environment, it is difficult to attract new workers, because skilled workers can earn higher income in private industry, and another round of early retirement buyout might result in a loss of a great deal of talent and capability. These problems are compounded by inflexible government personnel policies, resulting in a serious barrier to the flexible reassignment of workers in response to shifting workload allocations or simply to the termination of those with poor performance records.

1.4 Ramifications and Conclusions

The overall observations and summary presented above have a number of important ramifications for military depot sustainment:

- Whether and how well customer needs and requirements are being satisfied in a timely manner is made difficult to assess. Consequently, the depot repair system is not able to tailor, reconfigure, or redeploy existing resources and processes to respond to changing customer priorities.
- Specific initiatives aimed at bringing about significant efficiency gains are stymied by a complex web of entrenched and change-resistant stovepipe organizational and management structures and policies.

- Opportunities are missed for achieving more efficient and effective solutions that would benefit customers; continuation of waste is allowed to occur; continuous improvement is impeded.
- The absence of an overriding discipline or imperative for maximizing efficiency is impeding or slowing down the determination for reducing costs, shortening factory flow time, and increased responsiveness to customer needs.
- Responsibility and accountability for concrete goals and objectives are ill-defined; unity of purpose and vision is blurred; and measurable progress toward specific performance targets, such as reducing costs and factory flow time, is impeded.
- Overall productivity, cost efficiency, and competitiveness of the depot repair process is made difficult to assess in the absence of accurate, reliable, and timely cost and other performance data.
- The flexibility and responsiveness of the depot repair system is impeded by many institutional and organizational rigidities and constraints, including inflexible supply-chain policies.
- The workforce finds itself with very little incentive for working harder or improving productivity.

To counter the challenges currently facing the sustainment system, military maintenance, repair, and overhaul depots must implement an aggressive transformation plan for the future. The National Defense Authorization Act for fiscal year 2005, Title VIII, Subtitle F requires the secretary of defense to provide plans to increase the emphasis placed on lean manufacturing technologies and processes in acquisition programs, and the potential for broader application of such technologies and processes throughout the department, in particular sustainment. The DoD 2001 Quadrennial Defense Review has described the need to reduce the logistics footprint, improve our armed forces' global mobility, and increase the reliability of DoD weapons systems. In addition, the new DoD Defense Acquisition Management 5000 series directive 5000.1 (Defense Acquisition System) and instruction 5000.2 (Operation of the Defense Acquisition System) are oriented toward achieving these objectives while also reducing the time required for development and deployment of needed war-fighter capability through implementation of evolutionary acquisition strategies and spiral development processes. The goal of all these directives is to achieve a quantum leap in sustainability throughput and efficiency by transforming depot workloads and processes into those of a "best in class" facility using best practices, process improvement initiatives, and advanced manufacturing/sustainment processes and layouts. The process of change is clearly underway, is well-motivated, and is moving in the right direction. The DoD has committed leadership and support at the command level, dedicated and experienced management at the depot level, and a capable workforce at all levels, particularly at the shop floor level. Specific success stories and accomplishments, realized under very difficult circumstances, should be a source of pride. However, the transformation process is far from complete. In addition, any incremental improvements enterprisewide remain difficult to quantify. The challenges facing the depots are complex and daunting, but there is strong determination to meet these challenges successfully.

Chapter 2

A Lean Model for the Military Sustainment Enterprise

As existing weapons systems age and the costs and cycle times on the maintenance, repair, and overhaul of these systems increases, various organizations within the U.S. Department of Defense (DoD) are conducting independent studies to help the system become more efficient. Current research efforts on maintenance repair and overhaul operations focus on individual elements of this sustainment system. However, to more effectively solve the sustainment problem, research should be conducted on the whole enterprise, from raw material suppliers to final product delivery. To accomplish this objective, the authors developed a new "lean" framework for military systems sustainment. The goal of this model is to minimize non-value-added activities throughout the entire enterprise.

2.1 Introduction

In recent years, the nature and role of logistics have undergone dramatic changes. The old logistics system reflected the war-fighting strategy that dominated the decades-long Cold War period. During this period, primary emphasis was placed on nationwide mobilization to support prolonged war efforts designed to address large-scale theater conflicts spanning continents. The logistics base developed to support the Cold War military strategy reflected a "push" sustainment system characterized by layers of "just in case" inventories and organic depot repair and maintenance operations with stovepipe functionality. The logistics system was characterized by a long pipeline, huge inventories, and slow transportation.

With the end of the Cold War, the focus of logistics has shifted from the "just in case" ("push") system to a "just in time" ("pull") system, in response to a fundamental shift in military requirements. In the emerging global environment, strategic attention has shifted to the possibility of multiple concurrent regional contingencies requiring the application of focused efforts of limited duration, placing a high premium on readiness and stressing mobility, flexibility, and responsiveness. Also, significant cutbacks in military spending, mirroring global strategic shifts, are requiring a major downsizing and restructuring of the U.S. armed forces, including the nation's logistics infrastructure supporting all services. Although fewer resources are now available for the supply of logistics services, the demand for logistics support remains largely undiminished, thus putting extraordinary pressure on available resources. The end result is unprecedented emphasis on greater efficiency in providing logistics services, in order to avoid undercutting military readiness. Resources claimed by inefficient logistics, obsolete infrastructure systems, and wasteful, excessive inventories are scarce resources needed for building, maintaining, or modernizing war-fighting capabilities.

The military depot sustainment community has already initiated substantial changes in logistics thinking and practice—for example, with its Lean Logistics program. The new motto focuses on providing the right parts, at the right place, as soon as possible and with as few system resources as possible, by focusing on meeting customer mission requirements, applying modern business practices, and reengineering existing practices. The keys to change include customer-driven repair, tightened repair and manufacturing processes, innovation in contracting, consolidated inventory, and fast transportation to all points. A major enabler is the substitution of fast transportation for the traditional practice of maintaining costly inventory scattered throughout the logistics supply pipeline. The resulting "just in time" logistics system is thus geared directly to satisfying customer requirements on a timely basis. Expected results include streamlined processes and better customer support.

In embarking upon such a process of fundamental transformation, the maintenance depots face difficult challenges as well as major opportunities. While important near-term operational and organizational changes are currently being implemented, longer-term changes must also be addressed. What are the critical areas where the definition and adoption of lean principles and practices would yield the greatest benefits over the next several years? Over a longer-term time frame, what are the most important changes that can be introduced to achieve improved system-level integration and optimization resulting in significantly greater efficiency and responsiveness? Further, how should new weapons systems be designed for sustainment, particularly in view of the rather long life cycle of these systems and the fact that different sectors of the industry are moving at quite different "clock speeds" in terms of technological change? How should existing weapons systems be redesigned for block changes, to achieve improved affordability in sustaining them during the balance of their long service lives?

Further, these longer-term changes must be consistent with, and derived from, a coherent vision of the 21st-century battlefield and the supporting logistics infrastructure. The sheer complexity and arguably revolutionary nature of these changes requires an enterprisewide architecture for making informed strategic decisions.

Although the base realignment and closure process has reduced the number of depot facilities, it does not address opportunities to reduce inefficiencies in the remaining depots or in government-owned, contractor-operated facilities, or with respect to the department's efficiency in contracting for depot maintenance resources. Since then, the DoD has begun a series of initiatives to enhance the cost and effectiveness of its remaining depot activities. Some of these initiatives have focused on how to better utilize depot capability and capacity through workload consolidations, public-private competitions, and reengineering depot maintenance processes. Examples include agile combat support (Eady and Williams 1997), flexible sustainment (Performance-Based Business Environment 1997), the U.S. Army's Modernization through Spares program (Kros 1999), the Lean Aerospace Initiative,[1] and the Lean Sustainment Initiative.[2] However, these initiatives focus on individual elements of the sustainment system, not the whole sustainment enterprise. One approach to the problem is to turn to lean principles for guidance. Using these concepts, the idea is to develop synergies along the whole supply chain, from the original equipment manufacturer to the customer. These lean concepts provide a set of tools and an overriding philosophy on how to transform lean manufacturing into a lean sustainment supply chain. However, in order to effectively coordinate these efforts and to bring military sustainment into the lean paradigm, a new framework or model for the whole enterprise needs to be developed. This chapter will delineate the development of this lean framework/model for military systems sustainment. The goal of the model is to minimize non-value-added activities throughout the entire enterprise. The mission would be

- To identify and define lean principles and practices to help achieve significant cost savings, greater efficiency, and higher quality in providing responsive logistics and sustainment support to the military customer (war fighter) in an environment of flexible global operational requirements and constrained resources
- To design a framework for building an integrated lean sustainment system for the early 21st century, stressing affordability while also maximizing the operational availability, readiness, and capability of the nation's combat forces
- To develop a new design model for lean sustainment by defining a new product development, acquisition, and sustainment process based on platform-based, modular, and incremental design and technology insertion approaches that fully incorporate up front the lessons learned during downstream operations

and support stages in order to help minimize life-cycle costs (development, production, sustainment) while maximizing future readiness, mobility, and flexibility consistent with the battlefield vision of the future

This chapter begins by proposing a new Lean Sustainment Enterprise Model for how sustainment should be structured. The chapter concludes with a brief description of an initiative, the U.S. Navy and Air Force cartridge actuated device/propellant actuated device (CAD/PAD) program, which has some elements of the proposed lean sustainment model. This example is used to illustrate that the proposed model is realistic, and that it can be implemented.

2.2 The Lean Sustainment Enterprise Model

In order to achieve a truly lean approach, some organizational structures within the current military system must be integrated. The proposed Lean Sustainment Enterprise Model (LSEM) (Agripino, Cathcart, and Mathaisel, 2002) calls for the consolidation and integration of the following sustainment functions: in-service engineering, integrated logistic support, intermediate/depot maintenance, operational support, and supply support. This realignment of the military sustainment system mirrors a commercial maintenance repair and overhaul (MRO) operation. The goal is to achieve significant customer service levels while reducing total ownership costs. The new organizational framework allows close coordination between the operational community and the supporting sustainment network required to meet evolving life-cycle support requirements. The proposed enterprise model is illustrated in figure 2.1.

The key attribute of this framework is that it is organized around three primary sustainment structures: operational sustainment, sustainment engineering, and MRO operations. These three structures are consolidated into one life-cycle support facility, shown in the center of figure 2.1. The three structures are not explicitly illustrated in figure 2.1; they will be explained below. Rather, the authors chose to use the traditional acronyms (such as ILS, for integrated logistic support) within each structure so that a direct comparison can be made between this new framework and the current military sustainment model. The supply chain that feeds this new facility is illustrated in figure 2.1 to the right of the facility, and the operational (O) level and intermediate (I) level maintenance activities that benefit from the facility are illustrated on the left (as the operational support function).

Within the life-cycle support facility, there exist the traditional ILS functions such as training; packaging, handling, shipping, and transportation; and the computer resources, among others. These functions are now part of what the authors call the first structure, the operational sustainment structure. New information systems technologies allow many of these stand-alone ILS elements to be combined and integrated into a net-centric environment. Sophisticated interactive technical manuals are

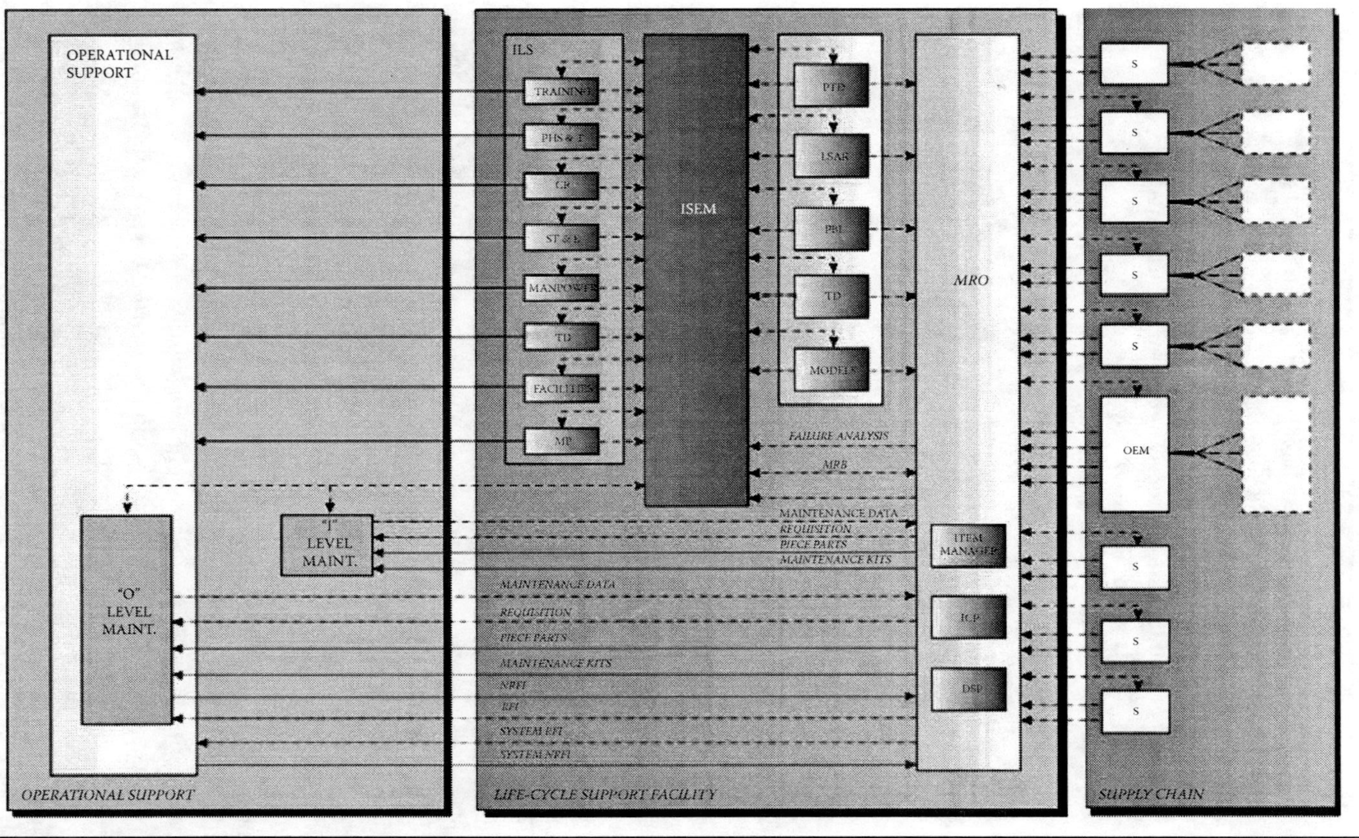

Figure 2.1 The Lean Sustainment Enterprise Model.

Table 2.1 Abbreviations Used in Figures 2.1, 2.2, and 2.3

CR	Computer Resources
DOP	Designated Overhaul Point
DSP	Designated Stock Point
"I" Level	Intermediate Level Maintenance
ICP	Inventory Control Point
ISEM	Integrated Systems Engineering Management
LSAR	Logistics Support Analysis Record
MP	Maintenance Plan
MRB	Material Review Board
MRO	Maintenance, Repair, and Overhaul
NRFI	Not Ready for Issue
"O" Level	Operational Level Maintenance
OEM	Original Equipment Manufacturer
PBL	Product Baseline
PHS&T	Packaging Handling, Shipping, and Transportation
PTD	Provisioning Technical Documentation
RFI	Ready For Issue
S	Supplier
ST&E	Special Tools and Equipment
TD	Technical Data

rapidly evolving to include training and elaborate diagnostics capabilities. Advances in both enterprisewide and specialized logistics-engineering-applications software packages are being designed with open architectures that would allow an integrated digital environment. These advances in information technology potentially could eliminate many traditional logistic infrastructure bureaucracies that were established during the Cold War. Operational sustainment processes must be reengineered to effectively use these new technologies and applications.

The second structure within the life-cycle facility, sustainment engineering, provides engineering services to the other structures, primarily the MRO structure. The sustainment engineering structure uses an integrated systems engineering management framework to maintain such traditional functions as provisioning technical documentation, product baseline maintenance, technical data packages, and engineering models. Intelligent engineering-analysis software tools could provide system engineers the capability to monitor and correct operational sustainment problems, such as technology obsolescence, aging systems, reliability performance degradation, and maintenance-engineering management. System effectiveness management practices are used to automate and monitor sustainment technical performance measures for rapid problem identification and resolution to minimize cost and mission readiness impacts.

The third structure, the MRO structure, provides spares and material support to the war fighter. The MRO organization structure will include inventory management and supply-chain management responsibilities, which is why it directly connects to the supply chain structure in figure 2.1. The MRO structure could perform remanufacturing services using new lean production concepts, such as "just in time" single-piece flow, and Kanban-based pull production systems.[3] Significant cycle-time reduction and increased service-level performance have been observed by many institutions using these lean concepts, including the Lean Aerospace Initiative (2001). In terms of inventory management, the traditional military logistics infrastructure designates the inventory control point (ICP) organization to perform inventory and asset management. The designated stock point organization performs warehousing and transportation coordination services for the ICP. These services are now consolidated in the new MRO structure to minimize cost and streamline asset movement. These responsibilities are routinely colocated in most commercial MROs.

From the perspective of the supply chain, figures 2.2 and 2.3 for the proposed model are analogous to figures 1.5 and 1.6 for the current sustainment system described in chapter 1. Note that with the new model there are just three levels to the supply chain—not seven, as in the current model. The new model also places the designated overhaul point (DOP), the depot performing the maintenance functions, in the center of the supply channel and distribution channel activity. The intent is to have the right part be available at the right place at the right time.

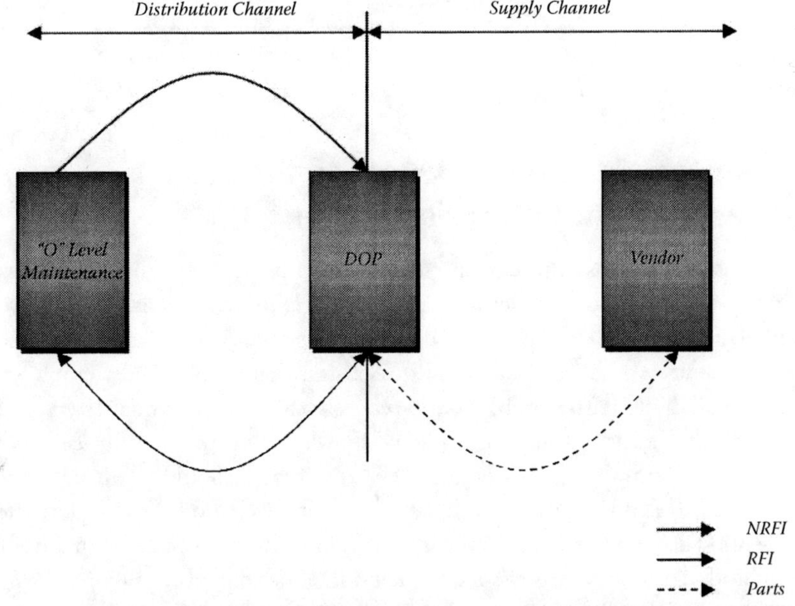

Figure 2.2 The Lean Sustainment Enterprise Model Supply Chain.

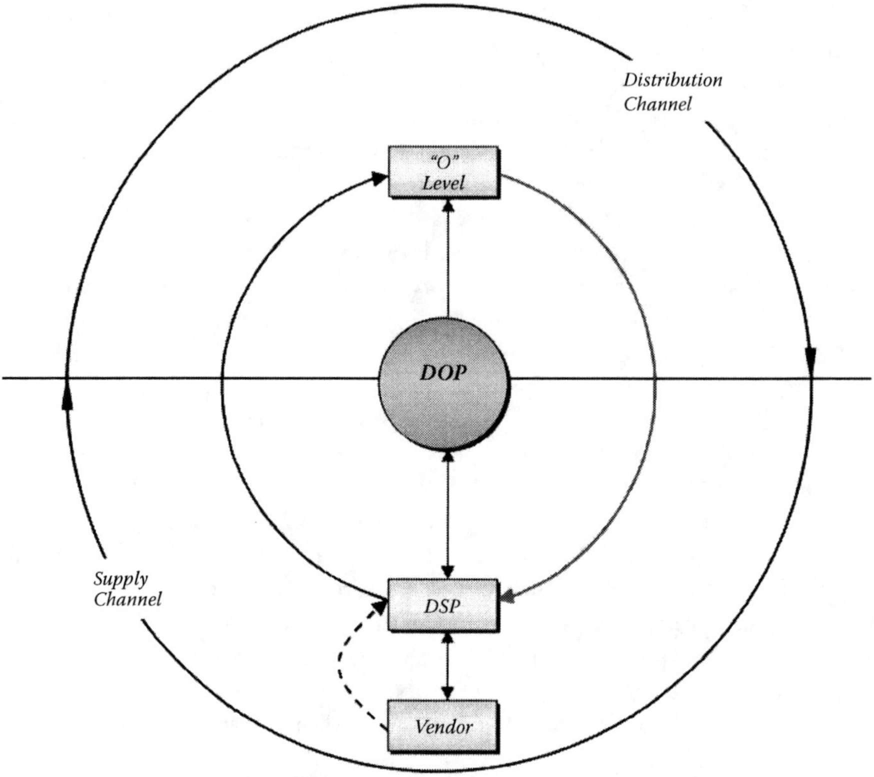

Figure 2.3 The Lean Sustainment Enterprise Model Distribution and Supply Channel.

2.3 Benefits of and Challenges to the Lean Sustainment Enterprise Model

The proposed Lean Sustainment Enterprise Model provides for the remanufacturing, refurbishment, modification/upgrade, testing, failure analysis, inventory control/management, and configuration control of a system and its associated critical subcomponents in one integrated enterprise. Fast depot operations, emphasizing low-cost availability with variable volume capacity, allows for standardized product production and refurbishment using focus shops, central purchasing, central distribution, and central processing. The integrated model should result in a significant cost savings and improved cycle-time performance, and it should outperform a conventional depot because it integrates the operational system with inventory control and the in-service systems engineering functions. The intent is that the right part will be available at the right place at the right time. Logistics delay time, a key metric for leanness, should be reduced as lead times and turnaround times are decreased to an absolute minimum in order to obtain low cost, high quality, and on-time material availability. The LSEM has the potential to reduce the cost of inventory and the cycle time of material refurbishment. It also offers considerable improvements to accommodate product redesigns and material sustainment efforts, which are required to ensure that the useful economic system life will be much longer than that of traditional weapon systems.

Systems effectiveness management in the proposed LSEM is a proactive approach to quickly identify and resolve sustainment problems. With over 60 percent of the total system life-cycle cost associated with operations and maintenance, there is great opportunity to optimize sustainment costs (Blanchard and Fabrycky, 1998). The system effectiveness management approach in the LSEM integrates failure data with knowledge-based decision models for quick resolution of sustainment problems. Early identification of "out of specification" performance problems of the sustainment system can be used to trigger sustainment engineering actions.

The traditional military sustainment model is based on systems design characteristics and performance specifications. During the system design and manufacturing development phases, reliability-based provisioning and inventory models are developed to support the initial fielding of these systems. After several years of operations, these models are updated with historical usage data to reflect the changes of the system as it ages. But in-service failures occur with greater frequency. This increase in system maintenance quickly created out of stock conditions in the supply system. Supplier problems also increased over time due to changing technology and business cycles. However, in the proposed LSEM all levels of system maintenance are monitored, including depot-level failure analysis and logistics performance measures. Failure data is loaded into systems-engineering models for analysis. The analysis provides the basis for product and process improvements and provides a "what if" system analysis tool for simulation-based trade-off studies.

In the LSEM, initial system deployments are sufficiently sustained because the initial support infrastructure and resource requirements are accurately computed based upon reliability-based systems-effectiveness analysis. This analysis is effective during early deployment, but it becomes less efficient as the system ages. Thus, real-time data collection and analysis is required to manage the sustainment system efficiently. To effectively collect the necessary data required for a systems-effectiveness management process, the sustainment system must be completely integrated, as is suggested in the LSEM. The sustainment-enterprisewide information system needs to be fully integrated to establish an effective system sustainment management process. The new systems-effectiveness management approach would allow the sustainment engineer to quickly identify any problem area and to conduct root-cause analysis. All data sources for the analysis can quickly be assessed from this information system. With the use of simulation-based decision-making tools and failure data integrated, as it is in the LSEM, the sustainment engineer is provided with powerful tools for continuous systems-engineering process improvement. This approach provides an effective life-cycle-management methodology to fully integrate both the sustainment engineering process with normal sustainment operations and maintenance. This integrated approach provides greater efficiencies in organizational coupling and real-time feedback for enterprisewide continuous improvements.

The LSEM is not without its challenges, however. Possible barriers include the amount of integration required among the depot, in-service engineering, inventory control, and supply-chain management. Close coordination and integration is mandatory to fully benefit from the concept. Special skills will need to be developed to perform the many new tasks. The level of understanding that is needed to successfully maintain and operate the LSEM will need to be reviewed and addressed in any implementation planning, but the intent is not to translate the opportunity into a job-reduction program. Existing personnel, and their skill sets, are in short supply and are just as important as in the old model. So personnel reductions are not recommended in the new paradigm.

Another challenge is that the in-service engineer must ensure that ordering times, shipping times, fill rates, maintenance turnaround times, as well as other metrics realistically portray the impact and interaction of the supply, transportation, maintenance, and procurement systems. Determining the range (number of different items) and depth (quantity of each item) of spares to be procured and stocked must be constantly evaluated and adjusted to provide a lean operation.

2.4 A Case Study: The Joint CAD/PAD Program

To illustrate that the proposed model is realistic and that it can be implemented, the author searched for an ongoing initiative that has some elements of the LSEM. Although no current initiative fully replicates the proposed LSEM, there are some excellent examples. One such example is the U.S. Navy and Air Force CAD/PAD program.

In 1998, the U.S. Navy and the U.S. Air Force began a unique management experiment: a joint program to manage the sustainment of the cartridge actuated device/propellant actuated device (CAD/PAD), which are explosive items used in aircraft escape systems and other applications. CADs/PADs all have defined service lives and must be replaced periodically. The joint program was born when visionary managers in the two branches of the armed forces saw the greater value of consolidating their previously separate activities and built the trust needed to overcome the risks of doing business in a new way. The key attributes of the program are

- Operation as a joint integrated product team/competency aligned organization with the service affiliation of team members transparent to users
- Assumption of responsibility by the U.S. Navy, as lead service, for an important factor (the escape system) in the operational readiness of aircraft in all services

- Employment of jointness in the sustainment phase of the life cycle rather than the more traditional development phase
- Use of best practices and continuous improvement with a strong emphasis on supporting the customer
- Management of a commodity rather than a weapon system
- Creation as an initiative from the working level, rather than a directive from the top

The joint program team consists of operating elements at the Indian Head, Maryland, Division Naval Service Warfare Center (near Washington, D.C.); the Naval Sea Systems Command; Hill Air Force Base in northern Utah; the Rock Island Arsenal in Garrison, New York; and the Naval Inventory Control Point, in Mechanicsburg, Pennsylvania. A small jointly manned program office, reporting to the conventional strike weapons program manager within the program executive office (PEO), manages the program.

In April 2001, the joint program received the David Packard Excellence in Acquisition Award, given for great innovation and results in acquisition. The award recognizes the program's reengineering of the process for resupplying CADs and PADs to U.S. Navy and Marine Corps users in the field. The old process was both labor- and paper-intensive, requiring up to four months from order to delivery. The reengineering team developed an "877" phone system that maintenance personnel use to order directly from the stock point at Indian Head, a common practice in the commercial world. The telephone operator is able to validate need in real time, using computerized maintenance records. Shipments are accomplished in most cases by an overnight commercial carrier, which allows for automated tracking. Actions by intermediate personnel have been greatly reduced and the average cycle time is reduced from 112 days to less than 8 days (Chappell and Taylor, 2002).

Minimizing duplication, optimizing joint resources, and applying the best practices of each service have all resulted in great savings, estimated by the program at $825,000 per year. Included in this figure are the savings from combined procurements of items that are common to two or more services, reducing the number of contract actions required and invoking economies of scale. Adoption of a Navy computer system for materiel planning will lead to more precise requirements determination and budget justification for Air Force needs. Under this system, the Navy has been able to defend successfully its annual request for procurement funds by predicting very accurately the readiness impact on specific aircraft of any reductions. The transfer of several former Air Force civilian personnel to the Navy will help preserve the technical and management capability to serve Air Force users. Personnel costs are included in the price of overhaul services for weapons systems and unit components.

2.5 Conclusion

Reduced DoD budgets are forcing the military to rethink how to manage the life cycle of the military systems. Initiatives such as the U.S. Army's Modernization through Spares program, agile combat support, the Lean Aerospace Initiative, the Lean Sustainment Initiative, and flexible sustainment present potential solutions to these budget problems, but they focus on individual elements of the sustainment system, not the whole enterprise. In order to take maximum advantage of the fundamental principles of being lean, a change in the military organizational structure is necessary. The change calls for the integration of the in-service engineering process, the inventory control points, and the MRO functions to ensure that a total systems engineering approach is used effectively in solving all parts of the problem. In other words, the synergistic effects of one solution can be magnified by other solutions in the chain. In utilizing a private industry type of approach, the author has developed an LSEM to provide the necessary framework to conduct research into development of this whole-system approach to lean sustainment for military systems.

Chapter 3

A Lean Enterprise Architecture for Military Sustainability

An increased military operational tempo, aging weapons systems, an aging workforce, limited financial resources, and the availability of new sustainment technologies are but some of the reasons why MRO depots must implement an aggressive transformation plan for the future. The goal is to achieve a quantum leap in sustainability throughput and efficiency by transforming depot workload and processes into those of a "best in class" commercial-type facility using best commercial practices, lean principles, and cellular manufacturing processes and layouts. A question arises as to whether to transform the entire enterprise (either the entire depot or each strategic business unit) all at once or incrementally one repair cell at a time. This chapter contributes to the question by defining and describing an architecture for the transformation of the enterprise. Three disciplines guide the design: the application of current process improvement initiatives in the transformation; generalized enterprise reference architectures; and systems engineering concepts. The lean enterprise architecture described in this chapter is a framework for organizing the activities for the transformation of the enterprise. It applies the latest systems-architecture methods to design, construct, integrate, and implement a lean enterprise using systems-engineering methods and practices. The design process incorporates lean manufacturing and cellular design attributes and values as requirements for improving the enterprise.

3.1 Introduction

Military readiness is dependent on its ability to operate and maintain its systems, and this requires a flexible, responsive, and robust organic depot MRO capability. MRO depot operations are vital to the support of the military force and Joint Command operations, and they are a critical element of our overall war-fighter capability. The rapidly changing global geopolitical landscape has elevated the importance of the depots as crucial instruments in the defense infrastructure, providing protection for our nation's borders and a worldwide environment in which free nations can survive and prosper.

The forces depend upon a highly responsive sustainment system, but the supporting facility infrastructure, equipment, processes, and personnel are operating with less-than-optimal flow processes, facility constraints, and outdated equipment. To effectively respond to the increased demand for mission-ready resources, the depots must confront the challenges with an aggressive transformation plan for the complete industrial complex and processes. Should the transformation be enterprisewide, or should the architecture support an incremental, cell-by-cell, transformation? The purpose of this chapter is to answer the question by describing a new Lean Enterprise Architecture (LEA).

3.2 The Life Cycle of an Enterprise

The military sustainment enterprise, as well as its products, follows a life cycle. Understanding this life cycle is key to an understanding of the Lean Enterprise Architecture presented in this chapter. An excellent reference for the life cycle of an enterprise is the Generalized Enterprise Reference Architecture (GERA) framework developed by an IFIP/IFAC (International Federation for Information Processing/International Federation of Automatic Control) task force on information processing (Bernus 1998). The structure is generic, so it would pertain to any enterprise or entity. Figure 3.1 illustrates the life cycle. The cycle begins with the initial concept for a system or transformation and then proceeds with development, design, construction, operation and maintenance, refurbishment or obsolescence, and final disposal of the system. The identification phase identifies the contents of the particular entity under consideration in terms of its boundaries and its relation to its internal and external environments. The concept phase includes the definition of the mission, vision, values, strategies, objectives, operational concepts, policies, and business plans of the system or transformation. The requirement phase is the set of activities that are needed to develop descriptions of operational requirements of the enterprise entity, its relevant processes, and the collection of all their functional, behavioral, informational, and capability needs. The design phases include all human tasks (those of individuals and organizational entities), all machine tasks concerned with the entity's customer services and products and related management

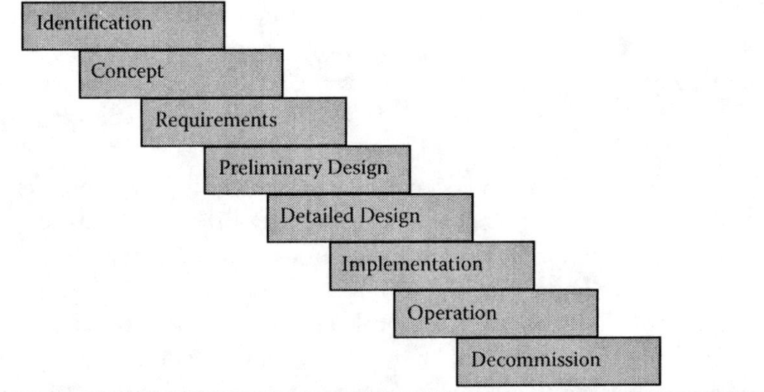

Figure 3.1 Life Cycle Phases for an Enterprise.

and control functions, and all necessary information and resources (including manufacturing, information, communication, and control, or any other technology). Dividing the design phase into preliminary design (or specification) and detailed design permits the separation of overall enterprise specifications. The implementation phase covers commissioning, purchasing, (re)configuring or developing all service, manufacturing, and control software as well as hardware resources; hiring and training personnel, and developing or changing the human organization; component testing and validation, systems integration, validation and testing, and releasing into operation. The operation phase includes the set of activities for producing the customer's product or service along with all those tasks needed for monitoring, controlling, and evaluating the operation. Finally, the decommissioning phase includes the activities for re-missioning, retraining, redesign, recycling, preservation, transfer, disbanding, disassembly, or disposal of all or part of the system at the end of its useful life in operation (Bernus 1998).

The Lean Enterprise Architecture follows this GERA life cycle structure. By doing so, it means that the transformation of the military enterprise should be designed with this "cradle to grave" concept in mind. It is not sufficient to simply apply a process improvement initiative to a cell without thinking about the preservation of those important improvement concepts for the entire life of the entity—or, in this case, the enterprise.

3.3 Why Is an Enterprisewide Transformation So Important?

An *enterprise* is, in this case, defined as the facilities, people, technologies, operating systems, logistics systems, and other resources that are allocated to the organization to perform its function and meet its performance goals and objectives. An enterprise can be an entire depot or an entire strategic business unit (SBU) within the depot. Granted, it is better to transform the entire depot rather than each SBU to take advantage of economies of scale (e.g., change management, culture, leadership, and reporting), but resources are not always available to change an entire depot all at once.

Why take an enterprisewide approach to a performance improvement transformation? Because viewing the implementation of the transformation across the entire enterprise minimizes the possibility of overlooking opportunities for further performance improvement. It eliminates the natural tendency to suboptimize functions and processes based on local metrics and organizational reporting. A "silo view" of lean implementation may allow gaps in performance to persist, with no one assuming responsibility for the entire enterprise (Delaware Manufacturing Extension Partnership 2004). It also helps improve enterprisewide quality, on-time delivery, and customer satisfaction by eliminating waste in the *entire* organization and supply chain, not just in one local repair/production cell. In turn, this helps drive enterprise operating costs to where they make a difference to the return on investment (ROI), and to minimize costs that don't. The Delaware Manufacturing Extension Partnership (2004) cites the following benefits:

- *Improved quality.* Quickly identifying potential problems and addressing them early in the process minimizes reworking and improves the overall quality of the end product. MRO enterprises can typically reduce defects by at least 20% per year and improve quality by up to 85%.
- *Increased productivity.* Lean techniques allow an enterprise to produce more with existing resources by eliminating non-value-adding activities. MRO enterprises can increase productivity by up to 30 percent per year.
- *Enhanced Customer Satisfaction.* Lean MRO enterprises deliver the quality products that customers demand—on time, every time. The military can enhance customer satisfaction by reducing lead times by up to 90 percent and increasing on-time delivery to almost 100 percent.
- *Reduced operating costs.* By improving quality, productivity, and customer satisfaction, lean military MRO enterprises can substantially reduce operating costs. For example, by eliminating or streamlining work processes, the military can reduce inventory more than 75 percent.

Furthermore, according to the National Institute of Standards and Technology, an enterprisewide lean transformation can lead to the productivity improvements shown in table 3.1.

Many North American manufacturers, eager for instant results, try to steal the "quick fix" parts of lean production and awkwardly force them into their existing

Table 3.1 Percent of Benefits Achieved through Enterprisewide Lean Transformation

Space Utilization	80%
Quality Improvements	90%
Work-in-Process Reduction	95%
Productivity Increase	55%
Lead Time Reduction	90%

Source: Schultz 2004.

plants to attack the "enemy"—waste. This *muda* (the industry term for such waste; literally, "waste" in Japanese) can look like the following:[1]

- *Overproduction*—that is, producing more than is demanded or producing it before it is needed. It is visible as storage of material, and is the result of producing to speculative demand.
- *Inventory, or work in process (WIP)* is material between operations due to large lot production or processes with long cycle times.
- *Transportation* does not add any value to the product. Instead of improving transportation methods, it should be minimized or eliminated (by, e.g., forming cells).
- *Processing waste* should be minimized by asking why a specific processing step is needed and why a specific product is produced. All unnecessary processing steps should be eliminated.
- The *motion* of the workers, machines, and transport (e.g., due to the inappropriate location of tools and parts) can be waste. Instead of automating wasted motion, the operation itself should be improved.
- *Waiting* for a machine to process should be eliminated. The principle is to maximize the utilization/efficiency of the worker instead of maximizing the utilization of the machines.
- *Making defective products* is pure waste. Preventing the occurrence of defects instead of finding and repairing them can help eliminate this form of waste.

To eliminate muda, manufacturers turn to the "quick fix" lean tool that is increasingly popular—the "kaizen blitz" (Laraia, Moody, and Hall 1999), which is a team set up to attack these wastes and inefficiencies in one element of a manufacturing process, not the entire enterprise (*kaizen* is Japanese for "incremental improvement"). But experts caution that stealing bits and pieces of lean production and performing an incremental implementation isn't enough: "You will never Kaizen your way to lean."[2]

Members of various other service companies involved in recent lean implementations have made similar public comments that identify incremental lean production as one of the causes of their firm's lean implementation breakdowns. The bifurcation of lean implementation within the firm meant that no one had the 25,000-foot view of what was happening across the enterprise; and this led to internal control shortcomings that were not identified (Bies 2004).

3.4 The Process of Architecting an Enterprise

Architecting an enterprise is the process of translating the strategic plan(s) of the enterprise into a structure or model that defines the phases of the transformation implementation. The model should spell out how an enterprise transforms itself to improve performance by specifying where it is positioned in the value chain of the military sustainment system. In the most basic sense, the model is the method of doing business by which an enterprise can sustain itself—that is, generate revenue. The traditional military sustainment enterprise is overstructured, overcontrolled, and overmanaged, but underled. The stakeholders in the enterprise should rather concentrate on that handful of leadership tasks that will bring success in the future. Thus, a new business model is emerging where "most of the key missions of the organization are distributed to the myriad individual pieces and unity comes from the vigor of people and the free flow of knowledge, not a burdensome central headquarters" (Pasternack and Viscio 1998). It should possess six components:

- *Value proposition.* A description of the customer problem, the solution that addresses the problem, and the value of this solution from the customer's perspective.
- *Market segment.* The group to target, recognizing that different market segments have different needs. Sometimes the potential of an innovation is unlocked only when a different market segment is targeted.
- *Value-chain structure.* The position and activities of the enterprise in the value chain and how the enterprise will capture part of the value that it creates in the chain.
- *Revenue generation and margins.* How revenue is generated (sales, subscription, support, etc.), the cost structure, and target profit margins.
- *Position in the value network.* Identification of competitors, complementors, and any network effects that can be utilized to deliver more value to the customer.
- *Competitive strategy.* How the enterprise attempts to develop a sustainable competitive advantage and use it to improve its competitive position in the market. (Chesbrough and Rosenbloom 2002)

There may be several models with these components in mind that meet the strategic plan(s), but each model must be evaluated and assessed for two objectives:

business strategic alignment and strategic fit. Strategic alignment is the consistency between the strategic plan and the business model used to implement it. An uncoordinated or unaligned approach to strategic planning across military agencies may result in "random acts of improvement," as illustrated in figure 3.2. If the work of each functional organizational structure is aligned, the organization will then have a direct and orderly kind of progress, as depicted under "aligned improvements."

Strategic fit, on the other hand, is the consistency between the business model and the enterprise architecture used to achieve the business model, and it indicates how well enterprise strategies fit its internal capabilities and its external environment.

The fit between the enterprise strategy and the business model has a significant positive and direct effect on performance. Fit is a more important determinant of organizational performance than is the type of strategy. The extent of the fit between the business strategy and the operational strategy determines organizational performance.

Enterprise architecting must occur at four levels in the organization: (1) the extended enterprise level; (2) the producer enterprise level; (3) the SBU level; and (4) the cell level. These levels are depicted in figure 3.3. The upper level of figure 3.3 represents the extended enterprise. It includes the inbound logistics network (parts and materials flowing into the base), the producer enterprise (the MRO production facility), and the outbound logistics network (the distribution channel for the resulting products). Combined, these three components become the extended enterprise architecture and represent the value-chain or value-stream network of enterprises and organizations that comprises the entire supply and production chain.

The lower level of figure 3.3 represents the tiered relationship within the producer enterprise. The enterprise is decomposed to include individual strategic business units with lower-level cells, or functional workspace components, that tie together resources, people, and technology to perform the mission of the enterprise. Overhead activities within the producer enterprise are represented as a cell or functional workspace. The tiered relationship illustrates the allocation and composition of the organizational structure as functional components.

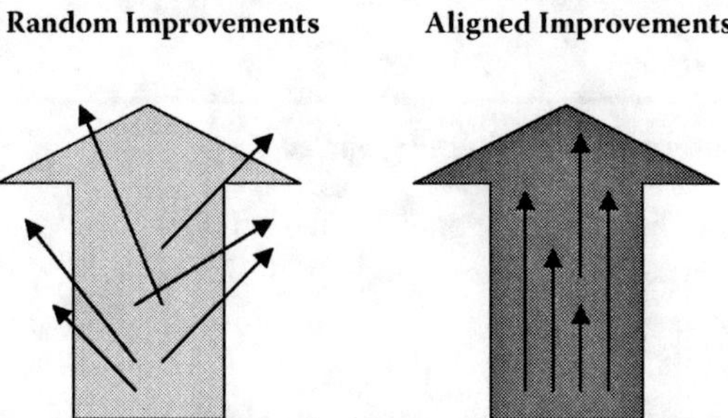

Figure 3.2 Strategic Alignment.

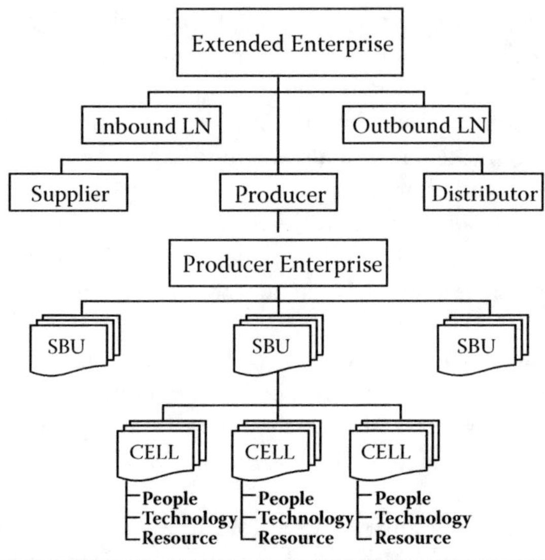

Figure 3.3 Business Enterprise Architecting Levels.

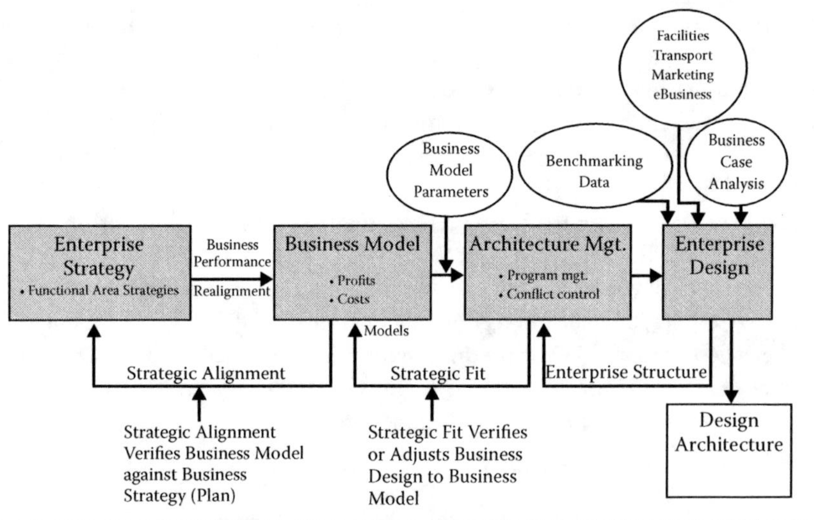

Figure 3.4 The Enterprise Architecting Process.

The process of architecting the transformation of the enterprise is a four-phase process: enterprise strategy, business model definition, architecture management, and enterprise design. These phases, illustrated in figure 3.4, are used to translate enterprise strategic plans into physical enterprise solutions. It starts with strategic planning for the enterprise (shown on the left side of fig. 3.4). Strategic business planning is used to position the enterprise to be competitive in the marketplace.

Functional area strategies are used to define the appropriate business model (in the middle of fig. 3.4) that provides the best strategic alignment for the enterprise. The business model, introduced earlier, is then used to define the overall enterprise transformation architecture with its associated financial and operational performance requirements. These requirements are necessary to implement the strategic plan(s). The architecture management phase (on the right side of fig. 3.4) is used to control the design process. It should utilize a Lean Enterprise Architecture and system engineering principles and practices for the design of the transformation architecture.

The process has three verification loops: strategic alignment, strategic fit, and enterprise structure. These loops (shown at the bottom of fig. 3.4) evaluate and validate the integrity of the architecture. The architecture is evaluated and validated against the initial design specifications. The specifications are evaluated for strategic fit against the business model. The business is evaluated for strategic alignment against the original strategic plans. The verification loops ensure that system engineering design solutions can be traced back to the strategic plan(s).

The business-model phase should be decomposed from the extended enterprise down to the functional cells, as illustrated on the left side of figure 3.5. The figure also illustrates how performance requirements and design constraints are used in conjunction with the architecting management and design activities to implement the various levels of the business enterprise (shown on the right).

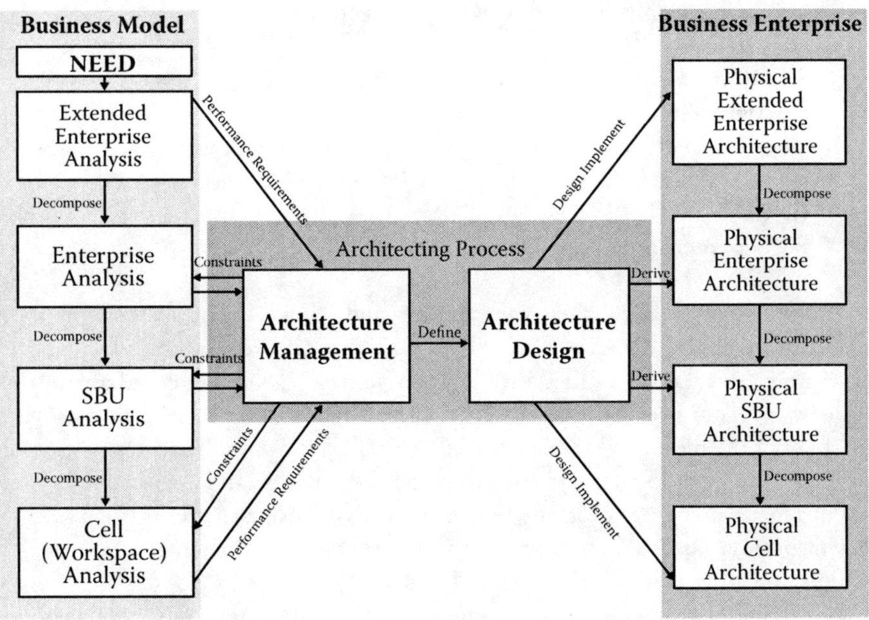

Figure 3.5 A Business Model Architecture.

3.5 Enterprise Architectures

What should this business model for the transformation look like? To address this question, one needs to turn to the body of literature on "enterprise architectures." Enterprise architecture frameworks describe the basic concepts, descriptions, and the related models (views) to provide a standard for enterprise engineering (Institute of Electrical and Electronics Engineers 1998). These frameworks are standards that are used to describe the enterprise from different points of view. These different points of view represent the system architecture with a specific focus, such as operational or technical architectures of the same system. A reason to focus on enterprise architectures is that in order to accomplish a successful transformation across the entire enterprise, the military does not have—and therefore requires—a guiding engineering architecture for its transformation.

Enterprise modeling frameworks, methodologies, and life-cycle concepts (such as the GERA concept described above) have previously emerged in the literature in the application domains of computer-integrated manufacturing (Petrie 1992; Yoshikawa and Goosenaerts, 1993) and information systems design (Olle, Hagelstein, and MacDonald 1998). In developing an architecture for the transformation of the military sustainment system, the authors searched for the most appropriate structure. The questions raised were, What reference architectures were already available? Are any of these structures suitable for military sustainment? And if so, which of these reference architectures was most appropriate? Our investigation revealed five significant and relevant architectures:

- Architecture of integrated information systems (ARIS)
- Computer-integrated manufacturing open system architecture (CIMOSA)
- Generalized enterprise reference architecture and methodology (GERAM)
- Groupe de Recherche en Automatlsation – GRAI integrated methodology (GRAI-GIM)
- Purdue enterprise reference architecture (PERA)

Table 3.2 summarizes these architectures and points to where the reader may obtain more details on each. One should note that all five structures support an enterprisewide approach. The GERAM framework is a good reference base for the framework of our Lean Enterprise Architecture. It is a good base because of its "recognition of the life-cycle life-history differentiation, allowing the representation of multiple change processes, and allowing the representation and characterization of various methodologies, according to their typical life-history patterns (such as top-down, bottom-up, inside-out, spiral, total re-engineering, incremental change—kaizen, concurrent engineering, etc.)" (Bernus 1998).

GERAM is an architecture for enterprise integration that was developed by the IFIP/IFAC Task Force on Architectures for Enterprise Integration. It obtained its start when the task force evaluated existing enterprise integration architectures

Table 3.2 Current Enterprise Reference Architectures

Framework	*Description*	*Application*	*Reference*
Architecture of Integrated Information Systems (ARIS)	ARIS provides a generic and well-documented methodological framework for an enterprise. The architecture distinguishes between organization, function, information and control views. It uses a graphic modeling system supported by software that models data movement and tasks. ARIS focuses on the analysis and requirements definition phase during the design of managerial information systems, not on the execution of business processes. In ARIS, business processes are described by process chain diagrams. The modeling is done using a tool set instead of a language.	Enterprisewide information system	Scheer 1992
Computer Integrated Manufacturing Open Systems Architecture Framework (CIMOSA)	CIMOSA is the European approach to enterprise modeling and integration, and is increasingly accepted as a basis for a common culture of enterprise modeling. The CIMOSA framework was designed mainly to support the model-driven enactment of manufacturing processes. Its orientation toward "run-time modeling" necessitates a formal process-description language. CIMOSA defines a comprehensive methodology of enterprise modeling. The modeling architecture is represented in a three-dimensional framework, the CIMOSA Cube. The first dimension, the generation axis, represents the four views through which a model can be seen: • the function view • the information view • the resource view • the organization view	Enterprisewide manufacturing	Bernus, Nemes, and Williams 1995; Vernadat 1993

(continued)

Table 3.2 Current Enterprise Reference Architectures (continued)

Framework	*Description*	*Application*	*Reference*
	The second dimension, the derivation axis, represents the different life phases of the model: • requirements definition • design specification • implementation description The third dimension, the instantiation axis, expresses the principle of building complex models out of reusable building blocks: • elementary models • partial models • particular model		
Generalized Enterprise Reference Architecture and Methodology (GERAM)	GERAM framework/standard is International Standards Organization Working Draft 15704. GERAM is intended to facilitate the unification of several disciplines in the change process, such as methods of industrial engineering, management science, control engineering, communication, and information technology to allow their combined use in the design process. This framework provides a description of all elements required in enterprise engineering and integration. GERAM provides a general framework for any architecture.	Enterprisewide manufacturing	Bernus 1998

Groupe de Recherche en Automatlsation – GRAI Integrated Methodology (GRAI-GIM)	The GRAI-GIM methodology, begun at the University of Bordeaux in the 1970s, was designed to help define a model of an integrated manufacturing system in order to specify a computer integrated manufacturing (CIM) system for subsequent purchase or development. Since this was done in conjunction with manufacturing industry partners, there is a strong emphasis on discrete (e.g., parts manufacturing) CIM concepts. Another major concept is the definition of reuseable modeling elements.	Enterprisewide manufacturing	Doumeingts et al. 1987; Doumeingts et al. 1992
Perdue Enterprise Reference Framework (PERA)	The PERA model includes three main components of any enterprise: • production facilities architecture • people/organization architecture • control and information systems architecture Each of these architecture “sets” exists at one phase (or really, at a point in time). During each phase of the enterprise, different diagrams are used to reflect the developing detail as the enterprise moves from initial definition to operations phase to dissolution. The PERA provides a life-cycle model that demonstrates how to integrate enterprise systems, physical-plant engineering, and organizational development from enterprise concept to dissolution. PERA was designed for process, manufacturing, and services industries.	Enterprisewide production	Williams 1989

(CIMOSA, GRAI/GIM, and PERA) and then developed an overall definition of a generalized architecture. The proposed framework that resulted from the work of the task force was GERAM, described as being "about those methods, models and tools which are needed to build and maintain the integrated enterprise, be it a part of an enterprise, a single enterprise or a network of enterprises (virtual enterprise or extended enterprise)." GERAM "defines a tool-kit of concepts for designing and maintaining enterprises for their entire life-history. GERAM is not 'yet-another-proposal' for an enterprise reference architecture, but is meant to organize existing enterprise integration knowledge. The framework has the potential for application to all types of enterprise. Previously published reference architectures can keep their own identity, while identifying through GERAM their overlaps and complementing benefits compared to others" (Bernus 1998).

Although the GERAM architecture was developed with information technology (IT) applications in mind, its generalized structure is clearly applicable to other enterprise domains, such as the military sustainment system. Of specific interest is the enterprise engineering methodology (EEM), which describes the processes of enterprise engineering and integration. EEM can be expressed in the form of a process model, which is exactly how Lean Enterprise Architecture can be described.

In addition to the GERAM model, the PERA is also very applicable to the Lean Enterprise Architecture because it covers physical space, information/control, and people/organizational issues—the three key aspects of transformation. The PERA provides a life-cycle model that clearly defines the roles and relationships among these three components. The PERA model breaks the enterprise life cycle into basically the same phases that were illustrated in figure 3.1: identification, concept, requirements, design, implementation, operation, and decommission (see table 3.3). Although this breakdown of the phases is not the only possible one, it is one that has been proven in a large number of projects in many industries. Smaller projects may

Table 3.3 The PERA Life-Cycle Phases

Phases	*Production Equipment*	*Human Factors*	*Control Mechanisms and Information Systems*
Enterprise Definition	1.1	1.2	1.3
Conceptual Engineering	2.1	2.2	2.3
Preliminary Engineering	3.1	3.2	3.3
Detailed Engineering	4.1	4.2	4.3
Construction	5.1	5.2	5.3
Operations and Maintenance	6.1	6.2	6.3
Decommissioning	7.1	7.2	7.3
Asset Disposal	8.1	8.2	8.3

combine phases to reduce overhead costs, but the deliverables between phases generally remain the same. At the end of each phase, a well-defined set of deliverables should be produced. These typically include documents, drawings, calculations, models, and economic analyses. Because the development of the next phase is based on these deliverables, approval to proceed on to other phases should be contingent upon acceptance and approval of all deliverables from the previous phase. Failure to do so virtually guarantees recycling, as well as lost time and cost, in the subsequent phase. Similarly, subsequent changes to even small details in these previous-phase deliverables will have a domino effect on current-phase deliverables. As the project proceeds, it becomes increasingly difficult to improve the design, because the cost and delay caused by changes become progressively greater.

As the PERA model indicates, there are also interfaces within the phase; at the highest level, these are among the three main enterprise components (physical space, information/control, and people). However, each of these is typically further subdivided on large projects. The number of subdivisions increases as the project progresses (and staffing increases). This is necessary to bring additional resources and skills to bear, yet each additional interface presents communication barriers, which are perhaps the most difficult aspect of large-project execution. For example, during the preliminary design phase, where a process is being defined, the performance metrics, information systems, and human roles should be developed in parallel. It is vitally important that these interfaces between groups who are designing the enterprise are clearly understood and coordinated. The design and implementation of an enterprise must be effectively integrated with enterprise systems planning and human and organizational development.

To summarize:

- The GERAM framework is appropriate to sustainment transformation because of its recognition of the life cycle of the transformation, its representation of multiple change processes, and its characterization of various methodologies such as EEM, according to typical life-history patterns such as top-down, bottom-up, inside-out, spiral, total reengineering, incremental change (kaizen), concurrent engineering, and so on.
- The PERA framework is also appropriate because it covers physical space, information/control, and people/organizational issues—the three key aspects of transformation. PERA provides a life-cycle model that defines the roles and relationships among these three components.

These conclusions suggest that a unique hybrid business model, embedded with the GERAM and PERA principles, may be the most appropriate architecture for MRO transformation in the military. The next section describes this hybrid model.

3.6 A Lean Enterprise Architecture for Military Sustainability

3.6.1 Definitions

Using the architecture models presented above as a basis for planning the transformation of the military sustainment system, Lean Enterprise Architecture (LEA) can now be described. But first, some common definitions to establish the context of LEA:

- A *lean enterprise* is an entity that creates value for its stakeholders (Murman et al. 2000).
- *Systems engineering* is a discipline that enables the realization of successful systems (International Council on Systems Engineering 2007).
- *Enterprise engineering* is the collection of tools and methods for designing and maintaining an enterprise (International Organization for Standardization 2003).
- *Systems engineering methods* are the set of processes used to accomplish systems engineering tasks (Institute of Electrical and Electronics Engineers 1998).
- *Systems architecture* is the arrangement of subsystems to meet system requirements (Institute of Electrical and Electronics Engineers 1998).
- *Systems architecting* is the art and science of creating systems (Rechtin 2000).
- *Organizational architecting* is the application of systems architecting to organizations (Rechtin 1999).
- An *architecture framework* describes the concepts and models for enterprise engineering (Institute of Electrical and Electronics Engineers 1998).

LEA is an architectural framework for enterprise reengineering in the design, construction, integration, and implementation of a lean enterprise using systems engineering methods, and was developed for the U.S. military aerospace MRO industry. The industry is in need of a complete redesign and reconstruction, and to do so it requires an architecture for the transformation. In searching for an architecture (Kaiser-Arnett 2003), the industry did not want a "design-build" approach (Pearce and Bennett 2005),[3] as is commonly employed in the construction industry, or a kaizen blitz approach (Laraia, Moody, and Hall 1999),[4] as is often used in lean manufacturing implementations. There are significant differences among these methods and the LEA, and the impact on the organization that is undergoing the transformation process. The design-build method is very conducive for enterprises that prefer to move quickly on a transformation and desire a single point of responsibility for both the design and the construction of the project. The most significant driving factor is the schedule. The transformation moves rapidly, and one must make decisions quickly. The kaisen blitz approach attempts to capture the "low-hanging fruit" by first leaning out waste in existing systems through the use of value-stream mapping (Tapping, Shuker, and Luyster 2002) and kaizen events (Imai 1986). The process continues until all cells have been made lean, at which time they are balanced and then integrated so that the system is "pull-based" rather than "push-based," pulling the requirements from the customer rather than pushing the requirements onto the customer. Often, lean success is defined as the existence of a kaizen culture in which lean tools are effectively applied, by enthusiastic employees, to eliminate waste every day. "If this is true," notes William Roper, "then many organizations should probably quit their lean programs now, as they will never succeed by this definition. There is no roadmap for achieving a kaizen culture, and left to their own devices, most organizations will run out of time and patience before they discover the path" (2002, page 1).

The design of the LEA incorporates lean attributes and values as baseline requirements for the re-creation of the enterprise. The approach is a structured systems engineering method for a lean enterprise transformation. LEA is meant to be complementary with lean and other continuous improvement processes, such as total productive maintenance (TPM; see Leflar 2001; Nakajima 1988; Robinson 1995). TPM focuses on the optimization of equipment and process productivity, and lean manufacturing addresses the elimination of waste (labor, time, cost, inventory, etc.) while establishing customer-driven ("pull," "just in time") production. LEA architecture uses a multiphase lean approach structured on transformation life-cycle phases and is developed from an enterprise perspective, paying particular attention to strategic issues, internal and external relations with all key stakeholders, and structural issues—such as TPM—that must be addressed before and during a significant change initiative.

3.6.2 The Lean Enterprise Architecture

In order to effect a successful transformation, depots require an integrated set of activities and support documents that execute their strategic vision, program concepts, acquisition strategy, schedule, communications plan, and implementation strategy. To this end, this author, with Tim Cathcart and Mario Agripino (Mathaisel et al., 2005), has created LEA (presented in figure 3.6), which is a structure to organize these activities for the transformation of the enterprise from a current state to a desired future condition. LEA uses a phased approach structured on the life cycle of the transformation. It portrays the flow of phases necessary to initiate, sustain, and continuously refine an enterprise transformation based upon lean principles and systems engineering methods.

The top of figure 3.6 represents the life cycle of the transformation. The bottom of the illustration represents the architecture that is used to create the life cycle. The architecture is comprised of three phases (shown at the bottom of the illustration).

The first component is the transformation strategic planning phase, which specifies the actions associated with the decision to adopt the lean paradigm. The second component is the transformation acquisition and integration phase, in which the environment and conditions necessary for a successful change in the enterprise are created.

The organization is then prepared for the launch into detailed planning and implementation, which is the third phase, the transformation implementation phase, in which the transformation of the enterprise is planned, executed, and monitored.

Each phase in this architecture creates the conditions necessary to put into effect the life cycle of the transformation. The description of each component of the life cycle is given in table 3.4.

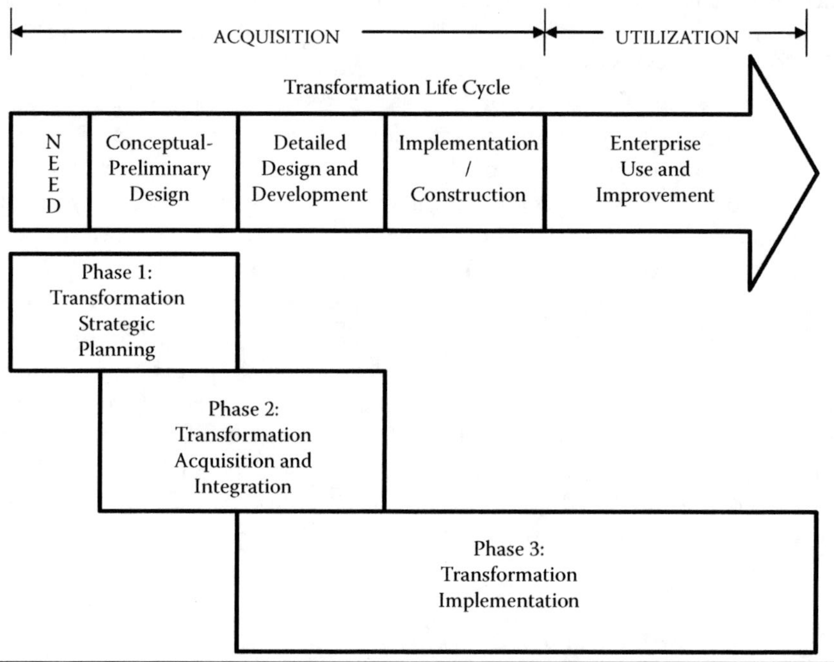

Figure 3.6 Lean Enterprise Architecture Phases.

Table 3.4 Transformation Life Cycle Components

Component	*Description*
Need	Wants or desires for transformation of the enterprise because of obvious deficiencies or problems.
Conceptual and Detailed Design	Market analysis, feasibility study, requirements analysis, enterprise system design and development, simulation, engineering prototyping, benchmarking, acquisition plans, trade-off analysis, and specifications development.
Implementation/ Construction	Modification, procurement, integration, installation, testing, training, and implementing the transformation of facilities, production systems, business systems, and policies.
Enterprise Use and Improvement	Operational use of the transformation, and continued review for improvement or modification.

Because the five principles of lean thinking (Womack and Jones 1996) are an important ingredient of the architecture, links can be drawn between the components of the framework and existing lean tools and techniques. These relationships are identified and further described in table 3.5.

In what follows below, the author describes the essential steps and documents that accompany each phase of LEA. These steps and documents are necessary to initiate, sustain, and continuously refine an enterprise transformation that will result in the implementation of lean principles and practices. The details of each document are provided in chapter 6.

3.6.3 Phase 1: Transformation Strategic Planning

Best commercial and government practices continue to demonstrate the benefits of a strategic plan (see table 3.6) to focus the effort and energy of an organization toward the achievement of common goals, objectives, and performance metrics. Thus, the first step in a transformation acquisition is to develop a strategic plan. The success of the organization is highly dependent on a focused vision set forth in a carefully conceived plan. The strategic plan should encompass the three crucial change elements of the transformation process: infrastructure, lean operations, and personnel change management. The strategic plan is part of phase 1 of LEA.

3.6.4 Phase 2: Transformation Acquisition and Integration

Transformation acquisition necessitates the development of a requirements package, an acquisition plan, an integration plan, and a change management and communication plan.

3.6.4.1 The Requirements Package

The requirements package (see table 3.7) consists of a statement of objectives/statement of work for the transformation, its scope and specifications, a contract data requirements list with acceptance criteria, and a delivery schedule. The package includes a compelling case for change in depot maintenance processes, procedures, and facilities; a clear future-state objective; meaningful performance metrics; realistic milestones and accountability; and a clear definition of success. The package addresses the need for urgent cultural transformation and identifies the need for IT integration. The package should also include a requirement to demonstrate and defend the expected ROI of the transformation against established performance metrics.

Table 3.5 The Relationship between Lean Enterprise Architecture and the Five Principles of Lean Thinking

Component	*Relationship to the Five Principles of Lean Thinking*	*Discussion*
Need	(1) Value	Every enterprise needs to understand what value the customers place upon their products and services. The need for the transformation is to eliminate waste and cost from the business process so that the transformation can be achieved at great value to the enterprise and its customers. Value is achieved through the use of the quality tools and continuous process improvement techniques espoused by Deming (1986; total quality management), Harry and Schroeder (2000; six sigma), Shewhart (1989; the plan—do—study—act cycle), and many others.
Conceptual and Detailed Design	(2) The Value Stream	The value stream is the flow of a product's life cycle from the origin of the raw materials used to make the product through to the customer's use and ultimate disposal of the product. In the conceptual and detailed design component of transforming the enterprise, it is only through a study of the value stream and its value-added or waste, using techniques like value-stream mapping (Tapping, Shuker, and Luyster 2002), can an enterprise truly understand the manufacturing process or service. Lean thinking advocates supplier and customer partnerships and radical supply chain management to eliminate waste from the entire value stream.
	(3) The Flow	One very significant key to the elimination of waste is flow. If the value chain stops moving forward for any reason, waste can occur. The principle of the

		transformation design is to create a value stream in which the product and its raw materials, components, and subassemblies never stop in the production process and where each aspect of production and delivery is fully synchronized with the other elements. Carefully designed flow across the entire value chain will tend to minimize waste and increase value.
Implementation/ Construction	(4) Pull	During implementation, the way to ensure that nothing is made ahead of time and builds up work-in-process inventory that stops the synchronized flow is to use a "pull" approach. A traditional Western manufacturer will use a materials requirements planning or enterprise resource planning style of production planning and control, whereby production is "pushed" through the factory based upon a forecast and a schedule. A "pull" approach posits that nothing should be made until the customer orders it. To achieve this requires great flexibility and very short clock speeds (Fine 1998) in the design, production, and delivery of the products and services. It also requires a mechanism for informing each step in the value chain what is required of them today based upon meeting the customer's needs.
Enterprise Use and Improvement	(5) Perfection	A lean enterprise sets its target for improvement. The idea of total quality management (Deming 1986) is to systematically and continuously remove the root causes of poor quality from the production processes so that the plant and its products are moving toward perfection. This relentless pursuit of perfection is a key component in the transformation of an organization that is striving for leanness.

Table 3.6 The Strategic Plan

Motivates and aligns the organization to achieve common goals and objectives
Aids tactical planning and execution
Assists in communications and workforce buy-in
Supports change planning and management
Supports development of processes and road maps

Table 3.7 The Requirements Package

Performance-based acquisition strategy
Performance work statement that captures the whats, not the hows
A compelling case for change in depot transformation
A clear future-state objective for depot infrastructure and process
Meaningful metrics to monitor progress and to drive acquisition objectives
A clearly stated definition of success (exit criteria)

3.6.4.2 The Acquisition Plan

The acquisition plan (see table 3.8) outlines the strategy for managing the acquisition elements of the transformation. Selection of the transformation contractor should be based on that candidates' early and continuous industry involvement, past performance, performance-based requirements, oral presentations, cost/benefit analyses, and full and open competition and briefings. The plan must also identify the risks associated with the transformation and develop a mitigation strategy to overcome them.

3.6.4.3 The Integration Plan

The integration plan (see table 3.9) is another aspect of phase 2. Integration encompasses an approach to establishing the appropriate lines of communication: vertically, for those stakeholders directly involved in the implementation of the transformation, and horizontally, to consider the impacts of other depot productivity enhancement initiatives (e.g., information system upgrades, contract repair financial/operational changes, supply support). The plan needs to consider how the transformation will affect, and be affected by, other initiatives. It may require a collaborative software tool that will enhance communications, review, decision making, and actions taken throughout the affected organizations. The commercially proven integrated process and product development (IPPD) approach is one tool that can help the transformation achieve its goals more efficiently and effectively by focusing on the integration and application of critical activities early on in the acquisition process. Two key pillars of IPPD are the integrated master plan (IMP) and the integrated master schedule (IMS). Together, these management

Table 3.8 The Acquisition Plan

Documents the acquisition strategy and high level program structure and schedules
Has an acquisition strategy that uses an evolutionary acquisition approach that leverages proven commercial best practices of lean/cellular MRO transformation
Has system engineering practices and methodologies that are used to design, develop, evaluate, test, integrate, and implement transformation activities

Table 3.9 The Integration Plan

Establishes appropriate lines of communication
Considers how the transformation will affect, and be affected by, other initiatives
May require a collaborative software tool to enhance communications
Uses the integrated process and product development approach
Develops an integrated master plan/integrated master schedule

tools provide the integrated plan of events and activities, the schedule in which these will occur, and the resources that will be used to execute them.

3.6.4.4 The Change Management and Communications Plan

Phase 2 also requires a change management plan (see table 3.10). The heart of change management is communication. However, that communication is effective only when it is focused in the context of an overall change management plan. Therefore, the scope should extend across all areas of change management, including strategy, training, and supporting management systems (Synergy 2003). A successful depot transformation depends, in large part, upon how effectively management communicates with those affected by the transformation. This communication must address, at a minimum, what's happening, why it's happening, and how it's happening. More important, each individual and organization affected by the transformation must understand how the transformation impacts him or her. There should be, at a minimum, three interrelated communications plans. These plans will be intra-agency, interagency, and extra-agency in scope. The intra-agency communication plan should keep all personnel levels at the depot informed about the transformation status and initiatives. The interagency communication plan should keep other organizations within the force informed about transformation status and initiatives. The extra-agency communication plan should promote and inform organizations outside the force.

Included in a change management/communications plan should be the development and maintenance of a website that will include briefings, presentations,

Table 3.10 The Change Management and Communications Plan

Establishes motivation for change and a sense of urgency
Builds a guiding coalition
Develops a vision and strategy for change
Communicates that vision
Empowers broad-based action
Generates short-term wins
Sustains the momentum: consolidates gains and produces more change
Anchors new approaches in the culture

Table 3.11 The Transformation Implementation Plan

Monitors schedules and performance
Manages risk
Sources selection planning
Prioritizes (and obtains funding for) the highest payback initiatives (measures and ensures return on investment)
Provides program/budget guidance and defends resources
Implements and monitors the difficult task of embedding cultural change within the depot
Fosters a sense of urgency for task completion coupled with a commitment of time and resources and establishes metrics that drive the proper behavior

contact lists, milestones, mission statement, organizational goals, streaming video shows, collaborative tools, and other communication tools.

3.6.5 Phase 3: Transformation Implementation

Transformation implementation is built on a strong centralized vision, continuous improvement, and progress measurement. Successful implementation also requires leadership, innovation, and organization. That basic leadership and organizational framework occurs when the necessary personnel are versed in program management, best commercial lean or cellular manufacturing processes, financial management, acquisition, source/vendor selection, administrative/office support, and other functions that are deemed necessary to help integrate government contractor and general contractor personnel efforts.

Thus, a good implementation plan (see table 3.11) is one of: monitoring schedules, performance metrics, and engineering changes; managing risks, costs, and vendor selection; prioritizing payback initiatives and resources; and fostering a sense of urgency in task completion.

3.7 The Role of Systems Engineering in the Lean Enterprise Architecture

The military sustainment enterprise is a complex collage of engineering components and interrelationships that exhibit dynamic stimulus-response characteristics, limits on its operations, and the emphasis on the reliability of its weapons systems. Being a "peopled" system, it presents special challenges to those who would transform it. Only leaders who are adept at the right kind of systems engineering can meet these challenges. The systems engineering view gives the enterprise a competitive edge over those who see the business as a functional organization or a set of processes (Ring 1999). Thus, the Lean Enterprise Architecture must be rooted in the concepts of systems engineering.

To demonstrate how the management tools of lean sustainment and the technical tools of systems engineering work together within the phases of LEA to ensure an effective transformation, the concept of lean enterprise transformation engineering needs to be explained. Earlier in this chapter, *enterprise engineering* was defined as the collection of tools and methods for designing and continually maintaining an enterprise (International Organization for Standardization 2003). Based on that definition, *lean enterprise transformation engineering* can be defined as a discipline that uses the tools of systems engineering and the management practices of lean sustainment to organize all of the tasks needed to design, implement, and operate enterprise transformation change. The structure for the transformation is based on the life cycle of the enterprise. The military and commercial MRO enterprises, as well as their products, follow this life cycle. The cycle begins with the initial concept for a system or transformation and then proceeds with development, design, construction, operation and maintenance, refurbishment or obsolescence, and final disposal of the system (Blanchard and Fabrycky 1998).

Lean enterprise transformation engineering uses an architecture framework to define and describe enterprise design and implementation solutions. An architecture framework describes basic concepts, descriptions, and the related models (views) to provide a standard for enterprise engineering (Institute of Electrical and Electronics Engineers 1998). The framework provides a description of all elements required in enterprise engineering and integration. It is intended to facilitate the unification of several disciplines in the change process, such as industrial engineering, management science, control engineering, communication, and information technology, to allow their combined use in the design process. It is structured using an enterprise life-cycle perspective that complements and integrates with the LEA transformation life-cycle phases. Lean/cellular transformation practices and methods are incorporated into the framework as design requirements for the future state enterprise. System engineering and enterprise engineering methods coupled with the framework will be used to design, develop, test, evaluate, integrate and implement the lean enterprise transformation.

How would an enterprise use the LEA framework for its lean transformation? As illustrated in figure 3.7, there are five fundamental tasks that should be followed: conceptual design, preliminary design, detailed design, implementation, and operation. The tasks are sequential; they follow the fundamental principles of systems engineering; and they are based on the life cycle of the enterprise. Specified within each task is the collection of process improvement tools and methods that one can use to design and continually maintain a lean state of the enterprise.

The five basic tasks in the framework given in figure 3.7 will now be described in the next four sections; the preliminary and detailed design tasks are described together in one section).

3.7.1 The Conceptual Design Task

For the conceptual design task, the strategic position of the enterprise is evaluated for competitive capability, organizational structure, and processes. Current business strategies and market research are used to define future-state enterprise architecture performance requirements. Feasibility studies, formal business case analysis, and ROI projections are used to select a conceptual enterprise architecture from various configuration alternatives. The conceptual enterprise architecture defines the enterprise performance, organizational and value-chain structures, technology, human resources, facilities, products, and operational requirements. The architecture defines operational interfaces and performance requirements needed to meet enterprise business strategy, vision, and mission objectives.

3.7.2 The Preliminary and Detailed Design Tasks

During these tasks, the conceptual architecture is evaluated and synthesized into functional and operational architectures. The functional architecture is developed during the preliminary design to describe enterprise functional and performance requirements. The operational architecture is developed during the detailed design task to describe the enterprise organizational structures and their individual configurations (organization structures, technology, human resources, facilities, products, etc.).

System engineering methods are used to design and develop these architectures using integrated product teams (IPTs). Each level of the architecture captures a stage in the design process as more detail evolves. The IPTs perform systems engineering analysis from previous architecture definitions and use trade studies to select architectural components. The architecture forces the IPTs to maintain a total enterprise solution. This approach provides an enterprise engineering method to meet organizational requirements. During the design tasks, facility and production system cells are designed in accordance with lean principles.

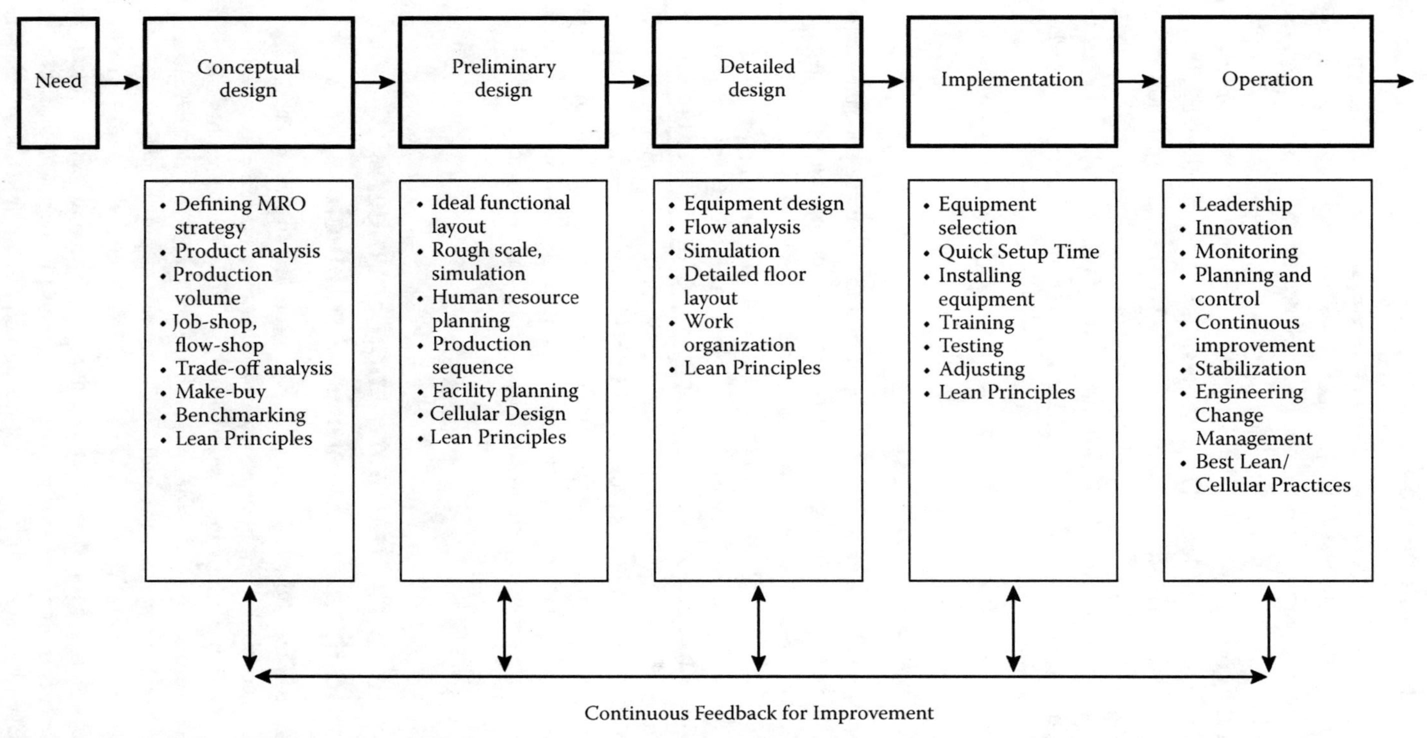

Figure 3.7 Lean Enterprise Transformation Engineering

3.7.3 The Implementation Task

During this task, the operational architecture is produced and implemented using project management methods. The operational architecture is used to develop the enterprise transformation plan. The plan will describe all tasks necessary to implement the future vision. During the implementation task, facility and production system cells are constructed and modified in accordance with lean practices. Specialized equipment and selected IT networks are procured, installed, integrated, tested, and certified. Workforce training is conducted for new enterprise operations.

Implementation can be either incremental or a one-time event, depending on risk. Implementation requires significant integration of people, technology, facilities, and operational processes. During this phase, great care must be taken to prevent disruption to current operations while simultaneously implementing enterprise changes. Implementation must consider both internal and external architecture interfaces.

3.7.4 The Operation Task

The operation of the transformed facilities and production system cells should ensure the continued strong centralized vision, transformation improvement goals, and progress measurement metrics that were designed in the earlier tasks of phases 1 and 2. All of the hard work in the tasks leading up to this point should not be in vain. The enterprise architecture is only as good as the leadership, organization, and engineering frameworks that are the foundation of the architecture. Thus, transformation operation requires continuous leadership, innovation, monitoring, control, and management of engineering changes. Such changes require a complete impact and cost assessment to either the production system or entire enterprise. In addition, the best operation of any transformation occurs when all personnel are versed in the most current best commercial lean or cellular manufacturing principles and practices.

3.8 Enterprise Transformation Engineering and the Lean Enterprise Architecture

Figure 3.8 shows how lean enterprise architecture and the concepts of lean enterprise transformation engineering work together to ensure an effective and successful transformation of the enterprise. The top of figure 3.8 represents the life cycle of the transformation; the bottom represents the three phases of LEA. Each phase in the architecture creates the conditions necessary to put into effect the life cycle of the transformation. The middle of figure 3.8 (the shaded region) is the framework for lean enterprise transformation engineering. This combination of lean enterprise and systems engineering methodologies portrays the overall flow of the action steps necessary to initiate, transform, sustain, and continuously refine an enterprise.

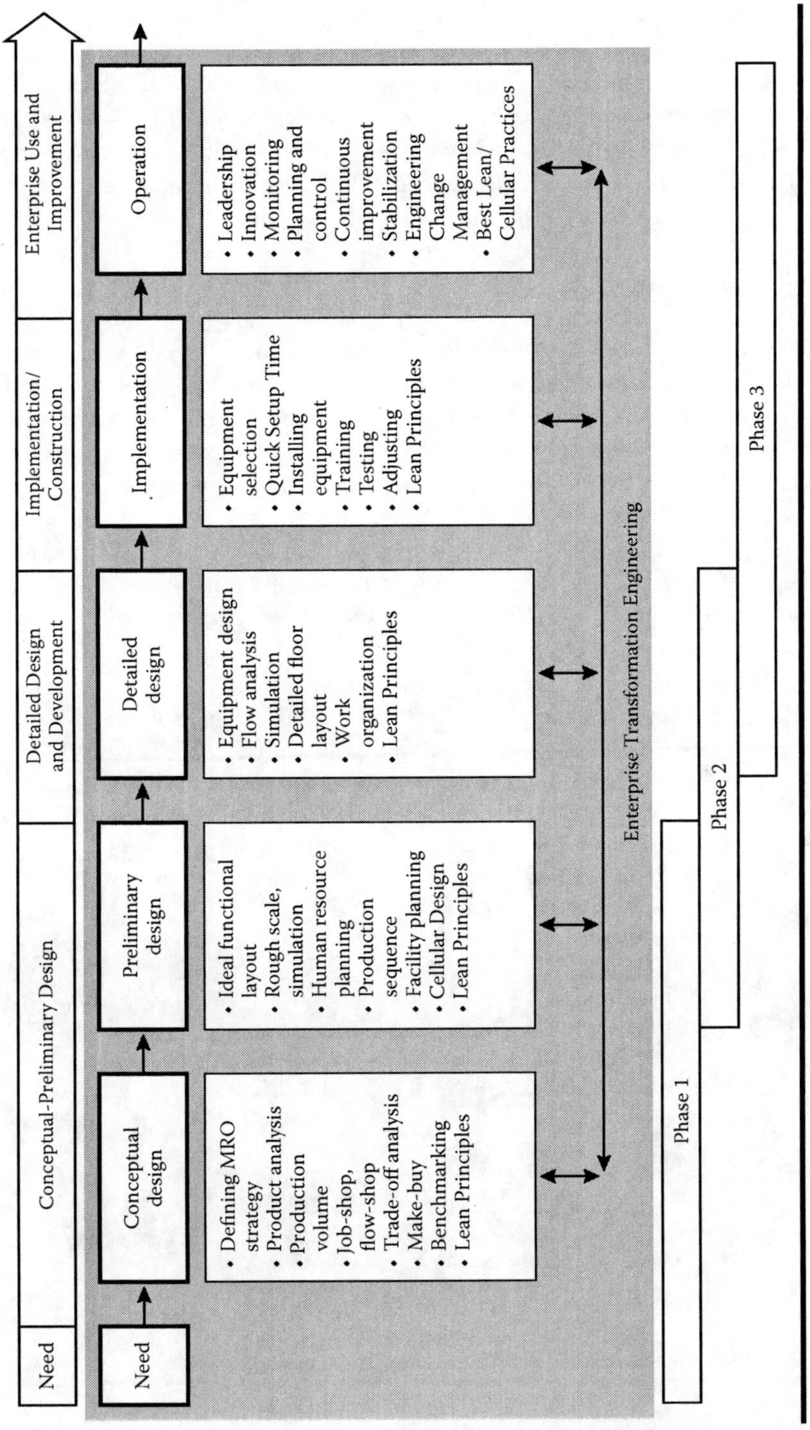

Need | Conceptual-Preliminary Design | Detailed Design and Development | Implementation/ Construction | Enterprise Use and Improvement

Need → Conceptual design → Preliminary design → Detailed design → Implementation → Operation

Conceptual design
- Defining MRO strategy
- Product analysis
- Production volume
- Job-shop, flow-shop
- Trade-off analysis
- Make-buy
- Benchmarking
- Lean Principles

Preliminary design
- Ideal functional layout
- Rough scale, simulation
- Human resource planning
- Production sequence
- Facility planning
- Cellular Design
- Lean Principles

Detailed design
- Equipment design
- Flow analysis
- Simulation
- Detailed floor layout
- Work organization
- Lean Principles

Implementation
- Equipment selection
- Quick Setup Time
- Installing equipment
- Training
- Testing
- Adjusting
- Lean Principles

Operation
- Leadership
- Innovation
- Monitoring
- Planning and control
- Continuous improvement
- Stabilization
- Engineering Change Management
- Best Lean/ Cellular Practices

Enterprise Transformation Engineering

Phase 1

Phase 2

Phase 3

Figure 3.8 Lean Enterprise Architecture.

At least one branch of the U.S. armed forces, the Air Force, has directed that all transformation activities use systems engineering methods and approved architectures. To provide guidance, it has released a preliminary draft of a document on robust engineering in Air Force acquisition programs (U.S. Air Force 2004). The term *robust engineering* is used to denote the use of a disciplined systems engineering process in conjunction with a robust product design. The appropriate application of robust engineering principles will enable acquisition programs to achieve the desired end state: to quickly deliver high-quality, low-cost products (capabilities) that fully meet the operator's needs and are designed to easily and inexpensively accommodate growth (scalability/expandability) of capabilities in subsequent increments. The process uses a classic V model (shown in fig. 3.9). The V model represents the decomposition and definition of user needs and systems design (on the left side) and the integration and verification of the systems (on the right side). The vertical axis represents the various levels of the system architecture, from system and subsystem to component design. The horizontal axis represents time and the various stages of the lifecycle.

The LEA of figure 3.8 correlates with this V model for life-cycle stages and decomposition detail. The left side of the V model represents phases 1 and 2 (the conceptual, preliminary, and detailed design life-cycle phases). The right side of the V model represents phase 3 (the implementation and operation life-cycle phases). Systems integration is considered part of the implementation phase.

The overall process of implementing the V model steps is called the *systems engineering process* (SEP) and is outlined in figure 3.10 (U.S. Air Force 2004). The SEP is used iteratively for each life-cycle phase of the LEA and the V model.[5] The

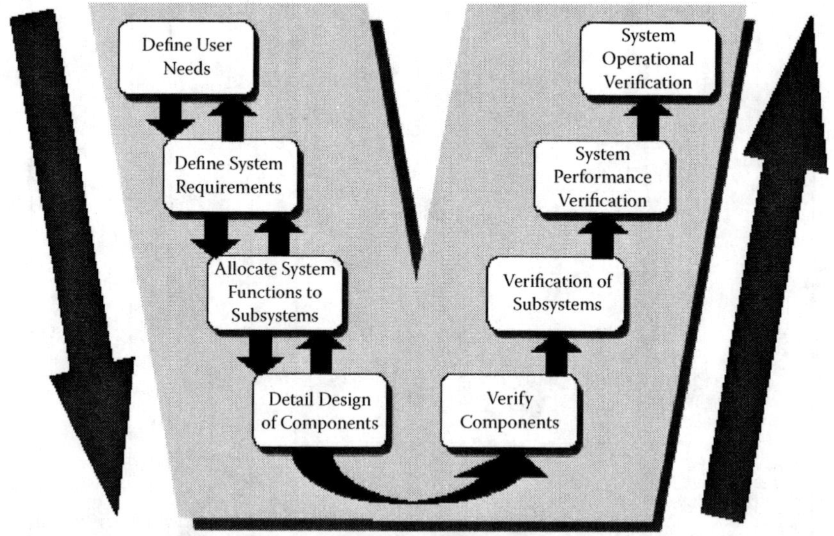

Figure 3.9 The Systems Engineering Model (from U.S. Air Force 2004).

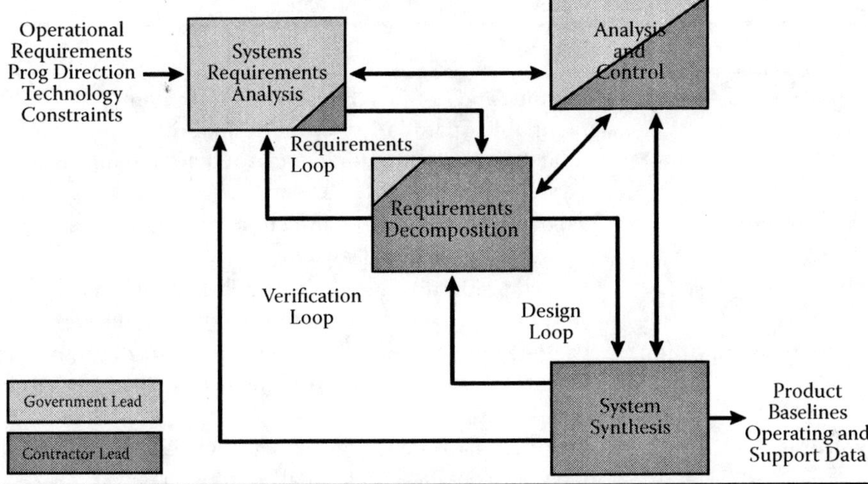

Figure 3.10 The Systems Engineering Process (from U.S. Air Force 2004).

process is always repeated, and it uses previously defined requirements, design allocations, and constraints as inputs for the next life-cycle activity. A description of each step in the process is provided in table 3.12. Note that in figure 3.10 a shaded color scheme is used to show the appropriate responsibilities for the government and contractor in the SEP process. The government has traditionally been responsible for the program management and requirements analysis portions of the SEP. Industry has traditionally performed the engineering design, integration, and verification activities in the SEP.

3.9 Preference for a Performance-Based Transformation

More than fifteen years ago, the U.S. Office of Federal Procurement Policy in Policy Letter 91-2 (1991) established that preference be given to performance-based contracting methods. This guidance was then incorporated into the OFPP document *A Guide to Best Practices for Performance-Based Service Contracting* (U.S. Office of Federal Procurement Policy 1998a). Current military policy continues to support a performance-based transformation approach, as demonstrated in the "Seven Steps to Performance-Based Services Acquisition" guide:

> ...over the next five years, a majority of the service contracts offered throughout the federal government will be performance-based. In other words, rather than micromanaging the details of how contractors operate, the government must set the standards, set the results and give

Table 3.12 Steps in the Systems Engineering Process

Step	*Description*
Requirements Analysis	Clarifies and defines the problem statement in verifiable quantitative terms. Requirements and constraints are identified and documented in the system requirements baseline.
Requirements Validation	Validates and resolves conflicting requirements and assumptions from all stakeholders.
Functional analysis	Is used to identify and develop all functional tasks required to execute the requirements baseline.
Functional Verification	Validates the functional architecture to ensure that it meets the minimum requirements baseline objectives.
Synthesis	Includes all of the design activities necessary to achieve specified functional architecture.
Design Verification	Is used to validate the system architecture against both functional and requirements baseline documentation.
Systems Analysis	A problem-solving step used throughout the systems engineering process to make decision trade-offs.
Control	A management step used to coordinate, document, and track the systems engineering process.

> the contractor the freedom to achieve it in the best way. — Presidential Candidate George W. Bush on June 9, 2000 (Interagency-Industry Partnership in Performance 2007)

Military transformation architects have not fully embraced performance-based transformation, but the commercial sector has, as will be demonstrated in chapter 5 on best sustainment practices. There are many reasons, such as unpredictable demands on the maintenance, repair and overhaul system, but the real reason is the traditional acquisition mindset that has entrenched the workforce. As a result, the Lean Enterprise Architecture was designed around a performance-based transformation.

3.10 Applications of the Lean Enterprise Architecture

Lean enterprise architecture was developed for the military MRO enterprise. It was chosen as the architecture for the U.S. Air Force transformation program at the Oklahoma City, Oklahoma, and Ogden, Utah, air logistics centers. In addition, it is beginning to appear in other U.S. commercial and military manufacturing implementations. Table 3.13 summarizes these known applications.

Table 3.13 Military and Commercial Applications of Lean Enterprise Architecture

Application	*Institution Performing the Application*	*Description*
Military maintenance, repair and overhaul depot	U.S. Air Force, Oklahoma City Air Logistics Center (OC-ALC) (Source: OC-ALC/MA-T Solicitation #FA8100-04-R-0001)	Customer: U.S. Air Force, Air Force Materiel Command Period of Performance: 2005–2015 Contract Value: $500,000,000 Brief Description: The scope of the Oklahoma City Air Logistics Center (OC-ALC) MRO transformation program is to design, develop, construct, install, implement, and deliver a dramatically improved MRO processes within existing facilities. The program will address a lean and cellular transformation of the MRO system for aircraft, engines, commodities, and weapons system software. OC-ALC/MA-T adopted the lean enterprise architecture strategy to transform the ALC industrial enterprise.
Military maintenance, repair and overhaul depot	U.S. Air Force, Ogden, Utah, Air Logistics Center (OO-ALC) (Source: OO-ALC/MA-T Solicitation #FA8201-04-R-0017)	Customer: U.S. Air Force, Air Force Materiel Command Period of Performance: 2005–2010 Contract Value: $37,500,000 Brief Description: The program objectives for this transformation effort are to design, develop, construct, install, implement, and deliver a dramatically improved MRO process and facilities. The program will address a lean/cellular transformation of MRO for aircraft landing gear, wheels, and brakes. Commodities will be addressed as they impact landing gear refurbishment production operations or as stand-alone business units as they are disrupted in the transformation process. This program is necessary to meet the OO-ALC objective of affordable increased throughput. OO-ALC adopted the lean enterprise architecture strategy to transform the ALC industrial enterprise.

(continued)

Table 3.13 Military and Commercial Applications of Lean Enterprise Architecture (continued)

Application	*Institution Performing the Application*	*Description*
Commercial	Lockwood Greene Engineers, Inc. (Lockwood Greene Engineers, Inc. 2005)	Customer: PACCAR (Kenworth and Peterbilt Trucks) Period of Performance: December 1997–present Contract Value: $5,109,749 Brief Description: PACCAR's lean transformation program is a multiyear effort involving their worldwide truck manufacturing complex. The lean transformation program is being executed in phases by plant site in several different North American and Central European countries. This is a production program involving program management services, lean manufacturing analyses, cellular designs, production equipment assessments, extensive facility modification design packages, and construction-phase support services at multiple production plant sites in North America and Central Europe.
Commercial	Lockwood Greene Engineers, Inc.(Lockwood Greene Engineers, Inc. 2005)	Customer: Thomson Multimedia, Inc. Period of Performance: June 2001–April 2003 Contract Value: $10,322,382 Brief Description: This was a production project involving program management; lean manufacturing analyses and design; production equipment condition assessment (over 5,300 pieces of equipment); equipment relocation and installation design packages; on-site construction management; and start-up services. Conducted a

		fast-paced lean manufacturing analyses (visioneering) seminar to gain consensus on facility concepts. Redesigned process flow line to accommodate existing and new equipment in a lean flow through process in new facility as opposed to departmental process from old facility. Performed detailed condition assessment on approximately 55 manufacturing systems comprised of approximately 5,300 individual pieces of equipment to determine if manufacturing equipment should be transferred, refurbished, stored or scrapped. Developed 94 detailed engineering layout drawings for all manufacturing areas for new picture-tube assembly line. Generated detailed performance and technical specifications for major equipment procurement or refurbishment. Generated cost savings and cost avoidances to the client totaling over $9 million dollars, including over $400,000 in annual recurring energy savings.
Commercial	Lockwood Greene Engineers, Inc. (Lockwood Greene Engineers, Inc. 2005)	Customer: U.S. Mint Period of Performance: October 2002–present Contract Value: $1,531,000 Brief Description: This is a production transformation involving program management services, lean manufacturing analyses, process modeling, lean/cellular designs, production equipment assessments, workforce planning, facility modification design packages, and eventual construction-phase support services at multiple U.S. Mint plant sites in America.

These applications have chosen to take an enterprisewide approach to their lean implementations. Why? Viewing lean implementation across the entire enterprise minimizes the possibility of overlooking opportunities for further performance improvement.

3.11 Case Study: The Lean Enterprise Architecture Implementation Process in the U.S. Air Force

Lean Enterprise Architecture was chosen as the architecture for the U.S. Air Force transformation of the Oklahoma City, Oklahoma, and Ogden, Utah, air logistics centers (ALCs). What follows is a case study on how the Oklahoma City ALC (OC-ALC) used LEA for its transformation.

3.11.1 Organization of the Implementation Process

The OC-ALC LEA uses a tiered approach for review, approval, integration and communication of transformation efforts and projects. Figure 3.11 shows the structure for the transformation. It is designed for the Directorate of Maintenance at the OC-ALC, and it integrates the systems engineering process within the life-cycle model framework of LEA. This integrated process will be applied in various contexts to new system development programs, to modifications of fielded systems, and to the reengineering of product support approaches for fielded systems. This process, including a decision matrix, will be put into place to assist in determining which plans and programs will be implemented and to resolve any conflict of overlapping, duplicative, or conflicting efforts competing for the same or precious resources. Synchronization will focus on a tiered approach, with the objective of increasing equipment availability to the customer, reducing cost of goods sold to the customer, increasing ROI, and effective integration/interaction of all transformation efforts. The organization chart associated with this tiered approach is provided in figure 3.12.

The vehicle for the review and approval process will also be a tiered approach with the Directorate of Programs–Transformation (XP-T) as the horizontal integrator for the ALC, and the Maintenance Program Transformation division (MAPT) as the integrator for depot maintenance (MX). Each wing and enabling organization will use a tiered approach (see fig. 3.13) with the transformation agent acting as the horizontal integrator within the organization. The four tiers at the wing/organization level are: the Program Requirements Teams (tier 4); the Program Review Council (tier 3); the Group Steering Council (tier 2); and the Executive Council (tier 1).

At the center level (see fig. 3.14), the tiers are: the group/organization transformation horizontal integrators (tier 4); wing/organization transformation horizon-

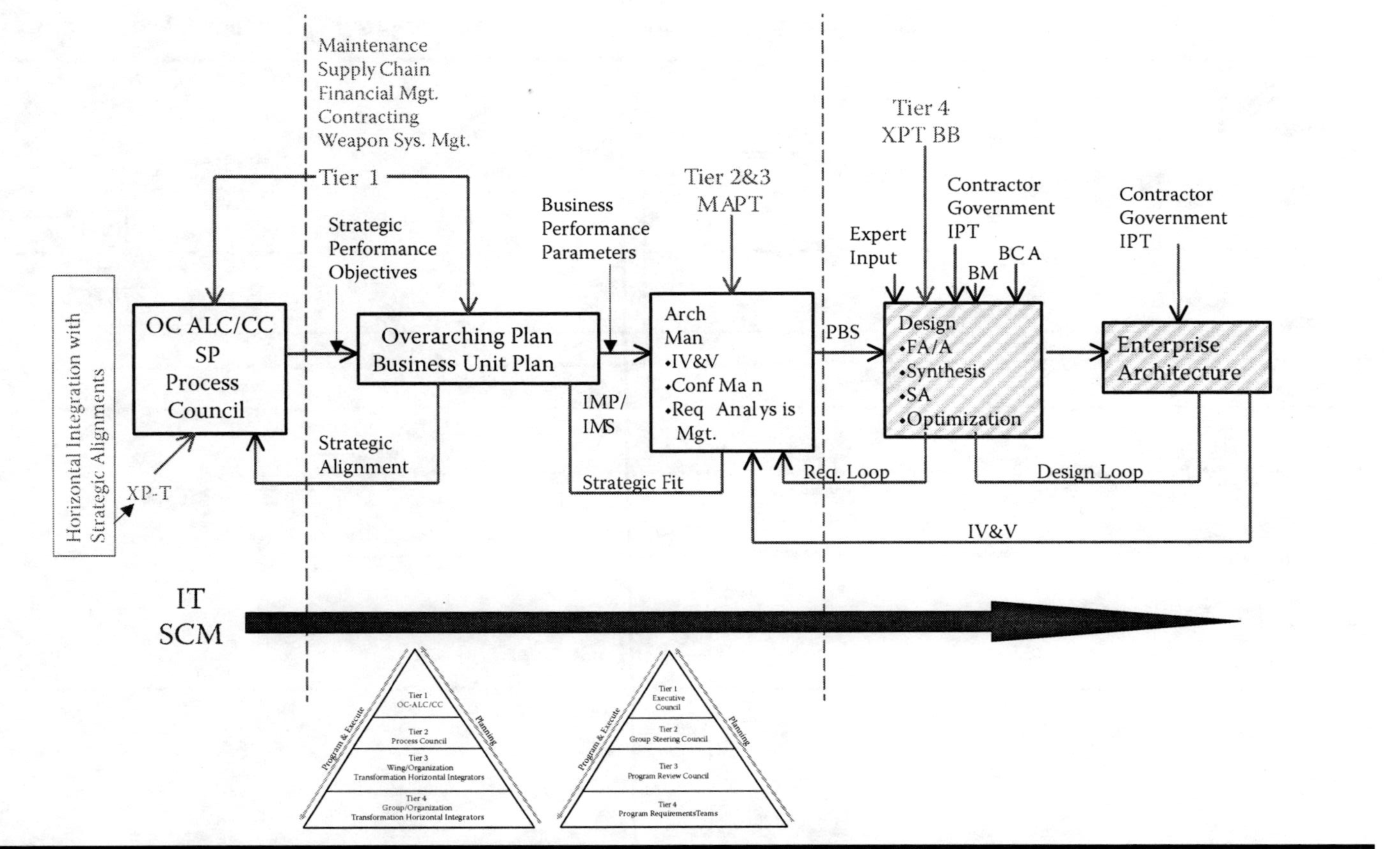

Figure 3.11 The Tiered Implementation Approach for LEA at OC-ALC.

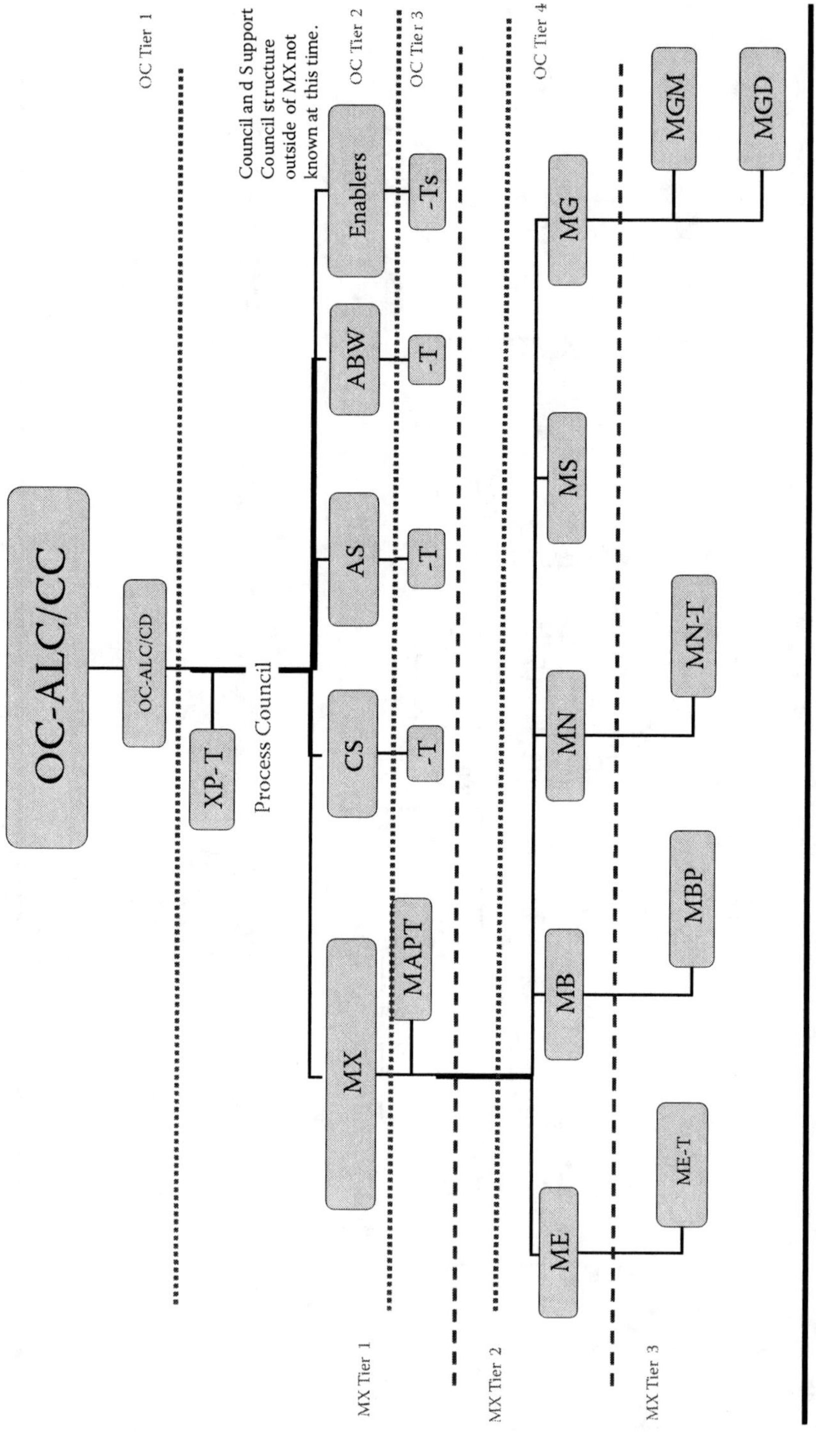

Figure 3.12 Implementation Organization Chart and Levels (Tiers) of Assistance.

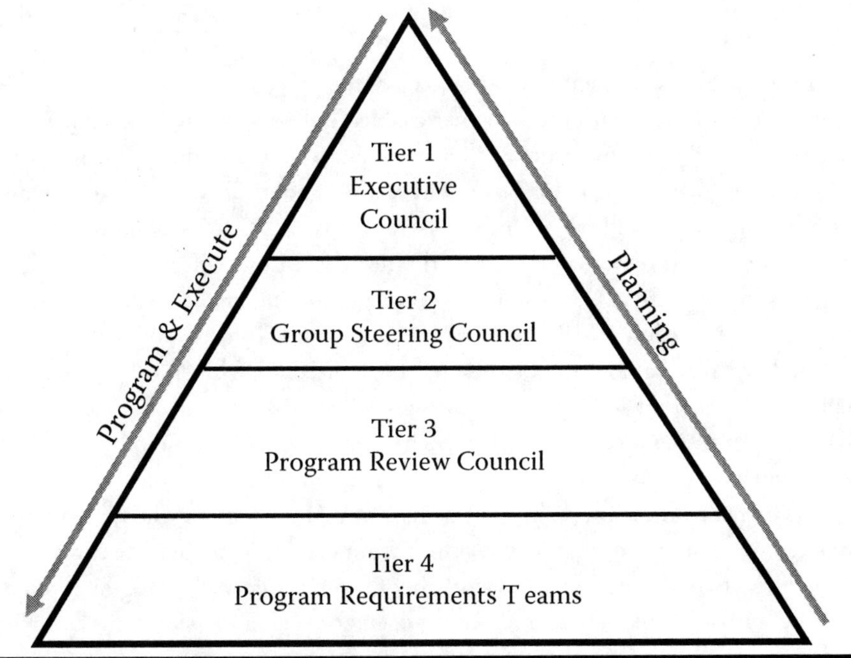

Figure 3.13 The Wing-Level Tiered Approach.

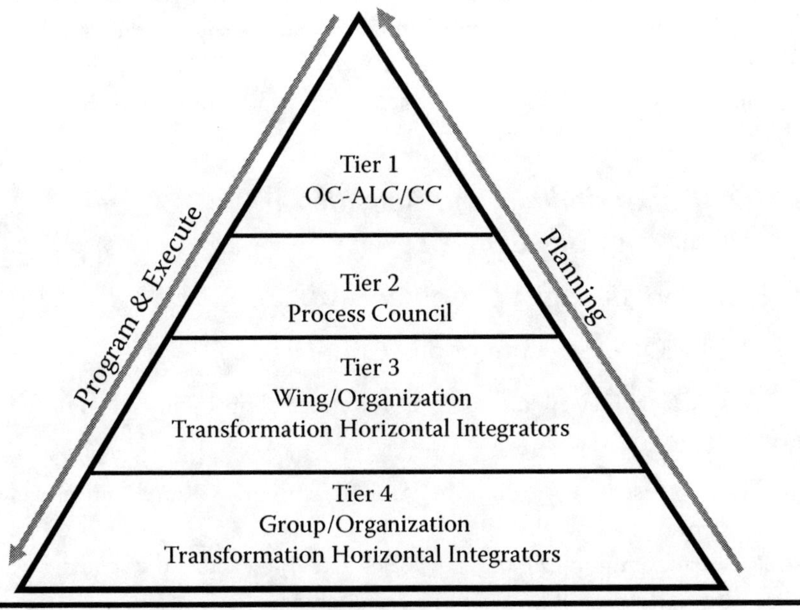

Figure 3.14 The Center-Level Tiered Approach.

tal integrators (tier 3); the process council (tier 2); and the OC-ALC Commodity Council (tier 1).

The OC-ALC Contracting Division chairs the process council, which includes representation from each process owner/enabler. All activities will be reviewed at one of the tiered levels to ensure full integration, acceptance, and compliance with OC-ALC goals and objectives. Tier 1 will retain responsibility for integration and support of the Center's Performance Objectives. OC-ALC/XP-T will monitor and coordinate transformation activities at the tier I level and will incorporate those activities in the OC-ALC transformation integration integrated master plan/integrated master schedule (IMP/IMS). In general, planning information will be generated and organized at lower tier levels and transmitted up, while program direction will flow down from higher levels. Currently there are processes in place for the management of the programs, such as technology insertion, commodity councils, command post platform, maintenance and repair, and military construction. The process owner of these programs will be represented throughout the tier structure in order to communicate and receive information necessary to integrate efforts. The intent is not to duplicate effort and work, but to communicate the program projects and the status via the tiered structure. Budgets for such areas shall interface with and complement the OC-ALC goals and objectives.

Thresholds for the appropriate level of review and approval (tiers 1, 2, or 3) are described below. These thresholds will be based on projected cost/resource requirements, number of touch points/impacts on other organizations, shops and areas, current directives, instructions and guidance, and the source/level of the transformation project. The methodology for identifying and initiating projects and the responsibilities and activities are outlined in figure 3.15 and described below.

3.11.2 Responsibilities and Activities at the Air Logistics Center Levels

3.11.2.1 The Air Logistics Center Level

Tier 1: The OC-ALC Commodity Council (CC)

OC-ALC/CC will review and approve projects that impact the center. Its four goals are:

1. Resolve issues that cannot be resolved at the tier 2 level and provide final approval of all projects.
2. Clearly communicate the transformation vision across the center.
3. Effectively coordinate the transformation process.
4. Precisely execute the transformation plan as budgeted and scheduled.

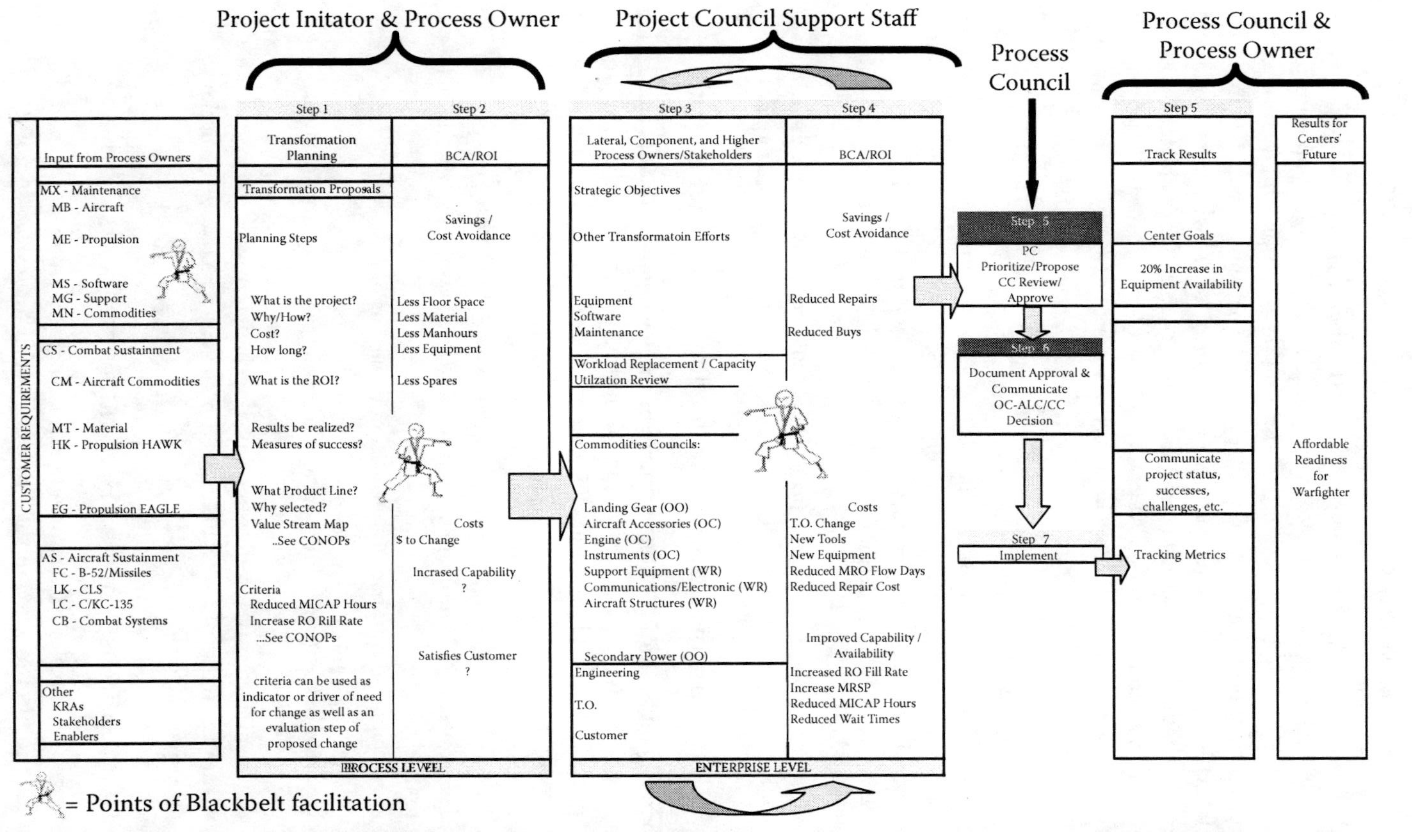

Figure 3.15 Methodology for Identifying and Initiating Projects in the OC-ALC Transformation.

Tier 2: The Process Council

The Process Council will meet to discuss transformation efforts and resolve any cross-wing issues that could not be resolved through the wing/organization transformation horizontal integrators. It will utilize the meeting as an opportunity to agree on a unified plan to present to the commander. Projects beyond the wing/organization transformation horizontal integrators' scope outlined below will be reviewed and approved by the Process Council. Tier 2 will approve projects for implementation or review and forward them to OC-ALC/CC for review and approval. Projects at this level of review/approval have the characteristics described below. Implementation project thresholds include:

- Project/process ownership within OC-ALC
- Projects implemented using available OC-ALC resources
- Zero change and impact to other organizations
- Coordination and agreement is accomplished within OC-ALC
- No requirement for resources and or funding outside the normal monies available to OC-ALC
- Approval authority for all aspects of the change (people, process, funds) is within the scope of OC-ALC directives, instructions and other guidance

Tier 3: Wing/Organization Transformation Horizontal Integrators

The horizontal transformation integrators from each wing/organization, along with the "black belts," are responsible for communication and integration of the projects that impact the center. Projects at this level of review/approval have the following characteristics:

- The process owner and area of impact are internal to OC-ALC
- The project can be implemented using available resources (no additional cost to implement)
- Zero change and impact to outside organizations or customers
- No coordination required outside OC-ALC
- No requirement for funding outside the normal monies available to OC-ALC
- Approval authority for all aspects of the change (people, process, funds) is within the scope of OC-ALC based on current directives, instructions, and other guidance

Tier 4: Group Transformation Horizontal Integrators

The horizontal transformation integrators from each group are responsible for sending the project forward to the Process Council for review, approval, and the resources required to execute the project.

3.11.2.2 The Wing/Organization Level

Tier 1: The Executive Council

The Executive Council is established as a communication exchange to promote the free flow of information between and among every level of each wing/organization. The council will act as the governing body responsible for overseeing each wing's transformation efforts. The four goals of the Executive Council are:

1. Resolve wing/organizational project issues that cannot be resolved at the tier 2 level.
2. Clearly communicate the transformation vision across the wing/organization.
3. Effectively coordinate the transformation process with every wing/organization.
4. Precisely execute the transformation plan as budgeted and scheduled.

Projects beyond the scope of tier 1 will be reviewed, and approved project packages will be forwarded to XP-T for review and approval by the OC-ALC tiered structure.

Tier 2: The Group Steering Council

The Group Steering Council (GSC) will meet to discuss transformation efforts and resolve any cross-group issues that could not be resolved by the Program Review Council (PRC). In addition, the GSC will utilize the meeting as an opportunity to agree on a unified plan to present to the wing commander during the Executive Council's meeting. Projects beyond the PRC's scope as outlined below will be reviewed and approved by the tier 2 GSC or forwarded to tier 1 for approval. Projects implemented by tier 2 must be fully documented and reported to XP-T throughout the project implementation and measurement phases. Tier 2 representatives should report these projects in tier 1 meetings and provide current status throughout the transformation cycle. Projects with this level of review/approval have the characteristics described below. Implementation project thresholds include the following:

- Project/process ownership within wings/organizations
- Projects implemented using available wing resources
- Zero change and impact to other wings or organizations
- Coordination and agreement is accomplished within the wing
- No requirement for resources or funding outside the normal monies available to the wing
- Approval authority for all aspects of the change (people, process, funds) is within the scope of the wing based on current directives, instructions, and other guidance

Tier 3: The Program Review Council

One goal of the center is continuous positive change to provide real-time, affordable, quality readiness to the war fighter. The transformation integrator is responsible for facilitation and institutionalization of process improvement programs. In light of this goal, it is recognized that local changes will be constantly implemented to improve work within offices, shops, and areas. OC-ALC's locally developed small projects can be implemented with the review and coordination of the tier 3 program review structure. A project description is required to be sent through tier 2 and XP-T to, at the very least, capture and communicate the project. When a project is completed a summary should be presented to the tier 2 GSC and include information such as metrics tracked/achieved and lessons learned that may aid other offices or work centers with similar projects. Projects at this level of review/approval have the following characteristics:

- The process owner and area are internal with no impact to outside organizations
- The project can be implemented using available resources (no additional cost to implement)
- No coordination required outside the project office/Resource Control Center (RCC)
- No requirement for funding outside the normal monies available to the office or RCC
- Approval authority for all aspects of the change (people, process, funds) is within the scope of the office or shop making the change based on current directives, instructions, and other guidance

Tier 4: The Program Requirements Teams

Transformation proposals require a sound business case analysis/return on investment (BCA/ROI) analysis, as shown in steps 1 and 2 of figure 3.15. Issues involving health, safety, and environmental issues will be considered as required outside of the BCA/ROI.

3.11.3 The Depot Maintenance Transformation Board

MAPT established the Depot Maintenance Transformation Board (DMTB) as a communication exchange to promote the free flow of information between and among every level of OC-ALC's maintenance (MX) directorate. Four tiers will comprise the DMTB, as previously depicted in figure 3.13.

Planning information will be generated and organized at lower levels of the four-tiered DMTB and transmitted up, while program direction will flow down from higher levels. The DMTB will also act as the governing body responsible for overseeing the MA-wide transformation. As such, DMTB is responsible for ensuring effective communication and programming throughout the maintenance directorate. The three goals of the DMTB are:

1. Clearly communicate the transformation vision across the MA.
2. Effectively coordinate the transformation process with every directorate, division, and shop.
3. Precisely execute the transformation plan as budgeted and scheduled.

Tier 1: The Maintenance Executive Council

The MX Executive Council is chaired by the MX director and is made up of MX group commanders; representatives from support organizations (such as contractors and those in IT) will be invited to attend as required. The Executive Council is responsible for setting the vision and the course for the MX transformation initiative and communicating that direction down through the tiers of the DMTB. The council will meet quarterly to discuss and fine-tune the MX transformation vision and to review, approve, and advocate transformation programs as brought forth by the GSC.

Tier 2: The Group Steering Council

The Group Steering Council (GSC) is chaired by the MAPT chief and made up of all MX group commanders. The GSC is responsible for reviewing and coordinating MA transformation efforts. The GSC will meet monthly to discuss transformation efforts and resolve any cross-division issues that cannot be resolved by the PRC. In addition, the GSC will utilize the monthly meeting as an opportunity to agree on a unified plan to present to the MX director during the MX Executive Council's quarterly meeting. Thus, the DSG will ensure the unified direction of transformation efforts throughout MX by communicating a unified plan to the MX Executive Council and vision and direction to the PRC.

Tier 3: The Program Review Council

The Program Review Council (PRC) is chaired by the MAPT senior program manager. Each MA divison is represented on the PRC by a single point of contact (POC) designated by the division chief. In addition, all MAPT program managers participate in the PRC. The PRC will meet monthly to share information about transformation efforts among the divisions. This information exchange includes direction from the higher levels of the DMTB and status of ongoing transformation efforts. The PRC is responsible for providing current transformation project status updates and coordinated plans to the DSG, as well as for informing the DSG of any issues that the PRC cannot resolve. The PRC also coordinates transformation projects with the program requirements teams, informing them of the directives handed down by the DSG.

Tier 4: Program Requirements Teams

Program Requirements Teams (PRTs) are established for each of the following MA divisons: aircraft, engine, and commodities. Each PRT is chaired by the maintenance directorate–transformation (MA-T) program manager responsible for transformation efforts within that division, and each team includes the division POC assigned to the PRC. Additional membership in each PRT is determined by the MA-T program manager and the divison POC, and may include other division personnel, contract resources, or personnel from other OC-ALC organizations. The PRTs are responsible for executing the MA transformation efforts within their respective divisions. Each PRT will meet weekly to provide project updates, share information, and review and execute division transformation projects as directed by the higher tiers of the DMTB.

3.11.4 Transformation Area Team Meetings

As plans for the transformation of each specific shop are developed, communication among the shop, management, and the transformation contractor team will be critical. Each transformation area shall form a transformation team (IPT) and hold regularly scheduled meetings to develop a list of the processes, flow, and unique requirements of each area being transformed. The IPT shall have regular contact with MA-T appropriate program managers participation and results from meetings shall be recorded and shared. A basic outline of each group's tasks should be developed by the IPT in conjunction with the transformation office (MA-T).

An example of focus areas for the area team meetings include:

- Shop requirements
- Workbenches
- Cranes
- Test stands
- Equipment
- Internal shop-flow recommendations
- How workers would organize the shop if given the chance
- Special requirements for clearances or floor space
- Utilities required: water, power, compressed air
- Coordination
- Defense Logistics Agency (DLA) delivery
- Commodoties and logistics supply support

- Engineers, item managers
- Supply and DLA warehousing

3.11.5 Transformation Evaluation Steps and Criteria

3.11.5.1 Determining Transformation Feasibility

When viewed by total cost, the drivers for the ALC, in ascending order, are commodities (spare parts), aircraft, and whole engines. When viewed by operating costs, the drivers, in ascending order, are whole engines, commodities, and aircraft. This contradiction points to the necessity to ensure that transformation efforts are fully integrated to achieve the center's objectives of a 20 percent increase in equipment availability and a 10 percent decrease in costs. Each area will use a standard set of criteria to evaluate the feasibility of initiating the transformation process. Examples for aircraft, commodities, and engines are provided below.

Aircraft

The goal for aircraft is to increase aircraft availability through decreased flow days and decreasing cost. Other criteria are reducing high overtime hours, cycle time, and mean time between failures (MTBF). If in reaching the goal, the primary mission aircraft inventory is exceeded and availability is not the driving factor, the improvements must be analyzed to determine if savings will enable additional aircraft workload to be brought to the ALC to utilize excess capacity.

Commodities

Eight commodity councils have been established by the Air Force Materiel Command. In keeping with the integration effort, transformation must be fully coordinated with the overarching plan, as well as laterally coordinated among the other ALCs as required. Key elements of the formula for analysis of commodities are: costs of purchases and determination of constraints driving to buy; mission capability (MICAP) hours and incidents; mission readiness spares package (MRSP) holes; customer wait time; high overtime hours; cycle time; work in process/on work order (WIP/OWO) quantities and their associated costs; EXPRESS failures; pipeline costs; MTBF; time on wing; and support to program depot maintenance (PDM) and production lines.

Engines

The criteria for measuring improvements to engine availability are twofold. First, war reserve engines and, second, leading indicators such as engine non-mission-capable hours and incidents, MRSP holes, customer wait time, high overtime hours, cycle times, WIP/OWO quantities and associated costs, EXPRESS failures, pipeline costs, support to PDM, MTBF, time on wing, and production lines and possible buys for modules sold separately.

3.11.5.2 Methodology/Evaluation Tools

Several steps and analysis techniques will be used to identify, develop, coordinate, and evaluate each transformation project. The Process Council, a key responsibility area owner, a business area, process owner, enabler, stakeholder, or other office is the starting point for a transformation project. The methodology for obtaining approval for a project is outlined below.

3.11.5.3 Transformation Planning Questions

The first step in the process for every new project is to provide basic identifying information and to prepare a plan by answering several questions. In answering the questions, a basic analysis is required. The result of this analysis is the development of a project plan. The basic identifying information includes:

- Task name
- Control number (document number, project/contract number, task/work order number, etc.)
- Project description
- Start date
- Completion date
- Process owner
- Product line
- Area supported by the process
- Project cost and whether it is currently funded
- The colors of money
- Stakeholders
- Status
- Why/how the project is transformational
- What methodology was used in selecting the project
- Whether or not a value-stream mapping process was conducted; if so, provide the reults; if not, undertake one or explain lack of such process
- Whether or not an action plan was developed; if so, provide results; if not, undertake one or explain lack of such plan
- How the Air Force benefits by investing in this project
- When the Air Force can hope to see results from this project
- What format is used to track and communicate status

- What the measures of success are
- Which visual management techniques will be used to measure project success
- Whether the transformation project is being accomplished with organic resources or contractor support
- If the project is contractor supported, what the contract period is for performance
- Whether there is a link to other projects (transformation to military construction)
- Which key responsibility area is supported

3.11.5.4 Criteria

Each transformation will be evaluated on specific criteria related to the equipment affected by the transformation effort. There will be different metrics for different product lines as described above. The evaluation will consider two categories: transformation factors and transformation results.

3.11.5.5 The Business Case Analysis/Return on Investment Process

Decisions will be based on a sound BCA/ROI process. A BCA/ROI study will be completed for each project that requires tier 1 and 2 review and approval. Health, safety, and environmental issues will be considered outside of the BCA/ROI as required. Additionally, improved support to the customer will be weighed heavily in this process. Evaluation of risks focusing on cost, schedule, and performance must be completed as part of the BCA. Air Force instructions AFPD 65-5 (Cost and Economics), AFI 65-501, and AFM 65-506 (Economic Analysis), and Department of Defense instruction 7041.3 (Economic Analysis for Decision Making) will be utilized in this process.

3.11.6 Project Identification and Coordination

As mentioned above, transformation ideas and projects can generate from several sources. Therefore, all programs and projects must be identified and coordinated with the process owner as well as the Process Council. In each area, the proposal must be evaluated against existing processes and ongoing transformation programs to identify conflicts and to determine the costs driven to other areas by the change, as well as savings incurred by others as a result of the change. The project initiator and process owner will develop a project charter to identify resources, including personnel from other organizations with emphasis on establishing cross-functional and multiskilled teams, and to establish a plan for the proposed team (e.g., whether this will be a short-term team or whether full-time personnel equivalents will be required to support the effort).

3.11.7 Impact Analysis

The transformation process will be mapped to all other organizations that will be impacted by the proposed transformation. For example, a decrease in PDM flow days could translate into an increase in parts supplied by another ALC, the DLA, or commercial suppliers. Coordination with these outside stakeholders is required to ensure successful implementation of the plan. Based on the multitiered approach, this evaluation would be accomplished at all levels: the transformation implementation level, component level, lateral level, and higher assembly levels up through to the ALC level. The analysis would also include evaluation of factors and results at the customer levels. One example is shown below (see fig. 3.16), where transformation efforts generated in one area are related to and have impact on other organizations and transformation efforts.

3.11.8 The Integrated Master Plan/Integrated Master Schedule

Process Council support staff will maintain and incorporate the council's actions into the OC-ALC IMP/IMS. There are several processes, programs, or projects that must be coordinated and synchronized to best leverage limited resources in achieving the objectives and vision. The IMP/IMS is the vehicle for this integration. Elements requiring integration include:

- Existing plans and programs
- Transformation projects across the ALC
- Command post platform for all years
- Military construction for all years
- Maintenance and repair projects
- Workforce development at all levels (blue- and white-collar, and leadership)
- Technology insertion
- Business operations: workload, current, projected, new (marketing)
- Material
- Change management/communication plans

3.11.9 Enterprisewide Business Case Analysis/ Return on Investment

Improvements in one area could drive either savings or cost in another. This requires an enterprisewide BCA/ROI analysis to capture the impact at the ALC level. As noted above, improved support to the customer will be weighed heavily in this process. Evaluation of risks that focus on cost, schedule, and performance must be completed as part of the BCA. At this point the evaluation needs to link

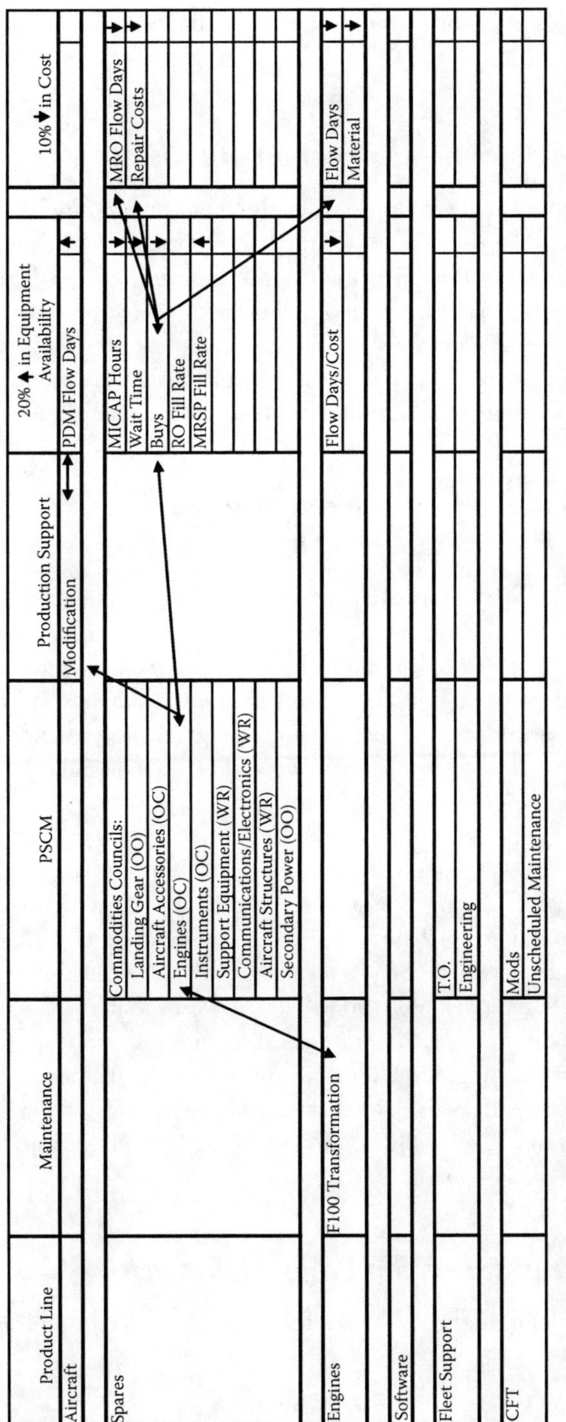

Figure 3.16 The Transformation Process Interaction Analysis.

to the center's goals of 20 percent increase in equipment availability and 10 percent reduction in cost.

3.11.10 Prioritization and Selection of Projects

When all the required analysis and coordination has been accomplished, the project will be presented to the Process Council. The Process Council will prioritize the transformation project against other ALC programs and goals, approve the implementation of the project, and allocate resources as required to meet project objectives. A commercial "off the shelf" decision support tool will be used for the prioritization process. The Process Council will establish evaluation thresholds to determine the appropriate level of review required for each project.

3.11.11 Documentation, Communication, and Change Management

Decisions on approved transformation projects will be documented by the Process Council and communicated to ALC personnel. All transformation efforts must be communicated to the stakeholders and included in the change management plan to ensure successful implementation. In addition, they will obtain buy-in from management as well as the workforce in order to ensure program success. This communications plan will provide the details on the flow of information about the program during the transformation.

The goal is to gain visible, unified support at every level by spreading the word about the transformation program, its approach to the transformation effort, and the progress on the program during its implementation. This goal can be accomplished by creating and maintaining a global transformation information flow that will ensure the open flow of information among all members of the OC-ALC team. In turn, the OC-ALC team will share the information with Air Force Materiel Command.

By consistently promoting the processes, benefits, and successes of the transformation, and establishing a free flow of information regarding the plan and its component projects, endeavors gain momentum for transformation through the support of a workforce that is fully knowledgeable and integrated into the transformation process (see fig. 3.17).

3.11.12 The Transformation Project Life Cycle

This section will delineate the processes for tracking and communicating project status (see fig. 3.18).

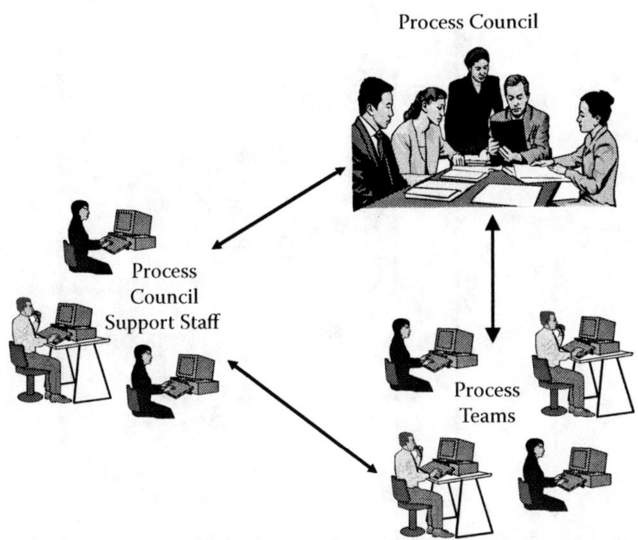

Figure 3.17 The Transformation Communication and Decision Process.

3.11.12.1 The Project Template

The project template will be sent to XP-T, and the project will be entered into the project database. Its timelines, milestones, and resources will be added to the OC-ALC integration IMP/IMS. A single IMP/IMS database will be maintained for the ALC. XP-T (Process Council support staff) will interface with the project initiator and process owner during the life of the project to track and report completed actions and progress as compared to the project milestones.

3.11.12.2 Metrics

Metrics will be established to measure the project savings and cost avoidance against actual savings to investment. It is important to note that metrics tracking in this phase will normally extend past the implementation completion date through to the scheduled/actual ROI date. However, it is important to track and capture this data against the original BCA/ROI anlaysis used to approve the project. Other measures of success, identified by the project initiator and process owner in the transformation planning step, will be gathered and documented monthly and reported quarterly to the Process Council. These measures can include, but not be limited to: cost of purchases and determination of constraints driving to buy; MICAP hours and incidents; MRSP holes; customer wait time; high overtime hours; cycle time; WIP/OWO quantities and associated costs; EXPRESS failures;

Steps of Transformation Project Methodology

IMS Project Timeline

Input/ Initiation

ROI DATE

Step 1 | Step 2 | Step 3 | Step 4 | Step 5 | Step 6 | Step 7 | Step 8

What and When

Transformation Planning

BCA/ROI

BCA/ROI

Coordinate - later, component, higher process owner/ stakeholders

Projects prioritized and selected

Approval documented

Implementation

Track Results

Communicate, Communicate, Communicate

Who (MX)

Project Initiator / Process Owner

Tier 3

Process Council Support Staff

Tier 3

Process Council

Tier 3

Process Council & Process Owner

Tier 2 & 3

Report to Tier 1

TRACKING
MAPT and/or XP-T
Track development of project from start to finish, ensure all actions are completed and validate findings.

Project template entered into Tracking Database, IMP/IMS, timeline/schedule established and BCA/ROI developed

- Establish Baseline Measurements for:
  – Cost
  – Schedule
  – Performance
  – Results

- Baseline:
  – Cost
  – Schedule
  – Performance
  – Results

-Track
  – Cost
  – Schedule
  – Performance
- Document Monthly
- Report to Process Council Quaterly

- Measures of Results

- Submit News Letters, Articles to Tinker Take-off, and Leading Edge
- Create and share historical and photographic record of transformation.

Figure 3.18 Transformation Tracking Steps.

pipeline costs; MTBF; time on wing; and support to PDM and production lines. XP-T (Process Council support staff) will track these metrics and the contribution of each project to the overall OC-ALC established goals.

3.11.12.3 Communication

Communication plans will be updated by the OC-ALC public affairs to include timelines/milestones for reporting the status of each project. At a minimum, articles will be prepared for relevant newsletters (the OC-ALC's *Tinker Take-Off* among them) to describe the approved project at project initiation. There will be at least two midpoint articles created and a final article (about goals achieved) at project completion. When facility changes are made, a photographic record will be created of changes, starting with the as-is state through to the final state. Along with the metrics, the Process Council will be briefed quarterly on the progress of each project.

3.11.12.4 Implementation

The process owner will implement the process in coordination with other stakeholders.

3.11.12.5 Measuring Results

The process owner will track and document the results with continuous reporting to the Process Council. The process owner will utilize the earned value management system and risk management tools to measure actual achievements versus the projections in the BCA/ROI analysis. The duration of the project will determine the reporting to the Process Council. Transformation efforts of one year will report findings quarterly. Efforts of two years, or greater duration, will be reported biannually. There will be a three-pronged approach to tracking transformation projects within the ALC. As with any major program, the cost, schedule, and performance of the project will be tracked and communicated to the community.

The responsible office for transformation integration is XP-T, which will function as the process owner for the reporting and communication of results to senior leadership.

3.12 Conclusions and Future Directions

Maintenance, repair, and overhaul depots must improve operational and financial performance to survive potential downsizing or reduction of infrastructure. The most efficient and effective method of supporting depot transformation is conversion to lean maintenance and cellular manufacturing philosophies and processes.

Failure to do so will result in an unresponsive, inefficient maintenance complex that increases material costs and decreases the competitiveness of the depot. That poor performance has a direct impact on the operational effectiveness of the war fighter. Transforming the military sustainment organizational structure is necessary. Four elements are essential to a successful transformation. The first is the recognition that the transformation should follow a life cycle. The second is that the implementation should be enterprisewide, not just for one cell in the manufacturing process. The third is the recommendation that the transformation be rooted in systems engineering principles (establishing need, conceptual design, preliminary design, detailed design, implementation, operation). The fourth element is that an enterprise architecture design should guide the effort.

In utilizing a private-industry type of approach, the author and his colleagues have developed a Lean Enterprise Architecture (LEA) that uses lean production, enterprise architecture, and systems engineering methodologies to portray the overall flow of the action steps necessary to initiate, sustain, and continuously refine the enterprise. The architecture was developed from an enterprise perspective, paying particular attention to strategic issues, internal and external relations with all key stakeholders, and structural issues that must be addressed before and during a significant change initiative. In today's environment, organizations that are considering a transformation to lean should embrace an enterprisewide architecture.

What is the next step in this research agenda? The author and his colleagues are now developing a more specific process for LEA that is intended to further define the performance requirements (improvement metrics), systems engineering processes, and architectural details that are necessary for a successful implementation, integration, and validation of the framework. The process needs to integrate all of the elements of an enterprise (its business systems, facilities, logistic networks, transportation systems, strategic business units, cells and other functional workspaces, and the workforce) in order to meet the strategic objectives of a lean implementation across the entire enterprise. Specific future research tasks are:

- To refine the fit between enterprise architectural frameworks and the systems engineering process
- To refine the design and details of LEA to conform to this fit
- To benchmark, through case studies, the performance of LEA and its processes against other traditional lean implementations
- To design an implementation road map for those enterprises that wish to undertake an LEA transformation

Chapter 4

Continuous Process Improvement Initiatives for Military Sustainability

Improving a process for a business enterprise is paramount to staying competitive in today's marketplace. Recently, military enterprises have been forced to improve their business processes because of an increased operational tempo, the need to improve performance (e.g., increasing weapons systems availability and mission capability) due to aging weapons systems, and military cost-reduction measures (e.g., base realignment and closure). A business process is a set of activities, using people and tools, that transform supplier material inputs into a set of customer outputs (goods or services). The business process can be pictured (in an elementary way) as a flow diagram, as in figure 4.1.

Many begin business process improvement with a continuous improvement model. Such a model attempts to understand and measure the current process and then make performance improvements accordingly. Figure 4.2 illustrates the basic steps: begin by documenting the current state, establish some way to measure the process based

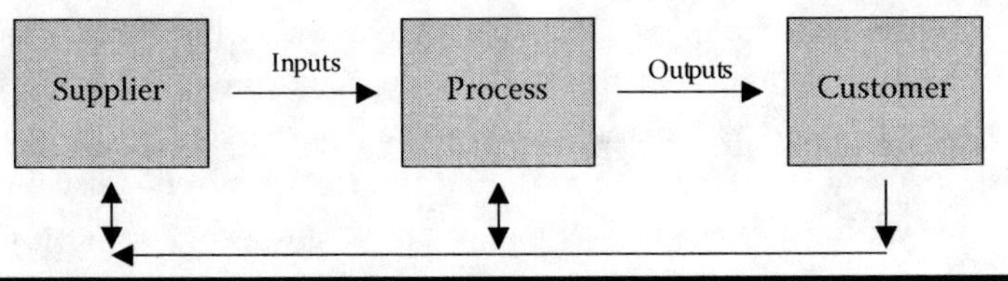

Figure 4.1 The Business Process Flow Diagram.

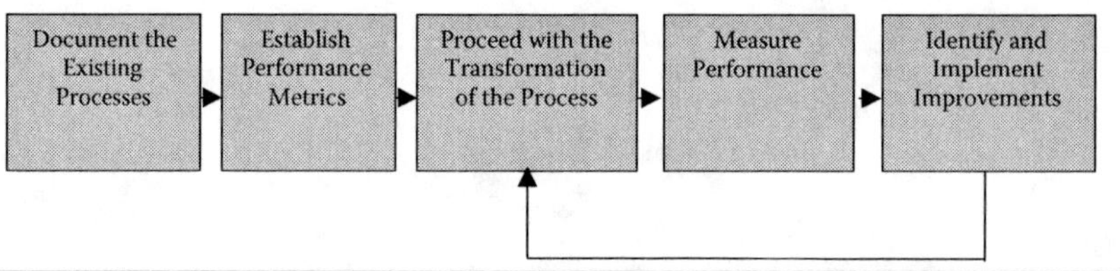

Figure 4.2 Continuous Process Improvement.

on what you and the customers want, implement the process improvement initiative, measure the results, identify further improvement opportunities based on the results, and then measure the performance of the new process. The feedback loop is why the method is called *continuous process improvement*. It is sometimes also called *business process improvement* or *functional process improvement*.[1]

Continuous process improvement is effective in obtaining gradual, incremental changes. However, over the last ten years several factors have accelerated the need to improve business processes. The most obvious is technology. New technologies, like radio frequency identification tags and the Internet, are rapidly bringing new capabilities to businesses, thereby raising the competitive bar and the need to improve business processes dramatically. Another motivation is the need to reduce cost and stay competitive relative to the commercial sector. Competing with the private sector becomes increasingly harder for the military. In today's marketplace, major changes are required to just stay even. It has become a matter of survival (ProSci 2005).

As a result, military sustainment, as well as the commercial manufacturing sector that supports the military, has sought out methods for faster business-process improvement. Moreover, these enterprises want breakthrough performance changes, not just incremental changes, and they want it now. Because the rate of change has increased for everyone, few can afford a slow change process. Some initiatives, such as total quality management, Six Sigma, and lean production, have been so popular that they have become academic disciplines in themselves, and many textbooks have been written specifically for them. Others, such as management by objectives, never gained a lot of popularity and are limited to references within other textbooks (Uzair 2001).

Before attempting to implement one of these performance improvement initiatives, the organization must establish and follow a particular set of steps for action. These steps are necessary to initiate, sustain, and continuously refine the enterprise. Chapters 2 and 3 have outlined these action steps and provide the tools to help the enterprise with its transformation. One of the first steps is for the organization to establish its overall performance goals and targets. This step is usually accomplished by developing a strategic plan for the entire enterprise, not just for a local business unit. However, some organizations start with a management-by-objectives approach to translate strategic goals to subordinate objectives, and then track the accomplishment of objectives in each department (McNamara 1999).

What follows are three sections: (1) an introduction to the transformation process; (2) a treatise on the most prominent approaches toward improving military enterprise performance; and (3) as a case study, a summary of U.S. Air Force continuous process improvement and transformation initiatives.

4.1 Transformation

The idea of transforming the DoD started with secretary of defense Donald Rumsfeld and has since permeated the department. The intent is to increase the emphasis placed on lean manufacturing technologies and processes in acquisition programs.

4.1.1 What Is Transformation?

Transformation is a wide-ranging concept that encompasses a variety of interrelated fields. Transformation processes, if thoroughly pursued, impact upon virtually all aspects of an organization's existence and, as such, require astute management if the success of such processes is to be ensured. For transformation processes to be successful it is essential that three mission success factors be acknowledged during the management of the process itself (Williams 2001):

1. The importance of providing decisive and strategic leadership over the process itself
2. The importance of ensuring that high levels of legitimacy ("buy-in") accrue to the process
3. The importance of determining the scope of the transformation processes itself—organizational culture, traditions, leadership styles, racial and gender composition, and so on

In essence, four major transformation "clusters" can be determined within the management of any transformation process (be this public sector, private sector, or civil society) and these are particularly relevant to the transformation of the military sustainment enterprise (Williams 2001):

1. *Cultural transformation.* This entails the transformation of the culture of the military sustainment enterprise with regard to the leadership, management, and administrative ethos of the military; its value system; and the traditions upon which it is predicated.
2. *Human transformation.* This entails the transformation of the composition of the military sustainment enterprise with regard to its composition and its human-resource practices. This component of the transformation process must be consistent with the DoD's broader policies.
3. *Political transformation.* This process strives to ensure that the conduct and character of the military sustainment enterprise conforms to the political

features of the democracy within which they are located—acknowledgment of the principle of civil supremacy, institution of appropriate mechanisms of oversight and control, and adherence to the principles and practices of accountability, transparency, and the like.

4. *Organizational transformation*. This cluster is the most relevant to a transformation of the military sustainment operation. It constitutes a more technocratic process within which the military will be the right size, its management practices and its diverse organizational processes made more cost effective, and its ability to provide services that are rendered more efficient in accordance with the broader principles of continuous process improvement, which have governed the transformation of the DoD to date.

During the process of managing a transformation, it is critical to ensure that the key areas of intervention are managed in such a manner that these interventions are strategically coherent and practically based. The restructuring of the military sustainment enterprise will be inextricably determined by the specific context within which such initiatives occur. Although one can formulate a general strategy for the transformation of each process, their institutional peculiarities and their local character will demand an approach that is flexible and context derived.

Within the DoD, transformation has several definitions. In its most broad sense, DoD transformation means refining operational processes, institutional constructs, acquisition and application of technology, and the strategic repositioning of forces. Each military service—the Air Force, Army, Marine Corps, and Navy—has its own ongoing transformation. Within the Army, for example, transformation also means changing the way units are structured, equipped, and deployed. Within the U.S. European Command, U.S. Army Europe forces will streamline under the Army's units of action concept, redeploy forces, gain new forces, and adopt a rotational manning construct to forward-operating sites and locations (U.S. European Command 2007). An excerpt of key points can be found in Cebrowski's overview of force transformation:

> Transformation is foremost a continuing process. It does not have an end point. Transformation is meant to create or anticipate the future. Transformation is meant to deal with the co-evolution of concepts, processes, organizations, and technology. Change in any one of these areas necessitates change in all. Transformation is meant to create new competitive areas and new competencies. Transformation is meant to identify, leverage and even create new underlying principles for the way things are done. Transformation is meant to identify and leverage new sources of power. The overall objective of these changes is simply—sustained American competitive advantage in warfare. (Cebrowski 2007, n.p.)

In an article on the transformation of NATO (the North Atlantic Treaty Organization), Garstka has examined the concept of transformation, the role it plays in both commercial and military organizations, and aspects of NATO's transformation. These concepts are very relevant to the transformation of the military sustainment enterprise:

> Transformation is about sustained, purposeful change, often on a large scale, undertaken with the strategic objective of creating or maintaining competitive advantage, or of countering an advantage put in place by an existing or a new competitor. The concept is relevant to organizations that are faced with challenges and opportunities that cannot be effectively dealt with by employing proven methodologies for making incremental improvements to existing organizations, processes, technologies, human resources management and business models. The need for transformation can exist in both private and public sectors.
>
> The impetus to transform may vary. In some cases, transformation is stimulated by rapid deterioration in an organization's competitive position resulting from unforeseen and unanticipated changes to the competitive environment, or by hitherto unknown rates of change. In other cases, transformation is opportunity driven, resulting from the desire to create or enhance competitive advantage by exploiting a new or emerging technology. This often requires organizational, process or people changes. In the case often referred to as a business turnaround, consistently ineffective leadership or management may cause a firm's competitive position to deteriorate to such a degree that a transformational perspective may be required to restore its competitive advantage.
>
> **Assessing competitive advantage**
>
> An organization is said to possess a competitive advantage when it achieves a superior competitive position vis-à-vis one or more competitors. Competitive position is a relative measure of performance. In a practical sense, it can be measured by comparing the integrated capabilities of competitors in a competitive environment. Examples of capabilities in business include product design, production, marketing, sales and distribution. In warfare, examples include maneuver, strike, logistics and command and control. Whether in business or warfare, an organization can assess its current and future competitive position by answering the following questions: . . .

Future competitive position

- Who are the likely future competitors and what are their likely capabilities?
- When are new competitors likely to appear?
- What are the anticipated future capabilities of the organization?
- What actions can be taken now to dissuade potential future competitors?
- What actions should be taken now to create future competitive advantage should dissuasion fail?

The answers to these questions will characterize an organization's current competitive position and provide an estimate of its future competitive position. In some cases, the answers are not clear-cut, since they involve uncertainty, ambiguity and the assessment of risk. This often leads to honest disagreement and stimulates debate within an organization. If consensus can be reached regarding the existence of a competitive shortfall — current or future — then dialogue can begin on potential courses of action to enhance the competitive position. It is at this point, after consensus has been reached regarding the need for change, that transformation should be considered as a means to accomplish it.

Capabilities as a focus of transformation

If one accepts the premise that capabilities are the primary basis by which organizations compete, then efforts to develop or enhance competitive advantage should be capabilities-based. In this way, a primary focus of transformation should be developing and enhancing capabilities.

Conceptually, capabilities can be viewed as having the components of people, process, organization and technology. This implies that capabilities can be enhanced through innovation and change at the component level. When incremental change at the component level involves sustaining innovation, traditional innovation methodologies are typically adequate. However, when capability enhancement or development requires synchronization of innovations in two or more components, or when innovation at the component level is disruptive, transformation methodologies are usually required.

A capabilities-based focus for transformation implies the following elements and relationships:

- Transformation is a continuous process that creates and maintains competitive advantage;
- Transformation encompasses the co-evolution of processes, organizations, technologies and human capital, which, when viewed together, enhance existing capabilities and enable new capabilities;
- Transformation broadens the existing capabilities base through the creation of new competitive areas and competencies, thereby re-valuing existing competitive attributes;
- Transformation seeks to affect current or future competitive advantage by identifying shifts in underlying principles or emerging rule sets;
- Transformation involves identifying new sources of power that, if exploited, could enhance competitive advantage; and
- Transformation focuses on the human component of change, developing leaders who can lead change and creating an organizational culture that is open to change and supportive of innovation, learning and risk-taking.

These elements provide a framework for thinking about transformation and structuring transformation initiatives. Clearly, the specifics of an organization's competitive situation will determine the scope, pace and intensity of initiatives required to achieve desired strategic objectives. Consequently, the correct answer to the question "What do you mean by transformation and what does it look like?" is often "It depends on the specifics of the competitive situation that an organization finds itself in."

Transformation and commercial organizations

In the commercial sector, an executive's decision to launch his or her company on a major transformation is typically driven by an eroded competitive position resulting from changes in the industry or the competitive environment. This may be the result of changes in the regulatory structure, the behaviour of competitors or the emergence of a new product or production technology.

Transformation efforts in the commercial sector to enhance or develop new capabilities can be proactive, as in the case of Dell's pre-emptive move into direct distribution and just-in-time manufacturing in the PC market. Transformation can also be reactive in response to a competitor's move, as in the case of competitor responses to Dell's relentless cost-reduction and share-gain drives. Compaq and HP merged in an attempt to gain scale advantage; IBM effectively surrendered, announcing the sale of its PC business to China's Lenovo and a new focus on services to corporate customers.

The opportunity for transformation to create or enhance competitive advantage by enhancing a capability through exploitation of a new technology is illustrated by Dell's shift to direct distribution. This shift was enabled and accelerated by the internet, which allowed for lower-cost direct distribution and supplemented a direct-sales force and telesales. The Dell experience also demonstrates that exploiting technology can require organizational, process and people changes. At Dell, the entire delivery system was reworked and the leadership team almost completely rebuilt with external talent as the business grew.

Transformation and military organizations

The US Department of Defense defines transformation as "a process that shapes the changing nature of military competition and cooperation through new combinations of concepts, capabilities, people and organizations that exploit our nation's advantages and protect against our asymmetric vulnerabilities to sustain our strategic position, which helps underpin peace and stability in the world."

This definition of transformation reinforces the centrality of capability development and enhancement to military transformation and highlights the proactive nature of the transformation process. In a defence context, the four principal components of capability—people, process, organization and technology—can be expanded to include additional capability building blocks. In the US Department of Defense, this corresponds to the construct of Doctrine, Organization, Training, Material, Leadership and Education, Personnel, and Facilities. The corresponding relationships between the four principal elements and the expanded US elements are as follows:

- People—Personnel, Leadership and Education, and Training
- Process—Doctrine
- Organization—Organization
- Technology—Material and Facilities

This simple framework highlights the principal dimensions of change for military forces and provides a mechanism to communicate clearly and succinctly the changes that can be pursued in "transforming" military forces. (Garstka 2005, n.p.)

In a report titled *The USAF Transformation Flight Plan FY03-07* the U.S. Air Force (2003) defines transformation as

> A process by which the military achieves and maintains advantage through changes in operational concepts, organization, and/or technologies that significantly improve its warfighting capabilities or ability to meet the demands of a changing security environment. (2003, p. ii)

Using this guiding document, the Air Force is transforming by taking advantage of technology that is rapidly evolving to the point that the military would be irresponsible not to exploit it in order to dramatically improve its war-fighting capabilities. Even if this were not the case, the Air Force must also transform in order to preserve the advantages the nation currently enjoys, which are in danger of eroding in the face of new challenges, and to meet the new security threats and environment. As stated by the 2001 Quadrennial Defense Review, "The purpose of transformation is to maintain or improve US military preeminence in the face of potential disproportionate discontinuous changes in the strategic environment. Transformation must therefore be focused on emerging strategic and operational challenges and the opportunities created by these challanges" (U.S. Department of Defense, 2001, p. 30).

4.1.2 The Transformation Process

Underdown (1997) describes transformation as the process of changing an entire enterprise from a current state to a desired future condition under the guidance of a plan. His plan is described using a transform enterprise methodology (TEM), which is a structured set of strategies integrated to transform an enterprise from a current state to a desired future condition—an organized collection of activities that describe what must be done to transform the entire enterprise. The TEM is composed of four primary activities:

Activity 1: Develop a vision and strategy
Activity 2: Create a desired culture
Activity 3: Integrate and improve the enterprise
Activity 4: Develop technology solutions

The TEM is written with a process paradigm, where all activities are considered part of a process. Under this paradigm, the vision is achieved through processes that have cultural, procedural, and technological components. Thus, the TEM begins with a vision of what the enterprise aspires to become and a plan to achieve it, as indicated in activity 1, "Develop a vision and strategy." The *vision* is a statement of what the enterprise aspires to become; the *strategy* is the transformation plan for achieving that vision. The cultural components are the norms, attitudes, and beliefs exhibited by the people involved in the process. The procedural components are the sequences of activities that transform an input into an output, provide direction for the enterprise, or gather resources with which the enterprise can operate. The technological components are the tools that enable the processes to perform.

Once the vision and transformation plan has been completed, the next activity, "Create a desired culture," begins. This is the process of creating a culture that has the competencies to transform the enterprise. A competent culture has the knowledge, attitude, and skills with which to facilitate a transformation. This culture is characterized by the constant desire of people to learn and develop critical thinking skills. Culture is the shared norms, values, and beliefs of the enterprise that have emerged over time. *Norms* are a set of standards governing appropriate or inappropriate behaviors for a group, and they often exist around issues such as quality, performance, flexibility, output levels, and conflict resolution. *Values* are preferences for the end conditions that are desirable. *Beliefs* include facts about the enterprise, how it works, and cause-and-effect relationships. Cultures are supported and maintained by management practices, procedures, measurement, and reward systems, as well as organizational structures. Because transformation is a process, cultural strategies are placed second in the dominance of activities in the TEM.

The "Integrate and improve enterprise" activity transforms how work is accomplished. This activity focuses on increasing the efficiency and effectiveness of all enterprise processes. Enterprise processes are those that transform inputs into outputs, such as lean production processes; provide direction for the enterprise, such as strategic planning; and gather resources to operate the enterprise, such as securing capital for equipment purchases. All enterprise processes should be considered for improvement. Process improvement is the focus of all enterprise strategies, but it cannot occur without people and an end condition to achieve. It is the third activity in the TEM.

The last activity, "Develop technology solutions," enables process improvements. *Technology* is any tool that enables a process to operate. As process improvements are made through the previous "Integrate and improve enterprise" activity, technologies are identified that enable the improvements to become reality. Technology can serve as the catalyst for continuous process improvements. Technological breakthroughs represent a small percentage of technology applications. Technology is placed last in the decomposition of the TEM to emphasize the belief that processes should be integrated and improved before implementing technology. Improving processes before implementing technology ensures that the process has achieved optimal efficiency and effectiveness before spending large amounts of resources on technology that has uncertain benefits. If technologies are introduced before improvement activities, the enterprise runs the risk of "automating chaos." This phenomenon occurs when a process is enabled to operate at a higher rate of speed only to produce the same mistakes faster rather than providing the expected improvements.

In the "USAF Transformation Flight Plan FY03-07" (U.S. Air Force 2003), the transformation process has two distinct components:

- Strategic planning to provide the general direction
- Innovation to actually conceive and examine new ideas and turn them into reality

Air Force long-range planning builds the strategy that provides the foundation of transformation. This strategy results from systematic examination of future demands the Air Force will face as a member of America's total military force. Producing a clear, long-range vision is the first step in planning. *Air Force Vision 2020*, the Air Force's strategic direction document (2006), sets the strategy for well into the first quarter of the 21st century. This vision guides the Air Force in developing the air and space capabilities key to meeting national security objectives and realizing the full spectrum dominance envisioned by *Future Joint Warfare* (U.S. Joint Chiefs of Staff 2007).

The purpose of Air Force innovation is to rapidly assess and implement new ideas, concepts, and technologies so as to field the best capabilities to the war fighter while also improving the associated doctrine, organization, training, materiel, leadership and education, personnel, and facilities. Its objective is the timely adoption and integration of new or improved technologies, capabilities, concepts, and processes into Air Force planning and acquisition activities, organizations, and operations. Air Force innovation must be continuous and comprehensive over the short-, mid-, and long-term time horizons.

Transformation in the Air Force can be accomplished in a variety of ways:

- Acquiring new technologies that perform new missions or significantly improving old systems or processes
- Using existing capabilities in new ways
- Changing how the military is organized, trained, and equipped
- Changing doctrine or tactics, techniques, and procedures that determine force employment
- Changing the way forces are led and leaders are prepared
- Improving how forces interact with each other to produce effects in battles or campaigns
- Developing new operational concepts

The process of transformation begins and ends with people. To ensure its ongoing transformation, the military must create an environment and a culture conducive to transformation. Then it must change its organization to institutionalize this culture (U.S. Air Force 2003).

4.1.3 Measuring Transformation

Unfortunately, there is no one quantitative metric or framework that allows one to say: "Above this line, a program, concept, or organizational change is transformational and below this line, it is not" (U.S. Air Force 2003). Is a technology that gives the military five times more capability in a certain area transformational, and one that provides four times more capability not transformational? This even assumes that transformational capabilities are quantifiable at all. Most metrics assume that transformation only comprises significant improvements in capability. This ignores the fact that many transformational efforts are geared to adapting to a post-Cold War security environment, which does not always require improvements in the same capability but different types of capabilities altogether that are not comparable to the status quo. Even when a capability is quantifiable, a different metric would need to be developed for each category. For example, measuring a weapons system availability rate is very different from measuring the turn time for a repairable unit or throughput, or awaiting parts. In the end, determining what is transformational comes down to qualitative judgment calls by informed senior leadership based on a set of agreed quantitative metrics.

According to the "USAF Transformation Flight Plan FY 03-07," the Air Force is trying to tackle the difficult problem of measuring transformation. The Air Force Studies and Analysis Agency (AFSAA) has recently developed a tool based on a concept called value-focused thinking (VFT), which makes it possible to measure the multiobjective goals of military transformation. The VFT methodology allows alternative technologies, concepts of operations, and organizational structures to be ranked in terms of contribution to military transformation using the same model. Using sensitivity analysis, transformational alternatives that dominate others and those that are sensitive to satisfying specific objectives can be observed. Alternatives may be ranked in terms of marginal contribution to transformation per dollar cost by dividing the change in transformation by the additional cost of a given alternative, which may be used directly as an input in trade-off analyses. The AFSAA will perform the transformational metrics analysis using this and other possible techniques for future presentation.

The key to a performance-based transformation is describing the requirements of the transformation as outcomes and not in terms of how to accomplish the transformation. Accordingly, the transformation team should conduct a series of three analysis-oriented steps to help identify and define the measures or metrics of the transformation performance: 1. defining the desired outcomes; 2. analyzing the outcomes; and 3. conducting a performance analysis to identify the appropriate performance standards and acceptable quality levels (AQLs).

4.2 Continuous Process Improvement Initiatives for Transformation

This section provides a brief description of the most prominent approaches to transforming and improving military enterprise performance. Table 4.1 lists these approaches, and the initiatives are described in several books and research papers. The most useful and common books and papers are listed in the references for this chapter. A good summary of some of these programs also appears in a study by Khusrow M. Uzair (2001). Partly to prove the popularity of these programs, Uzair also carried out an industrial survey. The results of this survey are presented in Uzair's thesis and not replicated here, but Uzair's work does prove that U.S. aerospace contractors and other manufacturing enterprises do employ these improvement programs. A brief comparison table of these programs is also presented in his thesis.

Table 4.1 The Most Prominent Approaches to Improving Military Enterprise Performance

Performance Improvement Initiative	*Approximate Date When Initiative Was Created*	*Good Sources of Information on the Initiative*
Total Quality Management	1950s	Deming 1982, 1986; Shewhart 1989
Six Sigma	1980s	Harry and Schroeder 2000
Business Process Redesign/Reengineering	1993	Hammer and Champy 1993; Teng et al. 1994
Quick Response Manufacturing	1993	Suri 1998
The Agility Forum	1991	Dove, Hatman, and Benson 1996
Agile Manufacturing	1991	Center for Automation and Intelligent Systems Research 2005
Variance Reduction	2000	Ruffa and Perozziello 2000
Lean Production	1990–1995	Womack and Jones 1996
Cellular Manufacturing	Late 1950s	Black 1991; Burbidge 1993
Total Productive Maintenance	1988	Nakajima 1988
Theory of Constraints	1990	Goldratt 1990
Flexible Sustainment	1997	Joint Logistics Commanders 1997

4.2.1 Total Quality Management

Total quality management (TQM) is a performance improvement initiative that has its roots in the statistical process control (SPC) techniques that were invented by Walter Shewhart of Bell Laboratories, who believed that the lack of information greatly hampered the efforts of control and management processes in a production environment. In order to aid a manager in making scientific, efficient, economical decisions, he developed the SPC methods and charts. Many of the modern ideas regarding quality were inspired by Shewhart, who also developed the Shewhart Cycle for Learning and Improvement, combining both creative management thinking with statistical analysis. This cycle (see fig. 4.3) contains four continuous steps: *plan*, *do*, *check (or study)*, and *act* (Shewhart 1989). These steps, Shewhart believed, ultimately lead to total quality improvement. The cycle draws its structure from the notion that constant evaluation of management practices, as well as the willingness of management to adopt and disregard unsupported ideas, are keys to the evolution of a successful enterprise. First, *plan* for bringing about an improvement by studying the process, defining any problem, thoroughly analyzing it, and determining its root causes and a possible solution for dealing with them. This must then be followed by pilot implementation, or the *do* step, in which we apply the solution determined in the previous step. A *check* step is then followed to see if expected results are being obtained. Finally, in the case of success, we take the improved process as a new work standard and start *acting* according to it. This leads back to a reanalysis of the process and *planning* for further improvements. In the case where expected results are not obtained in the *check* step, the *act* step may involve a reanalysis of the initial problem, which again leads to *planning*.

The concept was later advocated and implemented by W. Edwards Deming in Japanese industry in the 1950s. Deming, one of Shewhart's students and a consultant and statistician by profession, is now referred to as "the father of total quality management." Many of the TQM concepts originated with Deming's work, who guided the Japanese industry's recovery after World War II and who formed many of his ideas during the war while he taught American industries how to use statistical methods to improve the quality of military products. Since then, TQM has become steadily more popular (Deming 1982; 1986).

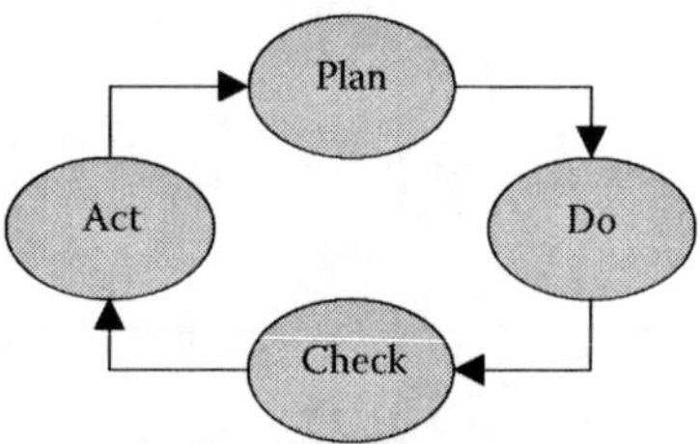

Figure 4.3 Plan, Do, Check or Study, and Act.

TQM has been defined by Schonberger and Knod to be customer focused, employee driven, and database oriented (1993). Because TQM is all about continuous improvement through data-based problem solving, it proposes the use of a number of problem-solving tools. The most famous of these are flow charts and diagrams, Pareto charts, cause-and-effect diagrams, histograms/graphs, SPC charts, check sheets, and scatter diagrams.

Important principles of TQM include customer-driven quality, top-management leadership and commitment, continuous improvement, fast response, actions based on facts, employee participation, and a TQM culture (see table 4.2). TQM brings about a slow but incremental and continuous process improvement. Perhaps because the process is slow, some people believe that TQM is no longer the "flavor of the month" in performance improvement initiatives. Managers and experts also disagree about how to effectively apply it. Some advise that customer

Table 4.2 The Principles of Total Quality Management

Customer-Driven Quality	TQM has a customer-first orientation. The customer, not internal activities and constraints, comes first. In the TQM context, "being sensitive to customer requirements" goes beyond defect and error reduction and merely meeting specifications or reducing customer complaints. The concept of requirements is expanded to take in not only product and service attributes that meet basic requirements, but also those that enhance, and differentiating them for competitive advantage. Each part of the company is involved in total quality, operating as a customer to some functions and as a supplier to others. The engineering department is a supplier to downstream functions, such as manufacturing and field service, and has to treat these internal customers with the same sensitivity and responsiveness as it would external customers.
Leadership from Top Management	TQM is a way of life for a company. It has to be introduced and led by top management, and this is a key point. Commitment and personal involvement is required from top management in creating and deploying clear quality values and goals consistent with the objectives of the company, and in creating and deploying well-defined systems, methods, and performance measures for achieving those goals. These systems and methods guide all quality activities and encourage participation by all employees. The development and use of performance indicators is linked, directly or indirectly, to customer requirements and satisfaction and to management and employee remuneration.

(continued)

Table 4.2 The Principles of Total Quality Management (continued)

Continuous Improvement	Continuous improvement of all operations and activities is at the heart of TQM. Once it is recognized that customer satisfaction can only be obtained by providing a high-quality product, continuous improvement of the quality of the product is seen as the only way to maintain a high level of customer satisfaction. As well as recognizing the link between product quality and customer satisfaction, TQM also recognizes that product quality is the result of process quality. As a result, there is a focus on continuous improvement of the company's processes. This will lead to an improvement in process quality. In turn this will lead to an improvement in product quality, and to an increase in customer satisfaction. Elimination of waste is a major component of the continuous improvement approach. There is also a strong emphasis on prevention rather than detection, and an emphasis on quality at the design stage. The customer-driven approach helps to prevent errors and achieve defect-free production. When problems do occur within the product development process, they are generally discovered and resolved before they can get to the next internal customer.
Fast Response	To achieve customer satisfaction, the company has to respond rapidly to customer needs. This implies short product- and service-introduction cycles. These can be achieved with customer-driven and process-oriented product development because the resulting simplicity and efficiency greatly reduce the time involved. Simplicity is gained through concurrent product and process development. Efficiencies are realized from the elimination of non-value-adding effort, such as redesign. The result is a dramatic improvement in the elapsed time from product concept to first shipment.
Actions Based on Facts	The statistical analysis of engineering and manufacturing facts is an important part of TQM. Facts and analysis provide the basis for planning, review, and performance tracking; improvement of operations; and comparison of performance with competitors. The TQM approach is based on the use of objective data, and provides a rational rather than emotional basis for decision making. The statistical approach to process management in both engineering and manufacturing recognizes that most problems are system related and are not caused by particular employees. In practice, data is collected and put in the hands of the people who are in the best position to

	analyze it and then take the appropriate action to reduce costs and prevent nonconformance. Usually these people are not managers, but workers. If the right information is not available, then the analysis—whether it be of shop-floor data or engineering test results—can't take place and errors can't be identified; thus, errors can't be corrected.
Employee Participation	A successful TQM environment requires a committed and well-trained workforce that participates fully in quality improvement activities. Such participation is reinforced by reward and recognition systems that emphasize the achievement of quality objectives. Ongoing education and training of all employees supports the drive for quality. Employees are encouraged to take more responsibility, communicate more effectively, act creatively, and innovate.
A TQM Culture	It's not easy to introduce TQM. An open, cooperative culture has to be created by management. Employees have to be made to feel that they are responsible for customer satisfaction. They are not going to feel this if they are excluded from the development of visions, strategies, and plans. Their participation is important. They are unlikely to behave in a responsible way if they see management behaving irresponsibly—for instance, saying one thing and doing the opposite.

Source: Management Assistance Program for Nonprofits, 2007.

satisfaction is the driving force behind quality improvement; others suggest that internal productivity or cost improvement programs achieve quality management. Advocates of TQM indicate that if an enterprise pursues the satisfaction of the internal and external customers in everything that it does, profitability and market-share improvements will follow automatically. In either case, all members of a TQM (control) organization strive to systematically manage the improvement of the organization through the ongoing participation of all employees in problem solving efforts across functional and hierarchical boundaries.

4.2.1.1 Awards for Quality Achievement

The Deming Prize has been awarded annually since 1951 by the Japanese Union of Scientists and Engineers in recognition of outstanding achievement in quality strategy, management, and execution. Since 1988, the similar Malcolm Baldrige National Quality Award has been awarded in the United States. Early winners of the Baldrige Award include Motorola (1988), IBM (1990), Milliken and Xerox (both 1989), and AT&T and Texas Instruments (both 1992).

4.2.2 Six Sigma

Six Sigma began as a measure of quality that is defined in terms of the number of defects present in a given product or process, and has now matured into a process improvement initiative that strives for near perfection. First initiated at Motorola in the early 1980s and later pioneered by Mikel Harry and Richard Schroeder (2000), the Six Sigma initiative is distinct from other improvement efforts in that it emphasizes setting up quantifiable improvement targets and employs statistics for getting increasingly closer to that target (Uzair 2001). The objective is to reduce process output variation so that on a long-term basis—which is the customer's aggregate experience with a process over time—the process will result in no more than 3.4 defective parts per million, 99.73 percent of the time. The 99.73 percent interval is the mean (μ) plus or minus three standard deviations (σ) found in a normal probability distribution in statistics (see fig. 4.4). Hence the name Six Sigma.

A Six Sigma defect is defined as anything outside of these customer specifications. Each sigma shift from the mean creates an exponential reduction in defects. The first sigma improvements from the mean are somewhat easier than later improvements because of the presence of more evident defects and problems. The improvement process could be slow, similar to TQM's style of incremental improvement. The closer an organization comes to achieving the full six sigma, the more demanding the improvements become. It is during this later phase that improvements might only be possible by a reengineering-type fundamental redesign of the whole enterprise.

The implications of a Six Sigma process improvement initiative go well beyond the quantitative eradication of customer-perceptible defects. The expanded objective of the original Six Sigma statistical concept is the implementation of a measurement-

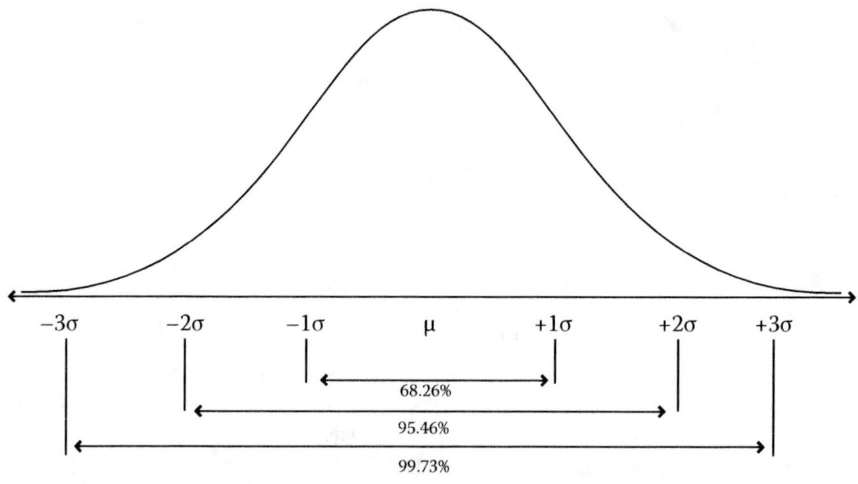

Figure 4.4 Normal Probability Distribution.

based strategy that focuses on process improvement and variation reduction. This expanded objective is accomplished through the use of two Six Sigma submethodologies, DMAIC and DMADV. The Six Sigma DMAIC process stands for *define*, *measure*, *analyze*, *improve*, and *control*. DMAIC is an improvement system for existing processes falling below specification and looking for incremental improvement. The *define* step consists of defining the problem and determining a road map for its solution. The *measure* step involves data collection and an assessment of the present state of defectiveness. The *analyze* step involves determining the root causes of the problem and then brainstorming and finding possible ways to eliminate them. The *improve* step involves implementing the determined solution, and the *control* step involves continuous monitoring and taking corrective actions to make sure that the defect or the problem does not recur.

The Six Sigma DMADV (*define*, *measure*, *analyze*, *design*, and *verify*) process is an improvement system used to develop new processes or products at Six Sigma–quality levels. DMADV can also be employed if a current process requires more than just incremental improvement. The approach that Six Sigma proposes for the elimination of defects is the same as the one prescribed by TQM and, perhaps, similar initiatives, although the terminology defined is a bit different, as indicated with the DMAIC and DMADV methodologies. Six Sigma proponents advocate the use of all of the TQM tools for detection of the defects. The overall strategy of Six Sigma is also similar to that of TQM: namely, to proactively discover the existence of problems and their root causes and to eliminate the root causes rather than implementing a solution to the problem. TQM proposes an incremental continuous improvement in individual operations, whereas Six Sigma sets out to transform a whole process with a focus on profitability and quantifiable elimination of defects. This transformation could be incremental as well as radical. It should also be noted that the term *defect* in Six Sigma has a broader meaning. It is not only anything that causes a failure to meet the customer's expectations or requirements, but also anything that blocks, or inhibits, customer satisfaction (Uzair 2001).

4.2.3 Business Process Reengineering/Redesign

Business process reengineering/redesign (BPR) is the "analysis and design of workflows and processes within and between organizations" (Davenport and Short 1990, p. 11). Teng, Grover, and Fielder define BPR as "the critical analysis and radical redesign of existing business processes to achieve breakthrough improvements in performance measures" (1994, p. 10). As defined by Hammer and Champy (1993), BPR is the fundamental rethinking and radical redesign of business processes to achieve dramatic improvements in critical, contemporary measures of performance, such as cost, quality, service, and speed. Unlike total quality management, reengineering does not seek to make businesses better through incremental improvements in an existing process. The aim is a quantum leap in performance improvements that can follow only from an entire revamping of the existing work processes and structures. Thus, reengineering is approached only when a dramatic improvement in performance is required. Such a need could be felt in the face of customer requirements, global competition, or unrelenting change in the market conditions. Such a dramatic improvement can only be achieved by challenging the very basic assumptions at the root of current business processes, and by restarting from scratch (Uzair 2001).

How does BPR differ from TQM? Teng et al. (1994) note that in recent years, increased attention to business processes is largely due to the TQM movement. They conclude that TQM and BPR share a cross-functional orientation. Davenport (1993) has observed that quality specialists tend to focus on incremental change and gradual improvement of processes, whereas proponents of reengineering often seek radical redesign and drastic improvement of processes.

Davenport notes that *quality management* (often referred to as *total quality management* or *continuous improvement*, refers to programs and initiatives that emphasize incremental improvement in work processes and outputs over an open-ended period of time. In contrast, *reengineering* (also known as *business process redesign* or *process innovation*) refers to discrete initiatives that are intended to achieve radically redesigned and improved work processes in a bounded time frame. A contrast between the two is provided by Davenport (1993).

BPR should focus on process. Process mapping can provide the tools and methodology with which to identify the current "as is" process, and can then be used to provide a "to be" road map for reengineering the product or service enterprise functions. Muthu (1999) provides a consolidated methodology for BPR (see fig. 4.5). Although the performance metrics may vary, the basic objective remains the enhancement of value provided to the customer. Some of the themes revolving around a reengineering effort are innovation, a focus on results, and reinvention of processes.

The Japanese word *kaizen*, meaning "incremental improvement," is a general term, but with a quality or customer satisfaction in focus, it becomes synonymous with TQM. Similarly, the Japanese term often used for reengineering-type radical or breakthrough improvements is *kaikaku* or *kaizen blitz* (Bicheno 2000). There is, however, a fine line between kaikaku and reengineering. Kaikaku, as originally defined, is applicable to any small area of the enterprise—mostly the shop floor—and despite bringing about a step function-like leap in performance, it does not necessarily have to signal a redesign from scratch. Reengineering, on the other hand, is only applicable to an entire enterprise process, and it is always a reinvention or starting over with a clean slate.

To elaborate on this point, whereas the concepts of TQM, kaizen, and kaikaku can be applied to any operation, a set of operations, or an entire process, reengineering is only applicable to a *process*, which is defined as a self-sufficient collection of activities that takes one or more kinds of input and creates an output that has some value to the final customer. An example of an operation would be bringing in a set

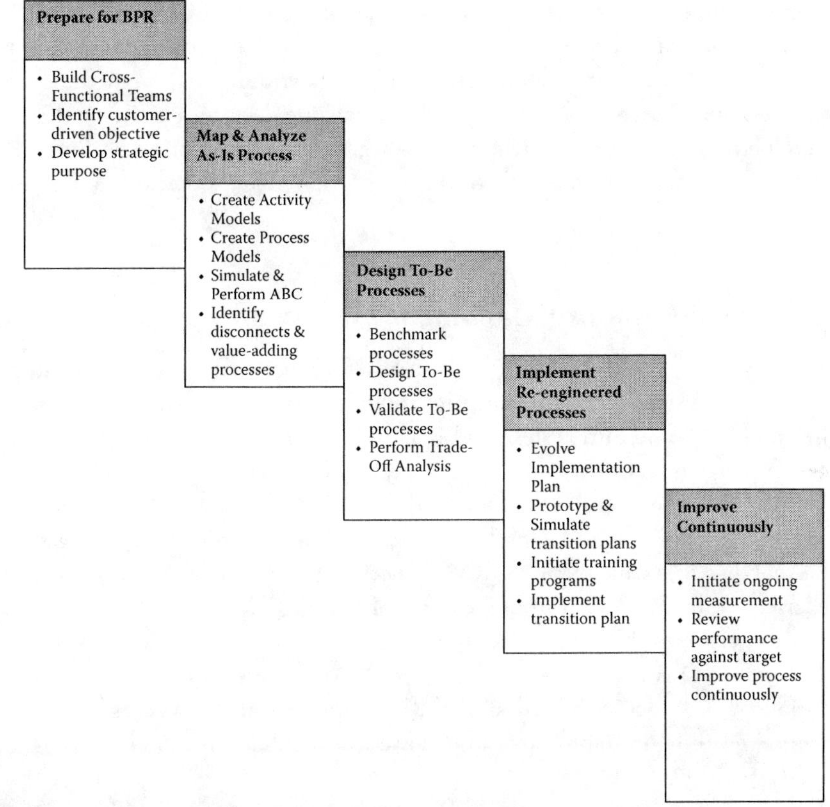

Figure 4.5 A Consolidated Methodology for BPR.

of documents from one office to the other, while that of a process would be "order processing at company X." Traditionally, reengineering has been applied successfully to white-collar enterprise processes only. In principle, however, the concept is equally applicable to a blue-collar process. In either case, information technology, because of its power of bringing about dramatic improvements, is considered an important enabler in reengineering.

Because of the dramatic improvements reengineering brings about in performance, it has been accused of leading to enterprise layoffs due to mass elimination of non-value-added operations from its various processes. This accusation was vehemently debated by Hammer, the founder of the reengineering movement (see Hammer 1990). According to Hammer, it is the enterprise leadership's responsibility to utilize the human resources saved by reengineering value-added tasks. It is even prestigious and satisfying for human resources departments themselves to contribute toward value-added tasks rather than being wasted away in redundant and non-value-added tasks. The objective of reengineering, notes Hammer, is the same.

Despite these criticisms, there are reengineering success stories galore in the corporate world. The most popular ones are those of Bell Atlantic, Hallmark Cards, and Taco Bell. Some of the common characteristics running through these stories are combining several jobs into one, decentralizing decision-making authority, starting performance improvement steps in a natural order, starting performance improvements where they make the most sense, and reducing checks and controls (Uzair 2001).

4.2.4 Quick-Response Manufacturing

Quick-response manufacturing (QRM) is an enterprisewide strategy for cutting lead times in all phases of manufacturing and office operations. QRM is described in Shalabi (2003) and Suri (1998), and is a concept that addresses two key factors: (1) the external aspect of responding quickly to customers by rapidly estimating, designing, and manufacturing customized or new products; and (2) the internal aspect, which focuses on reducing lead times for all tasks throughout an organization. Applying the principles of QRM reduces response times, improves quality, and lowers costs. From a customer's point of view, QRM means responding to that customer's needs by rapidly designing and manufacturing products customized to those needs; this is the *external* aspect of QRM. In terms of a company's own operations, QRM focuses on reducing the lead times for all tasks across the whole enterprise, resulting in improved quality, lower cost, and quick response; this is the *internal* aspect of QRM.

QRM achieves these lead-time reductions and other results through detailed management principles, manufacturing methods, analysis techniques, and tools that use basic concepts of system dynamics and ten basic principles. These principles are:

1. Find whole new ways of completing a job, with the focus on lead-time minimization.
2. Strategically plan for spare capacity: plan to operate at 80 percent or even 70 percent capacity on critical resources.
3. Measure the reduction of lead times and make this the main performance measure. Eliminate traditional measures of utilization and efficiency.
4. Stick to measuring and rewarding reduction of lead times.
5. Use MRP for high-level planning and coordination of materials. Restructure the manufacturing organization into simpler product-oriented cells. Complement this with paired-cell overlapping loops of cards with authorization, a new material-control method that combines the best of "push" and "pull" strategies.
6. Motivate suppliers to implement QRM, resulting in small lot deliveries at lower cost, better quality, and shorter lead times.

7. Educate customers about your QRM program, and negotiate a schedule of moving to smaller lot deliveries at reasonable prices.
8. Cut through functional boundaries by forming a quick response office cell (Q-ROC), which is a closed-loop, collocated, multifunctional, cross-trained team responsible for a family of products aimed at a focused target market segment. Empower the Q-ROC to make necessary decisions.
9. The reason for embarking on the QRM journey is that it leads to a truly productive company with a more secure future. Also, lower cost/price, higher quality, and shorter lead times result in highly satisfied customers.
10. The biggest obstacle to QRM is not technology, but mind-set. Management must recognize this and combat it through training. Next, companies should engage in low-cost or no-cost lead-time reductions, leaving expensive technological solutions for a later stage.

The objective is to improve the market share and profitability of an enterprise. This is also an enterprisewide program focused on operations and processes. Quick response manufacturing can be traced back to the Toyota Production System pioneered by Taiichi Ohno (1988) and Shigeo Shingo (1989). This production system was invented at the Toyota Motor Corporation in Japan in a direct confrontation with the mass-production system flourishing at the Ford Motor Company and General Motors Corporation in the United States (Womack, Jones, and Roos 1990). The situation demanded the birth of an entirely new way of manufacturing. Through analysis, Taiichi Ohno and Eiji Toyoda affirmed that in order to maximize the use of factory space, they had to produce a large number of different models and types of autos on the same shop floor. At the same time, they did not want to stock huge inventories of each model and type because they did not want to invest in building warehouses, and they knew that holding inventories for prolonged periods is in itself an expensive proposition. Further, they prophesied that they would have a great competitive advantage, from a customer satisfaction point of view, if they could change their production in synergy with changing customer demands. All this demanded that they devise a method for reducing the setup times to the least possible, so that changeover to different models and types of product did not entail long delays and inordinate person hours. Once this target for "single-minute changeover" was set, it was not an impossible goal to achieve for Shingo, the most capable of Ohno's engineers.

Negligible setup/changeover times, with concomitant low work-in-process, raw material, and finished good inventories form one-half of the premise of QRM (Suri 1998). The other premise is that a manufacturing company should also try continuously decreasing its lead time for manufacturing and product development, and for all enterprise processes, by a radical redesign or an incremental problem-solving approach. The idea is that on one hand, customer satisfaction is being achieved by minimizing the changeover/setup times, and on the other hand, a lead in achieving the same objective is being achieved by bringing one's products to the market faster than all the competitors. As mentioned before, the required continuous reduction in all these time parameters can be radical as well as incremental, depending on the need and situation. Means for achieving such a change include, but are definitely not limited to, such methodologies as worker empowerment, integrated product and process teams (IPPTs), total productive maintenance (TPM), and cellular layouts.

The primary performance metric considered by QRM for bringing about improvement is time. According to proponents of QRM, everything an enterprise does should be geared toward reducing the time spent in all pertinent organizational and industrial processes. Just like cost reduction was the competitive weapon in the 1970s, and quality in the 1980s, lead-time reduction was the weapon for the 1990s and into the 21st century. Of note, however, is that QRM also claims that—as a result of lead-time reduction—quality, cost, and other improvements take place automatically. The argument that Suri and De Treville (1986) propose runs as follows: If all the work-in-process inventories are minimized in a manufacturing system, problems become easier to be identified, and therefore process- and product-quality improvement opportunities increase. The analogy often presented in this regard is that of tidewater in a pond. If inventories are analogous to water, and the stones/rocks in the bottom of the pond are similar to quality problems, reducing the volume of water always highlights the presence of the stones, which hence become more likely to be removed. Likewise, because lead-time reduction involves elimination of non-value-added chunks of time, it automatically eliminates all kinds of waste and thus improves cost reduction (Uzair 2001).

Suri (1998) lays down the following prerequisites for a successful implementation of QRM:

- There must be a companywide understanding of the basics of QRM.
- Workers and managers need to understand some basic dynamics of manufacturing systems.
- The QRM program has to be implemented in both shop-floor and office operations.
- Firms must incorporate QRM policies in all areas.
- Shop-floor and office employees, as well as managers, need to thoroughly understand the concept of work cells.
- Obstacles to implementation should be anticipated as much as possible.
- Top management should not attempt to reorganize the whole company for QRM right away.
- Concrete steps for implementing QRM should be identified at the start of the initiative.

In the last few years, dozens of companies have implemented QRM strategies with astounding results. Typical results include reduction in lead times of 80–85 percent, on-time delivery performance improving from 40 percent to 98 percent, and reduction in scrap and reworking by 80 percent or more (Suri 1998).

4.2.5 Agility

4.2.5.1 The Agility Forum

In view of the rapidly changing global economy, technological advances, and increasing complexity of products and systems, management of change has gained unprecedented importance. This was particularly true for weapons systems, which take years to develop; yet some key technologies change about every three years (Goranson 1999). In the early 1990s, for the benefit of military industrial establishment in particular, the DoD and the National Science Foundation set aside 120 million dollars to develop tools to manage the problem of responding to unexpected change. Using these funds, the Advanced Research Projects Agency established the Agility Forum at Lehigh University in Bethlehem, Pennsylvania, under the auspices of the Iacocca Institute. Three NSF-funded university research centers were soon established, and 30 new research contracts were issued. Most of these programs digressed to other similar theories like quick response, supply-chain management, or electronic commerce, but a few core projects under the management of the U.S. Air Force were able to remain focused on the original idea. The work was further developed by the Agility Forum, as well as consultants and academicians (Uzair 2001).

Agile processes and strategic objectives for an agile enterprise have been the subject of a growing number of corporate investigations, research efforts, and government initiatives internationally since 1991; and each year a more vocal demand for an enterprisewide reference model has been raised. The Agility Forum answered that demand in 1996 with the development of a comprehensive agile enterprise reference model (see Dove 1996). The result serves two principal goals: (1) it provides a reference model structure that effectively captures and displays the state of enterprisewide competency at both proactive and reactive change; and (2) it validates the structure design with a rich and real example that is an instructive reference case for an entire enterprise. There are three elements in the reference model. The first is an enterprise framework provided by 24 critical business practices. The second offers a list of about 200 objectives for the proactive and reactive changes; and the third gives examples of how one company, Remmele Engineering, successfully addresses most of these changes. The reference model spans the 24 interrelated critical business practices in six categories: strategic planning, business case justification, organizational relationship management, innovation management, knowledge management, and performance metrics. Seven organizational relationships focus on business units, employees, partners, suppliers, customers, information systems, and production systems. Each of the 24 practices is presented in a three- to five-page structure that provides a generic definition, the framework and modules of a case-study practice that fits that definition, a set of generic proactive and reactive change issues, case-study responses for each issue, and a synopsis that evaluates and displays the competency of the case example using a change proficiency maturity model.

The reference model is intended to help both product- and service-based organizations begin the process of introspection and improvement prioritization. It identifies key issues that must be addressed, or at least considered, when an organization sets out to become more change proficient. Notably, it provides a means for competitive comparison and prioritizing improvement strategies. The creation of the model and case study was five years in the making as metrics, definitions, reference cases, critical practices, and concepts of change proficiency steadily emerged to build a foundation (Dove 1996).

4.2.5.2 Agile Manufacturing

Different groups have different definitions of the term *agile manufacturing*. The Center for Automation and Intelligent Systems Research at Case Western Reserve University in Cleveland, Ohio, adopted the following definition: "Agile manufacturing is the ability to accomplish rapid changeover between the manufacture of different assemblies" (Center for Automation and Intelligent Systems Research 2005, n.p.). *Rapid changeover* is further defined as the ability to move from the assembly of one product to the assembly of a similar product with a minimum of change in tooling and software. Rapid changeover enables the production of small lot sizes, allowing for "just in time" production. Agility demands increased flexibility in terms of the ability to

- ...determine customer needs quickly and continuously reposition the company against it's [*sic*] competitors
- ...design things quickly based on those individual needs
- ...put them into full scale, quality, production quickly
- ...respond to changing volumes and mix quickly
- ...respond to a crisis quickly (S. M. Thacker and Associates 2002, n.p.)

Today, agility is defined as the ability of an organization to respond well to unexpected change, and even to leverage that ability as a competitive strategy. This change could be external as well as internal. It could be a market change, because of unexpected mergers or acquisitions, or changing customer preferences because of some completely unforeseen external factors. It could also be technological changes, so critical to the viability of the enterprise. The objective of an agility initiative is to keep an enterprise continually competitive in the face of all these changes (Uzair 2001).

Whereas other improvement programs are built on the assumption of a static environment, agility is closer to reality in that it realizes the environment to be very dynamic. For example, the lean program assumes that "better, faster, cheaper" is always the guarantee of success. This is not entirely correct, because it benefits an organization to have some waste in its structure to cope with sudden changes in its internal or external environment. A good example of this situation is that of Wang Laboratories and IBM. When Wang Laboratories invented the word processor—an innovation that quickly created a billion-dollar company—shock waves hit the world's largest electric typewriter producer, IBM. IBM had dominated that market with the most-preferred (better, cheaper, customer-focused) products, but they were initially unable to respond to Wang's innovation. Wang successfully redefined and dominated this market precisely because they took advantage of change. However, Wang's market started eroding with the appearance of word processing software on personal computers. When IBM faced and responded to the new realities by creating the word processing personal computer, Wang was unable to change, and they were soon in bankruptcy. What put Wang out of business this time was IBM roaring back by entering (or creating) the personal computer business. IBM was able to respond successfully because of the previously underutilized skills of their many-layered, seemingly redundant, and expensive technical management pool.

To be a paragon of best management practices and to have a customer-focused, waste-free environment is important. But what is even more important in this new high-tech age is the ability to maintain this position, as well as to respond to any unexpected changes in an appropriate way—for example, to start making something else better, faster, and cheaper, or to become better, faster, and cheaper in a different way. This is what agility is all about.

It is important to note that the flexibility of systems and processes to quickly respond to changing customer requirements is a part of, but not the whole concept of, agility. Agility also includes taking an appropriate (not necessarily quick) action toward unexpected changes at strategic levels. The aim is to always keep the enterprise ahead of the competitors. This very much ties in with the profitability goal, the main target of all the improvement programs. According to Thacker, it is unlikely that this level of flexibility can be achieved without:

- ... Leanness.
- Specific individual customer focus.
- Regular Business Process Re-engineering....
- Partnering with other organizations....
- Selective, flexible use of performance management.
- Flexible manufacturing processes.
- Flexible business processes....
- Standardisation of products, processes and tools.
- Skill management processes.
- Empowered, innovative, flexible multiskilled, well trained... people....
- Low absenteeism levels.
- Low machine breakdown levels.
- Simultaneous engineering of product and process....
- Capable, reliable processes.
- Rapid response, supply chain....

- Pull systems....
- Regular customer feedback into the design process.
- Rethinking the management accounting systems....
- Excellent communications channels.... (Thacker 2002, n.p.)

Another concept commonly defined as a part of the agility movement is that of the *virtual enterprise*. The basic premise of the virtual enterprise concept is that keeping business partnerships (with suppliers, for example) fixed or in the long term can sometimes go against agility. An enterprise should also be able to form quick partnerships to cope with unanticipated changes in the market situation. These makeshift extended enterprises, known as virtual enterprise, have the added virtue of being very agile besides being lean because of minimum overheads (Uzair 2001).

4.2.6 Variance Reduction

Spurred by significant reductions in defense budgets, a joint initiative was taken by the DoD and the aerospace industry in the late 1990s to find out ways of reducing aerospace industry production costs. Spearheaded by Stephen Ruffa from the DoD and Michael Perozziello from the industry, extensive research was undertaken to determine the best methodology for carrying out significant and effective reductions in production costs. The findings were brought out in the form of a report and a book (Ruffa and Perozziello 2000), and the essence of their findings has since been called the *principle of variance reduction*. The giants of military and commercial aircraft engines and avionics production gave Ruffa unprecedented access. Their mission: to go beyond the age-old focus on flying farther, faster, and higher to discover how to effectively and permanently slash the cost of producing aircraft to allow this industry to continue its rapid pace of advancement. These findings, lauded by leaders across the industry and comprehensively explored in their book prove that production variation, as opposed to more common targets like labor utilization and inventory levels, is the chief cause of escalating production costs. More important, they reveal how companies can control spiraling production costs by first controlling the variability that has for too long been considered a necessary evil in manufacturing circles.

Whereas other improvement programs have profitability improvement as an implied target, variance reduction takes it as an explicit objective. Further, it proposes to achieve this target both for the enterprise in question and for the customers through a continuous reduction in cost of production. The basic concept of the principle of variance reduction is that inventory reduction and cycle-time reduction are the two primary metrics for reducing cost of production. In order for them to take place effectively, variance in all operations in the enterprise must be managed first. Thus variance reduction must be taken as the fundamental performance metric of the three (cycle-time reduction, inventory reduction, and cost reduction) in all enterprise operations. The success of all improvement efforts is dependent on whether variance in processes, operations, and systems has been managed well. The analogy presented by the proponents of the variance reduction program is thus: In a traffic stream, some disruptive behavior of a rash driver often causes a ripple effect and chokes down the whole stream. Putting in a few police cars on the highway to check such rash driving will remove all disruptions from the stream and, hence, will improve the overall efficiency of all the people driving on the road. This will also enable further improvements, like improving the speed limit, or improving the fuel efficiency of cars. If there is a roadblock or construction site on the highway, it needs to be fixed before putting in police cars, because if the roadblock is not removed, the police cars will themselves get choked in the narrow passages, instead of keeping rash drivers in check. Similarly, variance reduction is the primary metric to be controlled before any other improvement program can be put into action.

The variance reduction program does not end at reducing variances. Instead, it sees variance as a primary metric for improvement. The two other primary metrics it proposes are inventory reduction and cycle-time reduction. Strong improvement in both inventory and cycle time is seen only when variation in all processes and operations have been greatly mitigated. Variance reduction also has a set of six enablers for improving these three primary metrics, and thus for achieving the target of cost-of-production reductions. These enablers are:

1. Control of inventory
2. Control of manufacturing operations
3. Quality improvements
4. Supplier improvements
5. Flow improvements
6. Emphasis of manufacturing in design

Each of these enablers, in turn, is supposed to be implemented by a set of initiatives. The overall configuration is shown in Uzair (2001). The variance reduction program also suggests the implementation of these six enablers in a particular order. Lower-level enablers, if implemented first, will have a better impact on making higher-level enablers effective.

The improvement initiatives of each of the enabler supports could also be taken as tools or techniques for implementation. Thus, the tools and methodologies for improvement of variance reduction are not much different from those of other programs. Also, the scope of application of this program includes all enterprise functional processes, as in other programs. The degree of change brought about by this program can be dramatic or incremental depending on the approach taken for implementing each of the initiatives. The program itself has no specific guidelines regarding this approach (Uzair 2001).

4.2.7 Lean Production

The history of lean manufacturing goes back to the production system invented by the Toyota Motor Corporation in Japan. The concepts have been examined by Roos, Womack, and Jones at the Massachusetts Institute of Technology (1990). Based on this work, a whole philosophy of lean thinking and lean initiatives was developed by two of these researchers in the mid-1990s, and the same was presented in Womack and Jones (1996).

The lean initiative is somewhat different than other improvement strategies in that it is independent of either the speed or the mechanism of bringing about the improvement. It also does not advocate the use of a single performance metric for bringing about improvements. One, can therefore say that lean production is the basic framework within which the other improvement strategies work. Whereas TQM advocates customer satisfaction by working on what the enterprise already has and Six Sigma, reengineering, QRM, and variance reduction communicate the same thing by giving customer satisfaction different orientations, lean production goes an extra mile beyond what the enterprise already has. It talks about customer satisfaction by doing more for the customer than normally expected (creating value) and by using very carefully and effectively whatever it has (waste elimination). In other words, lean production is about doing only what the customer wants and also doing whatever the customer wants. The notion of continuous improvement seems to be shared by all of these programs (Uzair 2001).

There are five basic principles of lean thinking:

1. *Value.* The value that the customer places upon their products and services.
2. *The value stream.* The entire flow of a product's life cycle from the origin of the raw materials used to make the product through to the customer's cost of using and ultimately disposing of the product.
3. *Flow.* The key to the elimination of waste is flow. If the value chain stops moving forward for any reason, then waste will be occurring.
4. *Pull.* Do not make anything until the customer orders it.
5. *Perfection.* Set the targets for perfection. The idea of TQM is to systematically and continuously remove the root causes of poor quality from the production processes so that the plant and its products are moving toward perfection.

Value-stream mapping (described in the next section), pertinent to principle 2 above, is an important tool for implementing a lean initiative. It provides a basis for performing an in-depth analysis of each of the action steps leading to provision of value to a customer. As a result of this analysis, the steps that do not create value to the customer may be singled out and eliminated. These form what lean thinkers call *waste*—or *muda* in Japanese. Once this waste is eliminated, the remaining value-creating steps must "flow," the concept presented in principle 3 above. This involves discarding the traditional batch-and-queue mentality and implementing batch sizes to the order of single units. Setup-time reduction, cellular manufacturing, and IPPTs are all tools and techniques supporting this step. The next step (principle 4 above) posits that customers pull products and services through the enterprise, rather than the enterprise pushing them on to the customers, which is another key to the sustained competence of an enterprise. This "pulling" action reaches upstream, all the way to the supplier network. *Kanban*, "just in time," and production smoothing are all techniques supporting this principle. Finally, principle 5 is the same continuous-improvement philosophy common to all process-improvement programs. Here it says that there should be no end to the process of reducing waste and specification/creation of value for the customer, but a continuous improvement of the products and services and the way they are provided to the customer.

These five principles lead to "doing more with less," and at the same time coming closer to providing customers with exactly what they want. Although not explicitly stated, lean implementation is obviously customer focused, and it has to be knowledge driven. This is because continuous waste elimination and allowing customers to pull value through the enterprise are not possible unless they are supported by empowered teams of employees that are continuously trained and enabled to make knowledgeable, data-based decisions. To many lean thinkers, therefore, lean thinking is a knowledge-driven and customer-focused process through which all people in a defined enterprise continuously eliminate waste and add value, creating sustainable competitive advantage (Uzair 2001).

According to the Lean Aerospace Initiative (LAI), an enterprise that converts to lean production can achieve the following results:[2]

- Dramatic improvement in responsiveness to customers
- Elimination of factory-floor chaos
- Doubled or tripled labor productivity
- Greatly simplified production-control systems
- Reduction by 80 percent to 90 percent of warehouse space for purchased parts and materials
- Immediate shipment of completed orders to customers
- Total floor space of 55 percent to 65 percent in lean factories
- Reduction of inventory levels at all stages (raw materials, in-process, and finished goods) by greater than 90 percent

To support these claims, Womack and Jones (1996) report 50 to 90 percent improvements after converting to lean production.

4.2.8 Value-Stream Mapping

Value-stream mapping (VSM) was initially developed in 1995 to help researchers and practitioners identify waste in individual value streams and thus find an appropriate route for waste removal (Hines et al. 1998). The VSM tool ties together lean concepts and techniques by helping manufacturers think of flow instead of discrete production processes (Rother and Shook 1999). In this section, the VSM processes traditionally used in manufacturing will be applied to military sustainment. Two such case studies are presented later, in section 3 of this chapter. These VSMs are at a high level in the MRO process. The intent here is on identifying the waste at a strategic level (i.e., the major tasks) rather than on the specific details of how a system is maintained or repaired (i.e., how a system is disassembled, how each component is tested, diagnosed, fixed, etc.).

4.2.8.1 The Value Stream

A value stream is all the actions (both value-added and non-value-added actions) required to bring a product through the main flows of design and production. It is composed of the set of activities required to move a product through three key management tasks of business: (1) *problem solving tasks,* which transform the product from concept to design and engineering to product launch; (2) *information management tasks*, which follow order-taking through to MRO scheduling, delivery, and receipt of payment; and (3) *physical transformation tasks,* which make the most impact on a product's value and involve converting raw materials to a finished product—be it through maintenance or true manufacturing—that can be used by a final customer (Womak and Jones 1996). VSM is a technique that helps us see and understand the flow of material and information as a product makes its way through the value stream.

4.2.8.2 The Value-Stream Mapping Process

The focal point of VSM is to do only those tasks that add value to the final product from the viewpoint of the consumer. All other tasks can be divided into two groups. The first group adds no value and can be completely eliminated from the repair/sustainment process. These are considered to be the proverbial low-hanging fruit—quick and relatively easy to eliminate. The second group of tasks adds no value, but is required by a part of the MRO process. These tasks are harder to eliminate and will take a concerted effort on the part of managers and employees throughout the value chain to eliminate.

Step 1: Current High-Level State Mapping

In order to eliminate steps contributing no value, each major task in the process must be identified. Therefore, the first step in the VSM process is to define each individual action involved in the MRO of a specific product. Because drawing all product flows on one map is much too complicated, product groups or families are created, and it is the actions of these families that are mapped. To create product families, the following steps are recommended (Irani 2002):

- Create a binary product work center incidence matrix that lists products horizontally and work centers vertically. Based on each product's routing, enter a 1 in each work center or product cell for each work center used.
- Depending on the size of the matrix, use a computer to generate groupings of products based on like routings into another matrix called a block diagonal form (BDF). Each BDF matches a product family with a group of work centers that can be located together in a manufacturing cell dedicated to the manufacture of that product family. This becomes a basis for a design of a lean manufacturing facility.

In addition to defining each step of the process, mapping involves gathering or calculating the following information for each action; note that this is not an exhaustive list:

- Resources utilized (people and machines)
- Incoming storage time (includes transport time from previous step)
- Product throughput and cycle times
- Changeover time
- Finished storage time
- Process rate
- Cumulative days
- Cumulative scrap

Throughout the creation of the value-stream map, remember that it is not a plant layout, but rather a map of the flow of material through the MRO operation and the flow of information from the customer back to each process (Rother and Shook 1999).

Step 2: Identifying Waste

The second step of VSM classifies each part of the MRO process as value-added or wasteful from the viewpoint of the customer. Actual value-added time is calculated for each step so significant waste can be identified.

There are a plethora of places in which an enterprise can find excess waste, making identification relatively easy. When mapping the value stream, one should observe how often a product is touched and what value is contributed at each touch, or one can count the number of times a product is picked and warehoused. It is often these processes that comprise most of the total MRO time for a product or product family; however, these activities add no value to the end customer. The following are the seven traditional areas in which an enterprise can find and eliminate waste to realize valuable improvements (Walton 1999).

1. Waiting
   waiting for parts
   waiting for machinery
   waiting for approval
2. Transportation
   long distances between tasks
   long distances between organizations (if observing full value chain)
3. Inventories
   excess finished goods and raw materials
   gathering inventory "just in case"
   gathering information "just in case"
4. Excess Production
   producing more than required
   producing before required
5. Processing Time (Paperwork)
   poor communication
   multiple (excessive) iterations of documents
6. Reworking and Defects
7. Unnecessary Movement by Employees

One of the reasons that the amount of time spent on each of the above tasks is high is due to prevalent thinking in industry that mass production, often referred to as *batch-and-queue production*, is good, efficient, and something to strive for. However, it is proven that speeding up assembly when customers do not want more product creates high inventories and abundant waste. It allows individual enterprises to present themselves as efficient while passing on inefficiencies to other enterprises within the value stream. If, on the other hand, organizations refrain from focusing solely on their individual efficiency and, instead, focus on the overall efficiency of the value chain, results will be more streamlined and overall efficiency will be improved.

Step 3: Future-State Mapping

Creating a map of the future flow is the third step of the VSM process. The design should follow the continuous flow of a product family through its MRO process. Although the future-state map is a dynamic model, it represents a goal. Once goals are met, new goals need to be set in order to completely eliminate excess waste from the process.

Step 4: Eliminating Waste

The fourth step uses the future-flow map to create a plan that will allow the enterprise to eliminate waste. The previous steps demonstrate how products and services flow, providing insight into stagnation, inventory, and wait time; however, it is not until a plan is created and followed that waste can be eliminated.

4.2.8.3 Value-Stream Mapping as It Relates to Lean Sustainment

Identifying the value stream is just part of the lean thinking approach, and VSM is only the second step in the process of cutting extraneous waste from the MRO operation. The first step is identifying value, which can only be defined by the final customer. After mapping the value stream, the enterprise must implement continuous flow and eliminate the standard batch-and-queue methods found in most MRO organizations. In addition, the enterprise must be transformed to allow customers to pull products from upstream suppliers, instead of pushing the products to the customer. It is also important to recognize that the lean approach involves constantly revisiting the previous steps in a striving for perfection.

4.2.8.4 The Benefits of Value-Stream Mapping

Combined with the other steps of lean production, an enterprise that utilizes VSM can eliminate extraneous waste from its entire MRO process. Too often, organizations that implement lean bypass mapping the value stream. The result is that individual parts of the MRO process are remedied and isolated victories are achieved, but the overall process or entire enterprise still does not improve. Instead, if all of the steps of lean sustainment are utilized, an enterprise can increase the speed of delivery of a product and reduce or eliminate waste. Various improvement targets for an enterprise include:

- Reducing production lead time
- Reducing inventory
- Reducing cost
- Increasing available capacity
- Improving factory-floor usage
- Reducing order lead time
- Improving customer order fill rate and satisfaction

On its own, VSM allows an enterprise to view the material and information flows of a specific product or product family. According to Rother and Shook, value stream maps identify what is happening to a product family as it travels through the production line (1999). This may seem simplistic. However, delving into a step-by-step visualization of the MRO operation and identifying wasteful processes can only lead to improvements that will allow an enterprise to meet its business goals cheaply and more efficiently.

4.2.9 Cellular Manufacturing

Cellular manufacturing got its seeds from the pioneering work by S. P. Mitrafanov on group technology (see Black 1991). Research into the application of group technology for manufacturing first began during the late 1950s. Around this time, researchers began to recognize that some parts share common manufacturing approaches. They soon concluded that parts with common manufacturing attributes could be grouped together and processed in a manner similar to mass production. Using this theory, they would create groups of similar parts and then dedicate groups of machines and tools specific to the production of these parts to reduce setup times. Group technology is the management philosophy that believes similar activities should be grouped and performed with similar methods. The activities include product design, process planning, fabrication, assembly, and production control. Apart from this, group technology can be applied to administrative functions as well.

It was Burbidge (1975) who was responsible for initiating widespread interest in cellular manufacturing through his production flow analysis approach. *Cellular manufacturing* (CM) as a system for production refers not only to the layout of the machines or work stations, but also to the flow of the product. A cell is an organizational unit designed to exploit similarities in how a company processes information, makes products, and serves customers. Cells closely locate people and equipment required for processing families of like products. Component parts and subassemblies may previously have traveled great distances to all the equipment and labor needed for their fabrication and assembly. And items with very different manufacturing requirements and market characteristics may have shared the same equipment and the same workforces. After reorganizing into cells, companies produce families of similar parts together within the physical confines of cells that house most or all of the required workers and equipment. This product-focused arrangement facilitates the rapid flow and efficient processing of material and information. Cell operators can be cross-trained on several tasks, engage in job rotation, and assume responsibility for jobs that previously belonged to supervisors and support staff. Local control fosters employee involvement and creates a platform for improvement (Hyer and Wemmerlöv 1989).

Figures 4.6 and 4.7 contrast traditional functional layouts with cellular operations. The example is from an "organic" military MRO depot.[3] In the functional configuration (fig. 4.6), departmental organization is by function (or process). Because each system that needs repair requires all (or most) processes, it travels to every department. In each department, it sits in a queue waiting for processing. Nine process steps require nine queues and nine waits, for example. Travel distances are long, communications difficult, and coordination messy. In the cellular layout (fig. 4.7), equipment and workstations are arranged in a sequence that supports a smooth flow of materials and components through the process, with minimal transport or delay.

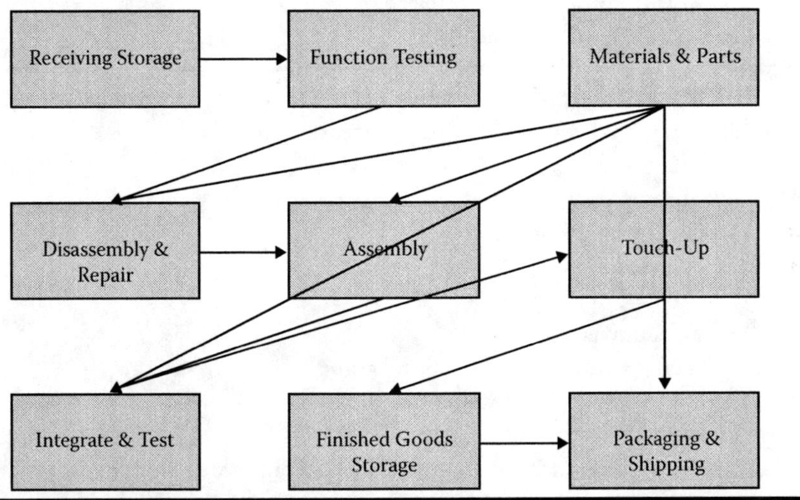

Figure 4.6 A Traditional Functional Plant Layout.

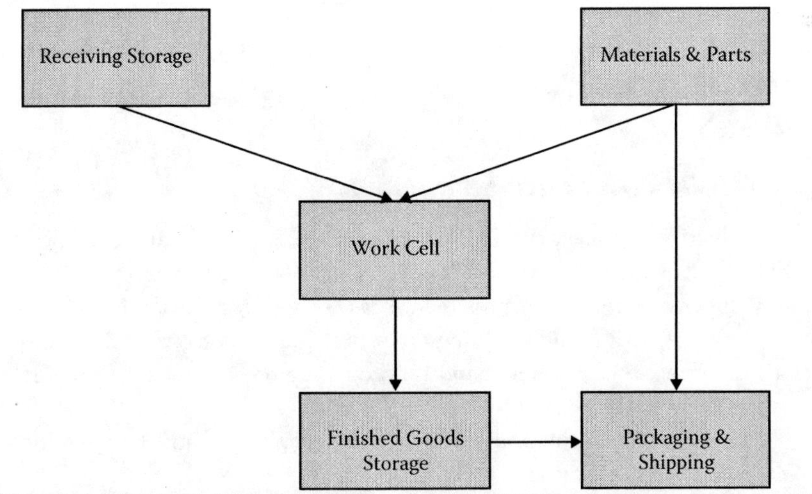

Figure 4.7 A Cellular Plant Layout.

Table 4.3 The Benefits of Cellular Manufacturing Layouts

Metric	*Traditional Layout*	*Cellular Layout*
Travel Distance	100′–1000′	10′–100′
Throughput	30 per year	60 per year
Quality (No Defects)	70% first test pass rate	85% first test pass rate
Turnaround Time (Days)	97	45
Equipment Utilization	75%–100%	60%–90%
Customer Wait Time	Weeks	Days

Benefits associated with cellular manufacturing include:

- Work-in-progress reduction
- Better utilization of space
- Lead-time reduction
- Productivity improvement
- Quality improvement
- Enhanced teamwork and communication
- Enhanced flexibility and visibility

Table 4.3 compares functional and cellular layouts along thirteen key metrics, and demonstretes typical improvements that are possible with cellular design. Cells negate many of the tradeoffs of conventional manufacturing approaches.

Despite these proven benefits, and despite over three decades of research in the area of cellular design, researchers have reported that much such research is not being used in practice (Marsh, Shafer, and Meredith 1999; Wemmerlöv and Hyer 1989; Wemmerlöv and Johnson 1997).

4.2.10 Total Productive Maintenance

Total Productive Maintenance (TPM) is a maintenance-program concept. TPM resembles total quality management (TQM) in that (1) total commitment to the program by upper level management is required; (2) employees must be empowered to initiate corrective action; and (3) a long-range outlook must be accepted as TPM may take a year or more to implement and is an ongoing process. Changes in employee mind-set toward job responsibilities must take place as well (Roberts 1997).

TPM aims to establish good maintenance practice through the pursuit of the five goals of TPM (Nakajima (1988):[4]

1. *Improve equipment effectiveness.* Examine the effectiveness of facilities by identifying and examining all losses that occur: downtime losses, speed losses, and defect losses.

2. *Achieve autonomous maintenance.* Allow the workers who operate the equipment to take responsibility for at least some of the maintenance tasks. This can be at the repair level (where staff carry out instructions as a response to a problem), the prevention level (where staff take proactive action to prevent foreseen problems), and the improvement level (where staff not only take corrective action but also propose improvements to prevent recurrence).
3. *Plan maintenance.* Have a systematic approach to all maintenance activities. This involves the identification of the nature and level of preventive maintenance required for each piece of equipment, the creation of standards for condition-based maintenance, and the setting of respective responsibilities for operating and maintenance staff. The respective roles of operating staff and maintenance staff are seen as distinct. Maintenance staff are seen as developing preventive actions and general breakdown services, whereas operating staff take on the "ownership" of the facilities and their general care. Maintenance staff typically move to a more facilitating and supporting role in which they are responsible for the training of operators, problem diagnosis, and devising and assessing maintenance practice.
4. *Train all staff in relevant maintenance skills.* The defined responsibilities of operating staff and maintenance staff require that each have all the necessary skills to carry out these roles. TPM places a heavy emphasis on appropriate and continuous training.
5. *Achieve equipment management early on.* The aim is to move toward zero maintenance through maintenance prevention, which involves considering causes of failure and the maintainability of equipment throught its design, manufacture, installation, and commissioning stages. As part of the overall process, TPM attempts to track all potential maintenance problems back to their root causes so that they can be eliminated at the earliest point in the overall design, manufacture, and deployment process.

To begin applying TPM concepts, the entire workforce must first be convinced that upper-level management is committed to the program. It is the responsibility of the coordinator to sell the TPM concepts to the workforce through an educational program. Then, the study and action teams are formed. These teams are usually made up of people who directly have an impact on the problem being addressed. Operators, maintenance personnel, shift supervisors, schedulers, and upper management might all be included on a team. Each person becomes a stakeholder in the process and is encouraged to do his or her best to contribute to the success of the team effort. The action teams are charged with the responsibility of pinpointing problem areas, detailing a course of corrective action, and initiating the corrective processes. In well-run TPM programs, team members often benchmark cooperating plants to observe and compare TPM methods and techniques and to observe work in progress. The teams are encouraged to start on small problems and keep meticulous records of their progress. Once the teams are familiar with the

TPM process and have experienced success with small problems, problems of ever-increasing importance and complexity can be addressed (Roberts 1997).

4.2.11 The Theory of Constraints

The theory of constraints (TOC) is a set of management principles developed by Goldratt (1990) that recognizes that organizations exist to achieve a goal. The TOC philosophy enables the managers of a system to achieve more of the goal that the system is designed to produce. Goldratt and Cox subsequently wrote a novel, *The Goal* (1992), that encourages organizations to think about the philosophy. A factor that limits the ability of an enterprise to achieve more of its goal is consiered a *constraint.*

There are two basic types of constraints: physical constraints and nonphysical constraints. An example of a physical constraint is the physical capacity of a machine; a nonphysical constraint might be the demand for a product or a corporate procedure. The TOC recognizes that the output of any system is limited, or constrained, by its least productive steps. The system would consist of multiple steps in which the output of one step depends on the output of one or more previous steps. In situations when the constraint can be easily identified, a five-step *process of ongoing improvement* provides the approach necessary to deal with the constraint. When the constraint is not as easily identified, the *thinking processes* provide the tools necessary to identify the core problem or core conflict and the approach needed to deal with it effectively. Goldratt uses a chain analogy to help illustrate why this is an effective way to get immediate results. A maintenance, repair, and overhaul enterprise can be thought of as a chain of dependent events that are linked together. The activities that go on in one link are dependent upon the activities that occur in the preceding link. The TOC posits that management needs to find the weak link in the chain, because a chain is only as strong as its weakest link. Thus, an enterprise should focus on chain strength (not link weight) by working to strengthen the weakest link, the constraint.

To manage constraints (rather than be managed by them), Goldratt proposes the five-step process of ongoing improvement, whose steps are:

1. *Identify the system's constraints.* This includes prioritization, so that only the constraints that really limit the system are the ones through which progress is made toward the goal.
2. *Decide how to exploit the system's constraints.* Once one has decided how to manage the constraints within the system, ask about the majority of the resources that are not constraints. The answer is to manage them so that they only provide what is needed to match the output of the constrained resources. Never supply more output than is needed. Doing so moves the enterprise no closer to the goal.

3. *Subordinate everything else to the decision made in step 2.* Because the constraints are keeping the enterprise from moving toward its goal, apply all resources available to assist in breaking them. Constraints are not acts of God; in practically all cases, their limiting impact can be reduced or eliminated.
4. *Elevate the system's constraints.* If one continues to work toward breaking a constraint (also called *elevating a constraint*), at some point the constraint will no longer be a constraint; it will be broken.
5. *Once the constraint is broken, return to step 1.* There will likely be another constraint, somewhere else in the system, that is limiting progress toward the goal.

The TOC provides a theoretical framework and the tools with which to continually identify constraints. There are five *thinking process* tools that allow executives to identify what to change in the organization, what to change it into, and how to implement that change:

1. *The current reality tree*, which captures the experience and intuition of the involved individuals.
2. *The evaporating cloud*, which identifies a solution to the core problem previously identified.
3. *The future reality tree*, which identifies what is missing from the solution.
4. *The prerequisite tree*, which identifies all the intermediate steps that are needed to reach the chosen solution.
5. *The transition tree*, which identifies those actions needed, given the current environment, to achieve the intermediate objectives that were identified earlier with the prerequisite tree.

In *The Goal* (1992), Goldratt and Cox also introduce the terms *drum–buffer–rope* and *buffer management*, the latter of which is an approach to managing production through constraints. The drum is the constraint; it is linked to market demand, which is the drumbeat for the entire plant. The buffer is the time/inventory that ensures that the constraint is protected from disturbances occurring in the system. The rope is the material released, which is "tied" to the rate of the constraint. The drum, buffer, and rope provide the basis for building a production schedule that is highly immune to disruption, avoids creating excess inventory, and uses small batches to minimize overall lead time.

The TOC must be reapplied, perhaps many times. It is very important not to let inertia become a constraint. Most constraints in an organization are of their own making. They are the entrenched rules, policies, and procedures that have developed over time. Many times, when a constraint is broken, organizations do not go back and review and change the rules and policies that initially caused the constraint. Most constraints in organizations today are policy constraints rather than physical constraints (Goldratt 1990).

The TOC defines three operational metrics that measure whether operations are working toward the goal: throughput, inventory, and operating expense. Given the measurements as described, employees can make local decisions by examining the effect of those decisions on the organization's overall throughput, inventory, and operating expense. A decision that results in increasing overall throughput, decreasing the overall inventory, or decreasing the overall operating expense for the enterprise will generally be a good decision for the business (Goldratt 1990).

4.2.12 Flexible Sustainment

Recent reductions in DoD resources have prompted the need for innovative acquisition and sustainment improvements. As a result, the secretary of defense has called for a simplified and flexible management framework for translating mission needs into stable, affordable, and well-managed acquisition programs. Flexible sustainment (FS) is the result (Joint Logistics Commanders 1997).

FS is intended to provide program managers in the military with assistance in implementing acquisition reform. The *Flexible Sustainment Guide* (Joint Logistics Commanders 1997) offers new and innovative ways to proceed with DoD acquisition and sustainment processes and contains useful ideas to help accomplish this objective. The material and concepts contained in the guide are included in the DoD Acquisition, Technology and Logistics Knowledge Sharing System (AKSS) website. FS is a process that encourages the program manager to use performance-based specifications and to develop innovative, cost-effective, life-cycle solutions. The guide was developed as a result of the Joint Aeronautical Commanders Group's action to implement performance-based business environment initiatives, and to address the many acquisition-reform initiatives. Innovative approaches to support of legacy systems, and the integration of logistics support concepts into the acquisition process for new weapons platforms, can be used to produce life-cycle savings, reduce cycle times, and improve performance. In essence, innovative logistics support can become an enabler for force modernization and aviation system readiness.

As the DoD's role continues to shift from that of being a technology producer to that of being a technology consumer, program managers are likely to rely more on commercial products to meet users' requirements. This requires the program managers to ensure the application of a rigorous system-engineering process that incorporates open systems concepts and principles. Supportability analyses, including comparison of commercial and organic cost-effective capability, should be conducted as an integral part of the systems-engineering process. It ensures delivery of systems that more readily accommodate commercial products whose design is not controlled by the DoD and whose lifetimes are much shorter and more volatile than the systems they support. This effort needs to begin at program initiation and continue throughout program development (design for support).

FS introduces two processes. The first is a reliability-based logistics (RBL), which suggests that increasing the inherent reliability of a system can result in significant reduction of the maintenance support structure. RBL is intended to assist the program managers in developing the best "design for support" solution. The second is trigger-based asset management (TBAM), which recommends assessment of fielded systems trends and a reexamination of the maintenance plan when "triggers" (such as changes in reliability or maintainability trends, a change in technology, or diminishing resources) are detected. TBAM is a cost-effective tool that enables a team to "support the design."

In addition to RBL and TBAM, other innovative support solutions, such as procurement of form-fit-function-interface spares, performance warranties, and obsolescence assessment are presented as cost-effective support alternatives.

DoD senior management has directed program managers to explore reasonably modifying performance requirements to facilitate the use of open standards and to develop standards-based architectures in designing systems. The guidance establishes the open systems approach as one of the best practices for avoiding imposing unique requirements, and it clarifies the use of open systems as an essential element of a program's acquisition strategy and a means to foster competition.[5] The guidance also stipulates that commercial and nondevelopmental items have open interfaces to the maximum extent affordable based on life-cycle considerations. Through the use of open systems concepts, the DoD can

- Reduce the life cycle costs of systems
- Maintain affordable superior combat capability
- Upgrade systems using new technology with less complexity and in shorter cycles
- Be resilient to changes in technology throughout the life of systems
- Mitigate obsolescence problems caused by current technology's shortened life cycles

4.2.13 Conclusions on the Continuous Process Improvement Initiatives

Any or all of the continuous process improvement (CPI) approaches described herein will improve performance depending on whether or not they are implemented comprehensively and correctly, and whether or not the focus is on performance of the entire enterprise, not just a local cell or business unit. The choice depends on the organization's nature, resources, and problems (McNamara 1999). One or more of the approaches can be combined. For example, cellular manufacturing can be combined with lean production to design the most optimal MRO cell possible.

Basically, the objective is to establish a baseline or current state and then develop a "to be" future state as part of the process improvement. The different methods are used to achieve the future state depending on the approach that is selected. Lean production can be interpreted as the basic framework in which any of these continuous process improvement strategies are implemented. CPI techniques are really the tools that can be used in enterprise transformation; they focus on enterprise processes and are usually constrained by existing legacy systems or other enterprise process interfaces. Typically, CPI suboptimizes selected processes due to the serial step approach used for implementation. These techniques also require significant workforce training and involvement in designing and implementing transformation activities. Process knowledge and expertise reside with the process owners who capture "low-hanging fruit" and then continuously strive to improve quality. These approaches typically have a mixed success rate, perhaps as low as 30 percent, due to the longevity and organizational change resistance inherent within these types of change initiatives.

Total quality management (TQM) and business process redesign/reengineering (BPR) are two different approaches to improving customer satisfaction. At the same time, both of them are aimed at the betterment of the competitive position of an enterprise by way of improving the value provided to the customers. Thus, they both could be described as leading the enterprise on a path toward leanness. Lean production still remains a superset of both because of the additional concepts of value creation/specification and its pull on the part of customers (Uzair 2001).

Six Sigma, quick response manufacturing (QRM), and variance reduction could be implemented either using the TQM approach or the BPR approach. What makes these programs specialties of TQM or BPR is their definition of a target metric for performance improvement. Six Sigma is TQM in its entirety, except that it has a statistical quantitative focus on reducing the number of defects. Similarly, QRM has a focus on the time parameter, and variance reduction on variability in processes. They are all siblings in a sense that they all define a primary metric and yet claim that focusing on that metric will automatically lead to improvement in all other performance metrics, thus leading to improved profitability and market share by way of improved customer satisfaction. Being specialties of TQM or BPR, they still fall under the framework of lean production (Uzair 1991).

Six Sigma, QRM, and variance reduction all address waste reduction from the enterprise perspective in one way or another. To Six Sigma, non-value-added operations indirectly lead to customer dissatisfaction; therefore, these non-value-added operations are defects. QRM proposes elimination of non-value-added chunks of time and inventory. Variance reduction also addresses the elimination of non-value-added chunks of time and inventory. None of them, however, address value creation or its pull (though QRM does have the "pull" concept). Hence, all three still fall under the lean framework.

Lean thinking has been implemented in many industries. Freudenberg-NOK, an automotive supplier and manufacturer of sealing, vibration control, and customer-molded components for various products, started implementing lean procedures in 1992. Since then, they have doubled labor productivity, increased factory floor space utilization by 200 percent, doubled inventory turns, improved margin rates by 14 percent, and reduced rejection rates by 96 percent. President and chief executive officer of Freudenberg-NOK, Joseph Day, attributes these improvements to the lean approach because first, there is greater employee involvement—which heightens awareness, creates a sense of ownership, and cultivates more creative contributions from the people who are closest to the product and the process; and second, profit margins are improved—which enables suppliers to invest more money in new technology, innovation, and research and development. In addition, products are more predictable and robust—which can lead to reduction, avoidance, and—ultimately—elimination of reworking costs (Day 2002).

Value-stream mapping (VSM) and its subsequent analysis is a process that takes effort and time to implement. Starting VSM with a few product groups in a single facility is the easiest way to gain practice and acceptance of the lean approach. When VSM is combined with other ideas and theories of lean thinking, the improvements and savings can be significant. However, it is not a process that can be undertaken once; rather, it is an evolving process that targets and eliminates waste from every product's MRO process. Beginning the process in one facility will ensure understanding of the process while gaining valuable experience in creating value-stream maps. Eventually, the process can be expanded to include processes in other facilities and organizations, which can only assist in making the MRO process much leaner.

Agility, on the other hand, seems to be on the other side of the picture painted by lean production. Whereas lean production gives a recipe for remaining ahead of competitors under the prevailing global and highly competitive environment, agility tells how to remain competitive if this environment starts changing. Lean production cannot be called a part of agility, because agility has no guiding principles for any particular static environment. Similarly, agility is not a part of lean production because lean production does not have a solution for a situation where everything (including the competitive environment) starts changing unexpectedly. Just as both a "head" and a "tail" are needed to make a coin, agility and leanness are both essential for survival and for remaining ahead of competitors. Just as the head and the tail share the same structure and material of the coin, agility and lean share a basic objective, yet they are different and complimentary in their concepts (Uzair 2001). Agility is the ability of an organization to respond well to unexpected change, and also the potential to leverage that ability as a competitive strategy. Agility is more of a conceptual enterprise attribute, one that can be incorporated into any production-system design methodology as a user requirement.

Cellular manufacturing (CM) is a production system that lays out machines or stations so that products flow through multiple cells. CM closely locates the workers and the equipment required for processing families of like products; thus, it is a type of production system. CM production systems are enablers of lean systems, and they are a key component in many production design methodologies.

4.3 Case Studies

4.3.1 A Case Study on Process Improvement Initiatives in the U.S. Air Force

All of the U.S. military branches have recently initiated process improvement. Most projects are aimed at improving operations and efficiencies at all levels in the organization. Many are created and developed with a specific target in mind, such as component repair. Within the Air Force, for example, there are projects driven out from the air staff, Air Force Materiel Command (AFMC), the air logistics centers (ALCs), specific ALC wings/business areas, as well as workers on the shop floor. Although all have creative solutions and ideas, issues do arise when enterprisewide integration is not factored into these well-intentioned projects. These issues can include:

Potential conflicts: for example, depot MRO developing a capacity to repatriate workload, while partnering or commodities councils contract out workloads.

Opposing initiatives: one program doing the exact opposite of another.

Duplication: essentially accomplishing the same tasks under different names or by direction of different agencies; for example, the AFMC's Lean Deployment Plan and an ALC's MRO transformation.

Wasted resources: completing one transformation, only to have it changed by another; for example, a component-repair process-improvement initiative at an ALC, and then an entire MRO transformation initiative at the same ALC.

In spite of such issues, process improvement projects are well worth the undertaking, and lessons can be learned from what others are trying to accomplish. With that intention in mind, table 4.4 provides an outline of several of the known Air Force transformation programs/projects. The hope is that others can benefit and learn from these experiences.

4.3.2 Value-Stream Mapping Case Studies

Two high-level value-stream maps are presented; one is a commercial avionics repair example, the other a military avionics repair example. The first maps the repair process in Boeing's avionics repair depot in Irving, Texas; the second maps the repair process of an Air Force F-15 heads-up display at Warner Robins ALC in Georgia. These value-stream maps were created using notation consistent with Rother and Shook (1999) and lean depot repair activities within the U.S. Air Force (see table 4.5).

4.3.2.1 Commercial Avionics High-Level Value-Stream Map

This section describes a commercial avionics repair value-stream map, which is shown in figure 4.8. The map was developed during two site visits to the Boeing Electronics Service Center in Irving, Texas. The map's creation was an iterative process between the authors and Boeing (Chase and Mathaisel 2001).

Currently, Boeing has an average total turn time of 14 days, including those repairs that are awaiting parts. Boeing's goal is to reach an average turn time of ten days. When items are received at Boeing, they are immediately put into the repair system. On average, Boeing receives approximately 25 to 30 avionics boxes a day for repair. On the day the boxes are received, they are moved from the shipping/receiving dock to the service center floor to begin repair. The actual movement from the dock to floor occurs approximately three times per day, based on the number of boxes in need of repair. "Aircraft on ground" boxes go through a slightly different process because they are earmarked as higher priority. However, this value-stream map was created based on an average box requiring repair.

Once the part has been physically moved to the incoming repair bins, the administrative staffer receives the initial paperwork from receiving and enters the necessary information into BaanERP, an enterprise resource planning (ERP) application. This person is also responsible for routing each package to a specific cell for repair. The entire process takes, at most, one day. While the administrative tasks are in process, the box itself sits in the incoming bins. Once the paperwork is complete, the box and the paperwork are reunited so that the repair process can begin.

The technician gives the box and paperwork a preliminary review, which takes approximately 30 minutes. He records any visual differences or defects on the box and ensures that the paperwork is correct. The next step is to obtain the required equipment and documentation to repair the box. The time to obtain the equipment and documentation varies depending on the technician's knowledge and the previous documentation, but on average it takes approximately 30 minutes.

At this point, the technician begins the initial round of testing and troubleshooting. If a failure is found, technicians "test down" to the component level to isolate the problem. On average, this step takes between one and six hours. Twenty-five to thirty percent of boxes sent to the repair facility are no-fault found and are sent back to the customer as is.

Assuming that there is a problem with the box, piece parts are obtained from Boeing's inventory. Current inventory levels are viewed using BaanERP. Once the order is placed, it takes between 5 and 15 minutes for the material handler to bring the ordered parts to the technician.

Approximately 10 percent of the time, "stockout" conditions exist for piece parts, meaning that the parts may be out of stock. Boeing avoids a larger percentage of stockouts by implementing last-time buys when vendors either go out of business or decide to stop making a part. If a stockout occurs, the box's paperwork is sent to the administrative staff and within one to three days the applicable

Table 4.4 Process Improvement Initiatives in the U.S. Air Force

Initiatives	*Description and Analysis*
1. Forcewide Initiatives	
1.1. Air Force Continuous Process Improvement	The Air Force continuous process improvement initiative uses industry-proven lean practices to continuously and systematically identify and eliminate waste. It involves the workforce in continuous improvement and effects a change in thinking throughout the Air Force to understand the value it delivers and to see and eliminate inefficiencies that do not contribute to that value. Process improvement methods used in the Air Force must have permanence, must be driven by leadership, must involve the entire workforce, and must make sense to all. These improvement methods focus on • methods to see and eliminate waste in any process • doing business with work tied to performance outcomes and war-fighter demand at lowest cost and highest quality • institutionalizing a way of thinking across the workforce to continuously improve the war-winning capability Phase 1 takes place in the first and second years of the initiative. It imposes, pushes, and manages early process improvement initiatives. It operates at a tactical level; looks at single activities (often narrow in scope); devotes activity to randomly selected areas; stages high-visibility events; is relatively easy to accomplish; has activity measures (e.g., number of events accomplished each month per percentage of organization's personnel devoted to core teams); and—most important—involves an early enterprise value-stream assessment by senior leaders in the organization to understand key business processes and value produced by the organization. Phase 2 should initiate around the second to third year of process improvement implementation and extend to approximately the fifth year. It is enterprise-focused, with a broad scope of implementation; is structured; is based on facts and priorities; follows an extended/enterprise VSM and analysis to achieve a future state; is integrated; measures performance or output; and has an established executive council type construct (e.g., a command- or wing-level executive council) for governance over process improvement activities.

	Phase 3 can initiate as early as the fourth or fifth year. This phase focuses on the evolution of the culture and is marked by extending process improvement efforts beyond the enterprise boundaries in pursuit of improvements with strategic partners within a given value chain. This phase is marked by having established process-improvement methods within the organization; having high-performance work teams; having real-time actions with actionable data available at all levels; having 90% of an organization at process-improvement maturity level 4 on a spider diagram/assessment; and includes Air Force self-sustaining process-improvement practices and principles.
1.2. Lean Process Engineering in the Operational Support Modernization Program	In 2004, the secretary and the chief of staff of the Air Force initiated the Operational Support Modernization Program to transform how the Air Force provides mission support or operational support. Because the Air Force had already achieved considerable success with the lean method of process reengineering in other areas, lean production was selected to reengineer critical operational support (OS) processes and to significantly improve OS effectiveness. Two lean engineering projects have been recently initiated: Air Force Deployment Management, and Operational Support Command and Control. The Air Force's ability to execute its mission is directly related to the availability of weapons systems (WS) spare parts. The Air Force possesses the most advanced forces in the world, but underfunding and a decline in supply support have led to a significant drop in readiness. To rectify this potential hazard, the Air Force is in the process of implementing a major redesign of the spares supply process through a set of initiatives designed to improve support to the war fighter. These initiatives, known as the Spares Campaign, promise a fundamental reshaping of the internal management processes and data systems used on a daily basis to buy, repair, and distribute the thousands of different items needed to maintain WS in a mission-capable (MC) status. This effort is being spearheaded by the Office of Supply Chain Integration and Logistics Transformation and an implementation team, consisting of civilian and career military personnel with logistical and supply expertise and defense contractors with experience in supply-chain management. The Spares Campaign initiatives are the result of four months of intensive review and analysis by five teams representing expertise from every level of the major commands (MAJCOM), air staff, air logistics centers, the Defense Logistics Agency, and commercial technical experts and consultants. The focus is

(continued)

Table 4.4 Process Improvement Initiatives in the U.S. Air Force (continued)

Initiatives	*Description and Analysis*
	on increasing WS availability and MC sorties and ensuring spares support in the expeditionary aerospace force (EAF) operating environment. The teams analyzed the strategic processes to identify disconnects, deficiencies, and areas for improvement. The events resulting from this review and analysis are: • 47 process disconnects were identified and then organized into 12 major categories • 190 implementation options were developed and considered to fix these disconnects; ultimately, 86 were deemed viable and considered for implementation. • these implementation options were aggregated into 20 initiatives. A red team made up of eight senior Air Force logisticians reviewed the work done by the five teams. • these 20 initiatives were then presented to the MAJCOM logistics commanders, who provided comments and ranked the initiatives. Given the MAJCOM logistics commanders' priorities, the impact of the program, and the time needed to implement them, the initiative selected eight objectives for immediate action. These eight objectives provide for a full spares process-improvement campaign. The eight objectives are: • Restructure defense logistics requirements by setting stable prices and allocating costs to the responsible commands. • Improve spares budgeting by establishing a single consolidated budgeting process for spares and consumable items, thereby meeting all spares requirements. • Improve financial management by tracking execution of WS support against approved requirements and budget. Simply put, determine whether the Air Force is getting an MC rate equivalent to the amount it is spending. • Improve item demand and repair-workload forecasting. This initiative calls for improved methods for calculating the type and time frame of maintenance needs for the future—that is, commercial technologies like advanced planning and scheduling systems. • Establish a virtual single inventory control point to centrally prioritize spares and funds allocation, passing the execution phase down to the air logistics centers (ALCs).

- Align supply-chain management to focus more on WS and MC rate goals.
- Standardize and expand the role of regional supply squadrons to support expeditionary operations.
- Adopt improved purchasing and supply management practices, thereby reducing purchasing costs and improving product quality and delivery.

Any one of these objectives taken by itself will not make a tremendous impact. But together, they will overhaul the entire spares process by getting spares into the hands of the maintainers and enabling the Air Force to improve WS support to meet current and future expeditionary requirements. The implementation of these eight objectives is the cornerstone in reshaping Air Force supply in the context of the EAF and readying the sustainment of them in the field.

1.3 Weapons System Supply-Chain Manager

A concept from the Air Force Spares Campaign initiative Align Supply Chain Management Focus, it

- includes a proactive identification of "weak links"
- is predictive, knowledgeable, and connected to suppliers and customers
- is a transformational approach
- ensures that supply-chain changes improve weapons systems availability
- utilizes balanced supply-chain management actions focused on WS
- utilizes dynamic adjustments of supply-chain actions to achieve effective WS support
- utilizes state-of-the-art business practices

WS supply-chain management actions

- are dual-facing, representing supply-chain issues to both the system program director and the war fighter
- negotiate WS requirements with the support community
- provide a central point for collecting, analyzing, and surfacing information that affects weapons systems availability (WSA)
- manage risk and mitigate constraints and risk factors
- develop and support robust, lean supply chains
- provide financial and process visibility

WS supply-chain management

- is value-added

(continued)

Table 4.4 Process Improvement Initiatives in the U.S. Air Force (continued)

Initiatives	*Description and Analysis*
	• allows for greater WSA • brings fewer surprises • allows earlier coordinated response to threats • allows accurate portrayal of supply factors impacting WSA • significantly reduces "firefighting" (solving individual problems)
1.4. The DLR Pricing Structure	This initiative sets stable prices and manages costs. One of the initiatives of the Spares Campaign is to change the depot-level repair pricing structure. Comprises: • direct allocable cost recovery: expenses can be directly linked to a specific supply-chain manager • business overhead cost recovery: expenses are not directly related to a specific supply-chain manager, both at ALC or headquarters levels.
1.5. The Demand Reduction Initiative	This project is intended to increase the reliability of parts, decrease repairs needed, reduce repair cost, reduce mission capability (MICAP) hours, and streamline item replacement.
1.6. The Regional Supply Squadron	This project is intended to extend centralized supply forcewide and expand responsibilities. Involves moving base supply functions—such as stock control, MICAP, war readiness supply package, and equipment management functions—to regional centers for MAJCOMs. This reduces the number of supply personnel required at each wing. The only functions left are warehousing and pickup and delivery functions that have been merged with the transportation squadron.
1.7. Spares Forecasting	This project is intended to develop an integrated model for forecasting and budgeting spares requirements.
1.8. Financial Management	This project is intended to track execution of WS support according to approved plan and budget.
1.9. Strategic Sourcing	This project is a strategic center-led approach to purchasing that utilizes a commodity-focused strategy and sourcing perspective with robust governance. Includes leveraged spending, performance, and total supply-chain costs, performance-based contracts/catalogs, and decentralized ordering.

1.10. Demand and Repair Workload Forecasting	This project is intended to improve demand forecasts and enhance workload planning.
1.11. Corporate Contracts	This project contains revised definitions: • Corporate contracts include prepriced and prenegotiated three- to ten-year contracts that allow decentralized ordering of spares, repairs, or both. • Long-term supplier contracts consolidate multiple requirements with major suppliers, are prepriced, and generate multiple buy actions against single contracts. Corporate-like contracts include technology task order engineering services, contract field team, and contractor logistics supply engineering services. Successes include pipeline reduction, cost avoidance, and contractor advanced release. Challenges include valid baseline: reduce total ownership cost, cost benefit analysis Focuses on projected requirements: comp data, commercial item definitions: • "of a type": command-wide interpretation • senior management buy-in: government and contractor
1.12. Logistics Enterprise Architecture	Logistics Enterprise Architecture (LogEA) is an in-depth focus on logistics functions within the Air Force enterprise. The architecture and governance provide for use of portfolio management, data strategy, and balanced score cards. LogEA's focus is on product support and engineering. Key elements are total life-cycle system management, condition-based maintenance, serial number tracking, demand management, operations safety suitability, and effectiveness tools/management. Portfolio management centers on supply-chain management, which includes future supply systems, advance planning systems, purchasing supply-chain management, strategic sourcing, commodity councils, supplier management tools, strategic distribution, bill of materials, and WS supply-chain management. Expeditionary operations and command and control includes agile combat support, a closed loop, a supply-chain common operating picture/enterprise single system, and decision tools. The maintenance focus is on field maintenance and regional maintenance, reengineering depot maintenance, depot shop improvement, and lean maintenance.

(continued)

Table 4.4 Process Improvement Initiatives in the U.S. Air Force (continued)

Initiatives	*Description and Analysis*
	Major thrusts include: • total life-cycle systems management and performance-based logistics • depot partnering • condition-based maintenance, plus end-to-end distribution • executive agents • enterprise integration
1.13. Supply-Chain Operations Reference Experiences	This initiative provides a common framework for communication within the Air Force and with partners (e.g, Office of the Secretary of Defense) and specific supply-chain process redesign. The focus is on a well-structured disciplined process evaluation. It is an excellent framework for comparing common or like practices. Incorporates best practices but needs better integration with lean principles. Commonly available within commercial modeling tools. Best practices are not defined at a uniform level. Is difficult to apply at a strategic level across multiple commodities and without geographic specificity. Not robust enough in return and repair areas for a global repair and return operation, although it is getting better. Not robust enough for a very technical intensive design/redesign product-support environment.
1.14. Cost and Economic Analysis	This initiative is with the Directorate of Economics and Business Management and the Air Force Cost Analysis Agency. It is intended to provide expert cost and economic decision support to the Air Force, the Department of Defense (DoD) and the U.S. Congress, enhancing Air Force capabilities through sound analysis. It is also intended to provide objective cost analyses, estimates, and information to the Air Force, the DoD, and Congress, thereby supporting effective stewardship of national resources. A diverse mix of highly motivated individuals with quantitative skills, experience, and professional certification in business, engineering, mathematics, operations research, and science. Forcewide economic analysis policy and review: Air Force inflation indices, competitive sourcing and privatization, financial support to Air Force services, corporate-level oversight of financial activities, nonappropriated financial analyst policy, training, support finance and audit committees. Activity-based costing policy and training: monitoring financial status of defense industry, economic impact of bases on local community. Economic developments affecting Air Force.

	Supports Defense Acquisition Board and overarching integrated product teams' milestone/program reviews: develops component cost analyses for acquisition category 1D, develops independent cost estimate for acquisition category 1C, leads cost-integrated process teams developing the Air Force service cost position. Supports major automated information system program milestone reviews: develops independent cost estimate. Credible cost and economic analysis requires: qualified analysts, data, objectivity, and realistic technical baseline. Evolutionary acquisition, price-based acquisition, technology advancement. Emphasis on Clinger-Cohen Act certification, evolutionary acquisition with return on investment (ROI) calculations—estimating costs and benefits. Impact of aging aircraft, working capital fund pricing, and contingency operations on depot level repairs. Contractor logistics support visibility. ROI impact of reliability and maintainability investments on operational and support costs. Cost and economic analysis has an important role in the Air Force. Cost and economics is an important consideration in almost every decision. Cost and economic analysis is a growth industry.
1.15. E-Business: Transformational Vision for Information Technology	This initiative is an establishment of a centrally governed enterprise information technology (IT) infrastructure. Access to information: worldwide, robust, real-time, "24/7/365," protected, scalable, assured. Seamless information exchange. Responsible data stewardship. Pursuing an enterprise approach, continuing transformation efforts to increase business and combat efficiencies, Partnering across Air Force to achieve successful IT initiatives. Migrates from base-level to Air Force enterprise services and expands from the non-classified Internet protocol router network to the secret Internet protocol router network. Increases standardization and furthers consolidation: regional, MAJCOM, forcewide. Standards-based, enterprise purchasing (IT Commodity Council). Develops a consistent model for resourcing infrastructure and applications/services. Transforms commodity procurement to enable "e-procurement" at point of need: adapts flexibility to changing conditions and optimizes buying power. Plans to provide an enterprise architecture that defines the Commodity Council's operations and systems, communicates rationale widely to all stakeholders, implements Commodity Council's business rules, and supports their processes with automation and systems.

(continued)

Table 4.4 Process Improvement Initiatives in the U.S. Air Force (continued)

Initiatives	*Description and Analysis*
	Enterprise architecture mission: Establishes clear picture of mission, strategies, and supporting technology across the enterprise; underpins a change-control process over IT projects; enables reuse; reduces duplication of effort; and leverages economies of scale. Promotes information and knowledge sharing and communicates standards and guidance.
1.16. Civilian Processes Become Lean	The initial target to be made lean is the civilian personnel fill process, where the current Air Force standard for a fill action is 100 days. There are three teams working to improve the vacancy fill process for several civilian occupational series. These five- to eight-member teams include members from the work area being studied, customers, and others from outside the area. A key mechanism for implementing the lean process is the "rapid improvement event." The first three weeks are spent creating the teams and confirming targets. At the end of the fourth week the team is expected to have a fully functioning new process. Seven-week program.
1.17. Expeditionary Combat Support System (ECSS)	This enterprise resource planning (ERP) project will replace Air Force retail and wholesale logistics legacy systems with commercially available core ERP packages, and with specific commercial off-the-shelf "bolt-on" solutions. It will involve transforming antiquated current-state logistics business processes into an enterprisewide and network-centered set of future-state business processes. It is based on commercial best practices and standards. Significant business process reengineering, change management, and training. ERP is a set of business process solutions using an integrated relational database system to manage enterprise operations: sales, planning, purchasing, maintenance, inventory control, financials. Attributes: Shares common data and practices across the enterprise. Provides real-time information for decision making and performance measurement. Key enabler of business process reengineering, incorporating best practices. Although the ERP methodology has been around for nearly 30 years, it is only within the last decade that software to integrate the many business processes within a large enterprise has become widely available. The five companies that have developed large-scale ERP software packages are Baan, JD Edwards, Oracle, PeopleSoft, and SAP.

	ERP is called a business process solution because it guides or directs an organization to change its current business processes to the most effective processes. It also goes beyond a single function (like budget allocation); ERP is a multimodule system. It performs all financial operations as well as procurement, maintenance management, and so on. Integrated means that all the business functions interact with each other. If data is entered or modified in one area, it automatically moves through the system and becomes instantly available for other processes. ECSS Program Content: • forcewide supply and asset management capability • forcewide maintenance capability • Air Force distribution network management tools • advanced planning and scheduling tools • product life-cycle management: engineering, configuration, data • customer-relations management and balanced scorecard • e-business/e-procurement for supplies and services • supply/maintenance-related financial management as a minimum • capacity-related human resources • deployment and facilities management
1.18. The Lean Aerospace Initiative (LAI)	In 1993 the Aeronautical Systems Center commander asked the Air Force Manufacturing Directorate, "Can the concepts, principles and practices of the Toyota Production System be applied to the military aircraft industry?" This inquiry formally launched the Lean Aircraft Initiative (LAI) when leaders from the Air Force, labor unions, defense aerospace businesses, and the Massachusetts Institute of Technology forged a trailblazing partnership to transform the industry, reinvigorate the workplace, and reinvest in America using a lean philosophy. Today, LAI is the Lean Aerospace Initiative, combining both aircraft and space systems. The initiative's stated mission is to research, develop, and promulgate practices, tools, and knowledge that enable and accelerate the envisioned transformation of the greater United States aerospace enterprise through people and processes. The LAI accelerates lean deployment through identified best practices, shared communication, common goals, and strategic and implementation tools honed from collaborative experience. It also promotes cooperation at all levels and facets of an

(continued)

Table 4.4 Process Improvement Initiatives in the U.S. Air Force (continued)

Initiatives	*Description and Analysis*
	aerospace enterprise, thus eliminating traditional barriers to improving industry and government teamwork. The greatest benefits are realized when the operating, technical, business, and administrative units of an aerospace enterprise strive for across-the-board lean performance, transforming itself into a totally lean enterprise. As a consequence, LAI is now in the enterprise value phase, engaged in transforming aerospace entities into totally lean enterprises, and delivering more value to all stakeholders than is possible through conventional approaches.
2. Air Logistics Center Transformation Initaitives	
	Air Force depot maintenance transformation (DMT) is taking a lean approach to integrate process improvements on the shop floor with production-support processes. This initiative will transform the depots into a "world class" maintenance, repair, and overhaul (MRO) operation. DMT "Trailblazers" will define and demonstrate improved production processes and provide production support to a lean repair line. Trailblazer teams will take the basic business process framework defined by the DMT team and, through a series of lean events and actual implementation, detail the lean solutions for the Air Force Materiel Command (AFMC). The four Trailblazers are WS-related, involving the three ALCs in sharing ideas and coordinating to define the depot maintenance business processes at the right level to export the best practices to the rest of the depot maintenance community. The four WS product lines at the ALCs that will be used to develop the detailed DMT processes are • the F-15 program depot maintenance line at the Warner Robins ALC in Georgia • the F-100 engine facility at the Oklahoma City, Oklahoma, ALC (OC-ALC) • the F-15 landing gear facility at the Ogden, Utah, ALC (OO-ALC) • the F-15 avionics shop at Warner Robins ALC in Georgia (WR-ALC)
	Lean sustainment is a major pillar in Air Force depot maintenance transformation and is broadening out to other mission areas in the ALCs. Leadership across the ALCs are implementing lean practices well beyond the DMT Trailblazers to deliver improved support to their war-fighter customers and improved ALC performance.

2.1. The Advanced Planning System	The advanced planning system is a sponsored transformation initiative that will provide a suite of tools for optimizing elements across the entire supply-chain network. The goal is to synchronize the entire supply chain to meet actual end-user demand and to enhance the visibility of demand and supply transactions through an integrated, capacity-focused system. Targeted improvements include increased war-fighter collaboration, enterprise WS optimization, increased forecast accuracy, and reduced cycle time and flow days.
2.2. Business Capability Planning for Logistics	Business capability planning for logistics is an AFMC program. It is meant to evolve with a global operational doctrine and concept of operations to improve support and affordability. The constraint of the program is that it must work within current business and IT architecture. The goal is to achieve 20% improvement in aircraft availability at 0% cost. Attributes desired for a future state are • well-led, motivated, skilled people with the right tools to accomplish their assignments • to establish an integrated, enterprisewide, end-to-end focus • to create an organization that is scalable and responsive, for both deployed and in-place capabilities • reliable, time-certain effective support • network-centered operations • simple and effective resource process • a learning culture • to establish a real-time, global expeditionary network requiring no transition from a peacetime state to wartime footing. The business management modernization program/financial management enterprise architecture is a broad look at functions across the DoD enterprise with in-depth focus on financial aspects. The supply management mission area would have as desired business effects the provision and delivery of reparable and consumable items (the right product at the right place and time at the right price). The depot maintenance mission area would have as desired business effects the provision of organic and contract depot repair capability for fielded and emerging WS; ensurance of the ability to rapidly respond to user requirements driven by contingency operations. Air Force Installations and Logistics (AF/IL) portfolio management would focus on a process for instituting system/solution change and a systems baseline supported by the AF/IL Registry.

(continued)

Table 4.4 Process Improvement Initiatives in the U.S. Air Force (continued)

Initiatives	*Description and Analysis*
2.3. Commodity Councils	Commodity councils are cross-functional teams that will develop and execute forcewide commodity-sourcing strategies. In July 2003, senior leadership committed to guiding principles that have driven the implementation of the commodity councils. This commitment was reaffirmed in February 2004. The councils operate under the following principles: • Knowledge of the commodity yields greater sourcing value. • Implementation of cross-functional approaches and skills to leverage existing technical and sourcing expertise. • A commodity-centered focus. • Following a persistent structure of enterprise commodity expertise. • Commodity councils work at an enterprise level. These principles were derived from leading practices in the commercial and public sectors. In essence, this council is an integrated product team (IPT) with no ownership of resources or processes. Purchasing and supply-chain management (PSCM) is transforming how the Air Force plans, contracts, works with suppliers and customers, manages assets, and responds in a more agile manner to the war fighter's material needs. The PSCM transformation will eliminate waste, reduce or streamline processes, and integrate purchasing and supply chain responsibilities. The disconnect at the Oklahoma City ALC (OC-ALC)—with the assumption that this will happen forcewide—is that OC-ALC Maintenance (MX) is the supplier for about 80% of the items managed by OC-ALC Combat Support (CS). Yet there is no discussion or interaction between MX and CS. In trying to establish discussions between MX and CS there are comments like, "We'll figure out what we need then tell you [MX] what you'll do," and, "We want to contract out all the work that has a regular and steady projected requirement. MX will retain the work where low quantity demands come once every year or two." There is a clear disconnect when the MX strategic goal is to increase throughput with decreased flow days and cost per unit so work can be repatriated. Since February 2003, the PSCM team has developed a road map for successful commodity council implementation. This road map includes the development of new AFMC-wide business processes and

	organizational design principles, such as requirements for resources, positions, and training. The road map also includes a "spiral" (iterative) implementation plan. The OC-ALC enterprise approach will have members of the CS community ("loggies" and item managers) and Defense Logistics Agency (DLA) representation to first use accurate requirements projections in designing business units and cells and ensuring material support is at the correct levels to sustain the even flow of work. Such planning cannot be done in a vacuum of only one function. The processes are interrelated and require integration from the very inception of projects.
2.4. Total Component Management	Total component management is a project to build spare-parts kits to be shipped when needed to support specific job control numbers. It will eliminate wasted time on the part of the mechanic, who will no longer have to spend time hunting and gathering parts to accomplish a job. While this plan will increase mechanic "touch time" improving efficiencies, it does not take into account the transformation contractor's approach. The contractor is tasked to build a cell based on a business case analysis/return on investment (BCA/ROI). The contractor's BCA/ROI may look at other options, such as contractor support delivery of spare parts. This may represent wasted resources. This would be a phased-approach starting with engines, aircraft, and commodities. The contractor may not follow this schedule.
2.5. Lean Depot Engine Repair	Lean depot engine repair is a set of projects generated to support lean improvement projects for engine repair at the Oklahoma City Air Logictics Center. Production enhancement technologies would improve effectiveness and efficiency of the center, specifically research and development projects such as engineering studies and prototype equipment. MX is looking for tangible results, clear benefits, and improved war-fighter support. Two projects are • to develop and provide a water jet drill to replace the manual drill process for augmentor parts • to develop and provide water jet strip hardware, which will increase pound per square inch pressure when striping thermal spray coatings The steps are (1) to analyze, engineer the new application, and document handheld laser welding technology and purchase new prototype handheld laser welding equipment; and (2) to analyze, engineer the new application, and document a high-velocity oxygen fuel (HVOF) flame diagnostic tool/process/method with purchase of new prototype HVOF equipment.

(continued)

Table 4.4 Process Improvement Initiatives in the U.S. Air Force (continued)

Initiatives	*Description and Analysis*
2.6. F-100 Cell design	This project involves the development of F-100 cell design, and implementation of the F-100 plan. Risk is conflict with higher headquarters programs like Trailblazer and Elog-21. Lean/cellular redesign of the F-100 MRO provides a holistic/system engineering approach that includes design, modeling, implementation, equipment, and training and totally transforms the F-100 MRO. The benefits include: \$20.8 million direct labor savings (ten years), \$260 million direct material savings, \$61 million reduced production overhead, 60% flow time reduction, 50% production capability increase, \$90 million Working Capital Fund (WCF) cash flow improvement, increased war readiness engines (WREs), reduced MICAPs, parts on shelf.
2.7. General Electric Family Cell Design	This project involves the development of a GE family business unit, cell designs, and implementation of the GE Engine Family Plan. Risk is conflict with higher headquarters programs like Trailblazer and Elog-21. Phase 1 and 2 benefits include: \$9.1 million direct labor savings (ten years), \$232.2 million direct material savings, \$18.8 million reduced production overhead, 69% flow time reduction, 12% production capability increase, \$75 million WCF cash flow improvement, increased WREs, reduced MICAPs, parts on shelf.
2.8. TF-33 Engine Repair	This project involves the development of a business unit plan and cell designs for TF-33 engines. Changes include: parts movement reduced 61%, ownership changes reduced 54%, flow days reduced 34%, material in process reduced 44%. Benefits include: \$8.6 million direct labor savings (ten years), \$111.6 million direct material savings, \$17.7 million reduced production overhead, 54% flow time reduction, 20% production capability increase, \$126.4 million WCF cash flow improvement, increased WREs, reduced MICAPs, parts on shelf.
2.9. The KC-135 Aircraft	This project involves the development of a business unit plan and cell designs for the KC-135 aircraft. Benefits include: flow days reduced from 413 to 207, number of docks reduced from 12 to 9, on-time delivery up 48%.
2.10. Multiskilled/ Multitasking Approach	Purpose: Our workforce has become far too specialized, and this emphasizes the need for a more diversified, multiskilled approach in matching workforce with workload. The goal is to create a more flexible workforce history. Until recently, multiskilled efforts have been focused on trades and crafts

	position in maintenance. Implemented air logistics center airframe rating system (ALCARS) in 2003. Eighty-five positions created in maintenance, blending aircraft mechanics' jobs with sheet metal mechanics' and electricians' positions filled by training and developing existing wage grade employees. Additional 14 jobs combining painters and equipment cleaners have been created outside of the ALCARS initiative. Future Direction: IPT formed with representatives from all four wings. Goal is to develop implementation plan that expands multiskilled approaches to other air expeditionary wing and wage schedules (GS) occupations. Integrate with ongoing lean/transformation initiatives throughout the ALC. Examine possibility of developing multiskilled positions during reorganizations. Apply national security personnel system flexibilities to reward multiskilled employees through new pay-for-performance appraisal system implementation plan.
2.11. Public-Private Partnering	This partnering is a cornerstone to the Air Force Depot Maintenance Master Plan. This public-private partnering initiative involves: • driving new workload and technology insertion • standardizing processes • cooperative versus competitive approaches Partnering is not meant to take jobs away. Its purpose is to utilize the expertise of each party and carefully weigh each party's needs and objectives and achieve a successful support solution, ultimately providing the war fighter a weapon system when he needs it. Partnering is a definite "win/win" opportunity for the parties involved, from the war fighter on down. Partnerships currently in place at OC-ALC: • Pratt & Whitney (P&W): Overarching umbrella engine support. Phase I includes F-100 foreign military sales (FMS) test cell, F-100 eddy current, special technology coating; P&W invested $7.5 million for low observable spray booth). Phase 2 includes: F-119 MRO; P&W invested $13 million for the heavy maintenance center. • Kelly Aviation Center (KAC): Propulsion Business Area F-100-LM: OC-ALC teamed with Lockheed Martin KAC to jointly prepare a bid for a workload split for F-100, TF-39 and T-56 engine support. Contract valued at over $10.1 biilion over the life of the partnership.

(continued)

Table 4.4 Process Improvement Initiatives in the U.S. Air Force (continued)

Initiatives	*Description and Analysis*
	• Boeing: C-17 core requirements agreement: a partnering agreement signed August 2002 includes core workload for: hydraulic, oxygen, instruments, and engine-related items. Strategic alliances in process/under development at OC-ALC: • Honeywell and OC-ALC signed a strategic directorate document in February 2005 to explore partnering opportunities in integrated avionics, engines, aircraft accessories, and systems and service solution workloads. • KAC and OC-ALC signed a memorandum of understanding in February 2005 for the evaluation of OC-ALC performance of KAC workload for the F-110 FMS, F-118, and TF-39 engine programs at OC-ALC facilities. • Standard Aero and OC-ALC signed a memorandum of understanding in September 2004 for the C-130J Engine (AE-2100) to explore the possibilities of moving the AE-2100 repair and overhaul operation to an OC-ALC facility. • General Electric and OC-ALC signed a strategic directorate document in February 2003 to pursue partnering opportunities in material support, work shares, direct sales agreement, and supply-chain management activities.
2.12. B-2 Avionics Test Program Set Upgrade	This initiative is intended to provide an updated method of repair and test for the B-2 avionics components that enhances the ability to complete the repair faster. The project calls for the upgrade of the depot-level test and repair capability of B-2 shop-replaceable units and line-replaceable units by providing test program sets that execute on existing B-2 automatic test equipment (ATE). No ROI has been accomplished at this time. Organic resources will be used to accomplish this project at a cost of $6.5 million using certified protection professional (CPP) funds. Cost of ownership and organic production costs will be reduced substantially, resulting in a lower shop end-item sales price. Additional cost savings result from the termination of interim contractor support ($5 million per year).
2.13. B-52 Maintenance Work Stand Set	This project provided engineering and fabrication of one prototype work stand. The work stand supports one aircraft dock and is capable of being moved and used in any of the Building 2121 aircraft work stations at OC-ALC. The supplier provided the complete, turnkey work stand. Measures of success

	included reduced labor and material costs, work stand repair and maintenance reduced 90%, direct product standard hours (DPSH) reduced by 0.4%, improved health and safety, and reduced flow days.
2.14. OC-ALC Building 3001 Revitalization	This initiative will rebuild the 60-year-old Building 3001 infrastructure and revitalize the building through internal redesign. This will be done with lean shop floor rearrangement. The goal of the lean redesign program is to increase throughput and war readiness levels for all engines, commodities, and aircraft repaired at OC-ALC. This is a ten-phase effort with numerous projects included in each phase. Phases 1 and 2 consist of the F-100, F-110, TF-33, F-101, and F-108 engines and the KC-135 aircraft. No ROI has been done at this time. This 15-year program will use military construction (MILCON) and CPP money. The world class transformation of Building 3001, and its related production operations, is expected to yield an average reduction in process flow times of 25%, accompanied by an average of 50% reduction in work in process (WIP). The average maintenance and operation costs are expected to reduce by 11% over time.
2.15. Flight Control Repair Modernization	This project is to purchase and install in Building 2101 at OC-ALC a programmable six-axis routing/ultrasonic cutter and a phosphoric acid anodizing system for C-135 and E-3 tab repair. Today, heavily damaged assets must be condemned and new parts must be purchased at three times the cost of repairing. The six-axis router and phosphoric acid anodizing system represent a linked equipment purchase that provides the enhanced repair capability needed to support the C-135 and E-3 fleets as well as any future workload requirements such as the F-119 engine and the C-17 aircraft. No ROI has been accomplished. No additional resources are required. This project will take nine or ten months after contract award and should be completed by the first quarter of fiscal year 2007 at a cost of $3.2 million using CPP funds. Success measures include lower cost, greatly improved production capability for both current and future workload repairs, and quicker turnaround times for C-135 and E-3 tabs.
2.16. The Lean Facilitator Contract	This is a contract established between the Marine Aircraft Group and Boeing to establish a robust self-sustaining lean program with organic technical expertise and experience for the 76th Aircraft Maintenance Group. This is a contractor-supported effort, which will provide deliverables such as lean manufacturing assessment tools, value-stream mapping, data repository, specialized training, and rapid improvement event (RIE) facilitator certification. No ROI has been accomplished at this time. No other supporting organizations are required at this time. There are four contractor/facilitators in place. The

(continued)

Table 4.4 Process Improvement Initiatives in the U.S. Air Force (continued)

Initiatives	*Description and Analysis*
	deliverable is for each to facilitate two to four lean events per month. This is duplicative of the maintenance directorate transformation contract. The risk is redundancy or conflict with the final overarching plan and aircraft business-unit plans. It could also be training in a different methodology than the winning contractor and could cause confusion and frustration within the workforce. At the very least, there is potential for wasted resources as areas have changed multiple times. The project will use Depot Maintenance Activity Group (DMAG) dollars and the money will be spent over a three-year period. The project will track flow day decreases, increased capacity, and decreased cost thru MX tier meeting, data repository, and the 76th MX Executive Steering Council.

2.17. The Lean Institute at OC-ALC	This project is intended to provide adequate training to the workforce in order to develop organic capabilities to implement transformation activity. Enterprise program to develop a trained credentialed workforce in lean sustainment, Six Sigma, and supply-chain operations reference (SCOR). We will track the number of students that are trained, and as projects are developed and completed they will be reported to the Depot Maintenance Transformation Board. Provides training on lean sustainment, SCOR, and Six Sigma. Upper-level undergraduate or graduate credit to be awarded for designated classes where appropriate. All course materials, manuals, handouts, and the like will be provided as needed. Educational records will be maintained on all class participants.
	Lean training will be on four distinct levels:
	• employee: 4 hours of training
	• executive: 8 hours of training
	• midlevel manager: 16 hours of training, 1 hour college credit
	• implementer: 80 hours of training, 2 hours college credit
	• SCOR training will be on four distinct levels:
	  • core business team: 4 hours of training
	  • executive: 8 hours of training
	  • evangelist: 16 hours of training, 1 hour college credit
	  • coach: 120 hours of training, up to 9 hours college credit

	Six Sigma training will be on four distinct levels: • executive: 8 hours of training • green belt: 40 hours of training, up to 3 hours college credit • black belt: 80 hours of training, up to 6 hours college credit • master black belt: 120 hours of training, up to 6 hours college credit When initiated, narrow and rigid responsibilities with risk of using training different from selected transformation contractor. Now under same management team. Risk is slight.
2.18. Trailblazer Initiative	HQ AFMC selected the F-100 product line to be the product line made lean by their newly formed Trailblazer teams. The F-100 fan drive turbine shop was the area designated to be made lean at OC-ALC. The cross functional OC-ALC Trailblazer team was formed in March 2004. The team was trained during March and April in Trailblazer lean methodology and value-stream mapping by a team of Altarum consultants. This training concluded with a value stream map of the F-100 fan drive turbine being created. From this value-stream mapping, strategic points for RIEs were noted and an action item plan was developed. To date, five of six RIEs are complete, with personnel training and prework being done for the sixth at this time. The production space on the floor has been reworked and redesigned to meet lean, one-piece flow objectives. Standardization of work, sorting, straightening, shining, standardizing, sustaining, and safety ("5S + 1"), and continuous improvement efforts are ongoing. It was determined that actual flow times could be reduced from 113 days to 15 days by moving key back-shop processes into the same cell as the front shop. This move eliminates waste in the form of travel time, ownership changes, and sleep time between changes. The front-shop production areas have been moved to incorporate this change. New material movement processes through the shop will be implemented with the integration of the front and back shops. Kitting will no longer be needed, and this will eliminate the need for a kitting cage and the software program that deals with it. All administrative and support personnel will be located in a production support facility located right on the production floor in the shop area. This will increase the communication between cognizant entities as well as improve the quality of that communication. In addition, members of the Trailblazer team are utilizing the Trailblazer methodology to facilitate an IPT with OC-ALC PSCM representatives. Also, an initiative is underway to institute a "pull" system through

(continued)

Table 4.4 Process Improvement Initiatives in the U.S. Air Force (continued)

Initiatives	*Description and Analysis*
	the back-shop processes that will benefit all product lines (not just the F-100) by streamlining the flow and by developing and adhering to a takt time.
2.19. The Gearbox Lean Initiative	The gearbox shop is currently a stand-alone maintenance repair center at the OC-ALC for 14 different types, models, and series. It is one of the premiere shops that contain approximately 60% of their special processes, and primarily consists of TF-33, F-100, and GE-series engines. Currently the shop contains approximately 42 personnel and maintains an assembly/disassembly and a machining unit to complete gearbox major and minor overhauls. The core gearbox lean team consists of the following personnel: • facilitator (1) • unit chief (1) • work supervisor (1) • work leader (1) • mechanics (3) • program management team members (3) • scheduler (1) • planner (1) • engineers (3): electrical, mechanical, facilities The purpose of this lean initiative is to reduce asset/operator travel, reduce sleep time, and reduce flow days. In order to implement this lean initiative the team had to decide which asset took the longest lead time to go through the entire system. As a result, we needed to conduct a time study to build a baseline for the other additional assets—namely, the TF-33 and F-100 gearbox types, models, and series. We also determined that the special processes—such as painting, stripping, chromating, and chemical cleaning—were clear indicators that parts were sleeping in between processes. The assets chosen for this time study were part of the GE gearbox housings. The housings primarily consist of the front, main, rear, and fan frame adapter housings.

The main focal points of these project time studies are as follows:

- Currently the gearbox shop takes up approximately 22,892 square feet.
- assembly/disassembly covers 8,609 square feet
- machining covers 14,283 square feet

Gearbox stats are as follows (averaged out due to four separate assets):

- total asset travel: 34 miles
- total number of shops involved: 6
- total number of handoffs: 19

To date, the gearbox team is working to realign the shop to create a smoother process flow. Additionally, they plan to bring in two key processes that will decrease their sleep time significantly. Those two processes are painting and blasting. However, in the future the plan is to bring in additional processes such as chemical cleaning. The team determined that the best course of action for this initiative to take place was to build an implementation plan that will transform the gearbox shop into a more productive repair shop with increased capacity. The plan includes floor painting, new consolidated tool kits, and adding computers to each work station. The plan consists (tentatively) of a seven-phase approach to move the shops out of the area to a predetermined swing space. Next, the engineers will determine which parameters need attention, such as electrical, structural, or equipment, and make necessary adjustments. Afterward, the 5S + 1 team will paint the floor and the shop will move back and be realigned according to the final engineering layout. Currently, the plan is being revised to reduce the current projection completion date of 463 days. This may be done by combining phases to shorten the lead time.

The gearbox lean implementation plan will allow the gearbox shop as a whole to potentially

- reduce sleep time by 80%
- reduce asset travel by 53%
- reduce operator travel by 25%
- reduce tool costs by 73%
- reduce square footage 13%
- increase throughput

(continued)

Table 4.4 Process Improvement Initiatives in the U.S. Air Force (continued)

Initiatives	*Description and Analysis*
2.20. F-108 Air Force/ Navy Processes	Current historical data show that the flow times of the F-108 product line average 186 days. The Navy has raised concerns with flow days to senior levels of the Propulsion Division. The F-108 Air Force engine configuration/variations have a targeted 35 flow days. The CFM56-2A-2 Navy engine configuration/ variations have a targeted 45 flow days. Propulsion Division senior leadership selected this project to improve customer support through a drastic reduction of flow days for both customers with emphasis on the CFM56-2A-2 Navy engine configuration/variations. The CFM56-2A-2 Navy engine configuration/ variations maintain the highest priority for supportability and therefore a reduction of flow days for this program is paramount for national security. This project encompasses multiple divisions and support organizations—the Propulsion Division (MAE), the Commodities Division (MAN), the Maintenance Material Support Division, and the DLA. The project encompasses multiple support organizations within each entity—production, planning, scheduling, and the System Program Office (LP). The MAE project was started on 28 June 2004. Production requirements required a delay in the project, but the project was reinitiated 23 August 2004 and team members are currently online. Planning for the MAE/MAN partnering of the project was started at/between the division level (with Mr. Allen of the MAN and Colonel Diehl of the MAE) on 29 July 2004. The MAN project was actually started on 18 August 2004. Both teams are currently in data-collection mode. In addition to the actual leaning of processes, the MAE is providing its change agent to mentor MAN personnel in developing organic MAN lean change agents' skills and development of organic lean methodologies. MAN value-stream mapping on the concerned products (F-108 fuel nozzles) is in process. The MAN has videotaped the fuel nozzle and is preparing to perform a throughput analysis on the critical paths of the process. Flow days have been averaged at 27. Process has been mapped with approximately 250 minutes of process time. The MAN value-stream mapping on the concerned products (F-108 aft air/oil seals) has not been started. MAE lean team personnel initially mapped and thoroughly documented MAN processes and have and

	are assisting the MAN. MAE lean team personnel are now focusing on mapping MAE long-pole processes to eliminate flow days. The plan is to aggressively attack the ownership changes and sleep time of minor/major modules and parts thereof that contribute to the 186 flow days. Three parts have been initially selected that have been identified as major contributors. Additional parts and modules will be examined and made lean as applicable. Each entity that is to be examined will be challenged to reduce its possession time to five flow days or fewer. Although this may not be realistically achievable in all cases, it is achievable for many portions of this product. The Air Force should see results in three to six months.
2.21. Nonconforming Material Review Board (MRB) Process Improvement Initiative	The purpose of this initiative is to improve inconsistencies and streamline administrative processes within the engine Material Review Board (MRB)/non-conforming material report (NCMR) environment. The broad-scoped product line includes the following: • TF-33 • F-100 • F-108 • F-119 • F-101 • F-118 • F-110-100 • F-110-400 (phasing out) A cross-functional IPT was formed in November 2003 and is being led/facilitated by OC-ALC/MAE-T. Data gathering was initiated and began in December 2003. The method of data collection and action-plan development included process-flow mapping due to the complexity and unique headquarters/AFMC–authorized "engines only" administrative process flow. Process-flow mapping was the first step toward developing value-stream mapping of selected areas. Lean methodologies accompanied by Six Sigma tools (such as supplier–input–process–output–customer diagrams) are being utilized to identify inputs/outputs of the process flow.

(continued)

Table 4.4 Process Improvement Initiatives in the U.S. Air Force (continued)

Initiatives	*Description and Analysis*
	Benefits/gains (to date): • depot maintenance activitation planning accountability being established • communication enhancement/centerwide points of contact established (increased response times) • refinement/rewrite of operational instructions and corrective action requests within the propulsion directorate (in process) • the value of NCMR activity identified: metrics identified and displayed in front of MRB pool work area • continuous improvement and reduction of administrative bottlenecks • prototype of I-POMX system phase 1 completed; phase 2 in process • 5S + 1/continuous improvements in process
2.22. The Front-Shop Assembly and Disassembly Augmenter F-110-100 and F-110-129 Refurbishment Program	The purpose of this project is to prepare for refurbishment of the General Electric F-110-100 and F-110-129 jet engine augmenters, which started in fiscal year 2006. A value-stream map has been conducted. At this time, space has been identified for placement of the refurbishment shop. Making the shop leaner will reflect many of the process-improvement philosophies, such as the theory of constraints, takt-time applications, Six Sigma, lean concepts, value-stream mapping, and other valuable tools. Participation will include shop-floor mechanics, first-line supervisors and higher, union stewards, engineering, industrial engineering technicians, and scheduling. Tangible benefits that will impact aircraft availability include longer time on wing by removing tired iron, which will increase dependability of the engine. Creating a takt-time environment will help managers increase their ability to manage to the minute and be assured of producing two augmenters per day by adjusting workload and efforts to different phases of the refurbishment.
2.23. Augmenter Parts Repair Value-Stream Flow Implementation	This ongoing project has already reduced flow time for the augmenter parts repair process, has increased availability of equipment and personnel, and has reduced sytem work in progress. The project started in February 2004 and included the creation of value-stream maps for many different part-process flows. Having these data available has aided in reducing flow times (e.g., starting early September 2004 the flow time of the GE F-110 outer flap will be reduced from 23 to 8 days).

	Implementation of the GE F-110-100 flame holder and F-110-129 mixing duct are currently ongoing, and flow times are already being reduced.
2.24. Machine Shop Modernization	This project is a four-phased approach to transforming engine machining operations from the current 1950s technology to modern state-of-the-art technology. Phase 1 is for the purchase of seven new pieces of industrial support equipment that is used for precision metal measurement, preparation, and removal on turbine engine components. Phase 2 purchases an additional five computerized numerically controlled machines. This project will cost $3 million in CPP funds spread over five years. Success measures include reduced equipment down time, reduced recyclables, reduced flow times, increased war-ready engines, and reduced maintenance costs.
2.25. The Software Support Facility	This project consolidates software engineering and replaces five separate areas into one 72,000-square-foot facility. The new facility will be specially equipped for computer resource development and maintenance for automatic test equipment and test program sets for jet engine controls, engine testing and trending software, and industrial automation of various overhaul processes supporting 8 WS and 11 different jet engine types. A project return on investment is expected starting in fiscal year 2007. This project will take approximately 24 months to accomplish using MILCON funds of $14.2 million and $0.8 million indirect operating expense for equipment. Success is measured in terms of organic support cost savings due to improved work processes from better work facilities and conditions and a more efficient and economically operated facility.
2.26. The WR-ALC Lean Process Improvement Model	The WR-ALC lean process improvement model has been designed to achieve bottom line results that will affect the war fighter and create capabilities that will support the mission of the Air Force. The model reflects the use of "lean tools" that will expose waste in processes that are targeted for improvements. The cornerstone of the improvement process is the value-stream map/analysis of the process to determine current and future states. Other important tools include RIEs (how processes get changed quickly); strategy alignment and deployment/policy deployment; corrective action/Six Sigma; people, product and process breakthroughs; visual management; sort, straighten, scrub, safety, standardize, and sustain breakthroughs; total productive maintenance; standard work development; standard work deployment; and benchmarking. Each of these tools is part of the overall lean backbone that focuses on continuous process improvement.

(continued)

Table 4.4 Process Improvement Initiatives in the U.S. Air Force (continued)

Initiatives	*Description and Analysis*
	The WR-ALC lean enterprise journey is divided into three phases. Phase I, lasting from one to three years, imposes, pushes, and manages the lean process; operates at a tactical level; looks at single activities, often narrow in scope; devotes activity to randomly selected areas; stages high-visibility events that are relatively easy to accomplish; has activity measures (the number of events accomplished each month/percentage of organization's personnel devoted to core teams); and conducts a lean forum. Phase 2, lasting through the fourth and fifth years, is seen as having an ALC strategic focus; is enterprise based, with broad scope; is structured, based on facts and priorities; follows an extended/enterprise value-stream map/analysis to achieve a future state; is integrated; measures performance or output; and conducts lean sustainment in a business forum- or executive council-type construct. Phase 3, which focuses on the evolution of the culture, spans the sixth and seventh years and is marked by having strategic partnerships; having truly lean organizations; having high performance work teams; having real time actions with actionable data available at all levels; and having 90% of the organization (ALC) at lean maturity level 4 on the spider diagram/assessment.
2.27. WR-ALC Lean Aircraft Component Repair	WR-ALC is the technical repair center for the depot maintenance and support of the C-5, C-130, C-141, and F-15 weapons systems; it also provides maintenance support to the C-17 weapon system. In order to be lean and competitive, its processes are undergoing continual improvement, striving to provide world-class support to the war fighter by reducing production cycle times and improving delivery rate while maintaining the quality of its products. Ensuring it maintains state-of-the-art infrastructure in the form of both facilities and equipment will enable it to increase production flows and enhance the working conditions for our workforce. The WR-ALC transformation strategy is focused on allowing it to "provide combat capabilities for DoD warfighters and our allies through superior acquisition and sustainment.... now and in the future." Its depot strategy and implementation plan is the road map for its transformation efforts. The framework of its strategy is grounded in three distinct areas: aircraft, avionics, and software. This project is in support of the aircraft section of that strategy. That transformation strategy and how it will implement aircraft transformation is as follows:

	• Goals: reduced flow days and improved due date performance for less cost. • How do we get there? Identify and rectify bottlenecks; implement lean initiatives by reducing movement of aircraft and aircraft components; provide inside dock positions for aircraft; create lean backshops; and expand and develop partnerships.
	This project is in direct support of the "lean backshops—aircraft components" portion of the transformation. Specifically, the project will provide for the construction of a facility designed for state-of-the-art sheet metal repair of aircraft components being funded with MILCON dollars. This project continues lean efforts to improve the cellular flow of aircraft components by minimizing transportation and thereby reducing aircraft component flow days. The project provides a centrally located 120,000-square-foot modern efficient facility that consolidates and improves productivity of aircraft component repair functions at WR-ALC. It will provide a facility large enough to accommodate repair of C-5, C-17, C130, F-15, and HS-3 aircraft components and consolidate repair operations closer to the industrial (flight line) area. This project will enhance WR-ALC's ability to support the existing cargo and fighter aircraft core workload. WR-ALC has a core shortfall in cargo aircraft. This initiative will help position the center toward bringing in additional core capability and reducing the cargo aircraft core shortfall.
2.28. WR-ALC Advanced Metal Finishing Facility	This project is in direct support of the "lean backshops—aircraft components" portion of WR-ALC's transformation. Specifically, this project will provide for the construction of a facility designed for state-of-the-art sheet metal repair of aircraft components being funded with MILCON dollars and CPP. It will transform metal plating and treatment, nondestructive inspection, blasting, and shot peening processes into technologically cutting-edge, low-pollution processes. This will be accomplished by building a specialized facility complete with the latest processing technology, waste minimization and recycling equipment, automation, and lean manufacturing concepts. The transformation will dramatically change the processing of parts, resulting in a reduction of the environmental burden and labor requirements while increasing shop capabilities and customer support. The workload supported by the existing plating shop is extensive, including C-5 pivot arms and struts; C-17 tubes and skins; C-130 blades, propeller hubs, pump housings, and fasteners; C-141 bell crank drives, bell cranks, and wing attach fittings; and F-15 canapies, flaps, ailerons, and stabilizers. As such,

(continued)

Table 4.4 Process Improvement Initiatives in the U.S. Air Force (continued)

Initiatives	*Description and Analysis*
	this project will enhance ability to support the existing cargo and fighter aircraft core workload. WR-ALC has a core shortfall of 580,000 DPSHs in cargo aircraft. This initiative will help position the center toward bringing in additional core capability and reducing the cargo aircraft core shortfall.
2.29. WR-ALC Cargo Aircraft Maintenance Transformation	This project will specifically provide for the construction of a depot maintenance hangar funded with MILCON dollars. The hangar will be sized to accommodate midsize aircraft (cargo, tankers, and special-mission aircraft) and will be used to support aircraft maintenance operations for the C-17 and C-130 weapons systems. The facility will be capable of supporting four C-17 aircraft or eight C-130 aircraft work positions with office, support, and utility space for the operations listed above. This project will enhance WR-ALC's ability to support the cargo airframe core workload. The project will transform midsize cargo aircraft maintenance operations to a more efficient and flexible process by consolidating the C-130 depot maintenance workload in a central location and providing additional inside maintenance spots. The project directly supports the war-fighting support capability of the C-17 and C-130 weapons systems. Increasing capacity and flexibility will reduce flow days and improve the efficiency. Decreased flow days equate to more cargo aircraft available in the active fleet to support missions.
2.30. Ogden ALC (OO-ALC) Landing Gear Process Improvement Programs	This project is intended to conduct an initial lean improvement of landing gear, wheels, brakes, and struts, bringing antiquated processes and equipment into a lean, cellular process. Cost: $13 million; 100% executed. Benefits: Investment-to-savings ratio of 2:8. Transformational merit: incorporates lean cell concepts; configured for equipment upgrades; new technology and right-sized equipment. Measures of success: reduced flow days by 30%; reduced rework by 60%; reduced WIP by 51%.
2.31. OO-ALC Aircraft Transformation	This initiative is intended to reconfigure aircraft production docks and facilities and implement lean cell operations. Cost: $16.7 million.

	Transformational merit: integrates processes to minimize non-value-added tasks; initiates cellular flow process; reduces equipment/labor constraints. Benefits: savings-to-investment ratio of 4:2; payback in 3.58 years. Measures of success: reduced aircraft WIP, Common Configuration Implementation Program first success (20 to 11); increased throughput; reduced flow days 25–50%.
2.32. OO-ALC HVOF Transformation	This initiative is intended for the application of a tungsten-carbide cobalt coating that decreases reliance on chrome-plating processes. Cost $3.5 million. Transformational merit: reduces time and manual error; applies harder coating 20 times faster; reduces grinding and reworking. Benefits: savings-to-investment ratio of 7:5; payback in 1.1 years. Measures of success: reduced flow days by 20%; reduced WIP by 20%; improved throughput by 20%; increased quality and mean time between failures (MBTF).
2.33. OO-ALC Open Architecture Digital Test Stand	This project provides developmental test stands for digital test-station improvements, which will enhance organic ATE software sustainment capability. Cost: $4.4 million. Transformational merit: supports new and upcoming WS needs; reduces life-cycle costs; increases flexibility. Benefits: savings-to-investment ratio of 4:2; payback in two years. Measures of success: reduced flow days by 50%; reduced WIP by 33%; MBTF increased by 85%; reduced training time by 96%.
2.34. OO-ALC Shop Replaceable Unit (SRU) Test Stands	This project enhances repair of multiple mission design series (MDS) SRUs. Replaces 14 single-purpose stations; 9 common automated test stations; all capabilities; work routed to any repair cell. Cost: $14.69 million. Transformation merit: combines seven test processes; creates a single cellular work center; multi-MDS support from single tester.
2.35. OO-ALC Coatings Process	This project procures an automated coating and automatic removal system. High-quality application. Suitable to thin skins and composite.

(continued)

Table 4.4 Process Improvement Initiatives in the U.S. Air Force (continued)

Initiatives	*Description and Analysis*
	Cost: $8.83 million. Transformation merit: eliminates manual processes; implements lean cellular configuration; eliminates reworking with manual. Benefits: investment-to-savings ratio: 2:56; payback in six years. Measures of success: reduced flow days; reduced direct labor hours by 34,000; reduced flow two days per item; increased efficiency 90%.
2.36. OO-ALC Software Facility	This project repatriates software maintenance from less efficient/more expensive sources and improves efficiency by colocating software development teams. Aids in eliminating core shortfall. Cost: $21.4 million. Transformation merit: leverages capability maturity model level 5 capability; reduces waste (cost) by utilizing more efficient source; reduces waste (time) by colocating software maintainers.
2.37. OO-ALC C-130 Docks	This project provides a wraparound maintenance stand, complete with lighting and electricity. Cost: $2.53 million. Transformation merit: centralized, self-contained unit; eliminates fall-protection harness; increases efficiency. Benefits: investment-to-savings ratio of 2.63; payback in 5.74 years. Measures of success: reduced C-130 flow time by seven days; reduced labor costs.

Source: U.S. Air Force Oklahoma City Air Logistics Center

Table 4.5

Function	*Notation*	*Information collected*
Transportation		Number of movements per day
Inventory	Inventory	Average amount of inventory
Repair process		Average time to complete process
Outside source		No information necessary

parts are located and ordered. Depending on the vendor and the part, the box will have an awaiting parts (AWP) status for days or months. Once the part is received, it takes approximately one day to induct the part and put the box back into circulation for repair.

Once the piece part is obtained, the length of repair is estimated. If the repair is estimated to take more than one hour, the technician places the box, piece parts, and documentation into a bin for an electronic assembler to repair. This allows the technician to focus on diagnosing problems and making quick repairs and allows the assembler to focus on more difficult repairs. Therefore, the technician spends about one to three hours repairing boxes, whereas the assembler spends one to three days completing a repair.

Upon completion of the repair, the box is tested and the paperwork is verified. Depending on the magnitude of the repair and the complexity of the paperwork, retesting can take anywhere from one hour to three days. A final inspection is completed by administrative staff to verify the paperwork. Transportation between the repair benches and shipping occurs approximately three times per day. Depending on when the box is transported, and on the shipper's availability, packaging and shipping could take between one and two days.

Observations

The main drive is to minimize turnaround time. Boeing does not allow cannibalization of parts. This is partly because each customer owns the box that is sent in for repair. Therefore, according to Federal Aviation Administration regulations, Boeing

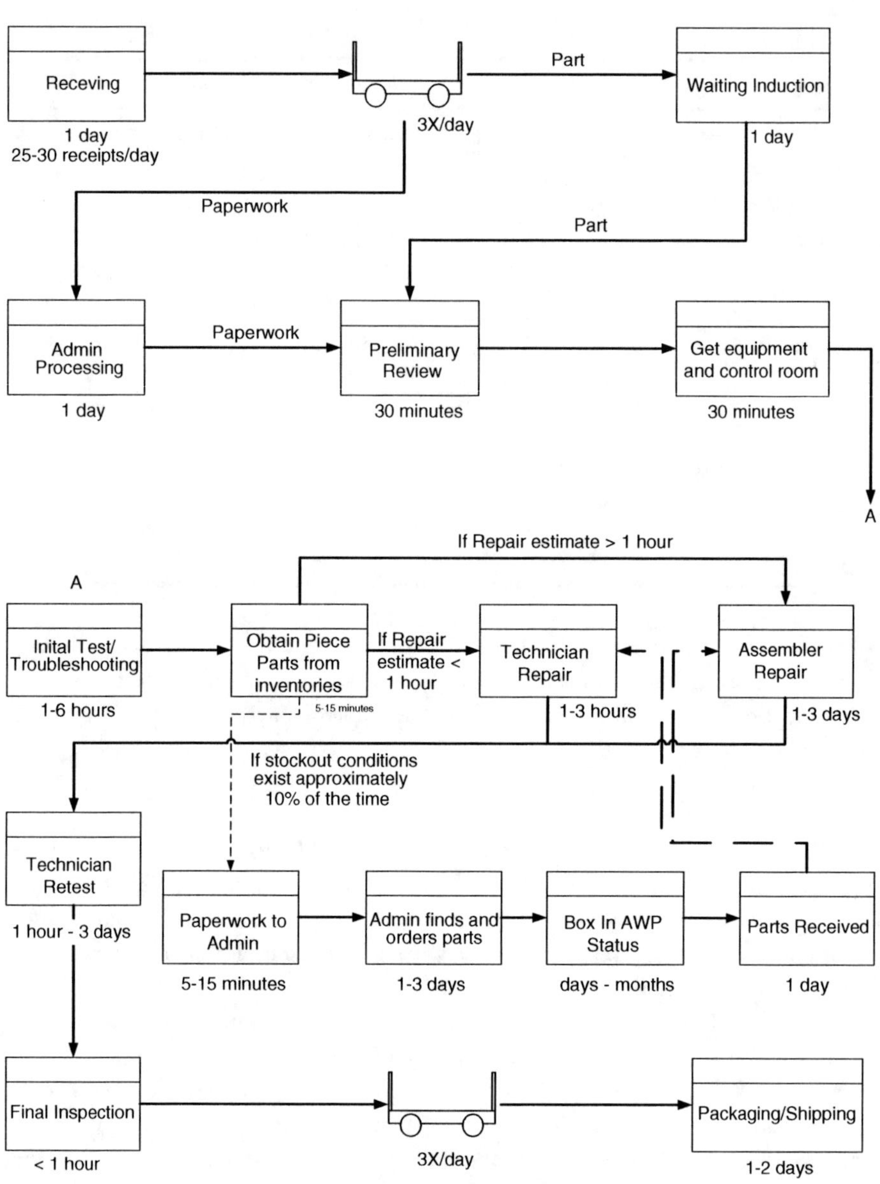

Figure 4.8 A Commercial Avionics Value-Stream Map.

cannot simply take parts from a working avionics box and place them in a nonworking box. Instead, Boeing must repair each box and find fault for each repair. Boeing also services avionics boxes on a first come, first served basis, unless an aircraft is grounded. This provides Boeing the opportunity to meet its turnaround-time goals, because turnaround time is calculated from the time the box is received to the time it leaves the depot. This procedure also ensures that boxes are not warehoused and potentially overlooked.

Boeing has a good inventory management system and maintains a close relationship with its vendors. The inventory management system utilizes safety stocks and reorder points, and these minimize the risk of stockouts. In addition, inventory levels are monitored closely and reviewed quarterly to ensure that the right parts are being ordered at the right time and in the right quantity. Close relationships with vendors enable Boeing to identify obsolescent parts early; this allows them to prepare in advance for last-time buys or engineering changes. Without this close partnership and their inventory system, Boeing would have a much higher stockout percentage.

There is room for improvement. First, paperwork follows the box throughout the process; at almost every step technicians verify the information on the paperwork. Computerizing the information would help to minimize the time spent checking and rechecking the information. In addition, providing engineering data and illustrations on computers for each technician would minimize the need to search and obtain the requisite information for repairing avionics boxes.

4.3.2.2 F-15 Heads-Up Display High-Level Value-Stream Map

This case study describes an F-15 wide-field-of-view heads-up display (HUD) value-stream map, which is shown in figure 4.9. The information contained in the map was gathered during two separate site visits to Robins Air Force Base in Georgia. The map's creation was an iterative process between the authors and the Warner Robins ALC (Chase and Mathaisel, 2001). The case study also examined subcomponents to this system that present materials and parts problems for the Air Force sustainment community.

In 2001 the Air Force had an average turnaround time for HUD repair of 17.6 hours. The Air Force wants to improve this time throughout the repair process and will be using best practices from the commercial sector and other military operations to make improvements and modifications. The HUD starts its repair process in the field on the flight line. Once the HUD has been identified to be in need of repair, it is removed from the aircraft and taken to the test facility on base. If the problem is minor and there is sufficient inventory on base, the HUD is repaired. At times, repairs occur by cannibalizing components from other aircraft that are in need of other repairs. Once those aircraft are repaired, the components are either reinstalled on the aircraft or sent into the supply system for redeployment to another base. When there are no test or repair facilities on base or the repair is too severe to be completed on base, the HUD is shipped to the Warner Robins Air Logistics Center (WR-ALC) to be repaired. It is accompanied by Air Force form 350, which describes the problem, date of initial malfunction, and other relevant information. The length of this process varies. Because the Air Force owns all HUDs and treats

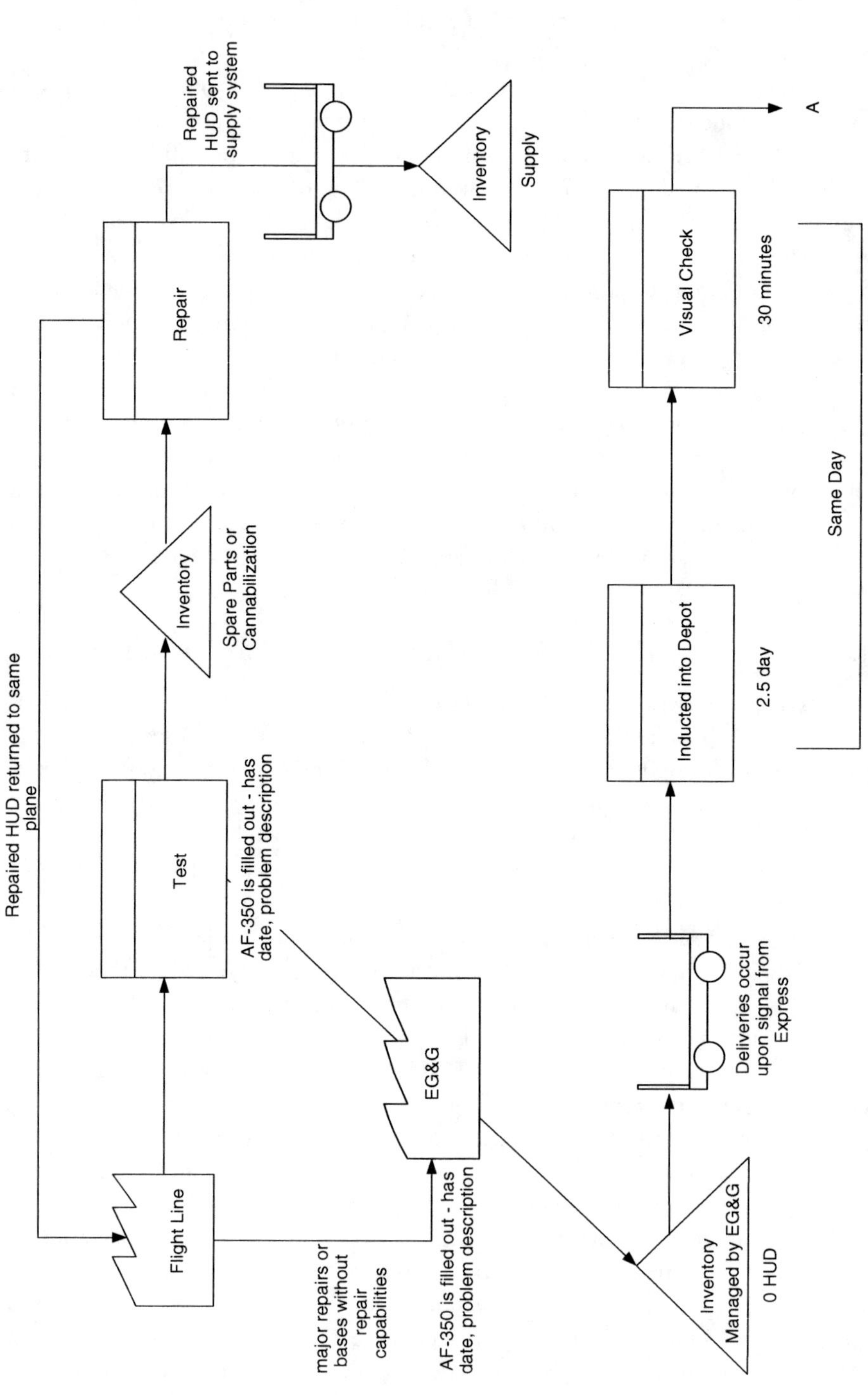

Flight Line

major repairs or bases without repair capabilities

AF-350 is filled out - has date, problem description

EG&G

Inventory Managed by EG&G

0 HUD

Deliveries occur upon signal from Express

Inducted into Depot

2.5 day

Visual Check

30 minutes

Same Day

A

Test

AF-350 is filled out - has date, problem description

Inventory

Spare Parts or Cannabilization

Repair

Repaired HUD returned to same plane

Repaired HUD sent to supply system

Inventory

Supply

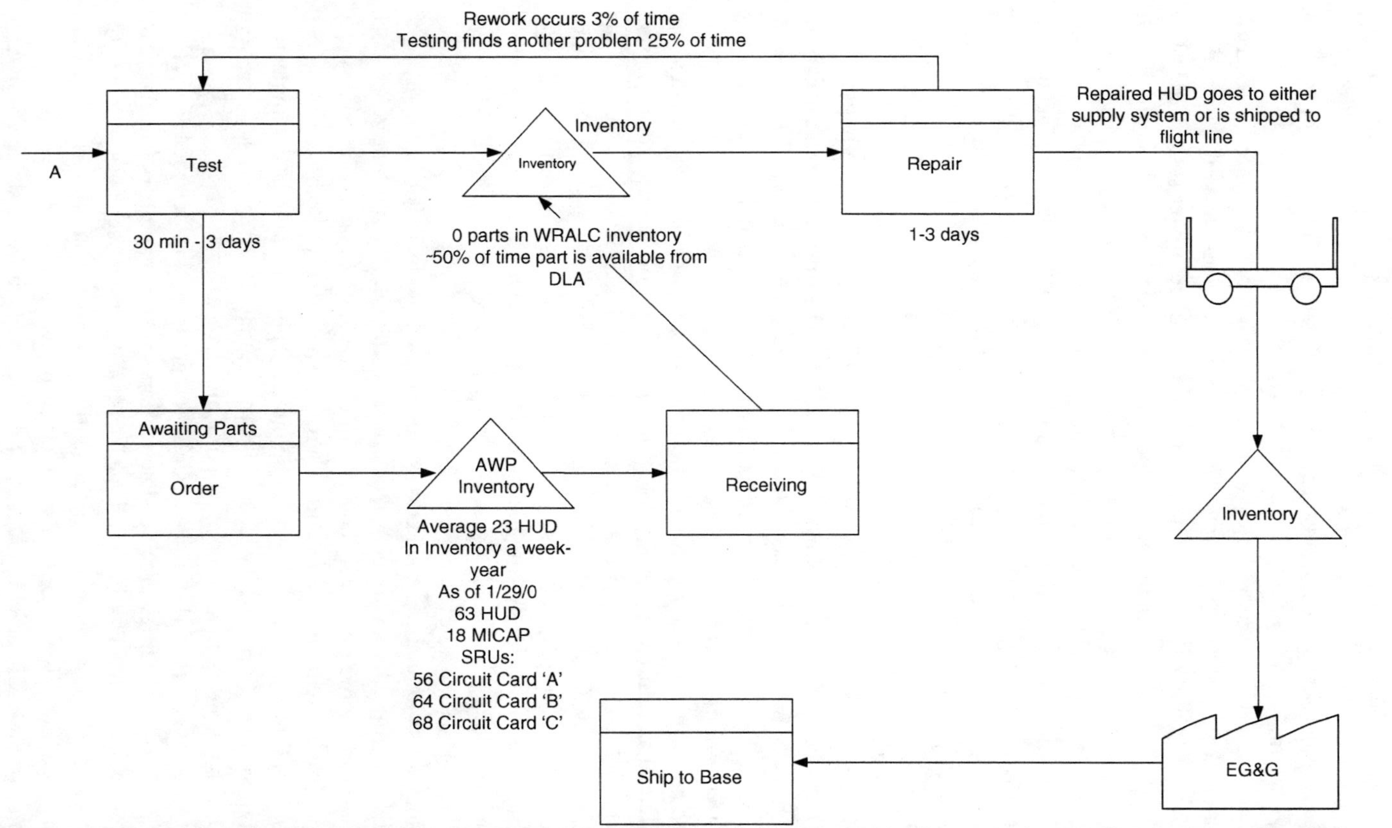

Figure 4.9 A Military Avionics Value-Stream Map.

them as interchangeable parts, pieces from numerous HUDs can be used to make one whole working HUD. Unless an entire HUD has been cannibalized for parts, it is usually not sent to the depot for repair. This could mean a repair of weeks or months from the time the initial problem was identified.

Once the HUD is sent to WR-ALC for repairs, it is held by EG&G, a Defense Logistics Agency (DLA) contractor, in a warehouse. Sometimes it is stored for months. EXPRESS, the Air Force production control computer system, identifies which HUDs should be inducted for repair. Until that decision is made, the HUDs sit in inventory at the DLA warehouse operated by EG&G. Once identified, the HUD is moved from the EG&G warehouse to the repair depot. The duration of time between movements from the warehouse to induction at the repair depot takes approximately five days. At that time, a technician completes a visual check of the box and notes any obvious differences or defects. The visual check takes about 30 minutes. Depending on the extent of the problems, testing can take anywhere from 30 minutes to three days. Testing is done at the component level and technicians can isolate a problem within six circuits.

Once the problem is identified, inventory is checked for parts. For the F-15 HUD, stockouts occur approximately 73 percent of the time. Often this occurs for DLA parts, but it mostly has been shown to occur for depot-level (Air Force-managed) parts. DLA's "stockage" effectiveness is about 40 percent. Air Force stockage effectiveness is 18 percent.

Component parts can be divided into two categories, *exchangeable* and *consumable*. Each has a different methodology for calculating stock levels. Stock levels for exchangeable component parts—managed by the Air Force depots in Ogden, Utah; Oklahoma City, Oklahoma; and at the Warner Robins ALC—are not controlled at the local retail-supply-account level. Stock levels for these items are calculated at the source-of-supply level using data system D200A. Overall, the stockage effectiveness rate for exchangeable items from the Air Force has been about 52 percent for all depot maintenance.

Stock levels for consumable items are determined by the depot supply data-system D035K using locally developed algorithms. The D035K will order for a stock level over and above an actual "hole" in an end item. The major sources of supply for consumable items are the DLA inventory control points in Richmond, Virginia; Columbus, Ohio; and Philadelphia, although local purchase and local manufacture are also possible. Overall, the stockage effectiveness rate for consumable items from the DLA has been 84 percent for all depot maintenance.

If a stockout occurs, the HUD is put back together and is identified as AWP. At this point, supply staff research possible vendors and place an order. The Air Force does not work on AWP orders until the parts have already been back ordered. The D035K requisition is routed electronically to the source of supply (either the DLA or the Air Force). The amount of time taken to award a contract will vary from part to part and from order to order (see the discussion above on stock levels). As in the commercial sector, HUDs wait in AWP inventory for days, weeks, or months.

Once the part is received, the HUD is reclassified as AWP-F. The box stays at AWP-F until EXPRESS drives a new requirement for it; only then will it go back into production. Currently, only 24 percent of all AWP end items have an active repair requirement.

Depending on the damage to the HUD, the repair time takes between one and three days on average. Once it is complete, the boxes are retested. Reworking occurs 3 percent of the time and testing leads to another problem 25 percent of the time. Currently, the Air Force's testing capabilities only allow them to locate one problem at a time. This means that a box could be inducted, tested, placed as AWP, repaired, and tested again only to find a new problem, and if there is another stockout, placed back into AWP. With the time necessary to obtain out-of-stock parts, the testing and repair system needs to be utilized more efficiently so as to minimize time spent in AWP.

Upon final testing, the HUD is transported to inventory that is managed by EG&G. At that point, it is either shipped back to a flight line or added to the supply system to be shipped to a flight line when a repair is sent in. In the case of the wide-field-of-view HUD, because of the long length of repair, the boxes are sent back to the flight line for immediate use.

Observations

The Air Force has many avenues to pursue to improve its turnaround time for HUD repair. Some will result in small changes to the repair process; others will require a broader scope and involve other departments within the Air Force in order to see results. Many of the hurdles that the Air Force needs to overcome have been previously dealt with at commercial repair operations. The commercial sector receives HUDs from aging aircraft; they, too, have obsolescence problems. However, they have made modifications to processes and procedures in order to handle these problems.

The Air Force's main problems are its lack of inventory and the processes and procedures that allow cannibalization to occur, both at the depot and in the field. As with most organizations, demand forecasting at its best is only slightly accurate and at its worst is totally inaccurate. In addition, there is a high variability in demand. For example, during one month, 20 HUDs may need the same repair, only to not see the problem again for months or years. The fact that there is no inventory to provide for this variability means that most boxes will sit AWP for a long period of time.

Cannibalization, as stated before, allows flight lines and bases to keep boxes indefinitely while using each working part to replace parts on other boxes. This allows the base to have a working box, but does not give the repair depot ample time and information to complete a repair. Because of the depot's inability to identify more than one problem at a time, sending a box with multiple problems will result in a repair that will take much longer than originally forecast. In addition, because of the large number of parts that are needed for a large repair, the chance that one part will be out of stock is much greater.

The Air Force also does not maintain supplier relationships (the Air Force and the DLA are still in the "lowest bidder" mode). This frequently prevents the Air Force from being informed of vendors who are going out of business or parts that will no longer be produced. (The Air Force does have a "diminishing manufacturing resources" program, covered in regulation AFMCI 23-103, and is therefore sometimes informed of vendor changes.) It also lengthens the amount of time necessary to locate and procure parts when stockouts occur. Creating and maintaining supplier relationships will allow the Air Force to be more knowledgeable of obsolescence issues and other parts procurement issues.

Invoking a first-come, first-served induction system will provide the Air Force with a smoother start to the repair process. In addition, to maintain a reasonable inventory level, all items should be prioritized based on predicted volume, value, and criticality. Therefore, the items that are commonly used should be in stock at all times and should be continuously replenished. Those that are not needed frequently should be maintained at a safety stock level but should be replenished on a less frequent basis. Until a sufficient inventory system can be installed, inventory should be located at only one location to avoid duplication of purchase and loss of parts.

4.3.2.3 A Comparison of Air Force and Commercial Avionics Repair

Figure 4.10 compares the repair operations of the military and commercial avionics value-stream maps. On the vertical axis, the major processes of the repair process are listed. The horizontal axis summarizes the amount of time (hours) required to complete each major process.

The times for commercial repair processes are generally lower than for military processes. However, it is interesting to note that there often is not a significant difference between the times. Repairing, retesting, and shipping are all completed in about the same amount of time. Two of the processes—induction and obtaining parts—can be significantly altered by invoking some of the aforementioned recommendations. The major discrepancy in turnaround time can be found when a box is classified as AWP. Here the average is 160 hours for commercial repair, and 848 hours for military repair.[6] The differences are observed because of the commercial repair industry's ability to partake in last-time buys and maintain supplier relationships. In addition, they are utilizing an inventory model that allows them to have consistent inventory in stock.

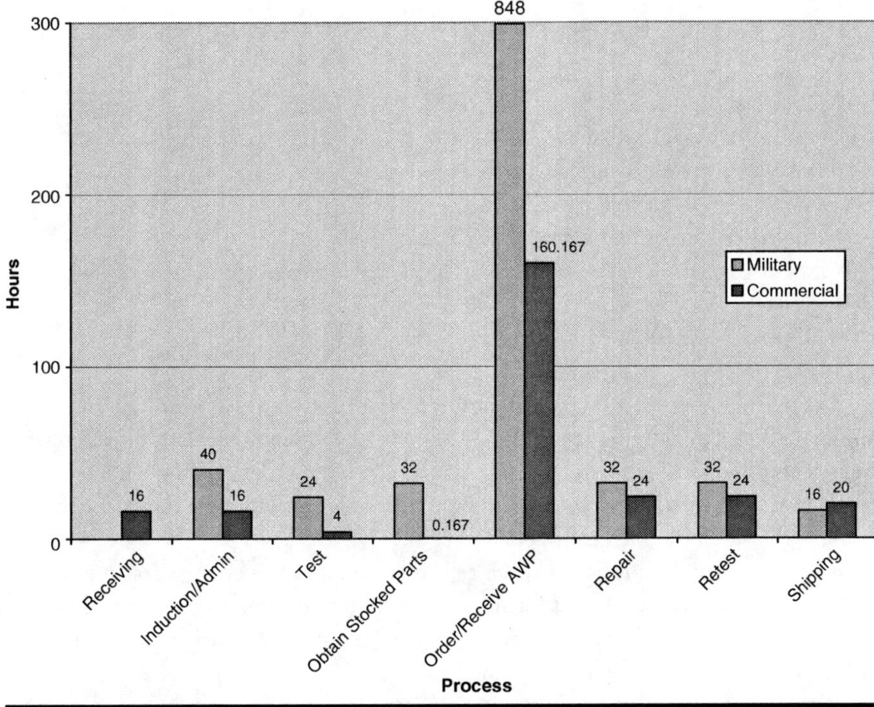

Figure 4.10 A Comparison of Commercial and Military Avionics Repair Processes.

Appendix: Performance Metrics for the Transformation of a Depot Maintenance Base

Transformation to lean MRO operations requires identified metrics to monitor depot performance and provide the feedback necessary to review and revise implementation plans. Performance metrics both display organizational performance and serve as diagnostic tools to uncover problems early in the repair process. Performance includes a balanced measure of cost, schedule, quality, and the like. Various benchmarking studies provide an initial list of relevant metrics, which are then used to establish a baseline of performance and produce successive (daily, monthly, quarterly) measures of performance. The high-level metrics are:

- Production
- Organic production hours
- Major system production
- Subsystem production
- Quality
- Major system quality defect rate

- Subsystem quality defect rate
- Component quality defect rate
- Cost
- Net operating result

The performance thresholds are designed to

- Align contractor performance with objectives
- Focus on critical success factors in meeting performance objectives
- Reflect performance goals
- Rromote continuous improvement in performance

The metrics also must be consistent with those used routinely throughout senior military reviews to judge depot operations. These higher-level metrics will be assessed and supported by evaluation of lower-level (cell, cluster) metrics, as shown in table 4.6. Such lower-level metrics can be aggregated to formulate and support the development of the higher-level metrics described above.

Metrics are posted throughout each cell and at higher levels of organizational management. They communicate performance throughout the organization to stakeholders at all levels, and serve as information for the independent financial and accounting process needed periodically for both internal and external audit purposes.

Table 4.6 Performance Metrics for the Transformation of a Depot Maintenance Base

Metric	*Definition*	*Timing of Measurement*	*Goal*
Schedule (Maintenance Turnaround Time)	Time from induction to serviceablility	Hours/days	Major weapons systems: 100 days Minor systems: 25 days Commodities: 17 days
Work in Process	Count and dollar value of assets in work	Daily, weekly, monthly	Reduce by XX percent
Cost	Labor, overhead, general & administrative for commodities and weapon system production	By product, by process	Reduce by XX percent; meet the Office of Secretary of Defense approved net operating revenue goals for fiscal year
Supply Parts Required	Material costs	By product	Reduce (or increase) by XX percent

Metric	*Definition*	*Timing of Measurement*	*Goal*
Quality (Defects)	Instances of reworking	Monthly	100% first-test pass rate for minor systems and commodities; less than two tests for major weapons systems
Back Orders	Number and time in status	Daily	Eliminated in less than 48 hours

Chapter 5

Best Sustainment Practices

This chapter presents a plan for benchmarking, classifying, and implementing best sustainment practices. A number of major research centers have identified, researched, and promoted exceptional practices, methods, and procedures in the design, testing, production, facilities, logistics, maintainability, and management of products. Some of these centers, such as the U.S. Office of Naval Research's Best Manufacturing Practices Center of Excellence (BMPCOE[1]) and the American Productivity and Quality Center,[2] exist to increase the quality, reliability, and maintainability of goods and services produced by American firms by providing benchmarking cases for manufacturing applications. In addition, a number of U.S. corporations that provide maintenance, repair, and overhaul (MRO) services to the commercial and military community have developed best practices. In an arena of cost reductions, aging systems, and the closure of military bases that sustain the Air Force, Army, Marines and Navy, the MRO community can benefit from the knowledge that exists at these centers of best sustainment practices, wherever those best practices may reside.

The investigation herein specifically focuses on MRO practices and how these practices can apply to the sustainment of U.S. military operations. The goals for this investigation are summarized in table 5.1. The discussion will have an enterprise perspective, as an MRO transformation is expected to follow the Lean Enterprise Architecture (LEA) outlined in chapter 3. The *enterprise* is, in this case, the facilities, people, technologies, operating systems, logistics systems, and other resources that are allocated to the organization to perform its function and meet its performance goals and objectives.

The best practice case studies that are presented in this chapter also have an enterprise-wide perspective to minimize the possibility of overlooking opportunities

Table 5.1 Goals for Benchmarking Best Sustainment Practices

Near-Term Goals:	Identify major research centers and maintenance, repair, and overhaul providers that possess best practices. Develop a framework for obtaining information on these best practices.
Long-Term Goals:	Make recommendations on practices that would directly benefit the military sustainment community. Implement the action. Make the process a standard part of the continuous process improvement approach to transformation.

for further performance improvement and to minimize the tendency to suboptimize functions and processes based on local metrics and organizational reporting.

To begin, a brief review of the benchmarking process is offered. Next, the research and methodology section describes how a benchmarking investigation should be conducted. Then, a plan is suggested for how the best practices should be identified and classified, and an implementation strategy for these practices is presented. This process has seven steps to it, and will be referred to as the *seven-step benchmarking process*. The subsequent section presents a schedule plan for executing this seven-step process. Finally, a few case studies are presented as examples of enterprise-wide best sustainment practices.

5.1 Benchmarking

Benchmarking is the process of identifying, understanding, and adapting outstanding practices from organizations to help improve enterprise performance, and is recognized as an essential tool for continuous improvement of quality (Dattakumar and Jagadeesh 2003). This statement is evidenced by the recent large number of publications in the field. If one looks historically at benchmarking in the United States, the Xerox Corporation is generally credited with the first major benchmarking project in 1979. Xerox was interested in how Japanese manufacturers produced less costly but high-quality photocopiers; the company learned how to increase design and production efficiency and reduce manufacturing costs of their machines by benchmarking Japanese manufacturers.

Benchmarking goes beyond just competitively analyzing the industry. It includes analyzing organizational processes and methods to assess how competitors have achieved their positions. Consequently, there are different types of benchmarking (see table 5.2). The earlier stages of benchmarking developments stressed a process or activity orientation. Recently, however, the scope of benchmarking appears to have expanded to include strategies and systems (Yasin 2002). A strategy or framework for benchmarking is one of the key issues in this investigation.

Table 5.2 Types of Benchmarking

Type	*Examples*
Internal: against best internal operations	Comparisons between shops within a depot Comparisons between shops within other maintenance, repair, and overhaul (MRO) providers or supply chains
Competitive: against external direct competitors	Comparisons between depots and other MRO providers or supply chains Comparisons between Goodrich and TIMCO MRO providers
Functional: against external functional best operations	Comparisons between depots and Boeing repair services
Generic: against generic functions regardless of industry	Comparisons between Honeywell (electronics MRO) and Caterpillar Logistics (supply-chain provider)

5.1.1 Best Sustainment Practices: A Definition

Best sustainment practices, from the perspective of MRO services, are methodologies, techniques, or innovative use of equipment or resources or processes that have a proven record of success in providing significant, continuous improvements in cost, schedule, quality, performance, or other measurable factors enabling an enterprise to deliver best value to the customer and thus positively impacting the overall health and success of the MRO enterprise.

This chapter will use this definition to identify practices that are considered "best in class."

5.1.2 Reasons for Searching for Best Practices

Based on information obtained by the author as a result of site visits to military and commercial MRO centers, an observation of the current MRO system reveals critical issues facing the sustainment community and its attempts to transform itself using continuous process improvement initiatives, such as lean or cellular manufacturing. Most of these issues, such as higher than desired maintenance cycle times, are due to "awaiting parts" conditions, where a system cannot be repaired in a timely manner because technicians cannot obtain needed parts to fix it. With the current issues of cost reductions, aging systems, and military base closures, everyone in the sustainment community is indeed working very diligently to support the MRO process. Systemic problems in the industry are, however, hampering their efficiency in terms of

- Technological obsolescence of parts and systems
- Diminishing manufacturing sources (industries) and resources (skilled labor)
- Lack of integration of in-service engineering functions with depot maintenance functions
- A poorly structured performance measurement (metrics) program
- Contracting philosophies that are inefficient.
- Lack of an integrated information systems architecture

Although not everything that is being done to correct these systemic problems has resulted in suboptimal conditions, a number of issues have nevertheless arisen:

- The sustainment community continues to re-create or reengineer old technology in order to address the issues of diminishing manufacturing resources and parts and systems obsolescence.
- Limited engineering resources have caused programs to *react* to critical problems instead of *anticipating* them.
- Ineffective goals and performance metrics have caused higher sustainment costs and misuse of performance drivers.
- The current contracting philosophy has resulted in delayed deliveries and higher sustainment costs.
- The accessibility, accuracy, and timeliness of information have resulted in a workforce-intensive information system that does not function effectively in real time.

5.2 Objectives of This Chapter

An investigation by the author into both government and industry practices that might provide solutions to the sustainment problems that have already been mentioned has revealed that there exist numerous documented practices that will be of value to the sustainment community. The focus was on finding those practices that are best suited to the sustainment community. The practices come from government organizations as well as commercial industry. These concepts encompass improvements in systemwide metrics, such as waste, design time, organizational layers, and suppliers, as well as improvements in flexibility, capability, productivity, and customer satisfaction.

The objective is to present a framework for identifying, classifying, and implementing these best sustainment practices. By cataloging and documenting these best practices, one can learn from others' attempts to maintain systems and avoid non-value-added processes. The intent is to increase the quality, reliability, and timeliness of the MRO services on products. A road map for how these practices can be implemented is presented.

5.3 A Methodology for Benchmarking

5.3.1 Identifying the Best Practices

A number of organizations implement best practices. Many of these practices can be beneficial to the entire sustainment community if they are identified and documented. Thus, the first problem is identifying these organizations and documenting their best practices. A few institutions, like the BMPCOE, exist exclusively to identify and define these practices. But the BMPCOE site is just for manufacturing, not sustainability. The goal is to find such institutions, organizations, military depots, and commercial providers to identify the knowledge that exists at these sites, and to make a determination as to whether or not they are "best in class. What follows are possible methods for identifying these institutions.

5.3.1.1 Conducting a Survey

One method for seeking best practices is to conduct a survey of enterprises engaged in the business of MRO of systems supporting the aviation community. The survey can be administered by questionnaire. The purpose is to identify industry practices that might offer potentially significant benefits for the logistics and sustainment community supporting the U.S. military.

The questionnaire can consist of five potential sections:

Section 1. General Background Information
Section 2. Performance Metrics
Section 3. Business Practices
Section 4. Supply Chain Service and Performance
Section 5. Information Infrastructure

Questionnaires can be mailed to enterprises engaged in the business of the MRO of major systems or components. They can be selected from the *World Aviation Directory* and other sources already known to the military. Response rates for surveys of this type are typically poor (about 30 percent), but they are relatively inexpensive, and follow-up telephone calls generally boost the response rate. Table 5.3 provides an example of the type of questions that may be asked in the questionnaire. The appendix to this chapter provides a more extensive sample questionnaire.

Table 5.3 Process Improvement/Benchmarking Questions

- What processes are being benchmarked?
- What primary metrics are used?
- Who does the institution benchmark against?
- What are the underlying conditions that cause the particular performance improvement?
- Do those conditions exist at the military installation under consideration? If not, how might performance be different or how should the specific activities be modified to make them applicable?
- What recommendations are there for implementation?
- What media is used for display of the best practices?
- What process improvement tools are used?
- How is the institution organized for process improvement?
- What are the site-specific examples of success?
- Is there a formal benchmarking program in place?
- What other process improvement techniques are routinely used (such as Six Sigma or lean processes)?
- How do you choose which processes to benchmark? Which metrics do you use?
- How do you make the determination which institution has a best practice for a process?
- What criteria are used to select candidate benchmarks?
- How long do typical benchmarking projects take to complete?
- How many people are typically involved? What disciplines are involved?
- What is the typical investment in process improvement (lean processes, Six Sigma, benchmarking, etc.) per year? Is this steady from year to year? What makes up this cost?
- Did you obtain top-management buy-in before conducting a benchmarking study?
- Did the process owners fight the process? How did you deal with that?
- Do you utilize a toolbox approach where you utilize different process improvement techniques such as lean processes, Six Sigma, or benchmarking, or is one technique utilized? Why?
- How do you measure the success of your process improvement initiatives whether they are lean processes, Six Sigma, benchmarking, or some other tool?
- Do benchmarking teams undergo training?
- How long did it take to implement the recommended changes?
- Do you post metrics for the changed process to demonstrate improvement?
- Was there a rewards and recognition program for participants?
- Do you benefit from membership in the American Productivity and Quality Center or other types of groups that relate to or are involved in benchmarking, lean processes, Six Sigma, or any other related technique?
- What methods are utilized to make improvements?
  - flowchart analysis
  - Pareto analysis

  - root-cause analysis
  - statistical process control
  - other
- Do you utilize shop-floor metrics, and are they standard across the institution?
- Do you post process-improvement results from benchmarking, lean processes, Six Sigma, or other programs on the shop floor for employees to see?
- What types of metric displays (bulletin boards, plasma boards, computer displays, etc.) are used on the shop floor, and why were they chosen?

5.3.1.2 Websearches

Using powerful websearch engines, a methodological investigation may reveal practices from the following media:

- Business websites, such as that of Goodrich Aviation Technical Services
- Research institutions, such as the RAND Corporation
- The American Productivity and Quality Center
- Benchmarking institutions such as the BMPCOE (see also those listed in table 5.4)

5.3.1.3 Reports and Papers

Beyond conducting surveys and searching websites, best sustainment practices can also be found from the following sources:

- Reports from the news media
- Conferences, such as *Aviation Week*'s overhaul and maintenance conferences
- Academic papers
- Military briefings

5.3.2 A Framework for Identifying and Classifying the Best Practices

The framework for identifying best practices in the context of MRO operations consists of four basic steps, as depicted in the first four (lower) steps of figure 5.1. The top three steps—steps 5, 6, and 7—will be discussed in sections 5.5 and 5.6 below.

5.3.2.1 Step 1: Defining the Issue or Problem

The first step in the process is to define the issue or problem that the sustainment community is facing. There may be best practices available to help solve the problem.

Table 5.4 Benchmarking Websites

Activity Based Costing Benchmarking Association: http://www.abcbenchmarking.com
Accounting and Finance Benchmarking Consortium: http://www.afbc.org/RoundTable.pdf
Customer Satisfaction Measurement Association: http://www.csmassociation.org/roundtable.pdf
Financial Services and Banking Benchmarking Association: http://www.fsbba.org/RoundTable.pdf
Human Resources Benchmarking Association: http://www.hrba.org/roundtable.pdf
Information Systems Management Benchmarking Consortium: http://www.ismbc.org/roundtable.pdf
International Contact Center Benchmarking Consortium: http://www.iccbc.org/roundtable.pdf
International Council Of Benchmarking Coordinators: http://www.icobc.com/roundtable.pdf
Procurement and Supply Chain Benchmarking Association: http://www.pasba.com/roundtable.pdf
Society for Inventory Management Benchmarking Analysis: http://www.pasba.com/roundtable.pdf
Six Sigma Benchmarking Association: http://www.sixsigmabenchmarking.com/roundtable.pdf

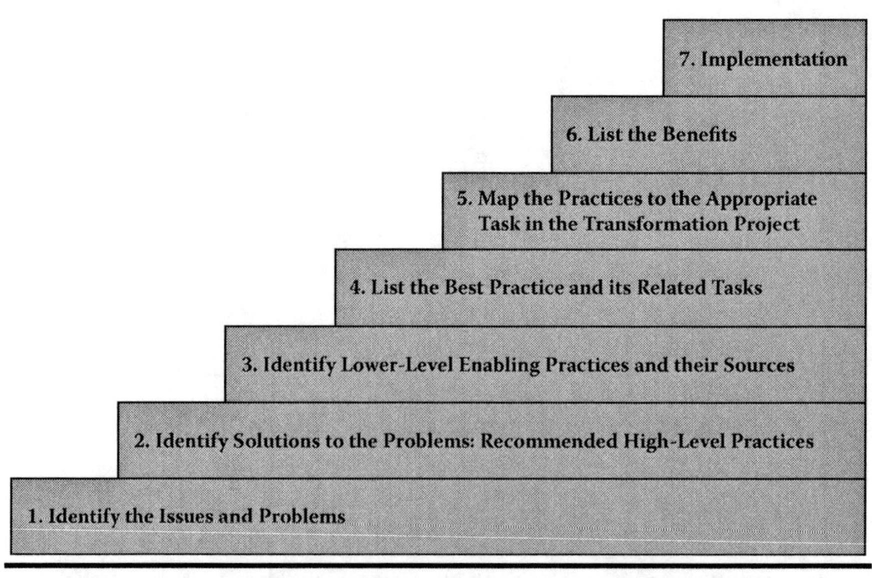

Figure 5.1 A Framework for Defining, Classifying, and Implementing Best Susutainment Practices.

Table 5.5 Identifying the Issues and Problems

	Supplier	*Maintenance, Repair, and Overhaul (MRO) Provider (Commercial/ Government)*	*Customer*
Issue	Parts availability decreasing	Depot cycle time increasing	Operational readiness decreasing
Source of Issue (Problems)	Parts obsolescence and diminishing manufacturing sources/resources	Lack of parts	Spares availability decreasing
Metric	Lead time	Logistics delay time	Mission capability

As an example, the parts-availability problem that pervades the MRO industry can be defined in the manner depicted in table 5.5. The problem may be slightly different for the supplier of the parts than it is for the (government or commercial) MRO operator who needs the piece or part to fix a subsystem. Further, the problem may also be different for the "customer"—in this case, the end user of the subsystem. In this table, the author lists the issue for each user (supplier, MRO provider, or customer), the source of the issue/problem, and the metrics that are commonly used to evaluate whether or not the problem exists.

Here it can be seen from the supplier perspective that the parts-availability problem is due to technological obsolescence (i.e., changes in the technology that cause older parts to be unavailable) and diminishing manufacturing sources (i.e., original equipment manufacturers going out of business) or resources (i.e., lack of skilled technicians due to retirement or improper training).

5.3.2.2 Step 2: Identifying Solutions to the Problem: Higher-Level Practices

The next step is to identify solutions that can possibly address the problem. These are the higher-level practices. Because there are three players in the sustainment arena (suppliers, MRO providers, and customers), the solutions would be different for each. A fundamental question to be answered when performing the benchmarking investigation is, What underlying conditions at the best-practice site cause the particular performance improvement? These conditions identify the higher-level practices that lead to solutions to the problems defined in step 1. To continue with the previous example, suppose the focus is on the supplier. What conditions or higher-level practices would help suppliers with their parts-availability problems?

Table 5.6 Identifying Solutions to the Problem: Recommended Practices for the Supplier

Source of Issue (Problems)	*Possible Solutions: Recommended Higher-Level Best Sustainment Practices*
Obsolescence	Technology insertion management
Diminishing Manufacturing Sources/Resources	Sustaining manufacturing capability Life-time buy
Long Lead Times	Buffer inventory Sustaining manufacturing capability Technology insertion management Lean manufacturing
Quality	Quality management systems Supply-chain management

In terms of technological obsolescence and diminishing manufacturing sources/resources, three possible solutions (i.e., higher-level best sustainment practices) can be identified (see table 5.6):

- New technology insertion
- Sustaining manufacturing capability
- Purchasing parts for the entire life cycle of the system

To solve the problem of long lead times in obtaining parts for suppliers, there are four possible solutions:

- Buffer inventory
- Sustaining manufacturing capability
- New technology insertion
- Lean manufacturing

Finally, to deal with the problem of poor quality piece parts for the supplier, there are two recommended higher-level practices: quality management systems and supply-chain management.

In the case of the MRO provider, seven recommended higher-level practices can be identified to help solve the parts availability problem, two for the documentation problem, one for the remanufacturing problem, and one for the resource constraints problem (see table 5.7).

Table 5.7 Identifying Solutions to the Problem: Recommended Practices for the Maintenance, Repair, and Overhaul Provider

Source of Issue (Problems)	*Possible Solutions: Recommended Best Sustainment Practices*
Parts Availability	Technology insertion management Sustaining manufacturing capability Life-time buy Buffer inventory Lean remanufacturing Quality management system Supply-chain management
Documentation	Configuration management Technical-data management
Remanufacturing Process	Lean remanufacturing
Resource Constraints	Resource requirements analysis

5.3.2.3 Step 3: Identifying the Enabling Practices and Their Sources

The third step in the process of identifying and classifying best sustainment practices is to list the lower-level "enabling" practices that are associated with the class of higher-level practices. These lower-level enablers help to further define the practices and their utility. For example, technology insertion management is a higher-level best practice. Some of the lower-level "enabling" practices within this technology insertion class are:

- Modernization through spares
- Continuous technology refresh
- Reducing total ownership cost
- Costs as an independent variable
- Rapid commercial off-the-shelf insertion
- Nondevelopmental item strategy

A framework for classifying these enabling practices is needed. The classification can be organized in a hierarchical manner to help keep them under the right category, ranging in scope from high-level lean practices to specific enabling best practices that are more context-specific in nature. This classification is illustrated by examining technology insertion management, which, as noted above, is a higher-level best practice, and there are six enabling practices in this category. So, one can

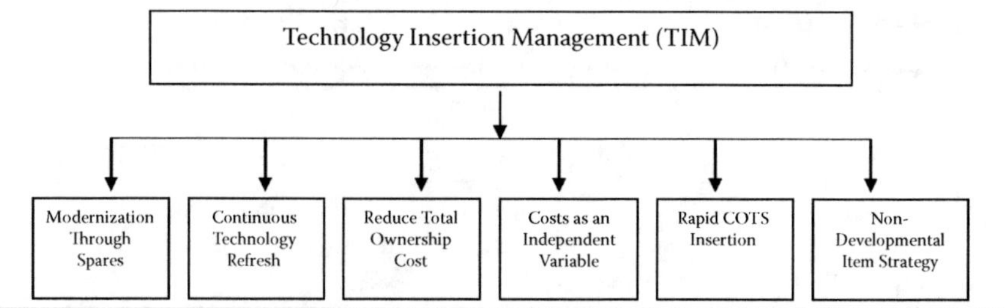

Figure 5.2 Classifying Best Sustainment Practices.

Table 5.8 Identifying Enabling Practices and Their Sources

Enabling Practices	*Source*	*Related Best Sustainment Practices*
Modernization through spares/continuous technology refreshment	U.S. Army	Service Life Extension Program
Reducing total ownership cost	U.S. Air Force	
Costs as an independent variable		
Rapid commercial off-the-shelf insertion	U.S. Navy, Lockheed-Martin	Sustaining manufacturing capability
Nondevelopmental item strategy	Department of Defense Acquisition Reform	Lean remanufacturing

classify these six enabling practices under the general category of technology insertion management, as illustrated in figure 5.2.

In a similar manner, other higher-level practices can also be classified hierarchically. In table 5.8, these enabling practices, along with those institutions that are believed to possess these practices, are identified. In this example, the U.S. Army has been identified as one source of best practices for Modernization through Spares program and its successor, Continuous Technology Refreshment. Similarly, the U.S. Navy and defense contractor Lockheed Martin possess best practices in the area of commercial off-the-shelf (COTS) insertion of technologies into their processes.

5.3.2.4 Step 4: Listing the Best Practice and Its Related Tasks

The last step in the process of identifying the best sustainment practices is to list the practices along with a more specific definition. One can accomplish this

Table 5.9 Tasks and Processes Related to Technology Insertion Management

Enabling Practices	*Related Tasks and Processes*
Modernization through spares/ continuous technology refreshment	Performance-based specifications
Reducing total ownership cost	Open system architecture
Costs as an independent variable	Market analysis
Rapid commercial off-the-shelf insertion	Technology assessment and management
Nondevelopmental item strategy	Supportability analysis
	Risk management
	Integrated product teams/concurrent engineering
	System requirements analysis/system engineering
	Integrated test and evaluation
	System modification and retrofit installation
	Technical data and configuration management
	Industry/government partnership
	Operational effectiveness assessment
	Warranty
	Acquisition streamlining and contracting

task with a definitive statement, or it can be done through example by listing a set of tasks and processes that are related to this practice. The latter approach is employed here. Continuing with the example of technology insertion management (TIM) as a higher-level task, TIM comprises the enabling practices that were identified above, and it represents the related tasks defined in table 5.9. In other words, institutions that practice any of these related tasks or processes are implementing TIM as a practice.

5.3.3 Generic Benchmarking Categories

Table 5.10 identifies some generic target areas for benchmarking research.

5.3.4 Key Operations, Functions, Processes in Sustainment to be Benchmarked

Table 5.11 lists the key functions and processes that would be the target of the benchmark institution.

Table 5.10 Generic Benchmarking Categories

Category	*Description*
Capacity	Amount, type
Facilities	Size, location, specialization
Technology	Equipment, automation, links
Vertical integration	Direction, extent, balance
Workforce	Skill, wage practice, tenure
Quality	Monitoring, intervention
Materials planning and control	Sourcing policies, centralization, decision rules
Organization	Structure, control systems, role of groups

Table 5.11 Key Benchmarking Functions and Processes

Functions	*Processes*
Maintenance Planning and Program Management (Line Maintenance and Base Maintenance)	Budgeting and cost accounting
	Evaluation of labor, aircraft, and engine productivity
	Workforce forecasts and workload leveling/planning
	Scheduled maintenance planning, maintenance scheduling-decision support tools, and location of maintenance checks
	Location of spares for maintenance support
Maintenance, Repair, and Overhaul (MRO)	Budgeting and cost accounting
	Aircraft and engine productivity (throughput)
	Workforce forecasts and workload leveling/planning
	MRO planning, maintenance scheduling-decision support tools, location of maintenance checks
	Location of spares for maintenance support
Inventory Management, Materials Control	Order quantity, reorder point
	Component and parts tracking
	Support equipment
	Facilities
	Location of inventory
	Costs
Transportation, Logistics Support	"Just in time" versus "just in case"
	Costs of logistics
	Transportation of personnel and parts to broken aircraft or engine
Supply Chain	Outsourcing, privatization
	Parts obsolescence
	Availability of supplier sources
Contracting	In house
	Outsourcing

Table 5.11 Key Benchmarking Functions and Processes (continued)

Functions	*Processes*
Human Resources	Training Turnover
Information Technology	Monitoring systems Decision support systems Enterprise resource planning
Engineering and Quality Control (Assurance)	Measurement systems Prediction systems
Administration and Support	Administrative structure, decision-making powers Redundancy, bureaucracy

5.3.5 Performance Characteristics/Metrics to Be Benchmarked

Table 5.12 has four performance characteristics and some of the supporting features that would be desirable in the operations functions to help achieve lean performance characteristics. These are the characteristics that should be researched in the best practice case studies and surveys.

5.4 Conducting Site Visits to Witness the Best Practices

The purpose of site visits is to witness the practice, not to validate that the practice is considered best. The understanding is that the center initially identifying the site as possessing the best practice had already validated the practices as best according to their own standards. Validating a best practice is a task for an official benchmarking institution, such as the BMPCOE or the American Productivity and Quality Center. If a practice cannot be validated as being best by a recognized benchmarking institution, then it should be classified as an *information practice.*

The steps for conducting site visits are:

- Request permission for a site visit
- Identify hosting organization point of contact
- Establish presurvey logistics
- Establish survey logistics presurvey: identify case studies
- Conduct site visit
- Give a presentation of reason for visit
- Validate best practices on factory floor, or discuss off-floor practices, send draft of results to host
- Incorporate changes from hosting organization
- Insuring technical accuracy
- Remove proprietary/sensitive information
- Share information: final report

Table 5.12 Benchmark Performance Metrics and Their Characteristics

Performance Metric	*Characteristics*
Cost Efficiency	Low overhead
	Special-purpose equipment and facilities
	High utilization of capacity
	Close control of materials
	High productivity
	Low wage rates and stable union contracts
	Cost per unit of output
Quality	Skilled workers
	Adequate precision of equipment
	Motivation for pride of workmanship
	Effective communication of standards or job requirements
	Reliability/effective scheduling
	Defects per units repaired
Dependability	Low equipment failure
	Low turnover
	High inventory investment
	Adequate training
	Reliability and maintainability: mean time between failure, mean time between maintenance, mean time to repair, etc.
Flexibility	Dependable, rapid suppliers
	Reserve capacity
	Multiskilled workers
	Effective control of work flow
	Versatile processing equipment
	Low setup time and cost
	Integration of design and production

Table 5.13 is a draft list of the possible best-in-class enterprises that have been identified for benchmarking.

5.5 Mapping the Best Practice to the Appropriate Task in a Transformation Project

Step 5 in figure 5.1 (the framework for identifying the best practices) involves mapping the practices to the appropriate task in a transformation project.

This step refers to the various phases and tasks of the LEA framework that a military depot transformation will be following. The main steps are conceptual design, preliminary design, detailed design, implementation, and operation. Table 5.14 suggests an approach for mapping each best practice to the appropriate task in a transformation framework.

Table 5.13 Possible Best-in-Class Enterprises for Benchmarking

Enterprise	*Location*	*Reason/Possible Best Practice*
Boeing	Irving, TX	Avionics
Boeing	Seattle, WA	Aircraft panel complexity analysis
Honeywell Avionics (Commercial)	Irving, TX	Avionics
Honeywell Avionics (Military)	Phoenix, AZ	Logistics
Goodrich	Seattle, WA	Aircraft MRO
Raytheon		Asset condition assessment
Naval Surface Warfare Center	Crane, IN	Asset condition assessment
Lockheed Martin Tactical Aircraft Systems (LMTAS)	Ft. Worth, TX	Integrated product development Performance management teams Risk management Supplier relationships Obsolescence and commercial technology insertion Variability reduction—separating the "critical few" from the "trivial many" Concurrent engineering—design for sustainability Conduct producibility engineering review Lean enterprise initiatives
Lockheed Martin Undersea Systems	Manassas, VA	Rapid commercial off-the-shelf insertion for electronics Reliability, maintainability and availability parameters as the critical design for sustainment
Rockwell Collins	San Jose, CA	Performance-based logistics for the Navy F/A-18 (A/B/C/D) fighter
Pratt & Whitney	San Antonio, TX West Palm Beach, FL	Flow lines Cellular repair and overhaul Implementing enterprise resource planning systems Flex sustainment for the military Depot production operations using the Toyota Production System
Navy Naval Sea Systems Command	Jacksonville, FL North Island, San Diego, CA	Total quality leadership Business process reengineering Baldrige National Quality Award

(continued)

Table 5.13 Possible Best-in-Class Enterprises for Benchmarking (continued)

Enterprise	*Location*	*Reason/Possible Best Practice*
		Performance-based logistics in partnership with Rockwell Collins Lean enterprise initiatives Lean-Pathways supplier programs Regional inventory and materials management concept
Corpus Christi Army Depot	Corpus Christi, TX	Advanced metal finishing processes and facility Bearing shop Programmed depot maintenance scheduling system on the webpage Strategic planning process High performance training Plastic media blasting process
Raytheon TI Systems	Dallas, TX	Commercial benchmarking for best practices Integrated product development Process failure mode and effects analysis Process capability analysis
Raytheon Missile Systems Company	Tucson, AZ	Risk management
Sandia National Laboratories	Albuquerque, NM	Quality function deployment Agile manufacturing facility "Just in time" procurement system Model-based design and manufacturing processes Inspection techniques for aging aircraft
Army Maintenance Center–Albany	Albany, GA	Manufacturing resource planning International Organization of Standards (ISO 9000) Earned value management Theory of constraints
Wal-Mart	Bentonville, AR	Supply-chain management Relationship management "Just in time" inventory program Radio frequency identification devices
Federal Express	Memphis, TN	Supply-chain management
Caterpillar Logistics	Peoria, IL	Supply-chain management Six Sigma/lean initiatives

Table 5.14 Mapping of Best Sustainment Practices to Lean Enterprise Architecture Tasks

Best Practice	*Conceptual Design*	*Preliminary Design*	*Detailed Design*	*Implementation*	*Operation*
Performance-Based Logistics		✔			
Integrated Product Development	✔				
Performance Management Teams	✔				
Risk Management				✔	
Commercial Technology Insertion					✔
Concurrent Engineering				✔	
Modular Design of Material Flow between Cells			✔		

5.6 Summarizing and Reporting the Results of the Benchmarking

Step 6 of figure 5.1 involves listing the benefits associated with implementing the best sustainment practices.

This step is where the best practice is formally documented. A possible format is illustrated in the Rockwell Collins best practice example in table 5.15. Although not illustrated in the example, the report should contain an abbreviated form of SWOT analysis:

- Strengths
- Weaknesses
- Opportunities
- Threats

Part of the SWOT analysis is identifying the benefits that the best practice will provide to a transformation. In addition, the report will address a question raised earlier (in step 2) concerning the underlying conditions at the benchmark site that caused the particular best practice to occur.

Table 5.15 Example from Rockwell Collins of Documenting a Best Sustainment Practice

Service Parts Provisioning

The types and quantities of repair parts are determined from the repair and repair part prediction models used in the preparation of the performance-based logistics (PBL) business case analysis. Initially, optics repair material, and combiner glasses are purchased to support the first two years of repairs with yearly options for the additional three years. Other low cost parts will be purchased at the predicted five year quantities to achieve economies of scale.

A material tracking system was implemented by the product support material analyst function that compares the actual parts used for repair to the predicted usage. The predictive model will be updated with actual data so piece parts predictions become more accurate over time. Future parts orders will use the updated parts model to determine quantities to order. Part usage will rely on parts requisitions from Rockwell Collins San Jose (RCSJ) and from the representatives at the Navy depots.

Repair piece parts are housed in carousels at the RCSJ plant, where the RCSJ repairs will be performed. The RCSJ repair line will order repair parts from the PBL portion of the RCSJ stockroom as needed. The PBL planning function will assure these parts get issued to the appropriate repair technician or operator for installation into the repairable. Lay-in material for supplier repairs will be required to support the first two years of the PBL demand with yearly options for the third through fifth years.

Table 5.15 Example from Rockwell Collins of Documenting a Best Sustainment Practice (continued)

Based on quarterly repair projections for the Navy depots (NADEPs), associated repair parts are positioned at the NADEP prior to the start of a quarter to support those projected repairs. The RCSJ on-site representative performs the repair part storage and issuing.
A repair part obsolescence plan was developed for the repair parts identified for the PBL. This plan will initially run the parts list through a program that will analyze the life cycle of the parts. Once the life cycle profile of the parts is known, a plan for that part will be generated to resolve that part's obsolescence profile. Identifying an alternate part, life-time purchase of parts, and/or redesign of the part are possible solutions for parts obsolescence.
Included in the repair parts procurement plan are parts for subassemblies to support repairs and spare assemblies identified in the models used for the PBL proposal. Those parts orders and build plans are generated and monitored by product support planning. Subassembly modules are put into the PBL stockroom carousels to be requisitioned as needed. The planning of these builds should take into account the set-back associated with the demand for the part, where the subassembly is used according to the repair demand prediction model.

Source: Rockwell Collins

5.7 Implementing the Best Sustainment Practices

Discovering practices at other best-in-class organizations is a relatively easy task compared to the implementation of the practice. Implementation is the last step—step 7—in the framework suggested in figure 5.1.

To assist in the implementation process, a road map has been designed for the task. This road map is presented in figures 5.3 and 5.4. The left side of figure 5.3 represents the organizations that possess the best practices related to sustainment. In the center is the benchmark investigation team that is attempting to discover these best practices. On the right are the transformation teams (stakeholders) that can benefit from these practices. The integrated benchmarking team identifies and documents the best practices. The individuals in the team consist of the key external investigators as well as the transformation team members. The rapid improvement teams (RITs) are the individuals who are responsible for implementing the transformation.

Figure 5.4 outlines the steps necessary for the RITs to implement the best sustainment practices. There are basically six steps. The fundamental questions that these steps raise for the RITs are: What are the underlying conditions at the benchmark site that cause that particular performance improvement? Do similar conditions exist at the depot undergoing the transformation? If not, how might the performance improvement be different, or how should the specific policies or activities that are different be modified to make the best sustainment practices applicable? The last step is important to continuous process improvement (CPI). It is the

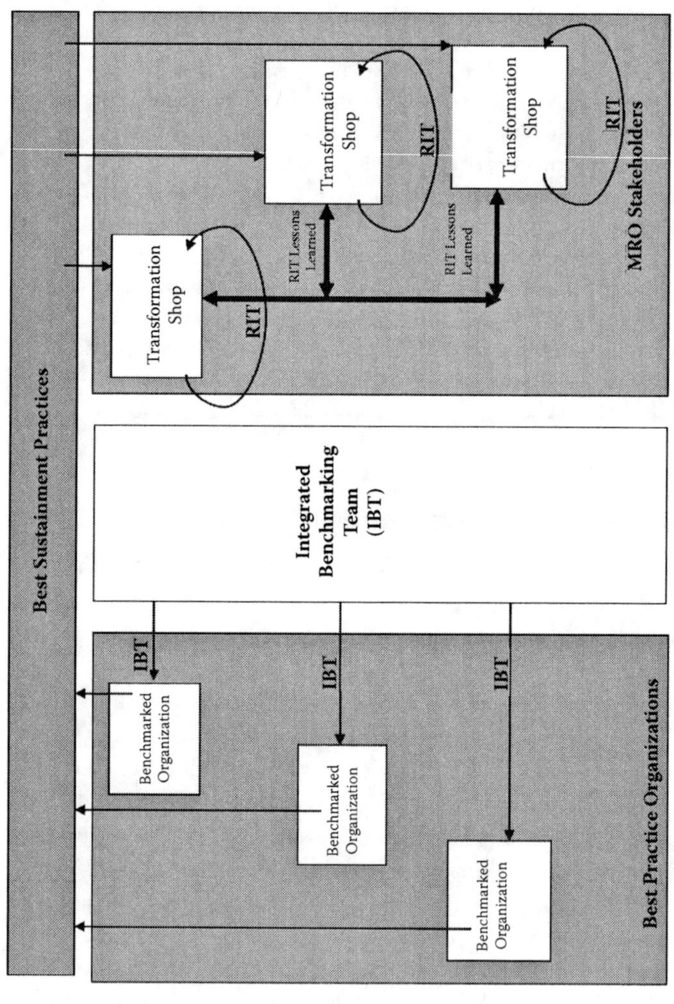

Figure 5.3 A Road Map for the Implementation of Best Sustainment Practices.

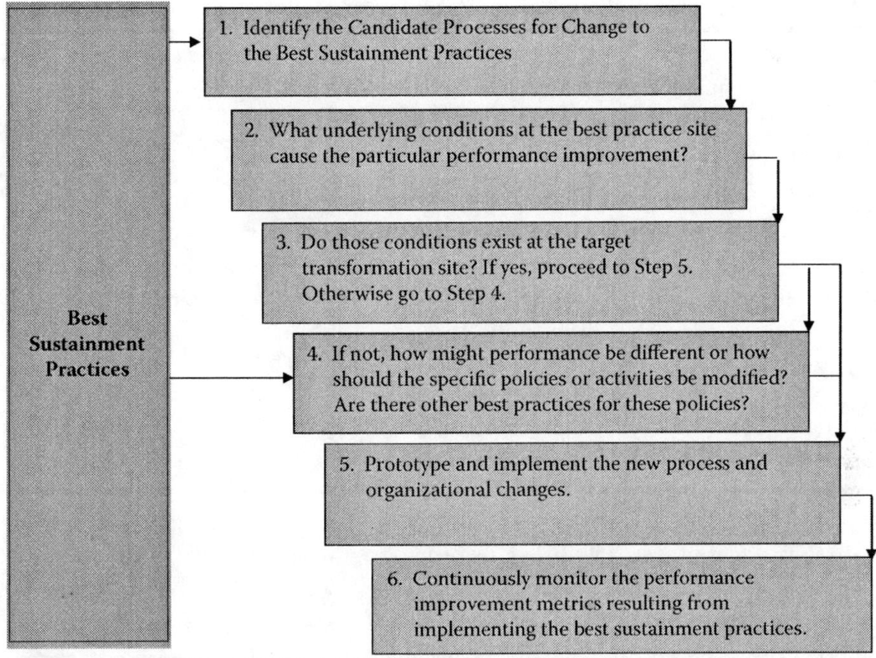

Figure 5.4 Implementation Steps for the Best Sustainment Practices.

task of continuously monitoring the CPI metrics pertaining to the best practice. These metrics are the same metrics used in a transformation, and the frequency of monitoring these metrics would be the same as in a transformation program.

5.8 Schedule Plan for Executing the Seven-Step Benchmarking Process

This section outlines a plan for executing the seven-step process described above. The benchmarking integrated project team (IPT) should perform the first six steps of the process, in collaboration with the appropriate stakeholders. The depot should perform the last step, the implementation of the best sustainment practices into the depot transformation. The benchmarking process should follow the schedule and tasks associated with the LEA implementation of a transformation (as shown in figure 5.5).

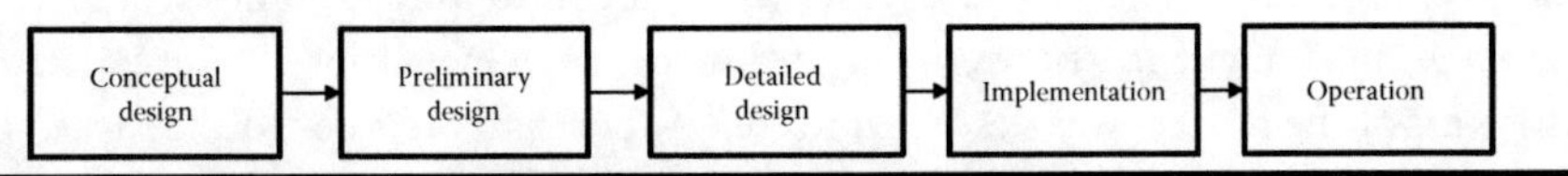

Figure 5.5 Steps in the Lean Enterprise Architecture.

Table 5.16 Executing the Benchmarking Process

Steps in Lean Enterprise Architecture	*Steps in the Benchmarking Process*	*Benchmarking Task Performed by:*
Conceptual Design	1. Identify problems	Integrated product team (IPT)
	2. Identify solutions	Consultant or IPT
Preliminary Design	3. Identify enabling practices	Consultant or IPT
	4. List the best practice	Consultant or IPT
Detailed Design	5. Map the practice to the Lean Enterprise Architecture task	Consultant or IPT
	6. List the benefits	Consultant or IPT
Implementation	7. Implementation	IPT
Operation	7. Implementation	IPT

As the depot proceeds with a transformation, the IPT should benchmark and document the institutions possessing the best practices that have been mapped to the appropriate task in the LEA. This mapping is described in task 5 of this benchmarking process, and the steps shown in table 5.16 should have been completed by that time. The idea is to carry forward to a transformation the lessons learned from the benchmark institutions to avoid costly and time-consuming duplication of effort.

Some of the candidate benchmark institutions were identified in table 5.13, above. Others can be identified using the MRO survey that was described in section 5.3.1.1. Thus, the first steps in executing the benchmarking process are to design the survey instrument, mail the questionnaire out to MRO-associated organizations, and process the survey responses to determine other candidate benchmarks. *Aviation Week*'s *MRO Magazine* can be very useful in providing a list of MRO-related organizations. In parallel with this survey, the benchmarking IPT should continue to search for benchmark institutions using other media described in section 5.3.1. These two tasks can be performed in parallel. The benchmarking IPT should approve the resulting list of benchmark institutions. The site visits by the benchmarking team should be conducted at the appropriate time in the LEA transformation schedule. Table 5.17 summarizes the schedule plan for executing the seven-step benchmarking process.

It is important to keep in mind that as best practices are implemented into a transformation the benchmarking IPT needs to continuously monitor the performance improvement metrics resulting from the implementation of the practices. This part of the process was described in step 7 above, and it is key to the successful

Table 5.17 Schedule Plan for Executing the Seven-Step Benchmarking Process

Sequence	*Task*	*Task Performed by:*
1	Design the benchmarking questionnaire	Benchmarking consultant or Integrated Product Team (IPT)
2	Mail the questionnaire to maintenance, repair, and overhaul-related organizations	Consultant or IPT
3	Process the survey responses	Consultant or IPT
4	Continue the search for best practices using other media (Internet, etc.)	Consultant or IPT
5	Document the best practices in accordance with the seven-step benchmarking process	Consultant or IPT
6	Begin site visits in accordance with the Lean Enterprise Architecture (LEA) schedule and a transformation plan (as described in table 5.16) prior to, but in accordance with, a transformation plan and LEA schedule for cell transformation	IPT

translation of the practice. The transformation team must continually ask: what underlying conditions at the best practice site cause the particular performance improvement? Do these conditions exist? If not, why and how might performance be different or how should the specific policies or activities be modified? Are there other best practices for these policies? Should the benchmarking team revisit the benchmark sites to discuss differences in the underlying conditions and what can be done to mitigate the risks?

5.9 Best Sustainment Practice Case Studies

The sections below document best sustainment practice findings at Pratt & Whitney and the U.S. Army. Each case study differs in terms of the practices implemented and the improvement themes (improvement in quality, reducing cost, inventory reduction, and improvement in process cycle times). The case studies presented here are examples of process variability reduction, process improvement, and flow optimization.

5.9.1 Pratt & Whitney

5.9.1.1 A Case Study in Implementing Enterprise Resource Planning Systems at Pratt & Whitney Space Propulsion

Pratt & Whitney Space Propulsion in West Palm Beach, Florida, has been providing leading-edge technology solutions to the commercial and military launch vehicle markets for more than four decades. Their product line includes both liquid- and solid-fuel rocket engines that satisfy a wide range of mission requirements. Pratt & Whitney's RL10 engine (see figure 5.6) has been the upper-stage liquid-oxygen and hydrogen-fueled rocket engine of choice for more than four decades. With the National Aeronautics and Space Administration's most reliable upper stage engine, the RL10-powered Centaur launched numerous satellites and space probes on a variety of exciting earth orbital and interplanetary missions. Under contract with NASA, Pratt & Whitney produces high-pressure turbopumps for NASA's space shuttles' main engines. Together, a pair of high-pressure turbopumps deliver liquid hydrogen and liquid oxygen to the shuttle engine's main combustion chamber for ignition. Pratt & Whitney's Chemical System Division's (CSD) booster separation motors are vital for NASA's space shuttle launches. Approximately two minutes into flight, 16 of these small but powerful motors (four each, mounted on the aft and forward sections of the two solid motor boosters) execute split-second timing to provide the precise thrust required for safe separation of the spent boosters away from the main fuel tank and the orbiter. The CSD has flown over 1,600 booster separation motors on the space shuttle (100 missions), and every one has performed flawlessly.

Figure 5.6 Pratt & Whitney's RL-10 Rocket Propulsion Engine.

This case study describes an enterprise resource planning implementation at Pratt & Whitney Space Propulsion in West Palm Beach. Enterprise resource planning (ERP) software attempts to integrate all departments and functions across a company onto a single computer system that can serve all those different departments' particular needs. That is a tall order: building a single software program that serves the needs of people in finance as well as it does the people in human resources and in the warehouse. Each of those departments typically has its own computer system, each optimized for the particular ways that the department does its work. But ERP combines them all into a single, integrated software program that runs off a single database so that the various departments can more easily share information and communicate with each other.

This integrated approach can have a tremendous payback if companies install the software correctly. Take a customer order, for example; typically, when a customer places an order, that order begins a mostly paper-based journey from in-basket to in-basket around the company, often being keyed and rekeyed into different departments' computer systems along the way. All that lounging around in in-baskets causes delays and lost orders, and all the keying into different computer systems invites error. Meanwhile, no one in the company truly knows what the status of the order is at any given point because there is no way for the finance department, for example, to get into the warehouse's computer system to see whether the item has been shipped. "You'll have to call the warehouse," is the familiar refrain heard by frustrated customers.

ERP is currently being implemented at Pratt & Whitney to improve the functionality and maintainability of all current and future business processes and to integrate these processes in order to

- Better manage and share business information
- Successfully meet productivity goals
- Increase the level of responsiveness to customers

Why use ERP? Pratt & Whitney is evolving, and is far more complex than in the past. This complexity will be magnified by future business plans. In order to successfully compete, Pratt & Whitney will need to begin to operate its business in a more integrated environment—one with more consistent, timely, and accurate information. Pratt & Whitney also has a complex, robust set of legacy systems. These systems were developed to mirror the existing organization. They were developed incrementally to automate the clerical functions in each department, driven by local efficiency needs with little inclination toward supporting enterprisewide needs. They have served the company well, but are old in terms of functionality, maintainability, technology, and ease of use. They were state-of-the-art systems when originally implemented, but they support obsolete business processes and cannot be changed as rapidly and cost-effectively as needed to meet Pratt & Whitney's productivity goals.

The case study herein is phase 5a of Pratt & Whitney's ERP rollout. The phases are:

Phases 1 and 2: Financial; hardware architecture
Phase 3: Singapore MRO center
Phase 3a: East Hartford, Connecticut, engine center
Phase 4: C-17, C-117 military engine repair center, Cheshire, Connecticut
Phase 5: JT9D engine overhaul center, Columbus, Georgia
Phase 5a: Pratt & Whitney Space Propulsion, West Palm Beach, Florida

The phases are configured partly by function and partly by location. The best practice is the phased-change implementation for the ERP systems at Pratt & Whitney. Rather than a "big bang" approach to implementing ERP, Pratt & Whitney used this phased approach. Another success factor is that there was a commitment from management for the implementation: training, exercising/testing the system, and modifications to the COTS version of the ERP system. Pratt & Whitney Space Propulsion made use of IPTs to integrate the ERP software into the organization. In addition, Pratt & Whitney software (user interface) code was written to dovetail with the COTS ERP system.

Performance improvements resulting from the ERP implementation include:

- Improvement in the management and sharing of business information through the provision of seamless interfaces and maintaining consistency in data
- Improved customer services and increased productivity
- Increased information flow among functional areas
- Maintaining a single database system that is a core feature of the integrated design and provides improved access to real-time, integrated information
- Data that sites can access from other functional areas—within a site and across multiple sites
- Accentuated transaction flow and mutual dependencies across modules
- Reduced inventory levels
- Better customer service

5.9.1.2 A Case Study on Cellular Repair and Overhaul at Pratt & Whitney's San Antonio Engine Center

Pratt & Whitney has MRO facilities in the United States, Europe, the Middle East, and the Asia-Pacific region. It also provides MRO services for non-Pratt & Whitney engines. For military customers, Pratt & Whitney offers a program called *flexible sustainment*, in which the company completely manages the engines for its customers using existing military or commercial overhaul and repair facilities. The program has demonstrated improvements in the readiness rate of its engines.

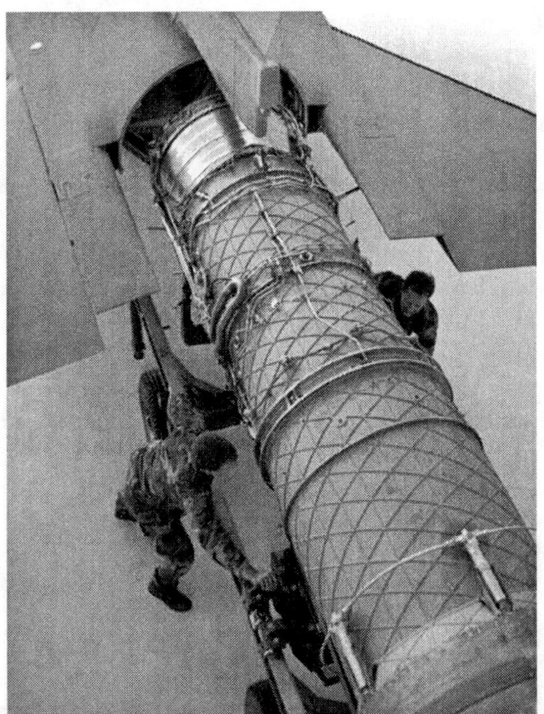

Figure 5.7 Pratt & Whitney's F-100 Engine.

The San Antonio Engine Center in Texas offers complete depot-level engine overhaul services for the F-100 engines (see figure 5.7). They perform scheduled and unscheduled depot-level maintenance for full engines and individual modules of the F-100-PW-100, -200, -220, -220E, and -229 engines. Additionally, they perform upgrades of F-100 engines to PW-220E configurations and analytical condition inspections. As the original equipment manufacturer (OEM), the center is electronically linked to Pratt & Whitney design engineering for instant technical guidance and the latest technical data. The center is recognized as a leader of continuous improvement and kaizen (incremental improvement) activity for improvement in module overhaul, engine overhaul, and kitting processes. The drive for quality results in cost-effective and responsive support for the center's customers. It has developed state-of-the-art material and supply-chain management systems that offer complete contractor-furnished material supply capability for all models of the F-100 engine. By using contractor furnished material, customers take advantage of the center's strength in vendor and distributor relationships to minimize awaiting parts delays and to reduce overall cost.

The San Antonio Engine Center is an ISO-9002 certified facility. It was identified as an institution possessing best practices in engine repair through an article that appeared in *Overhaul and Maintenance* (Weiner 2000). The focus of the article was on operational improvements using cellular manufacturing, kaizen, and flow lines in the engine center. The focus of the author's visit to the center was to investigate the use of flow lines in the engine repair/overhaul shop. The conventional overhaul process involved a stationary engine bay, where the engine remains for two months: the parts come in, the tools come in, the parts go out, and the tools go out. With the flow lines concept, there are five stations in which the engine gets torn down and five stations in which the engine is built up again. Each day, the engine moves down to the next station, where there are dedicated tools, parts, and people. All four of Pratt & Whitney's engine centers (in Cheshire, Connecticut, Columbus, Ohio, San Antonio, Texas, and Singapore) have the same flow lines. The concept is the same as the lean Toyota production system. Flow is a key principle in lean thinking, and the Pratt & Whitney flow lines use these basic principles. Variations make the process difficult: for example, different configurations of engines, different customer requirements, or the condition of an engine may vary. The lines are modular, grouped by families (e.g., turbine blades). The materials (parts) flow along the lines with the engine, but the employees move about depending upon their expertise. No toolbox is dedicated to an employee. All tool sets are located at the module site. The system uses parts kits, which are placed in carts that are numbered.

Pratt & Whitney was awarded a firm fixed price contract (FFPC) to provide depot services for a series of jet engines for the U.S. Air Force. Because of this type of contract Pratt & Whitney must reduce cost and increase productivity to maintain a profit margin. The company has implemented major changes in both depot operations and management resulting in the following performance improvements:

50 percent reduced floor space
25 percent improvement in productivity (measured by people)
60 percent reduced work in process
50–100 percent improvement in quality

Pratt & Whitney has stated that the FFPC provided them the proper contract vehicle with which to operate unconstrained by normal government requirements such as cost accounting and reporting. The company is unrestricted in extended business opportunities, such as providing foreign military depot services. Another example of innovative business practices and strategy that saved the government substantial savings occurred when the company reclaimed decommissioned assets for parts sharing. Pratt & Whitney inducted decommissioned assets to obtain obsolete parts that the Air Force no longer uses, but these assets can be used for resale in foreign military and commercial markets. In exchange for these decommissioned assets, Pratt & Whitney provided the government $60 million worth of common parts that are currently still in use by the Air Force.

The company adopted a team approach to depot operations and management, and has reduced many staff positions by delegating authority to the lowest possible level and by organizing business and operational processes around integrated teams. Management and work-cell teams are fully integrated with the day-to-day operational depot processes. Implementation of lean systems provides the proper environment in which team operations can occur successfully.

The Pratt & Whitney organization is structured around business management units. These business units are comprised of a number of key project managers that are colocated in an office area sharing an executive administrator. The program manager, contracting manager, and production engineer conduct daily business as an integrated product management team. This management approach has proven effective in integrating both business and depot operations. This management structure was a major problem with many senior and middle-level managers at Pratt & Whitney; it required strong leadership and commitment from top management.

Workforce positions are routinely rotated within the work-cell team structure. Each team member is trained in and assigned to the position of work-cell supervisor as part of the rotation process. The workforce is cross-trained and routinely attends training courses provided by the depot. On a monthly basis, process improvement goals are established for each team. The work-cell teams are not self-directed. Work cell leaders are provided performance goals from the production manager.

Depot workload and task scheduling are coordinated by the system program office manager located on the same base. The contracting officer is part of the program office staff and reports directly to the program manager. The depot is sponsor-funded and sponsor-operated to provide services to the war fighter. A bonus program and continuous process-improvement newsletter are examples of the openness and team spirit that exist at this depot. Each employee understands his or her mission and the performance objectives of his or her work cell (posted at each station). To understand the principles used in operations and management methodology, the quality manager referenced John Davis's *Fast Track to Waste-Free Manufacturing* (2000), in which Davis has created and developed links to four new drivers of waste-free manufacturing (workplace organization, uninterrupted flow, error-free process, and insignificant changeover), and details which order to approach these drivers in and when it is time to move from one driver to the next. He covers nearly every aspect of the lean revolution and provides the essential tools and techniques you will need to implement waste-free manufacturing. He also addresses the critical management issues that will arise in any plant that is striving to function on a world-class level.

To help Pratt & Whitney with its engineering analysis, the company established the Pacer Century Program, in which two or three engines per year undergo a detailed inspection analysis. The engines in this program are specifically chosen because of their high utilization rates. The forecasts are developed at Pratt & Whitney's West Palm Beach facility.

5.9.1.3 A Case Study on Depot Production Operations at Pratt & Whitney

Pratt & Whitney's depot production operations were modeled on the lean Toyota Production System (see chapter 4). The modular design of the material flowing between work cells allows for maximum flexibility in implementing unique one-time engineering changes and technical orders into the material refurbishment cycles. This best practice provides a new framework for system modernization by synchronizing technology cycles and maintenance cycles to provide the most cost-effective method to continue system life-cycle modernization. Quality management and continuous process improvement procedures are based on a quality management system from United Technology, which markets its quality programs and training services.

The depot uses the government supply system and OEM as sources for parts and consumable items. Supply-chain management has been a problem because of poor configuration accounting provided by the government. The technicians on the floor have been very successful in identifying configuration problems, and the technical baseline is continuously improving as each overhaul is conducted. The technician performs a miniature physical configuration audit during the overhaul process; configuration problems are documented and the engineering change process is used to update engineering, overhaul, and source control and procurement documentation.

The depot has developed flow lines based on the overhaul procedures and process. All materials and tools required to overhaul an engine are laid out in the standard U-shaped work cell configuration. Overhaul kits are stored in separate bins placed at each work cell. Separate disassembled parts bins are placed at the applicable work cell. Repairable assemblies are inducted in associated repair shops or shipped to other depots as directed. The depot turnaround time has decreased by 60 percent. Removed parts are inspected for material condition classification and possible reuse; these inspections are conducted after the disassembly parts bins are rotated and emptied. The depot is a mixed supplier/distribution system. Engines are "pushed" to the depot and, once inducted, they become a "pull" system for the overhaul and repair operations. Then they are "pushed" to a forwarded buffer-stock inventory.

The maintenance concept for these engines includes some preventative and corrective intermediate level maintenance with required scheduled depot-level overhauls. Condition-based maintenance is not used. The depot maintains "engine risk kits" as readiness spares to meet unexpected (surge) demands. The Air Force uses buffer stock at the operational unit locations to meet these surges. This two-layer approach can be streamlined and reduced with the one-level maintenance concept.

5.9.2 The U.S. Army

The U.S. Army has been identified as an institution possessing best sustainment practices through the BMPCOE. Examples are the Corpus Christi Army Depot (CCAD) in Texas, the Maintenance Center–Albany (MCA) in Georgia, and the U.S. Army Materiel Command (AMC) in Alexandria, Virginia. The CCAD performs overhaul, repair, modification, retrofit, and modernization procedures for Air Force, Army, Marine Corps, and Navy rotary wing aircraft as well as related engines and components. The MCA provides repair and overhaul capabilities to the operating forces and other customers. The AMC possesses best practices in its Continuous Technology Refreshment spares procurement strategy, formerly the Modernization through Spares program.

5.9.2.1 The Corpus Christi Army Depot

There are 32 practices listed for the CCAD at the BMPCOE website, of which 12 are best practices. The others are information practices, which are not deemed to be best practices by the BMPCOE but are given for information purposes. During a site visit to the CCAD in March 2000, the author focused on three of these best sustainment practices: the strategic planning process, rotor blade repair shop operations, and bearing shop operations.

The Strategic Planning Process

The strategic planning process grew out of a need by the CCAD to focus on the long term and a realization that the CCAD lacked a thorough knowledge of its industry position and environment. To help implement the process, the CCAD developed a strategic planning working group, an executive leadership team, and SWOT teams. These teams established a number of targets. The goals for its customers were to minimize customer complaints and to honor its agreements related to schedule, cost, quality, and safety. The goals for its workforce were:

- To become a multiskilled workforce with the ability to adapt to changing workload
- To establish and manage a multiskilled classification and job description system
- To have a high degree of effective communication
- To create a learning environment at the CCAD in which organization, group, and individual learning is fostered
- To design a strategy to maintain critical skills for the CCAD's business survival

Goals were also established for management information systems and costs. The process provided a road map for the CCAD, and has given the depot a tool with which it can control and manage the course and pace of change.

The CCAD developed and put in place a disciplined and well-implemented strategic planning process. Previously, the depot's strategic planning was difficult to integrate into the complex nature of depot operations. Very little external information regarding the position of the depot in the industry and the competitive environment was obtained in developing strategies. As a result, common business objectives had been sporadic.

In the early 1990s the depot began to develop marketing plans.The CCAD soon realized that it was necessary to develop a strategic plan before a meaningful marketing plan could be accomplished. The foundation of the strategic planning process developed by beginning with the best of past efforts, studying external forces (e.g., the Government Performance and Results Act of 1993, and the Strategic Plan for Year 2001 requirements), and focusing on the depot's customers and its business environment.

In 1997, the CCAD began to implement a strategic planning process for the years 1998–2001. A formal strategic planning regulation was put into effect that fully documented and defined the process. It begins with identifying the beginning and ending periods of the planning time frame, and it involves assessing the depot's current situation—its strengths, weaknesses, opportunities, and threats. Strategic planning includes reviewing the mission and any anticipated fiscal or resource constraints that are expected over the planning period which may stand in the way of achieving the mission. In the process, the leadership team visualizes what the depot wants to achieve (its vision) by the end of the planning period. The steps in a strategic planning cycle result in strategies, goals, objectives, and performance measures to achieve that vision for the future. Strategic planning involves all depot members to be successful and effective. Its success is measured ultimately by the depot's customers.

The planning process was kicked off by forming teams, which included a strategic planning working group, the depot's executive leadership team, and five SWOT teams. These teams worked in parallel to develop, customize, and implement the 26-step process for the CCAD. A customer survey was taken to get honest input from the depot's customers as part of the overall environmental scanning process. A six-question telephone survey was conducted with 20 customers, to which all 20 responded. The three most important items identified by customers were (1) reduced cycle time; (2) improved communications; and (3) adherence to the customer's statement of work objectives and tasks without compromising quality and safety.

Each of the five SWOT teams addressed a specific area: market knowledge, human resources, operations, financial matters, and management information systems (MIS). The MIS team received input from the others to develop an information strategy that supported the other four areas. The teams developed strategies for five aspects of depot management: planning, customers, the workforce, information, and cost. Each of these strategies had well-defined and clearly specified goals and objectives.

A strategic planning handbook for the next three years was then printed and distributed to all depot employees during a two-month time frame. An annual performance plan was developed by the executive leadership team and was distributed with the handbook. The strategies were implemented through the depot's continuous improvement process involving communication, coaching, and ownership to all levels of the command.

This process has increased communication across the entire organization, brought about a primary focus on the customer, and increased teamwork and creativity. A key to success has been coordination at all levels. The process has provided a strategic planning and management roadmap for the CCAD, and has given the depot a tool with which it can control and manage the course and pace of change.[3]

The Rotor Blade Repair Shop

The rotor blade repair shop inspects and repairs helicopter blades. Through the use of a Pareto analysis, the blade repair process fell out as a high-cost process, so it was a prime target for improvement. The CCAD also recognized that there was an opportunity for major market expansion into blade repair. The author observed the following practices in this shop:

Failure analysis for blades. This technique used a Six Sigma quality analysis process to determine the root causes of failure. The technique extended service life by 200 percent, and the CCAD was able to recover old decommissioned assets, saving new acquisition replacement costs and changing maintenance concepts for life cost savings.

Performance metrics. Each shop in the CCAD tracked performance metrics.

Lean implementation. The CCAD developed a local lean process/implementation procedure that included technology insertion for lean depot operations. Shop personnel also adopted lean principles for continuous process improvements.

The laser paint-coating removal process. This process reduced the time required to remove paint on helicopter rotor blades from 40 hours per blade to 8 hours per blade. A laser system was used to remove paint from the blades. It took several months to develop the process, but the return on investment time was only six months.

Composite remanufacturing. Using custom-made sectional heating pads, the CCAD was able to reduce repair times on the composite materials sections of the rotor blades. This process eliminated the need to use large environmental chambers for repairs. Employees developed this new process after being trained and highly encouraged by an implementation team. The cost savings was several million dollars.

Activity-based cost efforts. A special activity-based cost model was developed to benchmark technology-insertion-opportunity cost decisions. Since 1996, the CCAD has used activity-based cost (ABC) methods to support process improvements. ABC is being used to support the depot in its efforts to become certified in the Contractor Performance Certification Program (CP2/ISO 9002). Specifically, ABC analysis has been used to determine what percentage of total depot costs is used to support quality. The ABC analysis quantified the costs for the CP2 certification criteria. Cost figures have been collected at 374 different activities within the depot and then mapped to the six-core business processes of the CCAD. The ABC support team provides software support and training to all depot managers. This allows managers to focus on their sections within the depot and analyze how their decisions affect overall product costs charged to the customers. Although this is not a novel application of ABC, it is a very good use of it, and one that has provided the depot with useful data.[4]

Management-labor relations. The CCAD developed strong management-labor relationships to help implement their lean sustainment pilots. Capital funds were used to invest in these pilot implementations.

Academic partnerships. The CCAD developed a partnership with a local university (the University of Texas–Corpus Christi) for assistance and guidance in pilot implementation, support, and training.

The Bearing Shop

The CCAD has a state-of-the-art bearing shop for the inspection of new bearings, and for repair of used bearings for aviation use or other purposes. The majority of the work in the bearing shop is for aviation use. In 1997, 28,000 used bearings were processed through the shop, with 74 percent of the bearings being reclaimed for use. The 1997 cost savings for reclaiming bearings versus purchasing new bearings was \$9.8 million, with a cost avoidance of \$7.5 million. Approximately 13,000 new aviation bearings are checked in the facility per year to ensure that the bearings are functional and meet all requirements before use; approximately 1 percent of the new bearings fail to meet the requirements. Each bearing is assigned a “traveler” for traceability upon receipt. The bearings are weighed, cleaned, disassembled, and checked for all critical dimensions. New bearings are never handled without using gloves to prevent corrosive skin oils from contaminating them, and are cleaned, reassembled and process packed in a clean room environment. Each package contains a label printed with all critical measurements and the complete identification of the bearing.

Bearings that are used, or new bearings that fail to meet the requirements, may be reworked by honing their races up to 0.0003 inch if necessary, and installing new balls or rollers. These bearings are then cleaned, reassembled, and process packed in a clean room environment. Each package is marked with the same information found on new bearings, and also contains the number of operating hours on the bearing.

Bearings are typically processed through the facility in three days for normal-priority items, and in one day for high-priority work. Less than 0.1 percent of the bearings are ever returned by the customer due to their not meeting requirements. An example of one success story begins with a customer grounding some of its aircraft due to shortages/nonavailability of a particular bearing due to problems with the stock on hand of 664 bearings. The bearing shop was called on to assist in the problem. The shop was able to reclaim approximately 500 of the bearings in a two-day period and prevented extended grounding of the aircraft.

The personnel in the bearing shop are rotated every ten weeks to different jobs in the shop so that at the end of five and a half years every worker is familiar with all of the processes performed. The facility can process bearings ranging in size from miniature to large (three feet in diameter).[5]

5.9.2.2 The U.S. Army Maintenance Center–Albany

The U.S. Army Maintenance Center in Albany, Georgia, provides repair, overhaul, and "inspect, repair only as necessary" capabilities to the operating forces for the Marine Corps and other customers. The Marine Corps' depot concept is one of multicommodity operations, which allows for all ground and ground support equipment to be repaired at strategic locations on the East and West Coasts.

The MCA has implemented several better business practices—manufacturing resource planning II (MRP II), the International Organization of Standards (ISO 9000), and earned value management—since 1998 but had continued to miss customer requirements of cost and schedule targets as much as 50 percent of the time. Thus, in 2001 the MCA embarked on a theory of constraints (TOC) process-improvement initiative. The scheduling of principal end items and secondary depot reparables married well with the implementation of MRP II and resulted in a disciplined shop-floor control system that was not previously present. The concentration on customer requirements for cost, schedule, and performance resulted in all lines being on or ahead of schedule and within cost for fiscal year 2002, likely making MCA the only depot within the Department of Defense to do that. Following the TOC implementation was a lean "six S" manufacturing implementation—sort, straighten, scrub, standardize, observe safety, and sustain—that complemented the TOC and resulted in improved morale. It should be noted that the MCA is implementing lean practices with no contractor support, unlike its sister services, and consequently attributes its lean success to buy-in from its workforce. Additional morale boosters were the many quality-of-life initiatives—painting work areas, renovating the snack bar and cafeteria, installing magazine racks in the rest rooms, and the renovation of a fitness area, to name a few. Having upgraded to ISO 9001: 2000 standards in August 2002, the MCA recently finalized its first follow-up audit, and the Energy and Environment Accredited Quality Assessments registrar has stated that MCA is nearing world-class status in the integration of business practices. Hence, the MCA is becoming a benchmark for other Department of Defense depots and private industry.

Evidence of successes in addition to being force multipliers for the operating forces include:

- Meeting or exceeding customer requirements for cost, schedule, and performance.
- Significantly reducing repair-cycle times across all product lines.
- A reduction in field product quality deficiency reports (FPQDRs). As of 2003, the MCA had received only ten FPQDRs from its customers as compared to 21 the year before. Of the ten received that year, only one was deemed valid.
- Increased safety. As of 2003, the MCA has had 22 mishaps, as compared to 47 for the same period the year before. These include back strains, pulled muscles, and encompass minor mishaps with zero lost workdays.
- Since December 2002, hundreds of items have been added to the master work schedule for Operation Enduring Freedom and provided to the operating forces. These surge requirements have had very little impact on planned schedules. Additionally, the MCA has sent one maintenance team (with another on standby) into theater to support the war fighter.

5.9.2.3 The U.S. Army Materiel Command

The U.S. Army Materiel Command is transitioning from a defense-oriented industrial base to a commercially oriented national industrial base. The reasons for this change in military specifications are:

- The commercial market is driving new technology developments
- Defense budgets for new technology acquisitions are declining
- Military requirements are expressed in terms of what is needed, not how to make it
- The acquisition workforce is decreasing

The objective is to reduce military specifications on acquisitions as much as possible. The MilSpec Reform enacted in 1994 means doing business in a new way:

- Changing the acquisition culture

- Retraining the workforce on process improvement techniques and transformation objectives
- Restructuring management and policy
- Converting to performance-based acquisition
- Disposing of obsolete documents
- Eliminating cost drivers

Continuous Technology Refreshment

Best-practice examples of the MilSpec Reform successes in the U.S. Army that deal with continuous technology refreshment (CTR):

- New technology insertion, such as the implementation of new aviator night vision goggles
  - Procurement of new systems using performance-based contracting
  - Reliability has increased 33 percent
  - Range performance has increased 48 percent
  - Cost has been reduced 62 percent
- New technology insertion, such as the introduction of the M-157 smoke generator
  - Commercial technology is obtained with performance-based requirements
  - System readiness was formerly 60–70 percent; it is now 90+ percent
  - Spares were formerly obsolete; COTS technology is now employed
  - Commercial technology is obtained using performance-based requirements
  - Projected sustainment cost savings are $600,000 per year
- Commercial off-the-shelf technology insertion, such as the introduction of the AN/PRD-12 transportable radio direction finding system
  - Formerly there were high failure rates; now there is increased reliability
  - Formerly there was obsolete liquid crystal display technology; now there is new technology
  - Unit costs reduced 48 percent
  - Operating and sustainment costs savings of $11 million over ten years
- Battery-powered voice amplifiers: an example of new technology insertion
  - Battery-change interval increased from 8 hours to 20 hours
  - Battery costs reduced 65 percent
  - Soldier burden decreased 50 percent
- AN/PRC-112 survival radio 2000: an example of new technology insertion
  - Now a triservice program: Air Force, Army, and Navy
- Patriot PAC-2 low voltage power supply: an example of continuous technology refreshment
  - Formerly there was outdated technology; now there are COTS high-density modules

- Formerly the Patriot PAC-2 was high maintenance; now modular replacements allow rapid field maintenance
- Repair costs reduced 92 percent
- Cost savings of $3.36 million projected over eight years

Note that all of the above examples are best practices in the Army's CTR spares-procurement strategy. CTR in the Army is a spares-acquisition strategy applied throughout the materiel acquisition life cycle to reduce sustainment costs. It is based on technology insertion and commercial products and processes.

The Commercial Operations and Support Savings Initiative

The Army instituted the Commercial Operations and Support Savings Initiative (COSSI) to "improve readiness and reduce operations and support (O&S) costs by inserting existing commercial items or technology into military legacy systems." COSSI "emphasizes the rapid development of prototypes and fielding of production items based on current commercial technology. The program also implements the goals of the current Administration and the Secretary of Defense to: expand the use of commercial practices and products that will facilitate the modernization of our military forces; improve the acquisition process; and, make near-term investments to acquire modern capabilities based upon U.S. scientific and industrial pre-eminence" (Office of the Under Secretary of Defense 2001, p. 1)

Total Ownership Cost Reduction

The Army has also developed an overarching strategy for total ownership cost reduction" (TOCR), which is defined as "[t]he Army process to effect measurable improvements in our materiel solutions/systems, business processes, and infrastructure to reduce cycle time, increase support systems efficiencies, reduce ownership cost, and improve/maintain Readiness" (U.S. Department of the Army 2001, p. 14)

The basic principles behind the TOCR policy are:

- Life-cycle management
  - Establish single manager
- Cost management
  - Establish comprehensive program baseline
  - Quantifiable metrics
  - Continuous use of cost reduction incentives
- Incentives
  - Shared (originator, team, organization, contractor, Army)
  - Monetary and nonmonetary

- TOCR pilot programs
  - Program funding availability
  - Appropriate waivers/exemptions
  - Finite test period
  - Principles can be exported to other programs

Value Engineering

The U.S. Army has established the Value Concepts Office (VCO) to consolidate all acquisition reform and cost-saving initiatives in one office. The VCO is responsible for assisting buying activities in implementing value engineering efforts in all cost-saving initiatives. The office stresses the use of value engineering by using a certified value management specialist from the Society of Value Engineering. Lessons learned include:

- Educating the workforce in value management is much harder than anticipated.
- The value management strategy is overwhelming for most workforce personnel; an implementation guide would be useful.
- To many, value management is a fad, a "flavor of the month," because there are so often new programs with new names.
- No real funding is available to support legacy systems during the operational sustainment life-cycle phase.
- Successful efforts are a better "seller of strategy" than training is.

Acceptance of the strategy increases with pilot implementation projects.

An Integrated Technology Insertion Strategy for Sustainment

The Army has developed a comprehensive strategy for all phases of the life cycle of a weapon system. Early concept analysis for the Modernization through Spares program provided the foundation and framework for this effort. The Army uses technology insertion as both an acquisition storage and sustainment strategy. Integrating these two strategies would provide a good framework. Currently there is some conflict with the newer CTR strategy. The spares model used for a new CTR component still uses a lifetime sustainment computation, which was previously employed for legacy systems. The sparing practice is counter to the new strategies of CTR.

Rapid Improvement Teams for Pilot Implementation

Rapid improvement teams are used to implement pilots for new business processes and technology insertion systems and components. The RIT is a means of establishing collaborative stakeholder efforts; it focuses on the process of change by defining both the problem and its associated barriers for successful implementation. The RIT determines what actions are required to overcome these barriers within a 90-day period.

New Funding Strategy for Modernization

The current U.S. Army implementation pilot efforts employ a shared-funding concept. The Army has many programs that are used to fund the engineering efforts needed to find new technological solutions for components that are no longer supportable due to technology obsolescence. Once the new design is complete, the funding and fielding of the component is accomplished during normal system-refurbishment periods. The item manager coordinates the use and depletion of legacy-system spares inventory to help leverage the transition to a new technology-insertion sustainment strategy. Army comptrollers have determined that modernization of repairables is allowed with operations and maintenance funds as long as the upgrade does not change the fit, form, function, and interface of line repairable units. Research, development, test and evaluation funds are used to develop the engineering change proposals and test control officers, with the operations and maintenance funds being used to install the change into the fleet.

Appendix: Benchmarking Questionnaire

The purpose of this questionnaire is to identify best practices that would offer potentially significant benefits for the logistics and sustainment community supporting the U.S. military. It is designed to help facilitate an integrated world-class logistics and sustainment system for the military sustainment enterprise. In answering the following questions, please accept the definition of "leanness" as the minimization of non-value-added resources and the responsiveness to change in an enterprise.

Protection of Data Confidentiality

The confidentiality of all data you provide will be strictly protected in conformance with established data confidentiality and proprietary information practices. No information you provide shall be presented or published in a way that would permit the identification of any individual or any individual organization.

Section A: Performance Metrics

A1. From the following metrics, please identify the five most important ones, on a scale of 1 (most important) to 5 (least important).

- ☐ Downtime
- ☐ Total maintenance and repair cost
- ☐ Maintenance, repair, overhaul, or modification/upgrading cost time
- ☐ Percent of all fielded or in-service assets of a particular type (e.g., F-15, C-130) that are available and ready for operation or use on any given day
- ☐ Fill rate for orders
- ☐ Total cost of providing spare parts logistics and related product support services to your own customer base or, under contract, to customers of one or more of your client companies
- ☐ Total cost of providing inbound logistics and integrated supply-chain management services under contract with one or more customer companies
- ☐ Percent of all orders or shipments that are delivered on-time to receiving facilities of your customer companies (e.g., warehouses, plants, sales outlets) from their suppliers.
- ☐ Other (please specify) ______________________________

A2. Given the definition of *leanness* at the beginning of this document, what degree of leanness do you believe your organization has achieved, if any? Use a scale of 1 (highest rank/high impact of leanness) to 4 (lowest rank/no leanness at all):

____

A3. Have you recently initiated major improvements toward being lean in your organization?

☐ Yes ☐ No

If no, go to question A4

If yes, please rank the impact of each improvement on a scale of 1 (high impact) to 4 (low impact):

Schedule _______
Cost _______
Quality _______
Other _______
(If other, please indicate: ________________________________)

A4 . Are there target goals for future improvement?

☐ Yes ☐ No

If no, go to question A5.

If yes, please rank the relative importance of each improvement area, using a scale of 1 (high rank) to 4 (low rank). *Note:* Each improvement should have a different numerical ranking.

Schedule _______
Cost _______
Quality _______
Other _______
(If other, please indicate: ________________________________)

A5. Please indicate the extent to which the following factors may encourage or discourage a truly lean operation in your organization.

Factor	*Encourages*	*Neither Encourages nor Discourages*	*Discourages*
Customer-induced policies			
Regulation-induced policies			
Inconsistent and changing requirements from:			
Customers			
Government			
Prime contractor			
Technical limitations in:			
Processes			
Technologies			
Supplier-induced policies			
Organizational, managerial, or cultural policies			
Other (please indicate): ____________			

Section B: Customer Interaction and Performance Levels

This section addresses a number of key topics pertaining to how you organize and manage your extended enterprise, which is defined broadly as encompassing your organization's internal and external interactions that create value for your customers.

B1. Please check any of the following that best describe how maintenance and repair requirements are actually determined regardless of who performs the task.

- ☐ Predetermined time schedule
- ☐ "Use-based" schedule (e.g., number of hours)
- ☐ Follow a combination of the above two, depending on the product or system in question and depending on customer needs and preferences
- ☐ Other (please specify) ____

B2. What is the frequency of major maintenance tasks? ____________
What is the frequency of minor periodic checks? ____________
What is the frequency of major overhauls? ____________

B3. Please check which of the following best describe how repair requirements, repair priorities, and total quantities to be repaired are determined.

- ☐ Maintain uptime target for items by repairing within a given time interval and having all spares in stock
- ☐ Maintain uptime by maintaining spares of subsystems
- ☐ Focus on critical part inventories

B4. What is the service level on subsystems in terms of percent of demand filled from stock? ____________

B5. What is the average service level on parts range? __________

What is the minimum? __________

What is the maximum? __________

B6. What is your average inventory level of parts in days of supply? __________

What is the minimum? __________

What is the maximum? __________

B7. What is your average inventory level of subsystems in terms of days of supply? __________

What is the minimum? __________

What is the maximum? __________

B8. Elapsed time between a part's delivery to a repair facility or shop and its actual induction into repair process: __________(days/hours)

Elapsed time between part's induction into repair process and completion of the required repair tasks:__________(days/hours)

Elapsed time between completion of repair tasks and its receipt at the point of use: __________(days/hours)

Total elapsed time: __________(days/hours)

B9. How are customers notified of the mode of shipment and destination for unserviceable items?

- ☐ Electronically
- ☐ Fax
- ☐ Voice
- ☐ Other (please specify): ____

Section C: Service Processes

C1. Please check any of the following that best characterize how your organization's factory floor layout is designed for performing your maintenance, repair, or overhaul operations

- ☐ Job shop
- ☐ Batch flow process
- ☐ Functional departments
- ☐ Product groups
- ☐ Functional departments and product groups (e.g., using cellular manufacturing or group technology arrangements)
- ☐ Other (please specify) ______________________________

C2. Please check any of the practices, processes, or methods listed below that best characterize your current production operations.

- ☐ "Push" system
- ☐ "Pull" system (kanban)
- ☐ "Just in time" system
- ☐ Established process for tracing defects or errors discovered in the maintenance, repair and overhaul process to their source without assigning blame
- ☐ Common parts tracking system (e.g., using bar codes, color codes, etc.)
- ☐ Empowered multifunctional (i.e., multiskilled) work teams

C3. How many geographic sites typically hold identical spare parts? __________

C4. If the need for repair cannot be met either from on-site spare stock, wholesale spare stock, or another site's spare stock and must be satisfied, how is the repair accomplished?

- ☐ Repair is delayed
- ☐ Repair is sent to manufacturer or contractor
- ☐ Cannabilization
- ☐ Other (please specify) ______________________________

C5. If open needs exist for an asset, and the repair activity cannot proceed until parts become available, are those in the repair process alerted of the unserviceable shipment?

☐ Yes ☐ No

C6. Approximately what percentage of the items that need repair have multiple sources of repair?

Less than 25%	*25%*	*50%*	*75%*	*100%*

C7. For those items that have multiple sources of repair, what business rule is used to determine the split of work given to each source?

☐ Equally balance the additional workload
☐ User makes selection
☐ Algorithmically assign the workload based on current loads at these facilities
☐ Other (please specify) ______________________

C8. What percentage of the time is a recoverable item repaired without consumable part delays?

Less than 25%	*25%*	*50%*	*75%*	*100%*

C9. When delays occur, on average how long do they last? ________________

C10. For items repaired without delay, what is the average ratio of queue time to active repair time? ______________________________

C11. Are obsolete components traced?

☐ Yes ☐ No

Are obsolete components disposed of?

☐ Yes ☐ No

Section D: Information Infrastructure

D1. On a scale of 1 to 5, please indicate the degree to which you use information technologies in the following functional areas.

	Not at all 1	*Few Functions* 2	*Moderately* 3	*Most Functions* 4	*For everything* 5
Prioritization					
Inventory					
Demand/ Forecasting					
Work Order					
Billing/Finance					
Purchasing					

D2. Indicate which of the following activities are supported, and at what level.

IT Support (organizational hierarchy): How centralized are the following functions in your IT support operation?

	Companywide	*Physical location (a single, physical site—e.g., the Renton plant)*	*Functional division (all of the engine repair operations may not be physically colocated in a single site)*	*Functional division (single site—e.g., a sheet metal shop at one repair facility)*
Acquisitions				
Computer hardware				
Application software				
Networking hardware				
Networking software				
Hardware installation				

(continued)

	Companywide	*Physical location (a single, physical site—e.g., the Renton plant)*	*Functional division (all of the engine repair operations may not be physically colocated in a single site)*	*Functional division (single site—e.g., a sheet metal shop at one repair facility)*
Desktops				
Servers				
Application software installation				
Prioritization				
Inventory				
Demand/ forecasting				
Work order				
Billing/finance				
Purchasing				
Contract repairs				
Network maintenance				
Software				
Hardware				

D3. Architecture

How would you describe your organization (centralized, decentralized, hybrid) with respect to the formation and enforcement of policies that affect your operation and performance? Is your information systems and software maintenance managed in a centralized, decentralized, or hybrid strategy?

Individual organizations or departments manage their own software upgrades:
☐ Centralized ☐ Decentralized ☐ Hybrid
Backups and equipment purchases:
☐ Centralized ☐ Decentralized ☐ Hybrid
Are equipment purchases managed by central information systems (I/S)?
☐ Yes ☐ No
Are software upgrades and installations managed by central I/S?
☐ Yes ☐ No

Is networking maintained by central I/S?

☐ Yes ☐ No

Are contract repairs managed by central I/S?

☐ Yes ☐ No

D4. Commonality of Databases: Are your databases common to your internal organization, customers and suppliers? On a scale from 1 (least common) to 5 (most common or identical) rate the following:

Commonality Aspect	*Internal to organization*	*External*	
		Customers	*Suppliers*
Data definition			
Data structure (file, database)			
Data management systems (database management systems, file, spreadsheet)			

D.5 Data Quality: On a scale from 1 (lowest quality) to 5 (highest quality) please rate the quality of the data you use internally and that you share with other organizations:

Data Quality Aspect	*Internal*	*External*		
		Interorganization	*Customers*	*Suppliers*
Accuracy				
Timeliness				

D4. Please describe the most significant type of *exchange* or *flow* that best characterizes the form or content of the interaction between your own business unit and other parts of your parent organization, external government agencies or entities, or external firms. The form or content of interactions is defined in terms of major types of exchange or flow as listed below. Please select one or more items from this list and identify them by number, as applicable, in specific cells of the matrix provided below. In this matrix, rows represent organizational entities from which such exchanges or flows originate. Columns represent "destination" organizational entities that receive such exchanges or flows.

Types of interorganizational relationships (defined in terms of major types of *exchange* or *flow* between any given pair of organizational entities):

Type 1: Information (e.g., forecasts of parts failure, mission capability indication such as an aircraft not being mission-capable for lack of a component or part—mission capability, requirements for maintenance and repair, availability of capacity, availability of funds, etc.)
Type 2: Decisions (e.g., determining priorities, selecting suppliers, ordering parts)
Type 3: Money (e.g., funding or payment for services rendered, internal transfer payments for services rendered by other parts of the parent organization, payment to subcontractors and suppliers)
Type 4: Materials, parts and components needed for maintenance and repair services (e.g., from suppliers; from other parts of the parent organization to your business unit)
Type 5: Resources (e.g., labor, capital equipment)
Type 6: Unserviceable assets (i.e., parts, components or systems requiring depot-level repair)
Type 7: Serviceable assets (i.e., parts, components or systems that have been repaired and are available for customer use)

EXAMPLES:

Row G → Column A: 6
Row A → Column G: 7
Row F → Column A: 4
Row G → Column B: 3

FROM ↓ TO →	A	B	C	D	E	F	G
A. Operating units within your own organization	■						
B. Functional entities within your own organization		■					
C. Other operating entities within parent organization			■				
D. Other functional entities within parent organization				■			
E. Other gov't agencies or entities outside parent organization					■		
F. Other firms, subcontractors, and suppliers						■	
G. Customer organizations or units (and/or end-product users)							■

D5. For your answers to question D4, in what form does the information generally flow?

- ☐ Electronically
- ☐ Fax
- ☐ Voice
- ☐ Other (please specify): ____

D6. What are the principal methods used by your organization in managing its internal and external relationships, involving the types of interorganizational exchange or flow identified in D4? ________________

D7. Types of methods used for managing relationships (fill out the following form in the same manner as was done for D4 above):

Type 1: Adversarial or arm's length, reliance on complete contracts

Type 2: Transactional, with some information sharing

Type 3: Cooperative, with extensive information sharing

Type 4: Collaborative alliance, with extensive information, cost and risk sharing

Type 5: Long-term strategic partnership, based on mutual trust and obligation, involving high degree of strategic as well as tactical collaboration and interdependence

EXAMPLES

Between Row A and Column B: 3
Between Row E and Column B: 2
Between Row A and Column F: 1

FROM ↓ TO →	A	B	C	D	E	F	G
A. Operating units within your own organization	■						
B. Functional entities within your own organization		■					
C. Other operating entities within parent organization			■				
D. Other functional entities within parent organization				■			
E. Other gov't agencies or entities outside parent organization					■		
F. Other firms, subcontractors, and suppliers						■	
G. Customer organizations or units (and/or end-product users)							■

Section E: Business Practices

E1. How does your organization set prices for the various services or products you provide to your customers? Please check any of the items below that best characterize your current practices:

- ☐ The price for every new task, service, or product is negotiated separately ahead of time with each customer
- ☐ All customers are charged standard preestablished prices for the different types of services or products provided, where these prices are published or communicated openly, on an ongoing basis, to all customers and are not subject to any negotiation
- ☐ Customers are charged prenegotiated prices, including special or customized rates, under larger umbrella contracts, long-term purchase agreements, ongoing ("evergreen") service contracts, or indefinite quantity delivery contracts that are previously negotiated, where customers are invoiced for cumulative services rendered rather than for each separate discrete service or product provided

E2. Please specify below which particular types of contractual arrangements you use with one or more of your key customers (check one or more of the items listed):

- ☐ Long-term purchase agreement (three or more years)
- ☐ On-going ("evergreen") service contract
- ☐ Indefinite service or quantity contract
- ☐ Prenegotiated contractual arrangement for delivery of services on an as-needed or on-call basis
- ☐ Other (please specify) ______________________________
- ☐ A combination of the above
- ☐ None of the above (please specify your practice) ____________________
- ☐ Don't know

E3. If your organization provides services or products under umbrella service contracts, long-term purchase agreements, ongoing ("evergreen") contractual mechanisms, or indefinite service or quantity agreements, which of the following practices do you normally employ in charging your customers for services rendered or products delivered? Please check all that apply:

- ☐ Specified services are provided at fixed prices or rates that cannot be changed during the lifetime of the existing contract
- ☐ Prices or rates for services can be changed as needed, where you normally preserve the right to change your prices by invoking certain contingency clauses in your existing contract with your customer(s) to reflect rising costs of doing business

- ☐ Prices or rates for services can be changed during the lifetime of the contract, but only through mutual consent between you and your customer(s)
- ☐ Your prices can be changed during the lifetime of existing contracts, with or without mutual consent between you and your customer(s), but only to reflect the rising costs of materials and supplies, taxes and levies, and other expenses over which you may have little or no control, while your direct and indirect (overhead) labor rates remain fixed and cannot be changed before contract expiration
- ☐ Other (please specify your practice) ____________________
- ☐ Don't know

E4. How would you characterize the market in which your business unit operates? Please check any of the items below that best characterize your market environment:

- ☐ Your organization is the only supplier, or one of only several producers, of the type of product or service you provide to your customers
- ☐ Your organization is only one of many or numerous suppliers of the type of product or service you provide to your customers
- ☐ You provide your product or service to only one customer
- ☐ You provide your product or service to two or more customers
- ☐ You provide your product or service only to government customers
- ☐ You provide your product or service only to commercial and nongovernment customers
- ☐ You provide your product or service to a mix of government and nongovernment customers
- ☐ Other (please specify your practice) ____________________
- ☐ Don't know

E5. Which of the following business practices do you employ in determining your costs of production and deciding what prices to charge your customers? Please check all that apply.

- ☐ Use standard hourly direct labor costs for different types of tasks or activities established by independent external organizations, which are then "fully loaded" to include your other direct costs as well as indirect (overhead) costs
- ☐ Use actual incurred direct labor costs, which are then "fully loaded" to include your other direct costs as well as indirect (overhead) costs
- ☐ Use average total cost for all products or services per unit of time (e.g., month, week, day) or per unit of production, since specific cost data by function, process or activity are not available
- ☐ Use the activity-based costing method
- ☐ Other (please specify your practice) ____________________
- ☐ Don't know

E6. Does your organization obtain materials and supplies, parts and components from your suppliers under long-term purchase agreements (three or more years)?

☐ Yes ☐ No

If yes, do you know what percent of the total dollar value of the materials and supplies, parts and components your organization buys from your suppliers are obtained under long-term purchase agreements?

☐ Yes ☐ No

If yes, please insert your estimate here: _____________%

E7. Approximately what percent of your total dollar purchases of materials and supplies, parts and components do you purchase on a "best value" basis (i.e., based on the past performance, technological capability, management practices and overall reliability of the suppliers, reflecting best value to you) rather than on the basis of the lowest cost competitive bid?

Please insert your estimate here: _______%

E8. Approximately how long does it take for your organization to award a new contract or subcontract to a supplier, from first announcement to potential bidders to actual contract award, in the following dollar amounts? Please insert the number of elapsed business days in the spaces provided.

Under $10,000: _________ business days
$10,000 or more but under $25,000: _________ business days
$25,000 or more but under $50,000: _________ business days
$50,000 or more but under $100,000: _________ business days
$100,000 or more but under $500,000: _________ business days
$500,000 or more but under $1,000,000: _________ business days
$1,000,000 or more: _________ business days

E10. For a purchase decision of $10,000 or more (but under $25,000), how long does it normally take for your organization to obtain management approval from original formal request to signed approval to proceed?

____ business days

E11. Do you employ the same supplier performance evaluation, selection, and certification practices for other business units within your parent organization from which you regularly obtain goods and services as you normally use for your external suppliers?

☐ Yes ☐ No

E12. When you obtain goods and services from other business units within your parent organization, what prices do they use in charging your business unit for such goods and services? Please check any of the following practices that best characterize current interdepartmental or interdivisional pricing policy within your parent organization.

- ☐ Use internal transfer (accounting) prices that reflect actual competitive market rates outside the parent organization
- ☐ Use special internal transfer prices that are prenegotiated with other business units within the parent organization, based on normal internal costs of doing business, which may or may not reflect competitive external prices
- ☐ Use special "at cost" internal transfer prices that are determined by upper management, which may or may not reflect competitive external prices
- ☐ Other (please specify your practice) ______________________________
- ☐ Don't know

Section F: General Background Information

The purpose of this section is to gather information about your business unit's or organization's primary product or service, customer base, organization, corporate or organizational affiliation, management structure, employees, and financial information.

F1. Please give the name and address of your specific business unit, local organization, or facility: ____

F2. Please give your title : ____

F3. Which of the following types of service best describes the principal line of business or primary activity from which your business unit derives most of its sales revenue? *Business unit* means a company, division, department, facility, or organizational unit that is a self-contained cost, profit, or performance center. Please check where applicable.

- ☐ Maintenance, repair, overhaul, retrofit, modification, or upgrading of complete systems (e.g., aircraft, locomotives, copiers, etc.)
- ☐ Maintenance, repair, and overhaul of major subsystems, parts or components (e.g., aircraft engines, radars, landing gears, electronics, etc.)
- ☐ After-sales product-support services, including field support and maintenance, repair, service-parts inventory, and logistics operations and management
- ☐ Integrated inbound or outbound transportation and logistics services, including warehousing and distribution, involving multiple products shipped from one or more origins to one or more destinations
- ☐ Integrated third-party full-service contract logistics and supply-chain management services for one or more customers
- ☐ Other (please specify) ______________________________________

F4. For the past two fiscal years, please provide the average time to fill an order and ranges for major categories of orders:

Category	*Average Fulfillment Time*	*Minimum Time*	*Maximum Time*

F5. What was the total number of orders in the past two fiscal years?

First fiscal year: __________
Second fiscal year: ___________

General Information

Lead contact at your organization:
Name: ______________________________
Position: ______________________________
Phone number: ______________________________
Fax number: ______________________________
E-mail: ______________________________
How long did it take you to fill out this questionnaire? ________________

Chapter 6

Lean Enterprise Transformation Activities

A Guide

This chapter is a guide to the implementation of the Lean Enterprise Architecture (LEA). It is a "capstone" chapter portraying the overall flow of the activities necessary to sustain and continuously improve a military enterprise. Because an LEA transformation for the military is often assisted by outside contractors, it is inherently an "acquisition" process for services and products. As a result, it must follow the acquisition templates provided by the U.S. Department of Defense (DoD) and other government agencies. There are three DoD guidebooks to performance-based services acquisition (PBSA) (Interagency-Industry Partnership in Performance 2007; U.S. Under Secretary of Defense 2000; U.S. Office of Federal Procurement Policy et al. 1998) and one U.S. Navy guidebook to the contracting process (U.S. Office of the Assistant Secretary of the Navy 2000) that are particularly helpful.

The PBSA guidebooks are critical to a lean transformation because lean sustainment focuses on program performance and improvement, not simply on contract compliance. The 2007 guidebook states: "One of the most important challenges facing (the military) today is the need for widespread adoption of performance based transformation (PBT) to meet mission and program needs" (Interagency-Industry Partnership in Performance 2007, p. 3). In fact, the administration of

George W. Bush set a goal for FY2002 in U.S. Office of Management and Budget (OMB) Memorandum M-01-15 to "award contracts over $25,000 using PBSA techniques for not less than 20 percent of the total eligible service contracting dollars, increasing to 50 percent by 2005" (Interagency-Industry Partnership in Performance 2007, p. 3). But, although PBSA policies have been in place for a long time, the military enterprise has been slow to adopt them.

The first guidebook (Interagency-Industry Partnership in Performance 2007) breaks down performance-based acquisition into seven steps. We will follow these important steps, but we will also map them to the Lean Enterprise Architecture. The second guidebook (U.S. Under Secretary of Defense 2000) is "a cooperative effort among the components to help the acquisition team, and any other stakeholder, better understand the basic principles of PBSA and better implement performance based methodologies into services acquisitions."[1] The third guidebook (U.S. Office of Federal Procurement Policy et al. 1998) contains best practices that "have proven useful for drafting statements of work, solicitations, and quality assurance plans, and in awarding and administering performance based transformations. Many of these practices were identified through the government-wide Office of Federal Procurement Policy PBSC Pledge Program."[2] The fourth guidebook (U.S. Office of the Assistant Secretary of the Navy 2000) is intended to provide noncontracting personnel with an understanding of the contracting process.

In this chapter, all of these excellent guidebooks have been integrated with the LEA via eight activities. These activities are delineated in the LEA diagram in figure 6.1. The intent is to provide one template based on the many guidelines that the government provides, and to help make the subject of LEA enterprise transformation practical and logical. As the first guidebook states, the purpose is "to shift the paradigm from traditional 'acquisition think' into one of collaborative, performance-oriented teamwork with a focus on transformation performance, improvement, and innovation, not simply contract compliance" (Interagency-Industry Partnership in Performance 2007, p. 3). These transformation activities offer the potential to dramatically transform a military enterprise and "permit the federal government to tap the enormous creative energy and innovative nature of private industry" (Interagency-Industry Partnership in Performance 2007, p. 3).

The process of improving the military can be overwhelming. The intent is to offer a set of activities that will guide you through a lean transformation of your enterprise. Associated with each activity outlined in figure 6.1 is a generic document that has already been prepared to help you. These documents are identified in this chapter with a symbol. You will find them on the compact disk that accompanies this volume. Many of these documents, such as the acquisition plan (AP), statement of work (SOW), and performance work statement (PWS), are government documents that follow the strict acquisition policies and rules laid out by the U.S. Department

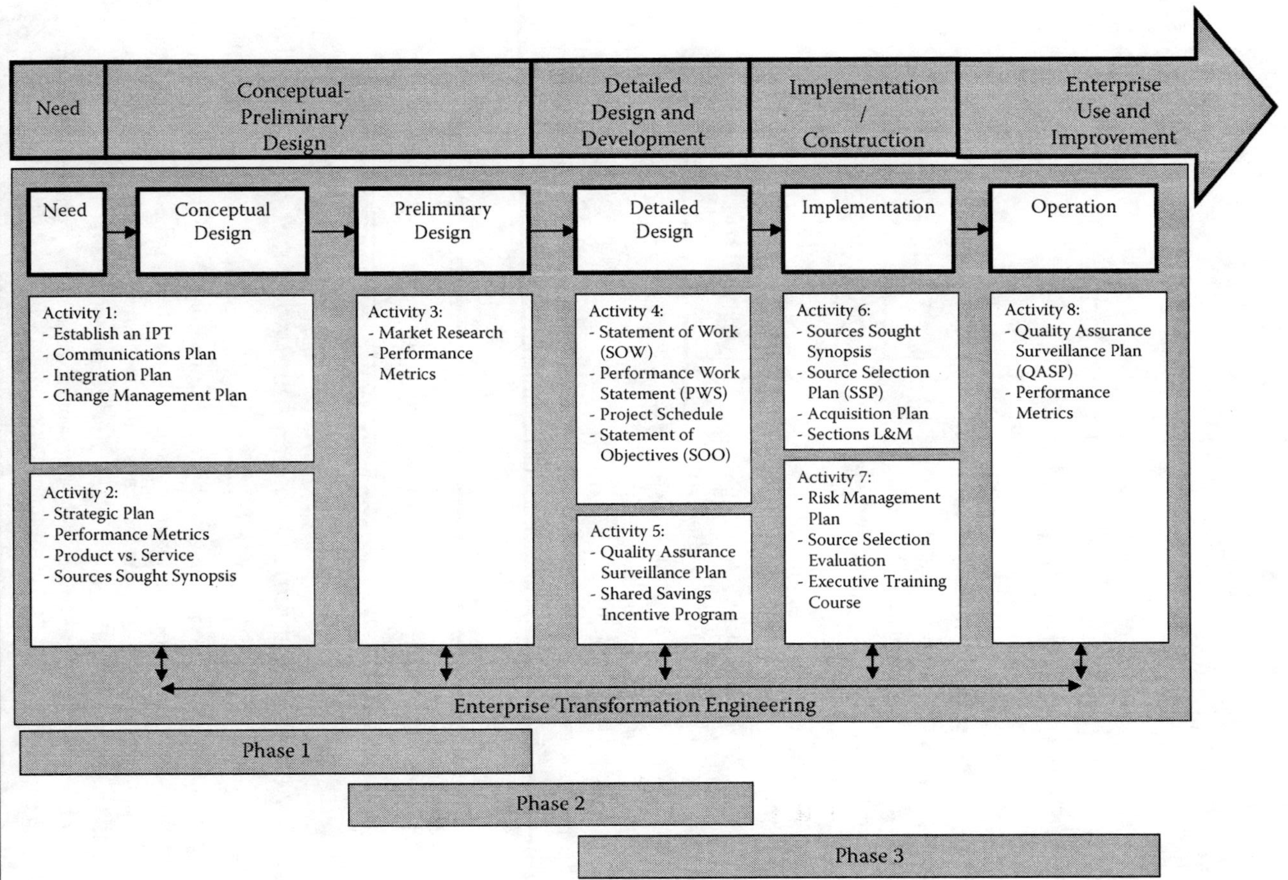

Figure 6.1. Lean Enterprise Transformation Activities (LEA).

of Defense. But, they have been modified to also adhere to the LEA principles. In addition to these government documents, the CD contains other documents of value to a lean transformation.

6.1 Activity 1: Establish an Integrated Product Team (IPT)

Enterprise transformation takes a team working cooperatively toward a common goal. As the first DoD guidebook states: "This is the model used by leading or breakthrough organizations, which have come to recognize the limitations of clearly defined roles, responsibilities, and organizational boundaries, and have adopted the use of transformation teams that integrate all stakeholders' efforts toward one goal: mission accomplishment" (Interagency-Industry Partnership in Performance 2007, p. 4). In this book, we call these teams "integrated product teams" (IPTs) in accordance with the fundamental principles of lean sustainment.

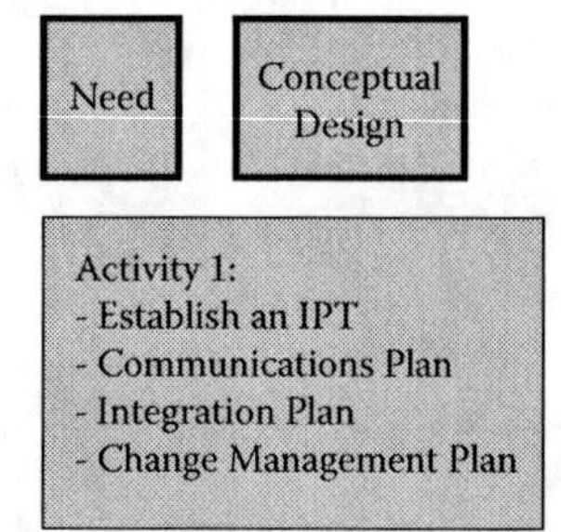

Figure 6.2. LEA Activity 1.

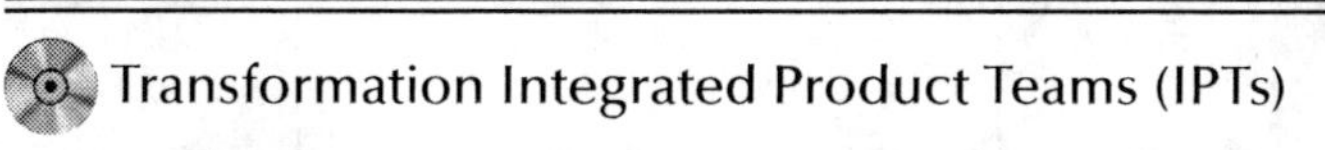

6.1.1 *Senior Management Involvement and Support*

For a lean transformation, an IPT should contain members representing all stakeholders, including senior management. Most lean initiatives start off with good intentions because senior management is usually involved at the start. But then as the initiative gets down into the trenches doing the hard work, management leaves the IPT, and the initiative loses steam. According to the first DoD guidebook, "Most best practice studies agree that senior management involvement and support is a predictor of success. Turf can become an issue unless there is strong, effective senior management support and a shared vision. Program decision makers should be on the team. Creating 'buy in' from leadership and establishing the realms of authority are essential to project success" (Interagency-Industry Partnership in Performance 2007, p. 5).

6.1.2 Empowerment

Members of the IPT must be empowered to make decisions. The project will slow to a crawl if the IPT has to go back to senior management every time a problem arises. The Statement of Guiding Principles for the Federal Acquisition System notes, "Participants in the acquisition process should work together as a team and should be empowered to make decisions within their area of responsibility" (Federal Acquisition Regulation 2007). The levels of empowerment, the specific tasks in the transformation, as well as the identification of the responsibility for the performance of that task, must reside within the IPT and be clearly defined.

6.1.3 Composition of the IPT

The IPT is the entity that plans and manages the activities throughout the lifecycle of the transformation. It should be customer focused, and it is essential that all stakeholders be involved throughout all of the three phases of the transformation life cycle, from establishing the need to implementation. The second DoD guidebook (Office of the Under Secretary of Defense 2000, pp. 2–3) recommends the following composition:

1. Customer/user: Responsible for defining the requirement, including an assessment of the risk that the government might assume when relying on commercial specifications and common marketplace performance and quality standards. The customer/user also plays an important role in deciding what tradeoffs can be made when considering a commercially available service to fulfill a depot requirement.
2. Technical specialist/project manager/program manager: These people serve as the principal technical experts and are usually the most familiar with the requirement and best able to identify potential technical trade-offs and determine whether the requirement can be met by a commercial solution.
3. Contracting officer/contract specialist: Serves as the principal business advisor and principal agent for the government responsible for developing the solicitation, conducting the source selection, and managing the resultant contract and business arrangement. This individual researches contracts in the marketplace

to identify best sustainment practices, such as commercial terms and conditions, contract type, bid schedule breakout, and the use of incentives.

4. Cost/price analyst: Analyzes and evaluates price and cost based data for reasonableness, completeness, accuracy, and affordability. Alternatively, some depots utilize cost engineering personnel from within an engineering division to conduct cost/price analysis from a technical standpoint.
5. Performance assessment personnel (quality assurance personnel): Performance assessment personnel are known by many names, such as quality assurance evaluator (QAE), contracting officer's representative (COR), or contracting officer's technical representative (COTR), but their duties are essentially the same. They serve as the on-site technical managers assessing contractor performance against contract performance standards. Performance assessment personnel are responsible for researching the marketplace to remain current with the most efficient and effective performance assessment methods and techniques.
6. Small and disadvantaged business utilization (SADBU) specialist: Serves as the principal advisor and advocate for small business issues. Also serves as the liaison with the Small Business Administration (SBA).
7. Finance/budget officer: Serves as an advisor for fiscal and budgetary issues.
8. Legal advisor: Ensures that the commercial practices and terms and conditions contemplated are consistent with the government's legal rights, duties, and responsibilities. Reviews for legal sufficiency and advises on acquisition strategies and contract.
9. Miscellaneous others: Personnel from outside the depot may also be useful, depending on their area of expertise. These include people from depots such as the Defense Logistics Agency, the Defense Contract Audit Agency, the Defense Finance and Accounting Service, the Defense Contract Management Agency, and the Environmental Protection Agency, to name a few.

6.1.4 Stakeholders

In addition to membership of the IPT, the stakeholders should include the customer, the general public, oversight organizations, even perhaps Congress. It is important for the IPT to know "who the stakeholders are and the nature of their interests, objectives, and possible objections. At a minimum, stakeholders should be consulted and, at times, may participate on the team" (Interagency-Industry Partnership in Performance 2007, p. 6). The stakeholders may include:

- Transformation areas affected by the changes
- Partners
  - Current and future production partners
  - Logistics
  - Item managers

- Product customers
- Workers, managers, supervisors
- Leadership
- Support agencies
  - Defense Logistics Agency warehousing
  - Vending companies
- Members of the worker unions

6.1.5 Communication

Goals for the IPT should be to gain the visible unified support at every level within the military by spreading the word about the LEA transformation, its approach to the transformation effort, and the progress on the program during its implementation. How does the IPT effectively communicate these activities to the stakeholders? To begin with, a communications plan (CP) should be developed. One such example document is available on the CD. There are a variety of communication vehicles to spread the word on the transformation program.

- Meetings
  - Staff meetings
  - Transformation area team meetings
  - Town hall meetings
- E-mail
- Websites
- Automated bulletin boards
- Newsletters

6.1.6 Change Management Plan

A good communication plan should address change and the impacts of those changes. There is nothing more frustrating than witnessing change when not informed about the change. Whether it is the workers, the customers, or the public, tell them about the change before it occurs. Change communication is effective only when focused in the context of an overall change management plan (CMP). A communications plan should be integrated with a CMP. A widely accepted view of change management by Kotter outlines eight stages of organizational change. Research on best practices validates that organizations who follow this framework have a high rate of success in their change efforts. The eight change stages according to Kotter (1996) are:

1. Establish the motivation for change and a sense of urgency
2. Build a guiding coalition
3. Develop a vision and strategy for change
4. Communicate the vision, including key communication action steps
5. Empower broad-based action, including key training action steps
6. Generate short-term wins
7. Sustain the momentum: consolidate gains and produce more change
8. Anchor new approaches in the culture

As transformation is implemented, unforeseen changes will emerge that will need to be incorporated in longer-term plans. More detail is provided for the near-term stages than for the longer term, but the IPT should evolve the future details as the plan is rolled out.

 Change Management Plan (CMP)

6.1.7 Integration Plan

An integration plan integrates the strategy, policies, processes, procedures, roles, responsibilities, and tool suites with other initiatives that may be ongoing in the enterprise. Integration not only facilitates good communication, but it ensures that all of the other hard efforts are not lost, or overwhelmed by the transformation, or not wasted. An integration plan is useful in building a foundation for planning, implementation, and management of the transformation to a world-class lean enterprise. The plan should apply integrated product and process development (IPPD)[3] methodology as a strategy to implement and subsequently manage the integration of the transformation.

Specific goals and objectives of the integration plan might include:

- Transformation life-cycle planning
- Optimizing the flexibility and use of approaches
- Minimizing cost and time of the transformation
- Encouraging multidisciplinary teamwork
- Streamlining communication and decision making
- Managing change

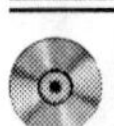 Integration Plan (IP)

6.2 Activity 2: Define the Need and Describe the Problem

6.2.1 The Need

The strategic plan is the document that defines the need for transformation. It is a dynamic document that is subject to review and change as activities are implemented and as the full spectrum of the transformation is coordinated and integrated. A key component of this transformational attitude is a dynamic enhancement approach that will ensure long-term success for the enterprise. Envision a pyramid structure for the approach to strategic planning. Outline the mission of the transformation at the top. Below, specify the overarching vision for accomplishing the mission with a set of general goals and objectives. The enabling tasks (ETs) are further down on the pyramid. They define the essential tasks for the mission areas and functions. ETs are the specific activities that make it possible to accomplish what are called "mission essential tasks" (METs). The METs represent each mission area's (MA) work breakdown structure (WBS) and the key outputs the MAs produce in support of the enterprise. Each ET has supporting objectives that are designed to improve the performance of the METs. The bottom of the pyramid describes the strengths, weaknesses, opportunities, and threats (SWOTs) for the enterprise, which is the data and information that is the foundation for the implementation of the strategy at the top. The strategic plan example provided on the accompanying CD has an example of this pyramid, and it includes:

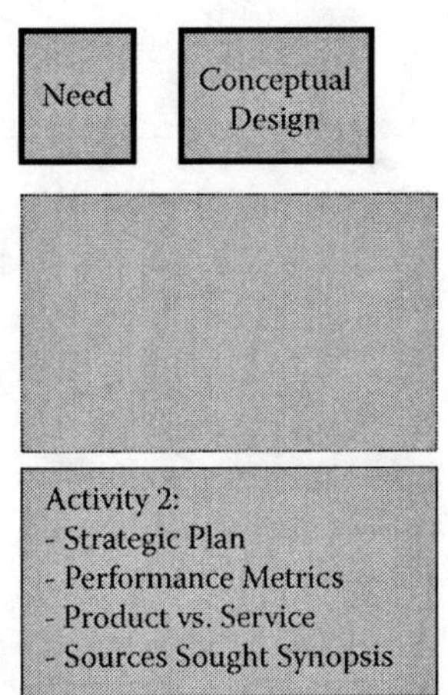

Figure 6.3. LEA Activity 2.

- A description of the strategic planning process as it applies to military depot maintenance
- A description of the depot maintenance mission, vision, and goals
- A listing of possible mission essential tasks and enabling tasks pertinent to such an effort
- Required mechanisms for controlling the transformation process, including:
  - Metrics
  - Benchmarking
  - Risk Management
  - Change Management

  - Communication
  - A timeline for implementation
- A description of the lean approach to transformation
- A description of the strengths, weaknesses, opportunities, and threats attendant on such an effort

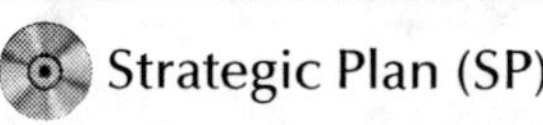
Strategic Plan (SP)

6.2.2 *The Requirements*

The second DoD guidebook (U.S. Under Secretary of Defense 2000) outlines a series of three steps to help specify the requirements of the transformation: first, defining the desired outcomes; second, conducting an outcome analysis; and third, conducting a performance analysis. These three actions really address the question: What, specifically, are the desired results (outcomes) of the transformation? Is it a reduction in system or component turn times, a reduction in awaiting parts problems, or is it the broader goal of increasing weapon system availability? It is one of the tasks that the IPT must face. These requirements are subsequently captured in the performance work statement (PWS) or statement of objectives (SOO). "To do this well, the team (IPT) will need to plan to seek information from the private sector during market research (another activity discussed below). Industry benchmarks and best practices from the 'best in the sustainment business' may help sharpen the team's focus on what the performance objectives should be" (Interagency-Industry Partnership in Performance 2007).

A transformation to lean requires metrics to be identified to monitor performance and to provide the feedback necessary to review and revise implementation plans. Performance metrics both display organizational performance and serve as diagnostic tools to uncover problems early in the transformation process. Performance includes a "balanced scorecard"[4] set of measures for cost, schedule, quality, etc. Benchmarking studies can provide an initial list of relevant metrics, which can then be used to establish a baseline of performance and produce successive (daily, monthly, quarterly) measures of performance. Examples of high-level metrics are:

1. Production
   a. Organic production hours
   b. Major system production
   c. Subsystem production

2. Quality
   a. Major system quality defect rate
   b. Subsystem quality defect rate
   c. Component quality defect rate
3. Cost
   a. Net operating result

Setting performance thresholds on these metrics can:

- Align performance with the objectives
- Focus on critical success factors in meeting military goals
- Promote continuous process improvement

The metrics must also be consistent with those used routinely throughout senior military reviews. These higher-level metrics should be assessed and supported by an evaluation of lower-level (cell, cluster, strategic business unit) metrics. The military enterprise does not necessarily have to be the one to do these measurements. The IPT should require a set of metrics as a deliverable from the contractor performing the work. An example of a performance metrics tasking document can be found on the CD.

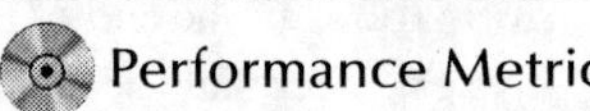

6.2.3 Is the Transformation a Product or a Service?

Is the government contracting for a "service" or a "product" when it undertakes a transformation? The question is an important one when the initiative is linked to the "colors of money,"[5] which addresses the disbursement of the different types of funds in the execution of a contract to perform a transformation. It becomes important if the type of contract (i.e., product vs. service) and the type of funds do not match. What is the difference? The *American Heritage Dictionary of the English Language* (2000) differentiates a product from a service in the following way:

> Product: A direct result, consequence. Something produced by human or mechanical effort or by a natural process.
>
> Service: Assistance, help. Installation, maintenance, or repairs provided or guaranteed by a dealer or manufacturer.

6.2.3.1 Product Type of Contract

From the supplements to various federal regulations, the definition of an "end item" establishes that an end item, or product, must include supporting elements, such as spares, technical manuals, and maintenance plans. A major weapon system, its subsystems, and its support elements are end items. So, one can say that a transformation of an enterprise that supports an end item is a product type of contract. For more information, the definition of a product and the criteria guidelines for an acquisition contract are provided in Section 5 of U.S. Department of Defense's MIL-HDBK-61A (1997).

6.2.3.2 Service Type of Contract

As the Department of Defense moves from contracting for deliverables defined by technical specifications to deliverables defined by performance specifications, one could argue that the DoD is moving steadily toward the acquisition of "services." The more reliance one places on a performance specification, the more likely it is that one is acquiring a service. In fact, *U.S. Code*, Title 10, Section 2306 makes reference to DFARS 217.171, which describes the maintenance, repair, and overhaul (MRO) of systems, such as aircraft, as a "service."

If one focuses on the specifications for a transformation, at one end of the argument the specifications are explicitly defined by physical, electrical, electronic, digital, and other criteria. However, at the opposite end of the spectrum are services, in which one could say: "I don't care what it looks like as long as it meets the requirement." In between the two ends of the spectrum lie many specification-compliant activities in which one might say: "It looks something like this." It is that middle region where a lot of the product-service turf issues arise. If a deliverable is primarily experience, expertise, brainpower, knowledge, and skill, then what is being acquired is essentially a service. However, this argument could be challenged by saying: "If that statement is true, the prime contractors for the F-22 and the Joint Strike Fighter aircraft are providing their experience, expertise, brainpower, knowledge and skill. So, they are providing services not products."

6.2.4 Synopsis of a Transformation Initiative

When one has completed the above activities, the end result should be a summary, or synopsis, of what the transformation is attempting to achieve. Such a synopsis should be only a page or two long, and it should be used subsequently as an executive summary for a solicitation for the transformation.

 Synopsis of Depot Maintenance Transformation

6.3 Activity 3: Transformation Preliminary Design—Possible Solutions

The third activity in the Lean Enterprise Architecture involves examining solutions and creating a preliminary design for the transformation. This activity is essentially market research, both in terms of seeking out solutions to problems as well as researching internal (military) and external (commercial) approaches. Some of the information that should be collected in this activity should be on military and commercial capabilities, best practices, performance metrics and measurements, costs, timetable, and incentive programs.

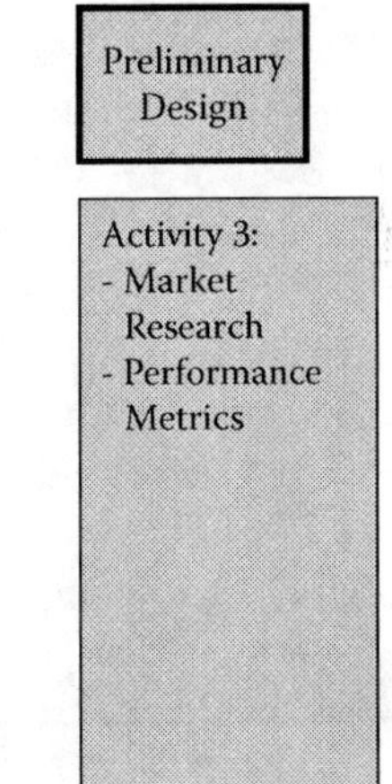

Figure 6.4. LEA Activity 3.

A number of tools can be used to conduct a market research study: benchmarking other sites, conducting a feasibility study, developing a sources sought synopsis, holding industry days, and conducting a survey on contractual issues. Benchmarking visits can demonstrate that a transformation program can be consistent with the way commercial industry does process improvement. A feasibility study can provide sufficient baseline production and cost information to justify a transformation initiative. Industry day is the process of inviting commercial contractors on site and holding one-on-one meetings to educate them about the proposed program and to brainstorm potential approaches. Finally, the responses from firms and institutions to a sources sought synopsis, and the questions and answers from a survey, can demonstrate that there exists a market expertise for transformation. This expertise can come from logistics contractors, IT professionals, manufacturers, maintenance contractors, and academia. One example of a market research report is available on the CD.

6.4 Activity 4: Transformation Detailed Design—Performance Work Statement or Statement of Objectives?

There are two approaches to a detailed design: a performance work statement or a statement of objectives. A PWS specifies a detailed description of the service or product to the contractor, whereas a SOO asks the contractor to develop the statement of work.

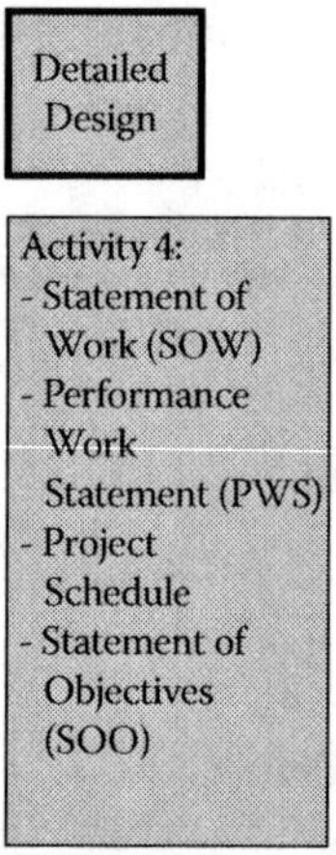

The PWS process is discussed in the DoD guidebooks and other guides offered by the government, in, for example, the Department of Treasury guide *Performance-Based Service Contracting* (2002). A list of these guides is given in the reference section. A review of these guides suggests that there is no standard template for a PWS. However, all the guides do specify that it should center on performance and quality, in addition to a description of the service or product that the enterprise desires. For a lean sustainment enterprise, the description should suggest improvements in eight areas:

Detailed Design

Activity 4:
- Statement of Work (SOW)
- Performance Work Statement (PWS)
- Project Schedule
- Statement of Objectives (SOO)

Figure 6.5. LEA Activity 4.

1. Workload/production
2. Financial operations
3. Infrastructure
4. Organizational structure
5. Work force management
6. Material support
7. Information technology
8. Balanced metrics

An example of a PWS is available on the CD.

Not to confuse the situation, but one can approach the organization of information in what is called a statement of work. A SOW includes: an introduction, background information, scope, applicable documents, performance requirements, special requirements, and deliverables. If a SOW approach is desired, an example is also presented on the CD accompanying this book.

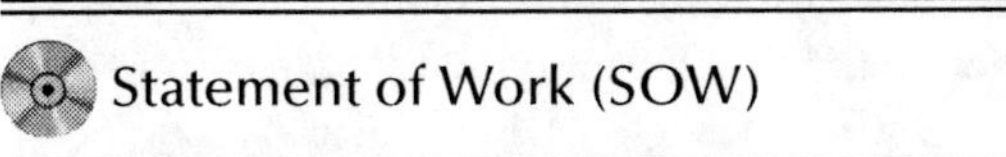

The alternative to a PWS is the use of a statement of objectives. A SOO turns the transformation process around and "requires competing contractors to develop the statement of work (SOW), performance metrics and measurement plan, and quality assurance plan, all of which should be evaluated before contract award. It is described briefly in the Department of Defense 'Handbook for Preparation of Statement of Work'" (1996) (Interagency-Industry Partnership in Performance 2007, p. 14). A SOO is usually incorporated into the request for proposal (RFP) from the contractors. It is incorporated either as an attachment or as part of section L of the RFP.

6.5 Activity 5: Transformation Detailed Design—Measuring and Managing Performance

Activity 5 is the development of an approach to measuring and managing the performance of the transformation initiative. This activity requires a consideration of performance standards, measurement techniques, performance management, and incentives. The DoD guidebook on performance-based services acquisition (Interagency-Industry Partnership in Performance 2007) encourages the use of existing commercial quality standards (identified during market research), such as International Standards Organization (ISO) 9000 or the Software Engineering Institute's Capability Maturity Models (Interagency-Industry Partnership in Performance 2007). "ISO has established

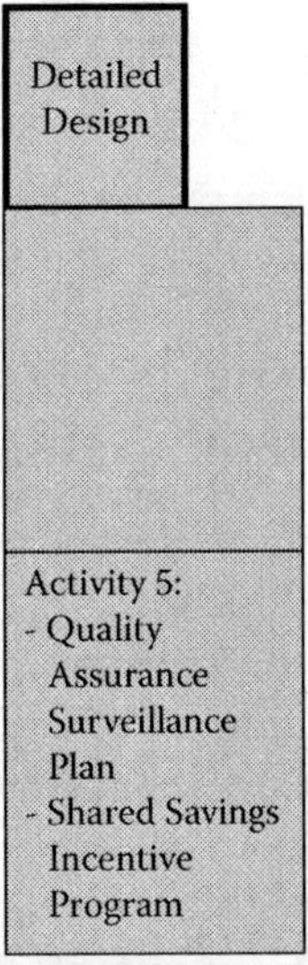

Figure 6.6. LEA Activity 5.

quality standards (the ISO 9000 series) that are increasingly being used by US firms to identify suppliers who meet the quality standards. The term 'ISO 9000' refers to a set of new quality management standards which apply to all kinds of organizations in all kinds of areas. Some of these areas include manufacturing, processing, government, software development, transportation, design, instrumentation, communications, and engineering. The Carnegie Mellon Software Engineering Institute, a Federally funded research and development center, has developed Capability Maturity Models (CMM) to 'assist organizations in maturing their people, process, and technology assets to improve long-term business performance'" (Carnegie Mellon Software Engineering Institute 2007). The Software Engineering Institute has assisted in the development of CMMs for Systems Engineering and Integrated Product Development. They are called the "IPD-CMM integrated product development capability maturity model" (Interagency-Industry Partnership in Performance 2007).

One approach is to ask the contractor to develop a quality assurance surveillance plan (QASP). The QASP provides a systematic method for evaluating the services the contractor is required to furnish. It is designed to provide an effective surveillance method of monitoring contractor performance for each objective listed on a service delivery summary (SDS). The performance thresholds identified in the SDS will be included in the QASP. The contractor, and not the government, is responsible for the management and quality control actions to meet the terms of the contract. Good management and use of an adequate control plan will allow the contractor to operate within specified performance requirements. The role of the government is quality assurance to ensure contract standards are achieved.

 Quality Assurance Surveillance Plan (QASP)

6.6 Activity 6: Transformation Implementation—Source Selection

Source selection is the process of selecting the right government or commercial contractor to perform the work of the transformation. When the transformation follows the lean enterprise architecture, the contractor must develop an understanding of the activities and requirements of the architecture, must have a history of performing these activities, and must have the resources to support the transformation.

One approach to finding the right contractor is "down-selection." "Down-selection is a means of limiting the competitive pool to those contractors most likely to offer a successful solution" (Interagency-Industry Partnership in Performance 2007, p. 32). There are four methods for down-selection: "using the Federal Supply

Service (FSS) Multiple Award Schedule (MAS) competitive process, using the 'fair opportunity' competitive process under an existing Government-Wide Acquisition Contract (GWAC) or multiple-award contract (MAC), using the multistep advisory process in a negotiated procurement, and using a competitive range determination in a negotiated procurement" (Interagency-Industry Partnership in Performance 2007, p. 32). The intent of these methods is to establish a small pool of qualified contractors who then compete for the contract.

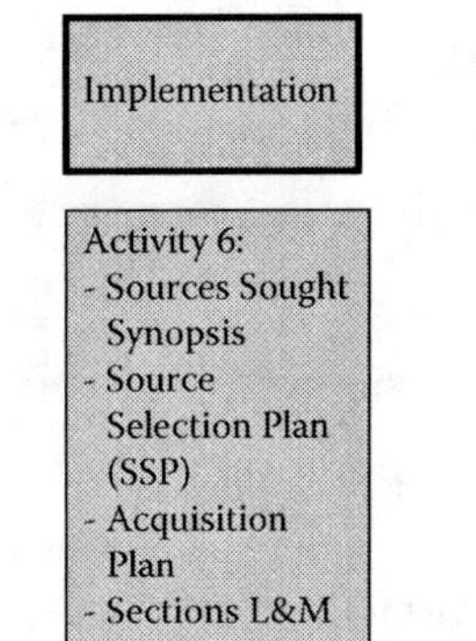

Figure 6.7. LEA Activity 6.

6.6.1 Source Selection Documents

There are a number of documents that accompany a source selection. To begin with, the sources sought synopsis (SSS) is a one-page document that announces the transformation and seeks the potential sources (contractors) of the transformation.

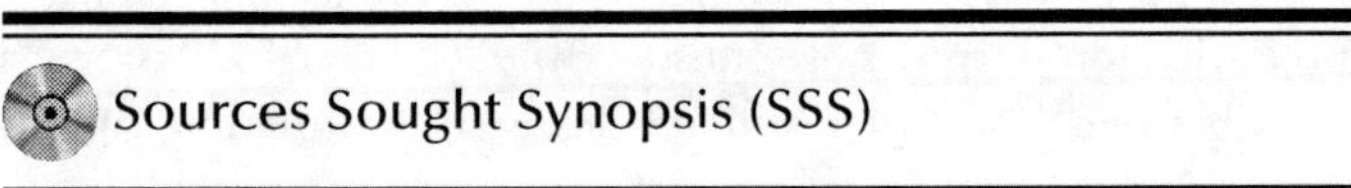

The source selection plan (SSP) contains the acquisition strategy and program management information provided to obtain approval for the selection of the contractor. The strategy should be to minimize the integration and economic risks through the selection of one highly qualified contractor to design, develop, construct, install, implement, and deliver the transformation. The use of multiple contracts for implementation would create unacceptable integration and economic risks due to conflicting methodologies and processes and redundant/duplicative activities. The one-contract strategy minimizes risk by leveraging and effective use of a "common" integrated set of methodology and processes.

The acquisition plan presents a plan of action for the government on the responses to the sources sought synopsis. The AP document considers such details as a small business set aside, the competition for the work, and the source selection procedures.

The single acquisition management plan (SAMP) contains the transformation strategy and program management information that is needed to obtain formal government approval.

Sections L and M are two separate documents that accompany the transformation solicitation (PWS, SOW, SOO, etc.). They help the contractors prepare response proposals. The performance work statement, section L, and section M are prepared and sent out to sources (contractors) together. PWS describes the requirement. Section L requests information on how the contractor will execute that requirement for evaluation purposes. Section M describes how the proposal response will be evaluated for source selection purposes. To illustrate the relationship between the three, Table 6.1 describes one aspect of a military depot transformation, program management. The sections L and M documents on the accompanying CD are examples of a two-phased down-select solicitation.

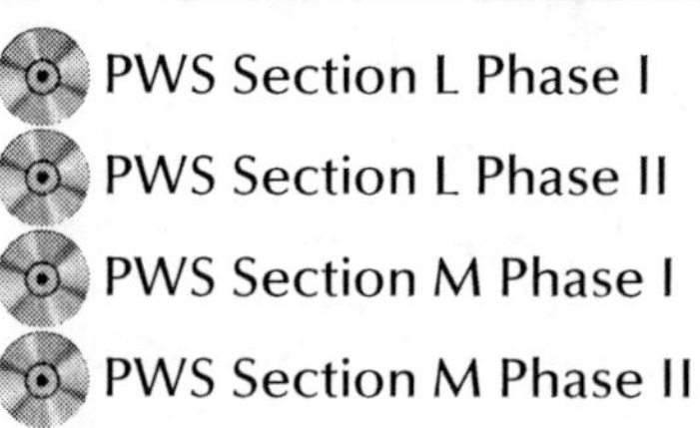

6.6.2 Evaluating the Proposal Responses

The integrated product team should craft a set of evaluation factors that are to be used for assessing the proposal responses. "To help ensure that selection decisions are based on significant determinants, evaluation factors should be kept to

Table 6.1 Program Management Plan for the Performance Work Statement and Sections L and M

Performance Work Statement	*Section L*	*Section M*
The contractor shall provide a program management plan, which encompasses the entire depot maintenance industrial complex and all current and known future workload/processes, including a layout of streamlined business units and implementation plans/milestones for the transition while continuing current mission support with minimal mission impact.	The proposal must describe and demonstrate how the prime offeror's experience (a minimum of five years) of program management with projects of the same scope and magnitude relates to the requirements specified in the PWS. The proposal must describe in detail a sound and rational approach to program management for the DMB MRO transformation program and demonstrate a clear understanding of total program requirements.	The source selection authority will select the best overall offer(s), based on an integrated assessment of mission capability, past performance, proposal risk, and price/cost. The proposal should demonstrate an effective, fully integrated program management approach for accomplishment of the government's requirements identified in the performance work statement, and the prime contractor should possess a minimum of five years of demonstrated program management experience with projects of the same scope and magnitude.

PWS, performance work statement; DMB, depot maintenance board; MRO, maintenance, repair, and overhaul.

a minimum. Each factor should receive the appropriate weighting based on its relative importance. Evaluation factors may include areas such as management approach, relevant experience, past performance, and price" (U.S. Under Secretary of Defense 2000).

 Source Selection Evaluation Work Sheets

6.7 Activity 7: Transformation Implementation—Managing Performance and Risks

No major project goes smoothly. There will always be surprises, modifications to the plans, and risk. That is why a change management plan should be developed as one of the first activities, and the performance of the contractors and government personnel should be continuously monitored. Because the IPT is the governing body to monitor change and performance, the success of the initiative depends on whether or not the IPT and military leadership remain in place throughout the initiative. After the source selection process is complete, the contractor should become a member of the IPT. In fact, FAR 1.102(c) provides: the IPT "consists of all participants in Government acquisition including not only representatives of the technical, supply, and procurement communities but also the customers they serve, and the contractors who provide the products and services" (Federal Acquisition Regulation System 2005). The first DoD guidebook suggests keeping the team together for the duration of the project: "Those on the team have the most knowledge, experience, and insight into what needs to happen next and what is expected during contract performance. Contract award is not the measure of success or even an especially meaningful metric. Effective and efficient contract performance that delivers a solution is the goal. The team should stay together to see that end reached" (Interagency-Industry Partnership in Performance 2007, p. 38).

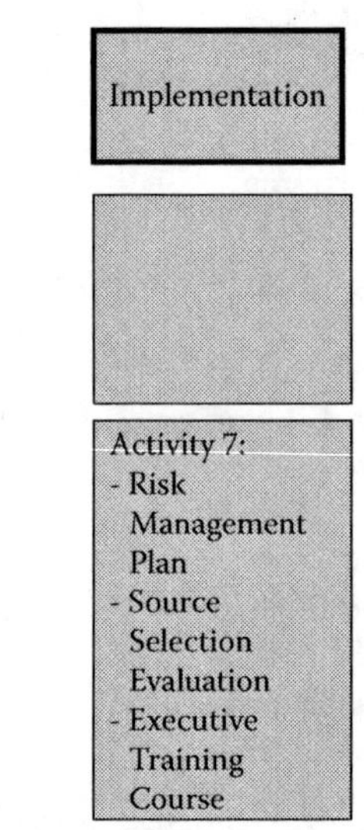

Figure 6.8. LEA Activity 7.

6.7.1 Risk Management

The Defense Acquisition Guidebook 5000 series requires that transformation managers continually assess risks by creating a risk management plan (RMP) to identify and control performance, cost, and schedule risks. A RMP helps formulate and implement a comprehensive and proactive risk management process as an integral part of the overall transformation approach. It is a tool to address situations that might adversely impact the transformation. The RMP:

- Identifies alternatives to achieve cost, schedule, and performance goals
- Assists in budget and funding priorities

- Provides risk mitigation strategies and information
- Monitors the health of the transformation during implementation

A DoD acquisition guidebook (Defense Acquisition University 2003) contains information on developing a risk management plan. It specifies three forms of risk:

- Technical risk: the risk that the transformation design, test, and implementation process will influence the nature of the service or product
- Cost risk: the risk that the transformation implementation will not meet the cost objectives as a result of a failure to mitigate technical risks
- Schedule risk: the risk that the timetable for the implementation is unrealistic and unreasonable, and the risk that transformation implementation will fall short of the schedule objectives as a result of failure to mitigate technical risks

Part of developing a risk management plan is assigning ratings to the levels and forms of risk. The ratings are the values that are given to a transformation event based on the analysis of the likelihood and consequences of the event. Ratings of low, moderate, or high are assigned to the types of risk based on established criteria. See the example RMP document on the CD.

 Risk Management Plan (RMP)

6.7.2 Create a Training Course

One proven approach to mitigating risk is to train everyone involved in the transformation. So, create a lean training course for your organization. Lean training is the ability to deliver the right level of training to the right individuals just in time to prepare them to be competent and effective in performing their work. The following are five helpful tips:

1. Develop a comprehensive and coordinated training plan that addresses the employee's needs just in time.
2. Build a central database of training offerings in order to determine and track the appropriate training for a given individual or project team at a particular time.
3. Provide lean sustainment awareness education to all employees prior to rolling out the improvement process.
4. Attend to middle managers' training needs first. They are the drivers of change and need to be well prepared and motivated to lead others.

5. Design and deliver lean sustainment training and team development training for the integrated product teams as they become involved in the process redesign.

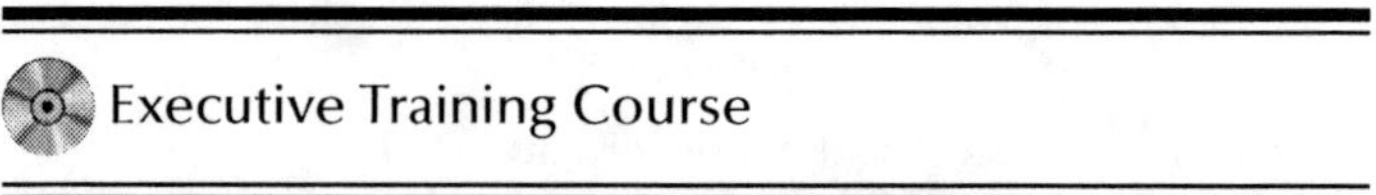

6.8 Activity 8: Transformation Operation

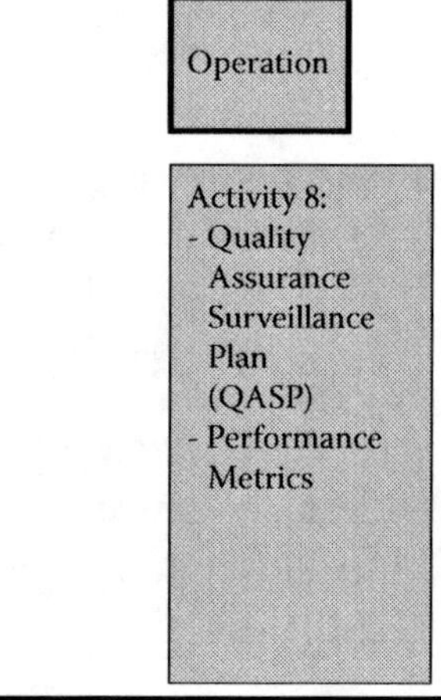

Figure 6.9. LEA Activity 8.

The operation of the transformation initiative embraces all the actions performed after the implementation to ensure the performance and delivery of the transformation requirements and metrics. It encompasses developing a systematic method to evaluate the services and products the contractor furnished. The quality assurance and surveillance plan should be reviewed, and the performance metrics should be tracked on a continuous basis. In the operation phase, both the contractor and the government should be responsible for the management and quality control actions to meet the transformation objectives. A good quality control program is the driver for service and product quality. Careful application of the process and standards presented in the QASP and performance metrics documents will ensure a comprehensive quality transformation.

In the end, it is the customer that must be satisfied with the product or service, and it is the customer that is the judge of the program's success. Customer surveys are just one way of verifying customer satisfaction, but the real metric for success is whether or not the transformation initiative has resulted in an increased workload, increased quality of product or service, and an improvement in the financial bottom line for the military enterprise.

6.9 Conclusion

This chapter relates the activities that are necessary for a performance-based transformation to the Lean Enterprise Architecture that was used to design the transformation. There are a number of government guidebooks that provide a roadmap for those wishing to use a performance-based transformation, and many of these guidebooks are mentioned and referenced in this chapter. There are also a number of documents that one must generate to satisfy the myriad of government policies and regulations that govern the implementation of such a transformation initiative. But, it is the intent and hope that this chapter and the LEA will provide a useful roadmap to guide you on your lean transformation journey, and that the accompanying documents on the attached CD are a good source for the tools and materials that you will need for the journey.

Appendix A: Useful Websites

Government Websites

Department of Defense policy on PBSA, 5 April 2000
  http://www.acq.osd.mil/ar/doc/ganslerpbsa.pdf
Defense Acquisition University Online Publication Resources
  Defense Acquisition Guidebook Series 5000
  Defense Acquisition Directive DoDD 5000.1
  Defense Acquisition Instruction DoDI 5000.2
  http://www.dau.mil/pubs/Online_Pubs.asp#Guidebooks
Federal Acquisition Regulation (FAR)
  http://farsite.hill.af.mil/VFFAR1.HTM
Air Force Contracting Toolkit on Services
  http://www.safaq.hq.af.mil/contracting/toolkit/part37/
Army Acquisition Support Center
  http://asc.army.mil/
Navy Acquisition Reform
  http://www.acq-ref.navy.mil/
Office of the Inspector General, Audit Report on Contracts for Professional, Administrative and Management Support Services, 10 March 2000, Report No. D-2000-100
  http://www.dodig.osd.mil/audit/reports/00report.htm
A Guide to Best Practices for Performance Based Service Contracting, Final Edition, October 1998
  http://www.whitehouse.gov/omb/procurement/pbsa/guide_pbsc.html
Department of Energy, Performance Based Contracting Guide, June 1998
  http://management.energy.gov/documents/pbiguide.doc
Health and Human Services (HHS) Performance-Based Contracting Desk Reference
  http://www.ogam2000.com/acquisition

Market Research Websites

http://www.imart.org/
A collection of search engines, directories, and databases to aid in market research.

http://www.cadv.org/
Disseminates information to enable exchanges of questions and answers and to share best practices and lessons learned.

http://govcon.com
A sourcing site for public sector contracting.

http://www.industrylink.com
Hundreds of links to companies grouped by technology.

http://superpages.com
Yellow pages of 16 million U.S. businesses.

http://switchboard.com

http://www.techweb.com
More than 100 links to industry, focused on electronics.

Notes

Chapter 1

1. See the Lean Aerospace Initiative website, http://lean.mit.edu/.
2. See the Lean Sustainment Initiative website, http://web.mit.edu/ctpid/www/lsi.html.
3. A second Navy undersea weapons center in Newport, Rhode Island is not considered a major depot facility because it employs fewer than 400 people—the minimum staffing level that the DoD names for facilities identified as major depots.
4. The Aerospace Maintenance and Regeneration Center is a facility whose primary function is to store aircraft removed from the inventory and provide parts to support Air Force requirements for in-service systems.
5. The Army refers to this practice as "controlled exchange." The Army's definition of *cannibalization* is the removal of components from equipment designated for disposal.
6. The Lean Sustainment Initiative at the Massachusetts Institute of Technology was a joint project between Headquarters Air Force Materiel Command and the Air Force Manufacturing Technology program in support of the Air Force Lean Logistics program. The Lean Sustainment Initiative project operated from May 1997 to December 2001. The author, Dennis Mathaisel, was one of the team leaders representing MIT in the project.
7. Sources: Honeywell Electronics, HQ Air Force Materiel Command.
8. The DBOF is a financial structure that was created to promote total cost visibility and full cost recovery of support services. It is structured around business areas that provide goods and services to customers throughout the DoD. DBOF business-area managers prepare their proposed budgets based on anticipated workload and expenses. At the same time, DBOF customers include in their budgets their planned requirements for goods and services from the various DBOF business areas. The budget process sets rates for each business area. Rates are keyed to a unit of output that is unique to each business area. The rates are stabilized for the budget year and are intended to ensure that customers pay for the full cost of goods and services they receive from the business areas.
9. Consumption rates.

Chapter 2

1. See the Lean Aerospace Initiative website, http://lean.mit.edu/.
2. See the Lean Sustainment Initiative website, http://web.mit.edu/ctpid/www/lsi.html.
3. Kanban is a software system that continuously monitors parts and supplies. Its name comes from the Japanese words *kan* ("card") and *ban* ("signal")—literally translated, "signal cards."

Chapter 3

1. See the Lean Aerospace Initiative website, http://lean.mit.edu/.
2. Thomas Jackson, Productivity Inc. (http://www.productivityinc.com), as quoted in Phillips (2000).
3. "Design-build," a popular term from the 1980s, is a fast-track building approach that evolved from the master builder concept of more than a hundred years ago. It is a delivery system for a construction project with strict scheduling demands, complex design issues, and a carefully controlled construction environment.
4. The kaizen blitz is "a sudden overpowering effort to take something apart and put it back together in a better way." (Dave Nave, modified by J. Keith Shiveley, 22 September 2003. http://www.isixsigma.com)
5. This systems engineering process is not unique to MRO applications. The same model has also been used in the design, prototype, development, construction, and use of manufacturing and industrial applications; see INCOSE, July 2000).

Chapter 4

1. For further information, see the ProSci BPR Online Learning Center website, http://www.prosci.com, 2005 (accessed 26 June 2007).
2. See the Lean Aerospace Initiative website, http://lean.mit.edu/.
3. *Organic* refers to MRO that is performed at a military depot, as opposed to outsourcing the MRO to a commercial contractor.
4. For additional information, see the Mid-America Manufacturing Technology Center website, www.mamtc.com (accessed 24 June 2007).
5. For additional information see the Plant Maintenance Resource Center website, http://www.plant-maintenance.com/maintenance_articles_tpm.shtml (accessed 24 June 2007).
6. Detailed information on open systems, guidance documents, and lessons learned in the application of open interface standards are available at the Open Systems Joint Task Force website, http://www.acq.osd.mil/osjtf (accessed 24 June 2007).

Chapter 5

1. See the U.S. Office of Naval Research's Best Manufacturing Practices Center of Excellence website, http://www.bmpcoe.org (accessed 2 July 2007).
2. See the American Productivity and Quality Center website, www.apqc.org (accessed 2 July 2007).
3. Source: Best Manufacturing Practices Center of Excellence website, http://www.bmpcoe.org (accessed 2 July 2007).
4. Ibid.
5. Ibid.

Chapter 6

1. J.S. Gansler, The Under Secretary of Defense, Cover Letter to the U.S. Department of Defense, "Guidebook for Performance-Based Services Acquisition" (2000), Washington, D.C., January 2, 2001.
2. Office of Federal Procurement Policy et al. (1998), Foreword.
3. See for example, U.S. Department of Defense, Office of the Under Secretary of Defense (Acquisition and Technology), "DoD Guide to Integrated Product and Process Development," Version 1.0, Washington, D.C., February 5, 1996.
4. The Balanced Scorecard is an approach to strategic management that was developed in the early 1990s by Drs. Robert Kaplan (Harvard Business School) and David Norton.
5. U.S. DoD Financial Management Regulation (FMR), Volume 2B, Chapter 5 is a good reference for the different "Colors of Money." The FMR can be accessed at http://www.dod.mil/comptroller/finman01.html.

References

Chapter 1

Blanchard, Benjamin S. 1998. *Logistics Engineering and Management*. Upper Saddle River, N.J.: Prentice Hall.

Blanchard, Benjamin S., and Wolter J. Fabrycky. 1998. *Systems Engineering and Analysis*. Upper Saddle River, N.J.: Prentice Hall.

Blanchard, Benjamin S., Dinesh Verma, and Elmer L. Peterson. 1995. *Maintainability: A Key to Effective Serviceability and Maintenance Management*. New York: Wiley-Interscience.

Brown, David. 2000. "Enterprise Architecture for DoD Acquisition." *Acquisition Review Quarterly* 7: 121–130.

Cordesman, Anthony H. 2000 (October). *Trends in U.S. Defense Spending: The Size of Funding, Procurement, and Readiness Problems*. Report. Washington, D.C.: Center for Strategic and International Studies.

Donnelley, Bob, and Ralph Proctor. 2005. *Defense Working Capital Fund Basics*. Report. Washington, D.C.: Office of the Under Secretary of Defense, Comptroller Program and Budget.

Eady, Walter B., and Anthony R. Williams. 1997 (March). *The Capabilities of Agile Combat Support under Wartime Conditions for the 21st Century*. Report no. AU/ACSC/0352/97-03. Retrieved 2006 from www.au.af.mil/au/aul/bibs/future/tf16.htm.

Gansler, Jacques S. 1999 (January). *Acquisition Reform Update*. Report. Washington, D.C.: Office of the Secretary of Defense, Acquisition and Technology, U.S. Department of Defense.

International Council on Systems Engineering (INCOSE). 1998. *Systems Engineering Handbook*. San Francisco: San Francisco Bay Chapter of INCOSE.

Jones, James. 1995. *Integrated Logistic Support Handbook*. New York: McGraw-Hill.

Kros, Todd C. 1999 (September). "Modernization through Spares: An Analysis of Implementation at the U.S. Army Aviation and Missile Command." MS thesis. Retrieved 2006 from http://handle.dtic.mil/100.2/ADA370762.

Lamming, R. C. 1993. *Beyond Partnership: Strategies for Innovation and Lean Supply*. Hemel Hempstead, England: Prentice Hall.

Lean Sustainment Initiative. 1998 (14 August). "Depot Repair Efficiency and Responsiveness." Unpublished research paper. Cambridge, Mass.: Center for Technology, Policy and Industrial Development, Massachusetts Institute of Technology.

Levasseur, G. (Jerry), Marilyn Helms, and A. Zink. 1995. "A Conversion from a Functional to a Cellular Manufacturing Layout at Steward, Inc." *Production and Inventory Management Journal* 36: 37–42.

Liker, Jeffrey, ed. 1997. *Becoming Lean: Inside Stories of U.S. Manufacturers*. Portland, Ore.: Productivity Press.

Mathaisel, Dennis F. X. 2001 (October). *Final Report: Sustainment Operations Team*. Report. Cambridge, Mass.: Center for Technology, Policy and Industrial Development, Massachusetts Institute of Technology.

Michaels, Kevin. 2004 (20 April). "The Military MRO Market." Paper presented at AeroStrategy, 2004 Aviation Week MRO Conference and Exhibition, Atlanta.

Mungwattana, Anan. 2000 (1 September). "Design of Cellular Manufacturing Systems for Dynamic and Uncertain Production Requirements with Presence of Routing Flexibility." PhD diss., Virginia Polytechnic Institute and State University.

Nightingale, Deborah. 2000. "Integrating the Lean Enterprise." Unpublished paper, Massachusetts Institute of Technology.

Performance-Based Business Environment. 1997 (23 January; rev. 2 July 1999). "Flexible Sustainment Guide." Retrieved 2007 from https://acc.dau.mil.

Sekine, Keniche. 1992. *One-Piece Flow: Cell Design for Transforming the Production Process*. Portland, Ore.: Productivity Press.

Sharma, Anand, and Patricia E. Moody. 2001. *The Perfect Engine: How to Win in the New Demand Economy by Building Order with Fewer Resources*. New York: Free Press.

U.S. General Accounting Office. 1987 (April). "Army Maintenance: Continuing Problems in Performing Maintenance at the User Level," Report to the Secretary of the Army GAO/NSIAD-87-104. Washington, D.C.: U.S. General Accounting Office.

U.S. General Accounting Office. 2001a (March). "Defense Maintenance: Sustaining Readiness Support Capabilities Requires a Comprehensive Plan," GAO Testimony before the Subcommittee on Military Readiness, Committee on Armed Services, House of Representatives, GAO/01-533T. Washington, D.C.: U.S. General Accounting Office.

U.S. General Accounting Office. 2001b (June). "Air Force Inventory: Parts Shortages are Impacting Operations and Maintenance Effectiveness," Report to Congressional committees GAO-01-587. Washington, D.C.: U.S. General Accounting Office.

U.S. General Accounting Office. 2001c (July). "Navy Inventory: Parts Shortages Are Impacting Operations and Maintenance Effectiveness." Report to Congressional committees GAO-01-771. Washington, D.C.: U.S. General Accounting Office.

U.S. General Accounting Office. 2001d (July). "Army Inventory: Parts Shortages Are Impacting Operations and Maintenance Effectiveness." Report to Congressional committees GAO-01-772. Washington, D.C.: U.S. General Accounting Office.

U.S. General Accounting Office. 2001e (November). "Military Aircraft: Services Need Strategies to Reduce Cannibalizations." Report to the chairman, Subcommittee on National Security, Veterans Affairs, and International Relations, Committee on Government Reform, House of Representatives GAO-02-86. Washington, D.C.: U.S. General Accounting Office.

U.S. General Accounting Office. 2003 (April). "Military Readiness: DoD Needs a Clear and Defined Process for Setting Aircraft Availability Goals in the New Security Environment." Report to the chairman, Subcommittee on Readiness, Committee on Armed Services, House of Representatives GAO-03-300. Washington, D.C.: U.S. General Accounting Office.

Watson, Gregory H. 1993. *Strategic Benchmarking: How to Rate Your Company's Performance against the World's Best.* New York: John Wiley & Sons.

Womack, James P., and Daniel T. Jones. 1996. *Lean Thinking: Banish Waste and Create Wealth in Your Corporation.* New York: Simon & Schuster.

Womack, James P., Daniel T. Jones, and Daniel Roos. 1990. *The Machine That Changed the World: The Story of Lean Production.* New York: Rawson/Macmillan.

Chapter 2

Agripino, Mario, Timothy Cathcart, and Dennis F. X. Mathaisel. 2002. "A Lean Sustainment Enterprise Model for Military Systems." *Acquisition Review Quarterly* 9: 275–298.

Blanchard, Benjamin S. 1998. *Logistics Engineering and Management.* Upper Saddle River, N.J.: Prentice Hall.

Blanchard, Benjamin S., and Wolter J. Fabrycky. 1998. *Systems Engineering and Analysis.* Upper Saddle River, N.J.: Prentice Hall.

Blanchard, Benjamin S., Dinesh Verma, and Elmer L. Peterson. 1995. *Maintainability: A Key to Effective Serviceability and Maintenance Management.* New York: Wiley-Interscience.

Chappell, Dennis and Tony Taylor. 2002. "The Joint CAD/PAD Program. Transition to Joint Program Building Trust, Achieving Economies of Scale." *Energetics & Program Management.* September–October. 2–5.

Cordesman, Anthony H. 2000 (October). *Trends in U.S. Defense Spending: The Size of Funding, Procurement, and Readiness Problems.* Report. Washington, D.C.: Center for Strategic and International Studies.

Eady, Walter B., and Anthony R. Williams. 1997 (March). *The Capabilities of Agile Combat Support under Wartime Conditions for the 21st Century.* Report no. AU/ACSC/0352/97-03. Retrieved 2006 from www.au.af.mil/au/aul/bibs/future/tf16.htm

Gansler, Jacques S. 1999 (January). *Acquisition Reform Update.* Report. Washington, D.C.: Office of the Secretary of Defense, Acquisition and Technology, U.S. Department of Defense.

International Council on Systems Engineering (INCOSE). 1998. *Systems Engineering Handbook.* San Francisco: San Francisco Bay Chapter of INCOSE.

Jones, James. 1995. *Integrated Logistic Support Handbook.* New York: McGraw-Hill.

Kros, Todd C. 1999 (September). "Modernization through Spares: An Analysis of Implementation at the U.S. Army Aviation and Missile Command." MS thesis. Retrieved 2006 from http://handle.dtic.mil/100.2/ADA370762.

Liker, Jeffrey, ed. 1997. *Becoming Lean: Inside Stories of U.S. Manufacturers.* Portland, Ore.: Productivity Press.

Nightingale, Deborah. 2000. "Integrating the Lean Enterprise." Unpublished paper presented at the Massachusetts Institute of Technology.

Performance-Based Business Environment. 1997 (23 January; rev. 2 July 1999). "Flexible Sustainment Guide." Retrieved 2007 from https://acc.dau.mil.

Saccomagno, Jeanna, 2000. Interview with the author, Indian Head, MD, October.

Warren, David. 1998. *Challenges Facing DoD in Implementing Defense Reform Initiatives.* Report. Washington, D.C.: U.S. General Accounting Office.

Watson, Gregory H. 1993. *Strategic Benchmarking: How to Rate Your Company's Performance against the World's Best.* New York: John Wiley & Sons.

Womack, James P., Daniel T. Jones, and Daniel Roos. 1990. *The Machine That Changed the World: The Story of Lean Production.* New York: Rawson/Macmillan.

Chapter 3

Askin, Ronald, and Charles Standridge. 2003. *Modeling and Analysis of Manufacturing Systems.* New York: Wiley.

Bernus, Peter. 1998 (19–20 November). "Position Statement—GERAM and Its Possible Implications to System and Software Engineering Applications." Paper presented to the International Federation for Information Processing-International Federation of Automatic Control Task Force on Enterprise Integration Strategic Workshop on Enterprise Integration and Enterprise Computing (Systems and Software Engineering Standards in the Context of Enterprise Integration), Enterprise Integration Group, School of Computing and Information Technology, Griffith University, Brisbane, Queensland, Australia.

Bernus, Peter, Laszlo Nemes, and Theodore J. Williams, eds. 1995. *Architectures for Enterprise Integration.* London: Chapman & Hall.

Bies, Susan Schmidt. 2004. "Enterprise-Wide Compliance Programs." *BIS Review* 7: 1–4.

Blanchard, Benjamin S., and Wolter J. Fabrycky. 1998. *Systems Engineering and Analysis.* Upper Saddle River, N.J.: Prentice Hall.

Brown, David. 2000. "Enterprise Architecture for DoD Acquisition." *Acquisition Review Quarterly* 7: 121–130.

Burbidge, J. L., and B. G. Dale. 1984. "Planning the Introduction and Predicting the Benefits of Group Technology." *Engineering Costs and Production Economics* 8: 117–128.

Chesbrough, Henry and Rosenbloom, Richard S. 2002. "The Role of the Business Model in Capturing Value from Innovation: Evidence from Xerox Corporation's Technology Spin-off Companies." *Industrial and Corporate Change* 11(3): 529–555.

Collet, S., and R. Spicer. 1995. "Improving Productivity through Cellular Manufacturing." *Production and Inventory Management Journal* 36: 71–75.

Delaware Manufacturing Extension Partnership. 2004. "Lean Enterprises." Retrieved 2006 from http: //www.demep.org.

Deming, W. Edwards 1986. *Out of the Crisis: Quality, Productivity and Competitive Position.* Cambridge: Cambridge University Press.

Doumeingts, Guy, Bruno Vallespir, D. Darracar, and M. Xavier Roboam. 1987. "Design Methodology for Advanced Manufacturing Systems." *Computers in Industry* 9: 271–296.

Doumeingts, Guy, Bruno Vallespir, Marc Zanettin, and David Chen. 1992 (May). "GIM, GRAI Integrated Methodology, A Methodology for Designing CIM Systems." Report, Laboratory for Automation and Products, University of Bordeaux.

Fine, Charles H. 1998. *Clock Speed: Winning Industry Control in the Age of Temporary Advantage.* Reading, Mass.: Perseus Books.

Fry, Timothy, M. Breen, and John Wilson. 1987. "A Successful Implementation of Group Technology and Cell Manufacturing." *Production and Inventory Management Journal* 28: 4–6.

Goldman, Steven L., Roger Nagel, and Kenneth Preiss. 1995. *Agile Competitors and Virtual Organizations: Strategies for Enriching the Customer.* New York: Van Nostrand Reinhold.

Harry, Mikel, and Richard Schroeder. 2000. *Six Sigma: The Breakthrough Management Strategy Revolutionizing the World's Top Corporations.* New York: Doubleday.

Howard, M. L., and R. G. Newman. 1993. "From Job Shop to Just-in-Time—A Successful Conversion." *Production and Inventory Management Journal* 34: 70–74.

Hyer, Nancy L., and Urban Wemmerlöv. 1989. "Group Technology in the U.S. Manufacturing Industry: A Survey of Current Practices." *International Journal of Production Research* 27: 1287–1304.

Imai, Masaaki. 1986. *Kaizen: The Key to Japan's Competitive Success.* Tokyo: McGraw-Hill.

Institute of Electrical and Electronics Engineers, Inc. 1998. *IEEE Standard for the Application and Management of the Systems Engineering Process.* Report. Piscataway, N.J.: Institute of Electrical and Electronics Engineers, Inc.

Interagency-Industry Partnership in Performance (U.S. Department of Commerce, U.S. Department of Defense, U.S. Department of the Treasury, U.S. Department of Agriculture, Acquisitions Solutions, Inc., U.S. General Services Administration). 2007. "Seven Steps to Performance-Based Services Acquisition." Retrieved 29 June 2007 from http://www.acqnet.gov/comp/seven_steps/index.html.

International Council on Systems Engineering (INCOSE). 2007. "What is Systems Engineering?", http://www.incose.org/practice/whatissystemseng.aspx.

International Federation for Information Processing / International Federation of Automatic Control Task Force. 1998 (June). *GERAM: Generalised Enterprise Reference Architecture and Methodology.* Report, version 1.6.3. Brisbane, Australia: available from http://www.cit.gu.edu.au/~bernus/taskforce/geram/versions/geram1-6-3/v1.6.3.html.

International Organization for Standardization. 2003 (July 15). "Industrial Automation Systems—Requirements for Enterprise-Reference Architectures and Methodologies." ISO/WD 15704. Geneva, Switzerland: International Organization for Standardization.

Kaiser-Arnett, Toby. 2003 (December). *Market Research for OC-ALC Maintenance Repair and Overhaul Transformation Program.* Report, Oklahoma City Air Logistics Center. Oklahoma City, OK: U.S. Air Force.

Kilpatrick, A. M. 1997 (February). "Lean Manufacturing Principles: A Comprehensive Framework for Improving Production Efficiency." MS thesis, Massachusetts Institute of Technology.

Kotter, John P. 1996. *Leading Change.* Boston, Mass.: Harvard Business School Press.

Lamming, R. C. 1993. *Beyond Partnership: Strategies for Innovation and Lean Supply.* Hemel Hempstead, England: Prentice Hall.

Laraia, Anthony C., Patricia E. Moody, and Robert W. Hall. 1999. *The Kaizen Blitz: Accelerating Breakthroughs in Productivity and Performance.* New York: Wiley.

Leflar, James. 2001. *Practical Total Productive Maintenance.* Portland, Ore: Productivity Press.

Levasseur, G. (Jerry), Marilyn Helms, and A. Zink. 1995. "A Conversion from a Functional to a Cellular Manufacturing Layout at Steward, Inc." *Production and Inventory Management Journal* 36: 37–42.

Liker, Jeffrey, ed. 1997. *Becoming Lean: Inside Stories of U.S. Manufacturers.* Portland, Ore.: Productivity Press.

Lockwood Greene Engineers, Inc. 2005. "Present and Past Performance Information." Unpublished report. Spartanburg, S.C.: Lockwood Greene Engineers, Inc.

Mathaisel, Dennis F. X., Timothy Cathcart, and Mario Agripino. 2005 (February). *Sustaining the Military Enterprise: Architecture for a Lean Transformation.* Defense Procurement Analysis: Military Policy Research, London.

Mathaisel, Dennis F. X., Timothy Cathcart, and Clare Comm. 2004. "A Framework for Benchmarking, Classifying, and Implementing Best Sustainment Practices." *Benchmarking: An International Journal* 11: 403–417.

Maskell, Brian H., and Bruce Baggaley. 2003. *Practical Lean Accounting: A Proven System for Measuring and Managing the Lean Enterprise.* Portland, OR: Productivity Press.

Monden, Yosuhiro. 1983. *The Toyota Production System.* Atlanta: Industrial Engineering and Management Press.

Mungwattana, Anan. 2000 (1 September). "Design of Cellular Manufacturing Systems for Dynamic and Uncertain Production Requirements with Presence of Routing Flexibility." PhD diss., Virginia Polytechnic Institute and State University.

Murman, Earl, Tom Allen, Kirk Bozdogan, Joel Cutcher-Gershenfeld, Hugh McManus, Debbie Nightingale, Erik Rebentisch, Tom Shields, Fred Stahl, M. Walton, Joyce Warmkessel, Stan Weiss, and Sheila Widnall. 2000. *Lean Enterprise Value*, New York: Palgrave.

Nakajima, Seiichi. 1988. *Introduction to Total Productive Maintenance.* Cambridge, Mass.: Productivity Press.

Nightingale, Deborah, and Ron Milauskas. 1999 (July). "Transition-To-Lean Roadmap Enterprise Level, Progress Report." Report presented to the Lean Aerospace Initiative, Cambridge, Massachusetts.

Ohno, Taiichi. 1988. *Toyota Production System: Beyond Large Scale Production.* Portland, Ore.: Productivity Press.

Olle, T. William, Jacques Hagelstein, and Ian G. MacDonald. 1998. *Information Systems Methodologies: A Framework for Understanding.* Wokingham, England: Addison-Wesley.

Pasternack, Bruce A., and Albert J. Viscio. 1998. *The Centerless Corporation: A New Model for Transforming Your Organization for Growth and Prosperity.* New York: Simon & Schuster.

Pearce, Sarah, and John Bennet. 2005. *How to Use a Design Build Approach for a Construction Project: A Client Guide.* Englemere, England: Chartered Institute of Building.

Petrie, Charles J., ed. 1992. *Enterprise Integration Modeling: Proceedings of the First International Conference.* Cambridge, Mass.: MIT Press.

Phillips, Todd. 2000 (January). "Building the Lean Machine." Retrieved 29 June 2007 from http://www.advancedmanufacturing.com/index.php?option=com_staticxt&staticfile=lean.htm&Itemid=39.

Rechtin, Eberhardt. 1999. *Systems Architecting of Organizations: Why Eagles Can't Swim*. New York: CRC Press.

Rechtin, Eberhardt, and Mark Maier. 2000. *The Art of Systems Architecting*. New York: CRC Press.

Ring, Jack. 1999. "When Enterprise = System." Unpublished article.

Robinson, Charles J., and Andrew P. Ginder. 1995. *Implementing TPM*. Portland, Ore.: Productivity Press.

Roper, William. 2002 (May). "The Missing Link of Lean Success." Retrieved 29 June 2007 from http://www.sae.org/manufacturing/lean/column/leanmay02.htm.

Rowe, Louis E. 1998 (1 April). "How to Develop a Successful Approach to Design/Build Construction." Retrieved 29 June 2007 from http://ecmweb.com/mag/electric_develop_successful_approach/.

Scheer, August-Wilhelm. 1992. *Architecture of Integrated Information Systems: Foundations of Enterprise Modeling*. New York: Springer-Verlag.

Schultz, Karl H. 2004. "Lean Management, Lean Results." Retrieved 29 June 2007 from http://www.leanscm.net/Articles%20Jan%2004/lean_results%20Schultz.htm.

Sekine, Keniche. 1992. *One-Piece Flow: Cell Design for Transforming the Production Process*. Portland, Ore.: Productivity Press.

Sharma, Anand, and Patricia E. Moody. 2001. *The Perfect Engine: How to Win in the New Demand Economy by Building Order with Fewer Resources*. New York: Free Press.

Shewhart, Walter. 1989. *Statistical Method from the Viewpoint of Quality Control*. New York: Dover.

Shingo, Shiegeo. 1989. *A Study of the Toyota Production System*. Cambridge, Mass.: Productivity Press.

Singh, Nanua, and Divakar Rajamaani. 1996. *Cellular Manufacturing Systems: Design, Planning and Control*. New York: Chapman & Hall.

Synergy, Inc., 2003 (October). "Team Synergy, OC-ALC Change Management Plan." Washington, D.C.

Tapping, Don, Tom Shuker, and Tom Luyster. 2002. *Value Stream Management*. New York: Productivity Press.

U.S. Air Force, Air Force Materiel Command, Depot Maintenance Transformation. 2003a. "Improving Production, Processes and Support to Provide Customers with Responsive, Predictable and Affordable Products and Services." Wright Patterson Air Force Base, OH: Air Force Materiel Command

U.S. Air Force, Air Force Materiel Command, Purchasing and Supply Chain Management (PSCM). 2003b. "Improving Warfighter Readiness through PSCM Transformation.Fact Sheet #1" 2003. Wright Patterson Air Force Base, OH. Air Force Materiel Command.

U.S. Air Force. 2004 (January). "Guidance for the Use of Robust Engineering in Air Force Acquisition Programs." Report. Fort Belvoir, VA: Defense Acquisition University.

U.S. Office of Federal Procurement Policy. 1980. *A Guide for Writing and Administering Performance Statements of Work for Service Contracts*. Pamphlet no. 4. Washington, D.C.: U.S. Office of Federal Procurement Policy.

U.S. Office of Federal Procurement Policy. 1991 (March). *Service Contracting*. Policy letter 91-2. Washington, D.C.: U.S. Office of Federal Procurement Policy.

Office of Federal Procurement Policy/Office of Management and Budget/Executive Office of the President. 1998 (October). "A Guide to Best Practices for Performance-Based Service Contracting" (final ed.). Retrieved 4 July 2007 from http://www.whitehouse.gov/omb/procurement/pbsa/guide_pbsc.html.

U.S. Office of Federal Procurement Policy. 1998b. *Service Contracting*. Policy letter. Washington, D.C.: U.S. Office of Federal Procurement Policy.

U.S. Under Secretary of Defense. 2000 (December). *Guidebook for Performance-Based Services Acquisition (PBSA) in the Department of Defense*. Washington, D.C.: U.S. Department of Defense.

Vernadat, Francois. 1993. "CIMOSA: Enterprise Modeling and Enterprise Integration Using a Process Based Approach." In *Proceedings of the IFIP TC5/WG5.12 International Conference on Enterprise Integration and Modeling Technique*, ed. Kluwer. Deventer, The Netherlands: Kluwer. 236: 25–33.

Wemmerlöv, Urban, and Nancy L. Hyer. 1989. "Cellular Manufacturing in U.S. Industry: A Survey of Users." *International Journal of Production Research* 27: 1511–1530.

Wemmerlöv, Urban, and D. J. Johnson. 1997. "Cellular Manufacturing at 46 User Plants: Implementation Experiences and Performance Improvements." *International Journal of Production Research* 35: 29–49.

Williams, Theodore J., ed. 1989. *A Reference Model for Computer Integrated Manufacturing (CIM): A Description from the Viewpoint of Industrial Automation*. Research Triangle Park, N.C.: Instrument Society of America.

Womack, James P., and Daniel T. Jones. 1996. *Lean Thinking: Banish Waste and Create Wealth in Your Corporation*. New York: Simon & Schuster.

Womack, James P., Daniel T. Jones, and Daniel Roos, *The Machine that Changed the World: The Story of Lean Production*. New York: Rawson/Macmillan.

Yoshikawa, Hiroyuki, and Jan Goosenaerts, eds. 1993. Information Infrastructure Systems for Manufacturing. IFIP Transactions B-14. Amsterdam: North-Holland.

Chapter 4

Bennettt, David, and Paul Forrester. 1993. *Market-Focused Production Systems: Design and Implementation*. Upper Saddle River, N.J.: Prentice Hall.

Bicheno, John. 2000. *The Lean Toolbox* (2d ed.). Buckingham, England: PICSIE Books.

Black, J. T. 1991. *The Design of the Factory with a Future*. New York: McGraw-Hill.

Boone, Louis E., and David L. Kurtz. 1999. *Contemporary Marketing* (8th ed.). Ft. Worth, TX: Dryden Press, 1999.

Burbidge, John L. 1975. *The Introduction of Group Technology*. New York: Wiley.

Burbidge, John L., and Barrie G. Dale. 1984. "Planning the Introduction and Predicting the Benefits of Group Technology." *Engineering Costs and Production Economics* 8: 117–128.

Burbidge, John L. 1993. "Comment on clustering methods for finding GT groups and families." *Journal of Manufacturing System* 12(5): 428–429.

Center for Automation and Intelligent Systems Research, Case Western Reserve University. 2005 (April). "The Agile Manufacturing Project." Retrieved 26 June 2007 from http://dora.cwru.edu/agile/home.html.

Cebrowski, Arthur K. 2007. "What Is Transformation?" Retrieved 23 June 2007 from http://www.oft.osd.mil/what_is_transformation.cfm.

Chase, Kathleen, and Dennis F. X. Mathaisel. 2001 (October). *Case Study: F-15 HUD.* Report. Cambridge, Mass.: Lean Sustainment Initiative, Sustainment Operations Team, Massachusetts Institute of Technology.

Davenport, Thomas H. 1993. *Process Innovation: Reengineering Work through Information Technology.* Boston: Harvard Business School Press.

Davenport, Thomas H. 1994 (July). "Reengineering: Business Change of Mythic Proportions?" *MIS Quarterly* 18(2): 121–127.

Davenport, Thomas H., and James E. Short. 1990. "The New Industrial Engineering: Information Technology and Business Process Redesign." *Sloan Management Review* 31: 11–27.

Day, Joseph C. 2002 (January). "Lean is the Only Way to Go." *Manufacturing Engineering* 28(1): n.p.

Deming, W. Edwards. 1982 (June). *Quality Productivity and Competitive Position.* Cambridge, Mass. MIT Press.

Deming, W. Edwards 1986. *Out of the Crisis: Quality, Productivity and Competitive Position.* Cambridge: Cambridge University Press.

Doumeingts, Guy, Bruno Vallespir, and David Chen. 1995. "Methodologies for Designing CIM Systems: A Survey." *Computers and Industry* 25: 263–280.

Dove, Rick, Sue Hartman, and Steve Benson. 1996. *An Agile Enterprise Reference Model with a Case Study of Remmele Engineering.* Report AR96-04. Boston, MA: Agility Forum.

Eckes, George. 2001. *The Six Sigma Revolution.* New York: Wiley.

Fine, Charles H. 1998. *Clock Speed: Winning Industry Control in the Age of Temporary Advantage.* Reading, Mass.: Perseus Books.

Garstka, John J. 2005 (April). "The Transformation Challenge," Report, U.S. Department of Defense, Office of Force Transformation. Retrieved 23 June 2007 from http://www.nato.int/docu/review/2005/issue1/english/special.html.

Goldratt, Eliyahu M. 1990. *The Theory of Constraints.* Croton-on-Hudson, N.Y.: North River Press.

Goldratt, Eliyahu M., and Jeff Cox. 1992. *The Goal* (2d ed.). Croton-on-Hudson, N.Y.: North River Press.

Goranson, H. T. 1999. *The Agile Virtual Enterprise: Cases, Metrics, Tools.* Westport, Conn.: Quorum Books.

Greiner, Larry E. 1998. "Evolution and Revolution as Organizations Grow." *Harvard Business Review* 76(3): 55–67.

Hammer, Michael. 1990. "Reengineering Work: Don't Automate, Obliterate." *Harvard Business Review* 68(4): 104–112.

Hammer, Michael, and James Champy. 1993. *Reengineering the Corporation: A Manifesto for Business Revolution.* New York: HarperCollins.

Harry, Mikel, and Richard Schroeder. 2000. *Six Sigma: The Breakthrough Management Strategy Revolutionizing the World's Top Corporations.* New York: Doubleday.

Hines, Peter, Nick Rich, John Bicheno, David Brunt, David Taylor, Chris Butterworth, and James Sullivan. 1998. "Value Stream Management." *International Journal of Logistics Management* 9(2): 25–42.

Hyer, Nancy L., and Urban Wemmerlöv. 1989. "Group Technology in the U.S. Manufacturing Industry: A Survey of Current Practices." *International Journal of Production Research* 27: 1287–1304.

Hyer, Nancy L., and Urban Wemmerlöv. 2002. *Reorganizing the Factory: Competing through Cellular Manufacturing.* Portland, Ore: Productivity Press.

Irani, Shahrukh A. 2002. *Value Stream Mapping in Custom Manufacturing and Assembly Facilities.* Report. Colombus: Department of Industrial, Welding, and Systems Engineering, Ohio State University.

Jablonski, Joseph R. 1992. *Implementing TQM: Competing in the Nineties through Total Quality Management* (2d ed.). Albuquerque, N.M.: Technical Management Consortium.

Joint Logistics Commanders, Joint Aeronautical Commanders' Group. 1997 (January 23) (Change 2, July 1999). *Flexible Sustainment Guide.* Washington, D.C.: Department of Defense.

Kaplan, Robert S., and David P. Norton. 1992 (January-February). "The Balanced Scorecard: Measures that Drive Performance." *Harvard Business Review* 70(1): 71–79.

Kotter, John P. 1996. *Leading Change.* Boston, Mass.: Harvard Business School Press.

Lee, Q., A. Amundsen, W. Nelson, and H. Tuttle. 1996. *Facilities and Workplace Design: An Illustrated Guide.* Norcross, Ga.: Engineering and Management Press, Institute of Industrial Engineers.

Liker, Jeffrey K. 1998. *Becoming Lean: Inside Stories of U.S. Manufacturers.* Portland, Ore.: Productivity Press.

Management Assistance Program for Nonprofits. 2004. "Total Quality Management." Retrieved 26 June 2007 from http://www.managementhelp.org/quality/tqm/tqm.htm.

Mansir, Brian E., and Nicholas R. Schacht. 1989. *Total Quality Management: A Guide to Implementation.* Bethesda, Md.: Logistics Management Institute.

Marsh, R. F., S. M. Shafer, and J. R. Meredith. 1999. "A Comparison of Cellular Manufacturing Research Presumptions with Practice." *International Journal of Production Research* 37: 3119–3138.

Mathaisel, Dennis F. X., Timothy Cathcart, and Mario Agripino. 2005 (February). *Sustaining the Military Enterprise: Architecture for a Lean Transformation.* Defense procurement analysis. London: Military Policy Research.

Mathaisel, Dennis F. X., Timothy P. Cathcart, Mario F. Agripino, Ulrik Petersen, Jeff Bradley, Toby Arnett-Kaiser, Gayle Davis, and Lee K. Levy II. 2005 (April). *Lean Enterprise Architecting for Military Sustainability.* Report to the U.S. Air Force Oklahoma City Air Logistics Center, Maintenance Repair and Overhaul Transformation Program OC-ALC/MA-T. Oklahoma City, OK.

McNamara, Carter. 1999. *Broad Overview of Various Programs and Movements to Improve Organizational Performance.* Report. St. Paul, Minn.: Management Assistance Program for Nonprofits.

Muthu, Subramanian, Larry Whitman, and S. Hossein Cheraghi. 1999. "Business Process Reengineering: A Consolidated Methodology." Retrieved 26 June 2007 from http://webs.twsu.edu/whitman/papers/ijii99muthu.pdf.

Nakajima, Seiichi. 1988. *Introduction to Total Productive Maintenance.* Cambridge, Mass.: Productivity Press.

Ohno, Taiichi. 1988. *Toyota Production System: Beyond Large Scale Production*. Portland, Ore.: Productivity Press.

Parnaby, John. 1986. "The Design of Competitive Manufacturing Systems." *International Journal of Technology Management* 1: 385–396.

Roberts, Jack. 1997. "Total Productive Maintenance: History and Basic Implementation Process." *Technology Interface* 2(1): 1–4.

Rother, Mike, and John Shook. 1999 (February). *Learning to See: Value-Stream Mapping to Create Value and Eliminate Muda*. Cambridge, Mass.: Lean Enterprise Institute.

Ruffa, Stephen A., and Michael J. Perozziello 2000. *Breaking the Cost Barrier: A Proven Approach to Managing and Implementing Lean Manufacturing.* New York: Wiley.

Schonberger, Richard, and W. P. Knod. 1993. *Operations Management: Continuous Improvement* (2d ed.). New York: HarperCollins.

Senge, Peter. 1994. "The Leader's New Work." *Executive Excellence* 11: 8–9.

Shalabi, Leslie, ed. 2003 (September). "Quick Response Manufacturing." Reprint of an article from OEM Off-Highway. Center for Quick Response Manufacturing, University of Wisconsin - Madison.

Shewhart, Walter. 1989. *Statistical Method from the Viewpoint of Quality Control*, New York: Dover.

Shingo, Shigeo. 1989. *A Study of the Toyota Production System*. Cambridge, Mass.: Productivity Press.

Suri, Rajan. 1998. *Quick Response Manufacturing: A Companywide Approach to Reducing Lead Times*. Portland, Ore.: Productivity Press.

Suri, Rajan, and Suzanne de Treville. 1986. "Getting from 'Just-in-Case' to 'Just-in-Time': Insights from a Sample Model." *Journal of Operations Management* 6: 295–304.

Teng, James T. C., Varun Grover, and Kirk D. Fiedler. 1994. "Business Process Reengineering: Charting a Strategic Path for the Information Age." California Management Review 36(3): 9–31.

Thacker, S. M., and Associates. 2002 (April). "Agile Manufacturing." Retrieved 26 June 2007 from http://www.smthacker.co.uk/agile_manufacturing.htm.

Tonaszuck, David M. 2002 (February). "The Impact of Leadership on Systematic Organizational Change." MS thesis, Massachusetts Institute of Technology.

Tushman, Michael J., and Philip Anderson. 1991. "Managing Cycles of Technological Change," *Research Technology Management* 34: 26–31.

Tushman, Michael L., and Charles A. O'Reilly III. 1996. "The Ambidextrous Organization: Managing Evolutionary and Revolutionary Change." *California Management Review* 38(4): 8–29.

Underdown, Damon Ryan. 1997 (December). "An Enterprise Transformation Methodology," PhD diss., University of Texas–Arlington.

U.S. Air Force, HQ AFMC/LGPP. 2000 (February). *Awaiting Parts (AWP)/Backorder Integrated Product Team (IPT) Study.* Report. Wright Patterson Air Force Base, OH. Air Force Materiel Command.

U.S. Air Force, HQ USAF/XPXT, Future Concepts and Transformation Division. 2003 (November). *The USAF Transformation Flight Plan FY03-07.* Report.

U.S. Air Force, HQ USAF, 2006. "2006 Vision Document."

U.S. Department of Defense. 2001 (September). "Quadrennial Defense Review." Report.

U.S. European Command. 2007. "Strategic Theater Transformation." Retrieved 26 June 2007 from http://www.eucom.mil/english/Transformation/Transform_Blue.asp.

U.S. Joint Chiefs of Staff. 2007 (August) "Future Joint Warfare." Joint Experimentation, Transformation and Concepts Division. Website: http://www.dtic.mil/futurejointwarfare/.

Uzair, Khusrow M. 2001 (Seprtember). "Development of a Framework for Comparing Performance Improvement Programs." MS thesis, Massachusetts Institute of Technology.

Walton, Myles A. 1999 (January). *Strategies for Lean Product Development.* MIT Lean Aerospace Initiative Working Paper 99-01. Cambridge, Mass.: Lean Aerospace Initiative.

Wemmerlöv, Urban, and Nancy L. Hyer. 1989. "Cellular Manufacturing in U.S. Industry: A Survey of Users." *International Journal of Production Research* 27: 1511–1530.

Wemmerlöv, Urban, and D. J. Johnson. 1997. "Cellular Manufacturing at 46 User Plants: Implementation Experiences and Performance Improvements." *International Journal of Production Research* 35: 29–49.

Williams, Rocklyn. 2001 (December). "Completing the Defence Transformation Process: The Transformation of the South African Reserve Force System." Institute for Security Studies occasional paper no. 54. Cape Town, South Africa: Institute for Security Studies.

Womack, James P., and Daniel T. Jones. 1996. *Lean Thinking: Banish Waste and Create Wealth in Your Corporation.* New York: Simon & Schuster.

Womack, James P., Daniel T. Jones, and Daniel Roos, *The Machine that Changed the World: The Story of Lean Production.* New York: Rawson/Macmillan.

Wu, Bin. 1994. *Manufacturing System Design and Analysis: Contents and Techniques* (2d ed.). London: Chapman & Hall.

Chapter 5

Dattakumar, R., and R. Jagadeesh. 2003. "A Review of Literature on Benchmarking." *Benchmarking: An International Journal* 10(3): 176–209.

Davenport, Thomas. H. 1993. *Process Innovation: Reengineering Work through Information Technology.* Boston: Harvard Business School Press.

Davis, John W. 2000. *Fast Track to Waste-Free Manufacturing: Straight Talk from a Plant Manager.* Portland, Ore: Productivity Press.

Goldratt, Eliyahu M., and Jeff Cox. 1992. *The Goal* (2d ed.). Croton-on-Hudson, N.Y.: North River Press.

Hammer, Michael, and James Champy. 1993. *Reengineering the Corporation: A Manifesto for Business Revolution.* New York: HarperCollins.

Harrington, H. James. 1996. *The Complete Benchmarking Implementation Guide: Total Benchmarking Management.* New York: McGraw-Hill.

Harrington, H. James, and James S. Harrington. 1995. *High Performance Benchmarking: 20 Steps to Success.* New York: McGraw-Hill.

Hayes, Robert H., Steven C. Wheelwright, and Kim B. Clark. 1988. *Dynamic Manufacturing.* New York: Free Press.

Hoppes, John Christian. 1995 (May). "Lean Manufacturing Practices in the Defense Aircraft Industry." M.S. thesis, Massachusetts Institute of Technology.

Kyro, Paula. 2003. "Revising the Concept and Forms of Benchmarking." *Benchmarking: An International Journal* 10(3): 210–225.

Manganelli, Raymond L., and Mark M. Klein. *The Reengineering Handbook*. Boston: American Management Association.

Millan, Juan L. 2000 (29 March). *Affordability Investment: Commercial Operations and Support Savings Initiative*. U.S. Army Materiel Command briefing. Washington, D.C.: U.S. Army Materiel Command.

Ohno, Taiichi. 1988. *Toyota Production System: Beyond Large Scale Production*. Portland, Ore.: Productivity Press.

Stalk, George. 1988. "Time—The Next Source of Competitive Advantage." *Harvard Business Review* 66(4): 41–51.

U.S. Department of the Army. 2001 (February). "Economic Analysis Manual." U.S. Army Cost and Economic Analysis Center.

U.S. Office of the Undersecretary of Defense. 2001 (December). "The Commercial Operations and Support Savings Initiative (COSSI) Challenges and Solutions for Success," Department of Defense. Acquisition, Technology and Logistics.

Watson, Gregory H. 1993. *Strategic Benchmarking: How to Rate Your Company's Performance against the World's Best*. New York: John Wiley & Sons.

Weiner, Robert (Pratt & Whitney Engine Services Overhaul and Maintenance). 2000. Interview with the author, San Antonio, TX, March 13.

Womack, James P., Daniel T. Jones, and Daniel Roos. 1990. *The Machine That Changed the World: The Story of Lean Production*. New York: Rawson/Macmillan.

Yasin, Mahmoud. 2002. "The Theory and Practice of Benchmarking: Then and Now," *Benchmarking: An International Journal* 9(3): 217–243.

Chapter 6

American Heritage Dictionary of the English Language. 4th ed. 2000. Boston: Houghton Mifflin.

Carnegie Mellon Software Engineering Institute. 2007. SEI Areas of Work: Management. Accessed August 2007 from http://www.sei.cmu.edu/managing/.

Defense Acquisition University. 2003. Risk Management Guide for DoD Acquisition 2003 (Fifth Edition, Version 2.0) Retrieved August 2007 from http://www.dau.mil/pubs/gdbks/risk_management.asp.

Federal Acquisition Regulation System. 2005 (March). Part 1.102(a). Retrieved August 2007 from http://www.acqnet.gov/far/reissue/FARvol1ForPaperOnly.pdf.

Interagency-Industry Partnership in Performance (U.S. Department of Commerce, U.S. Department of Defense, U.S. Department of the Treasury, U.S. Department of Agriculture, Acquisitions Solutions, Inc., U.S. General Services Administration). 2007. "Seven Steps to Performance-Based Services Acquisition." Retrieved 29 June 2007 from http://www.acqnet.gov/comp/seven_steps/index.html.

Kotter, John P. 1996. *Leading Change*. Boston: Harvard Business School Press.

U.S. Office of the Assistant Secretary of the Navy (RD&A), Acquisition and Business Management. 2000 (October). "Contracting for the Rest of Us: Some Basic Guidelines." Report NAVSO P-3689. Retrieved 4 July 2007 from http://www.acq.osd.mil/dpap/Docs/ctrrestofus.pdf.

U.S. Office of Federal Procurement Policy/Office of Management and Budget/Executive Office of the President. 1998 (October). "A Guide to Best Practices for Performance-Based Service Contracting" (final ed.). Retrieved 4 July 2007 from http://www.whitehouse.gov/omb/procurement/pbsa/guide_pbsc.html.

U.S. Air Force. 2003. *Performance-Based Service Contracts (PBSC).* Air Force Instruction (AFI) 63-124. Washington, D.C.: U.S. Air Force.

U.S. Department of Defense. 1996 (3 April). *DoD Handbook for Preparation of Statement of Work.* Publication MIL-HDBK-245D. Washington, D.C.: U.S. Department of Defense.

U.S. Department of Defense. 1997 (3 March). *Military Handbook Configuration Management Guide.* Publication MIL-HDBK-61A. Washington, D.C.: U.S. Department of Defense.

U.S. Department of Defense. 2003 (July). *Collecting and Using Past Performance Information (PPI) Deskbook.* Report. Washington, D.C.: U.S. Department of Defense.

U.S. Department of the Treasury, Office of the Procurement Executive. 2002 (November). *Performance-Based Service Contracting (PBSC).* Report. Washington, D.C.: U.S. Department of the Treasury.

U.S. Under Secretary of Defense. 2000 (December). *Guidebook for Performance-Based Services Acquisition (PBSA) in the Department of Defense.* Washington, D.C.: U.S. Department of Defense.

Index

A

Acquisition Plan, 62–63, 66–67, 250–251, 265–266
Agile Manufacturing, 113, 126
  agility, 113, 125–128, 145
  Agility Forum, 125
Agripino, Mario F., xiii, 36, 61,
Architecture, 3, 7, 38, 53, 58, 60
  enterprise, 35, 45, 51–52, 54–58, 153–154, 159
  framework, 69
Architecture of Integrated Information Systems (ARIS), 54

B

Babson College, xv, xiii
Benchmarking, 192–197, 203–208, 213–214, 257
  questionnaire, 232
Best Manufacturing Practices Center of Excellence (BMPCOE), 191, 195, 197, 205, 223
Best Sustainment Practices, 76, 191, 211
Boeing, 146–147, 207
Business Case Analysis, 52, 70, 88, 93–94, 210
Business Process Reengineering, 119, 156, 207

C

Cathcart, Timothy P., xiii, 36, 61
Cellular Manufacturing, xi, 2, 6, 45, 68–69, 71–73, 77–79, 130, 145, 193, 218
Change Management, 6, 48, 63, 67–68, 94, 96, 255, 268
Comm, Clare, xiii
Communications Plan, xi, 61, 67–68, 251, 255
Computer-Integrated Manufacturing Open Systems Architecture (CIMOSA), 54
Conceptual Design, 70, 100, 206, 213–214, 252, 257
Continuous Process Improvement, 24, 64, 101, 143, 193, 221–222
Current Military Sustainment System, 1, 10
  analysis, 13
  characterization, 7

D

Defense Logistics Agency, 16–17, 90, 184, 254–255

E

Enterprise Transformation Engineering, 69, 71–73, 251
Executive Training Course, 251, 270

F

Flexible Sustainment, 5, 35, 44, 113, 142, 218

G

Generalized Enterprise Reference Architecture and Methodology (GERAM), 54, 56
Groupe de Recherche en AutomatIsation (GRA), 54

I

Implementation, 47–50, 58–63, 68, 80, 99–100, 198, 211, 213–214, 264, 268
  Task, 72–73
Integrated Master Plan, 66–67, 84, 94
Integrated Master Schedule, 66–67, 84, 94
Integrated Product Team, 42, 70, 214–215, 252, 266, 270
Integrated Process and Product Development, 66–67
Integration Plan, 63, 66–67, 256

L

Lean, 33
  logistics, 34
  manufacturing 6, 61, 103, 200
  production, 130
Lean Aerospace Initiative, 5, 35, 39, 44, 131, 157
Lean Enterprise Architecture, 46–47, 60–64, 69, 72–73, 76, 100, 191, 209, 214, 249, 261, 264, 270
Lean Sustainment Enterprise Model, 36–37, 39–40
Lean Sustainment Initiative, xiii, 5, 18, 20–21, 23–28, 35, 44
Life Cycle, 36, 41, 43, 54, 58–59
  enterprise, 46, 69–70
  phases, 74
  transformation, 62, 96

M

Market Research, 70, 251, 258, 261, 272

P

Perdue Enterprise Reference Architecture (PERA), 54, 57
Performance Metrics, 187, 206, 233, 258–259
Performance Work Statement, 66, 250, 258, 262, 267
Performance-Based Transformation, 75–76, 112, 270–271
Pratt & Whitney, 163, 207, 216, 222
  San Antonio, 218
  West Palm Beach, 216
Product vs. Service, 259–260

Q

Quality Assurance Surveillance Plan, 264
Quick Response Manufacturing, 113, 122

R

Requirements Package, 63, 66
Risk Management, 99, 203, 207–208, 268–269

S

Single Acquisition Management Plan, 266
Six Sigma, 102, 113, 118–119
Source Selection, 251, 253, 264–268
Sources Sought Synopsis, 251, 261, 265
Statement of Objectives, 63, 251, 258, 262–263
Statement of Work, 63, 250–251, 262–263
Strategic Plan, 50–53, 62–63, 66, 223–225, 251, 257–258
Systems Engineering, 38, 40–41, 45, 60–61, 100
  role, 69–70
  process, 75–76

T

Theory of Constraints, 113, 140, 208, 227
Total Productive Maintenance, 61, 124, 138, 173
Total Quality Management, 64–65, 102, 113–116, 144
Transformation, 1, 6, 45, 62, 103–113
  activities, 249
  architecture, 52–54
  enterprise, 47, 49–50, 72
  implementation, 68
  life-cycle, 62
  measurement, 112
  performance-based, 75–76
  strategic planning, 63

U

U.S. Air Force, xiii, xv, 6, 14, 42, 74
  Oklahoma City Air Logistics Center, 76–77, 80
  Ogden Air Logistics Center, 76
  Warner Robins Air Logistics Center, 146
U.S. Army, 5, 35, 202, 231–232
  Corpus Christi Army Depot, 223
  Maintenance Center Albany, 227
  Materiel Command, 228
U.S. Navy, 42–43, 202, 249
  CAD/PAD Program, 36, 42

V

Value Stream Mapping, 60, 130, 131–132
  case study, 146
Variance Reduction, 113, 128–130, 144